TABOO OR NOT TABOO?

Developments in Psychoanalysis Series

Peter Fonagy, Mary Target, and Liz Allison (Series Editors)
Published and distributed by Karnac Books

Other titles in the Series

Developmental Science and Psychoanalysis: Integration and Innovation
Edited by Linda Mayes, Peter Fonagy, and Mary Target

Mentalizing in Child Therapy: Guidelines for Clinical Practitioners
*Edited by Annelies J. E. Verheugt-Pleiter, Jolien Zevalkink,
and Marcel G. J. Schmeets*

Orders

Tel: +44 (0)20 7431 1075; Fax: +44 (0)20 7435 9076
E-mail: shop@karnacbooks.com

www.karnacbooks.com

TABOO OR NOT TABOO?

Forbidden Thoughts, Forbidden Acts in Psychoanalysis and Psychotherapy

edited by

Brent Willock, Rebecca C. Curtis, and Lori C. Bohm

KARNAC

First published in 2009 by
Karnac Books Ltd
118 Finchley Road, London NW3 5HT

British Library Cataloguing in Publication Data

A C.I.P. for this book is available from the British Library

  ISBN: 978 1 85575 623 6

Edited, designed and produced by The Studio Publishing Services Ltd,
www.publishingservicesuk.co.uk
e-mail: studio@publishingservicesuk.co.uk

Printed in Great Britain

www.karnacbooks.com

CONTENTS

ACKNOWLEDGEMENTS

The editors wish to thank members of the original joint international conference planning committee (Drs Mary Anne Geskie, Cynthia Heller, Rebecca Curtis, Lori Bohm, Brent Willock, Don Carveth, and Yudit Jung), whose significant labours laid solid foundations for the stimulating discussions that eventually evolved into this book. For special mention, we would like to single out Dr Michael Stern, who chaired our committee with devotion, common sense, calmness, and good humour for several years. His imprint is on this book in many ways, most concretely in the title that he created in a moment of inspiration. The Board of Directors of the Toronto Institute for Contemporary Psychoanalysis (Drs Hazel Ipp, Judi Kobrick, Clarissa Barton, Don Carveth, Nira Kolers, Art Caspary, Gary Rodin, and Sam Izenberg) have enthusiastically supported this project that manifested in its preliminaray form on their turf. Our authors have blessed us with their unwavering commitment to this collective endeavour. It has been a pleasure to work with them through all phases in the epigenesis of our common dream. Thanks are due to the staff at Karnac Books, not only for embracing this project, but for their many years of outstanding support for psychoanalytic publishing. Our immediate families deserve special gratitude for accepting, with grace, significant periods of time in which we were otherwise preoccupied. For everyone's support, including many not mentioned, our heartfelt thanks.

ABOUT THE EDITORS AND CONTRIBUTORS

Robert Besner, PsyD, is a clinical psychologist and graduate of the Toronto Institute for Contemporary Psychoanalysis. A long-time student and practitioner of Buddhism, he lives in Toronto.

Lori C. Bohm, PhD, is Supervising Analyst and a member of the Faculty, William Alanson White Institute; Supervisor of Psychotherapy, Clinical Psychology Doctoral Program, City College of New York and St Luke's/Roosevelt Hospital Center; private practice in New York City and Hastings-on-Hudson.

Mark B. Borg, Jr, PhD, is a community/clinical psychologist and interpersonal psychoanalyst; graduate of William Alanson White Institute's psychoanalytic certification program; co-founder and principal partner of the Community Consulting Group, a community revitalization organization. He lives and practises in New York City.

Rebecca C. Curtis, PhD, is Faculty and Supervisor, W. A. White Institute; Professor of Psychology, Derner Institute, Adelphi University; Author of *Desire, Self, Mind, and the Psychotherapies: Unifying Psychological Science and Psychoanalysis*, and Editor of *Self-Defeating*

Behaviors, The Relational Self, and Co-Editor of *How People Change* and *On Deaths and Endings.* She lives and practises in Manhattan.

Michael Dalla, Jr, MA, is an industrial/organizational psychologist and co-founder of the Community Consulting Group, which is a community revitalization organization. He lives and practises in San Francisco.

Morris Eagle, PhD is Professor, Derner Institute of Advanced Psychological Studies, Adelphi University, Garden City, New York.

Peter Fonagy, PhD. Freud Memorial Professor, University College London; Chief Executive, The Anna Freud Centre, London.

James L. Fosshage, PhD, is Co-founder & Board Director, National Institute for the Psychotherapies; Founding Faculty, Institute for the Psychoanalytic Study of Subjectivity; Clinical Professor, New York University Postdoctoral Program in Psychotherapy & Psychoanalysis; President-elect, International Council for Psychoanalytic Self Psychology; Past President; Association for Autonomous Psychoanalytic Institutes.

Emily Garrod, PhD, is Co-founding partner, Community Consulting Group; Adjunct Professor, John Jay College of Criminal Justice; Clinical Supervisor, Saint Vincent's Hospital, Department of Psychiatry, New York City; graduate, William Alanson White Institute's psychoanalytic certificate program.

Daniel Gensler, PhD, Clinical Psychology, Yeshiva University; Assistant Director of Clinical Services, and Director, Child and Family Center, and Supervising Analyst, William Allanson White Institute; private practice in Manhattan and Great Neck, New York.

James S. Grotstein, MD, is Clinical Professor of Psychiatry, UCLA School of Medicine; Training and Supervising Analyst, Los Angeles Psychoanalytic Society/Institute and Psychoanalytic Center of California, Los Angeles.

Martha Hadley, PhD, is a psychologist, psychoanalyst, graduate of New York University's Post Doctoral Program in Psychotherapy and Psychoanalysis, practises in New York City and lives in

Western Massachusetts, where she teaches psychoanalytic theory at Hampshire College and Smith College School for Social Work.

Richard R. Hansen, PhD. Faculty and Supervising Analyst, Post-doctoral Program in Psychoanalysis and Psychotherapy, Derner Institute, Adelphi University, Garden City New York; Faculty and Supervising Analyst, Suffolk Institute for Psychotherapy and Psychoanalysis; supervisor, clinical psychology doctoral programs, Long Island University, C.W. Post Campus, and Ferkauf Graduate School, Yeshiva University. He lives and practises in Long Island, New York.

Anton Hart, PhD, Fellow Training and Supervising Analyst, W. A. White Institute.

Bruce Herzog, MD, studied psychology and medicine, University of Western Ontario; adult and child psychiatry, University of Toronto. Graduate, Toronto Psychoanalytic Institute. Faculty, Toronto Institute for Contemporary Psychoanalysis, and the Institute for the Advancement of Self Psychology. He lives and practises in Toronto.

Jill Howard, PhD. Adjunct Full Professor of Psychology, Long Island University; faculty member and supervisor of psychotherapy, William Alanson White Institute.

Harriette Kaley, PhD. Professor Emerita, Brooklyn College-City University of New York; Supervisor, Metropolitan Hospital, New York; Certificate in Psychoanalysis and Psychotherapy, New York University Post-Doctoral Program; independent practice, New York.

Jennifer McCarroll, PhD. Candidate, William Alanson White Institute, Adult Psychoanalytic program; staff psychologist, Fifth Avenue Center for Psychotherapy; clinical fellow, William Alanson White Psychotherapy Clinic; private practice, Manhattan.

Janet R. McCulloch, MD, is a graduate, Toronto Institute for Contemporary Psychoanalysis; Assistant Professor, Faculty of Medicine, Queen's University; practising individual psychoanalysis and group psychoanalytic therapy in Kingston, Canada.

Mark V. Mellinger, PhD, is a graduate, New York University's Postdoctoral program in Psychoanalysis; a member of the Faculty at Yeshiva University and The Institute for Contemporary Psychotherapy. He has a private practice in Manhattan and Westchester County.

Adam Phillips, MA. Formerly Principal Child Psychotherapist, Charing Cross Hospital; author; private practice, London.

Jeffrey B. Rubin, PhD. Visiting Lecturer, Union Theological Seminary; member of the Faculty, The Harlem Family Institute; private practice in psychoanalysis and psychoanalytically-informed psychotherapy, New York City and Bedford Hills, New York.

Ronald Ruskin, MD. Member of the Faculty, Toronto Psychoanalytic Institute, and Toronto Institute for Contemporary Psychoanalysis; Assistant Professor in Psychiatry, University of Toronto; Director of Day Treatment, Mount Sinai Hospital; private practice, Toronto.

Charles Spezzano, PhD, clinical psychology, City University of New York; certificate in psychoanalysis, Colorado Center for Psychoanalytic Studies; recipient of a New York Psychoanalytic Institute Heinz Hartmann Award for outstanding contributions to the theory and practice of psychoanalysis.

Janet Tintner, PsyD, is Supervisor of Psychotherapy, William Alanson White Institute; Clinical Supervisor, Rutgers Graduate School of Applied and Professional Psychology; Instructor of Clinical Psychology, College of Physicians and Surgeons, Columbia-Presbyterian Hospital. She has a private practice in New York City.

Brent Willock, PhD, is President of the Toronto Institute for Contemporary Psychoanalysis, and the Ontario Society for Contemporary Psychoanalysis. He is a member of the Faculty: Toronto Child Psychoanalytic Program; Institute for the Advancement of Self Psychology, and of the Advisory Board, International Association for Relational Psychoanalysis and Psychotherapy.

Foreword

Peter Fonagy

Few books on psychoanalysis deserve to be described as "page-turners". However, this collection of papers concerns all those topics in psychoanalysis that "cannot be spoken of". Inherently, therefore, it is one of the most intriguing books ever written by psychoanalysts for psychoanalysts. Each author reveals something that is known, yet not known, about the work that psychoanalysts do. In the current age of demand for greater transparency from professionals, this is a timely and important collection. Whether it is exploring the analyst's subjectivity in the consulting room, less of a taboo now than it has traditionally been, or the taboo of the financial gain that analysts seek and obtain through their work, the book is ground-breaking in its examination of taboo topics. Sometimes, what is revealed is practical and helpful in enabling the identification of ways of making traditionally emotionally difficult issues within the profession manageable, acceptable, and normative. This, of course, is the pattern for most social taboos. Taking a bird's eye view, what we see is that in many of the taboos of psychoanalysis, such as financial affairs, self-disclosure, or proscribed interventions, it is more what is projected into these actions by a cumulative psychoanalytic superego rather than the action itself that contains the shameful, not-to-be-spoken-about component. For example, self-disclosure has always been part of analytic work because it is impossible for all countertransference to have been thoroughly processed. It is an implicit agreement of psychoanalytic culture that allows self-disclosing analysts to be distinguished from their boundary-violating archetype and brings them in line with our general experience of the world, which underpins one of the major clinical achievements of relational psychoanalysts over the past two decades.

Perhaps because of our history, or perhaps because of the nature of our work, our profession is haunted by more taboos than most others. We find more projections of superego injunctions pervading our daily work than most other mental health or non mental health professionals. Some of these taboos serve our patients well, including the sexual taboo that analysts, for the most part, adhere to. We know that perhaps as many as 5% of psychologists and psychiatrists admit to violating this taboo in their practice. I do not for a moment believe that this figure applies to our profession. However, grappling with tenderness in psychoanalysis, as Janet McCullough puts it, needs to be talked about, and the feelings and thoughts that go into these experiences need to be publicly discussed in order to enable us to do our work better and under realistic conditions. Addressing taboos is about making the mind of the analyst real. Seeing the analyst's mind as it really is, as opposed to the idealized image that we would all dearly like to identify with in order to enhance our self-esteem, is a liberating experience.

I sincerely hope that this ground-breaking book will set a precedent for regular and systematic exploration of taboos in the profession as they shift and change, or, indeed, as they remain the same. Our clinical experience and our training have taught us that changes require taking the human mind to places where it least wishes to be. Taking the analyst's mind to these domains is in the best interest of unencumbered work, which is obviously in the best interest of our patients. We are indeed collectively indebted to Drs Willock, Bohm, and Curtis, and to the publishers, Karnac, for bringing this, in many ways controversial, book to the attention of the wider public. This book states nothing but the truth, and becoming publicly aware of an aspect of reality, as Freud pointed out in his speculations about identity of perception, brings us closer to the need to confront the past and the imperative to change. In bringing transparency to psychoanalytic practice, this book has not only appropriately grabbed our attention, but also facilitated a collective engagement with these difficult issues.

Introduction

Lori C. Bohm

Psychoanalysis has, from its inception, been a discipline concerned with overcoming the ill effects of certain social taboos. Freud's understanding of the underlying cause of the emotional disturbances of his hysterical patients was that they were suffering from the effects of repressing desires, due to taboos against sexual impulses. Patients in psychoanalysis are encouraged to speak about "whatever comes to mind", without editing, even if they believe their thoughts and feelings to be unacceptable, heinous, or scandalous. Given this focus, it might be assumed that psychoanalysis and its practitioners are free of the constraints imposed by restrictive taboos.

This book challenges this idea by examining a sampling of the taboos that are rife in the field. It is not intended to offer a complete summary of all of the forbidden ideas, clinical procedures, behaviours, and institutional practices in psychoanalysis, but rather to raise consciousness about the fact that, even within a field which encourages freedom of expression, many issues remain difficult to fully discuss both in the consulting room and in professional discourse. In some cases, the result is a limitation in the therapeutic results for the patient. In others, theory development is hampered by the taboo. In one case, that of the taboo against openly discussing a history of sexual contact between certain senior training analysts and their patients, future patients are potentially harmed.

Taboo or Not Taboo? Forbidden Thoughts, Forbidden Acts in Psychoanalysis is a book that was conceived as a result of a conference on the topic, held in July 2000 in Niagara-on-the Lake, Canada. At the conference, Dr Morris Eagle, the keynote speaker, suggested that if we are truly serious about confronting the unattended-to taboos in our field, a conference on the topic should be held every few years. This volume represents a beginning of what we hope will be an ongoing examination and re-examination of the taboos in psychoanalysis. It includes papers from a range of contributors, all practising psychoanalysts, including many of the field's contemporary luminaries.

The book begins with a consideration of the origins of taboo and the way taboos have made their way into psychoanalytic training Institutes. James Grotstein returns to Freud's remarkable treatise, *Totem and Taboo*, to remind us of the function of taboos in primitive societies. According to Freud, taboos in these pre-religious societies functioned as a group conscience, preventing incest and parricide. Grotstein notes that certain of the institutionalized taboos in psychoanalytic practice seem connected to these early taboos. For example, sexual (or even physical) contact between patient (as child) and analyst (as parent) is forbidden. Historically, there was also a taboo against a form of parricide, i.e., disagreeing too radically with Freud, as Ferenczi, Adler, Jung, and others discovered. The taboo against sexual contact between patient and analyst serves the vital function of protecting the safety of the analytic space. However, the taboo against challenging Freud, with its modern version, the taboo against experimentation in technique and against challenging Institute authority, have stifled theoretical development and supported the insularity of Institute life. We are reminded of the classic paper by Hans Loewald (1979), "The waning of the oedipus complex", in which he asserts that the development of the autonomous self, "is in psychic reality tantamount to the murder of one's parents, to the crime of parricide" (p. 757). The historical and current taboo against this symbolic form of parricide in psychoanalytic Institutes may help explain some of the developmental difficulties of the field as a whole. Grotstein recommends transforming certain taboos in psychoanalytic practice into principles that can then be questioned and revised where appropriate.

Whereas Grotstein emphasizes the importance of freeing psychoanalytic thinking from the constraints of taboos against new ideas, Morris Eagle, in Chapter Two, introduces the reader to the taboo implications of some of the newer ideas in psychoanalysis. For example, he considers the implications of the two-person model for psychoanalysis. This contemporary model acknowledges that the values and other personal qualities of the analyst shape what emerges in each therapist–patient dyad and have an impact on the outcome of each analysis. If this is so, Eagle wonders whether there are some people who just cannot be good therapists, due to personality problems. He also wonders whether patients who come to psychoanalysis believing they will learn more of the "truth" about themselves should be disabused of this idea, given the postmodern turn in psychoanalysis and its focus on the co-construction of a narrative, whose "truth" cannot be known. Eagle also offers a preview of a taboo topic, which is dealt with later in the book, the question of the role of money (specifically, potential diminished income) in a range of clinical decisions.

The next two chapters delve into taboos in an arena where psychoanalysis is traditionally considered to be particularly enlightened, that of the discussion of sexual feelings and actions. In Chapter Three, Charles Spezzano suggests that analysts do not fully confront sexual feelings, including their own, in the consulting room. He points out that while analysts are often quite comfortable dealing with patients' anger and aggression, and their own in response, there is a taboo against the full expression of sexual feelings. In the next chapter, Ronald Ruskin asks, given the "relaxed moral standards" of modern life, whether it is still advisable to retain the taboo against sexual activity between patient and analyst. He answers his question by giving several clinical examples of the serious damage done to patients in cases where the taboo was violated. He also describes the silence of various psychoanalytic Institutes about this behaviour on the part of senior training analysts, and the additional harm caused by this secrecy.

The third chapter in the section entitled "Expressions of Eros" moves away from sexuality to a discussion of the importance of the demonstration of tenderness in the psychoanalysis of individuals whose early lives were characterized by privation generally, and especially by deprivation of warmth and responsiveness on the part of care-givers. Janet McCulloch describes the theoretical conflicts and the taboo associated with the expression of tenderness in the analytic relationship, comparing the differing types of martial arts practice to different ways of working in psychoanalysis. She also uses teachings about when and how to "intervene" during martial arts combat as a model for when to intervene with tenderness in a psychoanalysis.

By directing our attention to the way psychoanalytic intervention can be informed by the teachings of a discipline, the martial arts, which is quite distinct from the psychoanalytic enterprise, McCulloch paves the way for the topics taken up in the next section of the book, "Buddhism and spirituality". In this section, both authors urge psychoanalysis to incorporate the wisdom of other disciplines to create a more comprehensive, possibly more accurate, and certainly more salubrious, notion of the place of the self in the world than the one presented in psychoanalytic theory. Robert Besner takes on the ambitious task of integrating human biology with psychoanalytic and Buddhist notions in order to fully delineate the nature of subjective experience. He reminds us that our moment-to-moment experience in the world is a function of complex physiological events, a fact largely ignored by psychoanalysis, with its focus on the subjective narrative construction of the self. He offers Buddhist meditation as a technique enabling the observation of momentary mental as well as physiological events.

Jeffrey Rubin directly confronts one of the original taboos in psychoanalysis, that of the role of spirituality in human experience. Rubin's notion of spirituality is certainly broader than that espoused by organized religion, which was clearly opposed by Freud (Rizzuto, 1998). Rubin argues that the self which is strengthened by psychoanalysis is an egocentric one that perpetuates the culture of narcissism, and that the psychoanalytic taboo against spirituality contributes to the alienation and depression from which many suffer. He suggests that incorporating spirituality into one's life will expand, rather than constrict, human potential.

The book then moves from the sublime to the practical by taking up some of the many taboos analysts have in dealing with money. As Adam Phillips points out in his contribution, "It is often far easier for people to talk about their sexuality now than about their money". Janet Tintner's candid chapter explores the benefits and pitfalls of charging a greatly reduced fee. For example, the low fee freed Tintner to confront her patient in ways she might not have confronted a full fee patient, for fear of losing the patient, and thus the income. However, the low fee also may have permitted the patient to consciously hold on to her belief that she did not need the analyst. This chapter serves as a reminder of the many subtle and often unattended-to ways that a low fee (or any fee) might provide fertile ground for enactment that the analyst might only be able to disentangle if she is comfortable with and able to fully discuss money issues with patients. Chapter Nine addresses a little discussed occurrence in psychoanalysis, the acceptance of cash as payment for treatment, and the resistance among analysts to doing so. Mark Mellinger argues that cash might, at times, provide greater anonymity for patients than do cheques, especially when the cheques are deposited with local tellers at a small village bank branch. He also advocates a full discussion of the patient's fantasies about the analyst's honesty in dealing with the cash, as well as any other thoughts and feelings that might come up when cash is used as payment.

In the next chapter, Jill Howard explores some of the issues that may arise when the patient has far greater wealth and real world power than does the analyst. She observes that the wealth and attitude of a rich, powerful patient in analysis might camouflage the fact that he or she is a patient like all others, with fears and needs, including the need to be loved by the analyst. This chapter provides a thoughtful counterpoint to Tintner's contribution about the low-fee patient. With both clinical cases, the importance of fully confronting and discussing money-related matters in the treatment is made abundantly clear.

The final chapter in this section is entitled, "The analyst and the bribe". In it, Adam Phillips uses a vignette in which a father offers to pay his son's analyst any amount of money to make his mute son speak to explore the role of money in our culture and to point out the analyst's possibly unique position as a professional who cannot be bribed with money. That is because paying more to an analyst than the customary fee cannot buy "more" of what the analyst has to offer. In his inimitable way, Phillips then connects the Freudian notion of pleasure, as always driven by what is forbidden or taboo, to bribery; only through bribery, through an "incentive bonus" can unconscious desire be satisfied. Consumers, including patients, might wish that money can solve the problem of taboo by providing access to the forbidden, but this is clearly impossible with the psychoanalyst. Phillips thus expands our thinking about the meaning of money in the psychoanalytic relationship, in a way that nicely complements the contributions of the other authors in this section of the book.

In the next chapter, Harriette Kaley tackles the thorny problem of whether published biographical material about famous people that includes information about a failed psychoanalysis should be open for discussion among psychoanalysts. Kaley had the experience of participating in a conference panel on the failed analysis of a famous person and was criticized for using the individual and his famous analyst's names, despite the fact that the information she used was already in the public domain. In her chapter, Kaley argues strongly for the importance of not censoring the use of clinical material of this type, as it can provide a powerful tool for learning and professional development.

From questioning whether psychoanalysis can rise above "political correctness" to openly discuss a failed analysis of a public figure, the book moves to an examination of other "real world" issues that have been taboo to discuss previously. Mark Borg, Emily Garrod, Michael Dalla, and Jennifer McCarroll challenge the reader to consider a community intervention, in which the practitioner violates many norms of standard analytic practice, to be a form of doing psychoanalysis. They suggest that interpersonal psychoanalysis and community psychology share common theoretical underpinnings, including the concept of the unconscious and of transference–countertransference enactments, and a common goal, to "expand self-experience". For these reasons, Borg and his colleages argue that psychoanalysis can indeed exist outside the consulting room.

Peter Fonagy raises another issue that has serious implications for psychoanalytic patients and candidates in training: the problem of the ageing senior analyst who is no longer competent to practise or supervise. After offering several illustrative case examples, as well as the political reasons why individual psychoanalytic societies find it impossible to deal with this concern, Fonagy provides a solution, the requirement of periodic formal re-accreditation of psychoanalysts.

In Chapter Fifteen, Richard Hansen dares to state out loud the often hidden fact that trying to maintain a practice consisting of purely or even mostly psychoanalytic patients is close to impossible in the present healthcare climate. He explores some of the possible ramifications of analysts' anger and disappointment about not being able to work with patients in the way that they believe they can be most helpful. This includes the propensity to be more "real" with patients, to more quickly self-disclose, possibly mitigating the patients' anger and aggression, and instead cultivating their appreciation. Patients may become too important to the analyst, to the detriment of the treatment.

Unlike prior sections of the book, which investigate areas that have been taboo to address in psychoanalysis, the next section explores an issue that has been a focus of recent theorizing in the field. As alluded to in Hansen's and Eagle's chapters, contemporary psychoanalysts, no matter their theoretical stripes, acknowledge that complete anonymity of the analyst is impossible, that the development of the work in each analytic dyad bears the stamp of the characters and values of both parties. Thus, some theorists have questioned the function of abstaining from self-disclosure with patients, an action originally designed to maintain analytic anonymity. Whereas Eagle raises important questions about other taboo implications of this reconceptualization of the analyst's contribution to the process, and Hansen raises questions about alternative and taboo motivations for the push to self-disclose, the papers in the "Self-disclosure" section of this book advocate for certain types of self-disclosure not previously described in the literature.

Daniel Gensler discusses what he calls "non-countertransferential self-disclosure," which is disclosure of personal information about the analyst's character, values, and issues, rather than disclosure about feelings and responses to the patient in the analysis. He argues that, whereas there are instances when this type of personal information is disclosed due to the analyst's unprocessed countertransference, there are also times when it may be disclosed for therapeutic reasons, to dislodge an impasse and to deepen the patient's self-exploration. He provides a detailed case example, including his own self-searching before and after his self-disclosure, which beautifully illustrates his theoretical contribution.

In the chapter that follows, Anton Hart takes up the question of what provides a patient with the feeling of safety that is essential for full and meaningful self-exploration in psychoanalysis. He proposes that it is the analyst's availability as a subject of analysis by the analysand that provides this sense of safety. In contrast to the traditional analytic position of "self-conscious censorship and privacy of the analyst's experience" as he is working with a patient, Hart encourages his patients to imagine what he is thinking and feeling during a session. He then carefully "tries on" their perceptions, wondering aloud about them, and at times sharing with the patient a qualified sense of what he understands himself to be experiencing at that time. He suggests that this less guarded way of speaking with patients provides them with a sense of safety and might also provide the analyst with an opportunity for personal growth while doing analysis.

Martha Hadley raises the issue of what to do when a patient describes, with uncanny accuracy, an aspect of the analyst's life that she has no possible access to in conventional ways. Telepathic knowledge or "thought-transfer" (Ferenczi, 1932) is a topic that has clearly been taboo in the field, to the extent that one prominent psychoanalyst, Robert Stoller, left a paper he had written on the subject unpublished, to be revealed only after his death (Mayer, 2001). In the chapter, Hadley grapples with whether or not it would be helpful or detrimental to tell her patient about several instances of apparent thought-transfer that appeared in the patient's dreams, and ultimately opts for self-disclosure. She describes the way in which this self-disclosure was therapeutic for the patient, helping to move the analysis and the patient's life in new directions.

Although some of the previous chapters in *Taboo or Not Taboo? Forbidden Thoughts, Forbidden Acts in Psychoanalysis* included actions by the therapist that heretofore would have been considered taboo, the final section of the book focuses in on two specifically proscribed interventions. In Chapter Nineteen, Bruce Herzog commissions a painting from a patient who has been trying to make her living as an artist, but has been crippled in her efforts by the belief that all of her productions are worthless. The therapy had reached an impasse because the patient could not believe verbal reassurances of the value of her art. Through agreeing to create a painting for her analyst, who paid her for it, she began to think of herself as an artist, and to take significant steps to advance her career. Herzog details his conflicts about using this intervention, including his reasons for deciding to do so, according to his theoretical formulation of what is therapeutic in the psychoanalytic situation.

James Fosshage ventures into the taboo realm of touch in psychoanalysis. His scholarly contribution includes a review of the literature on the prohibition of touch in therapy, the contemporary theoretical and research-based reasons to break this prohibition, guidelines for the use of touch in therapy, and clinical examples of the successful employment of this proscribed intervention.

Finally, Rebecca Curtis reviews the contributions to the book and the many taboos that have been presented and discussed, and Brent Willock, wittily using the biblical story of Lot, casts a backward glance while firmly facing the possible future of taboos.

The book, taken as a whole, provides a refreshing, thoughtful, honest look at many of the taboos present in psychoanalysis, even at this moment of greatly improved communication between the various theoretical schools in the field. Reading it provides a sense of freedom for the reader, as speaking of forbidden thoughts always does. We hope that the book will inspire others to seriously consider the taboos that hamper their practices, and that further ideas on these issues will come to light.

References

Ferenczi, S. (1932). *The Clinical Diaries of Sandor Ferenczi.* J. Dupont (Ed.), M. Balint & N.A. Jackson (Trans.). Cambridge, MA: Harvard University Press, 1988.

Loewald, H. W. (1979). The waning of the Oedipus complex. *Journal of the American Psychoanalytic Association*, 27: 751–776.

Mayer, E. L. (2001). On "Telepathic Dreams?": an unpublished paper by Robert J. Stoller. *Journal of the American Psychoanalytic Association*, 49: 629–657.

Rizzuto, A. (1998). *Why Did Freud Reject God?* New Haven, CT: Yale University Press.

To the courageous and innovative thinkers in our field who dare to look at and question matters one is not always encouraged to examine, doubt, or challenge.

PART I
ON TABOO

CHAPTER ONE

Taboo: its origins and its current echoes

James S. Grotstein

Introduction

*T*otem and Taboo (1912–1913) was one of Freud's most scholarly and profound works. The scholarship that went into it was exceptional. He filled in the missing links left over by notable anthropologists, such as James Frazer (1910, 1922), the author of *Totem and Exogamy* and *The Golden Bough*, who gave us the most detailed findings about the customs, relationships, and social practices of savage societies that had yet been garnered.

Freud was able to use what Bion (1970), following Poincaré (1952), termed the "selected fact" which, like the "strange attractor" of chaos theory, gives coherence and definition to what hitherto would have been called random or disconnected data. Freud analysed the anthropological customs of savages and was able to see a symmetry between the social psychology of taboos and the individual suffering from a psychoneurosis, particularly an obsessive–compulsive neurosis. The "selected facts" that gave coherence to these anthropological findings were Freud's theories of infantile sexuality, repression, talion law, and, especially, instinctual drives and their vicissitudes.

3

When one reads this monumental text from across the almost hundred years since its publication, one begins to realize how much psychoanalytic theory has changed. I found myself to be sentimental for this now arcane way of looking at phenomena. Classical ego psychology and its reactive descendants have opted to replace infantile sexuality, autoerotism, and the like for a more environmental–object focus. Kleinian theory comes closest to being the inheritor of Freud's original theories, but even modern Kleinians, especially in London, seem to be pulling away from its moorings in infantile mental life, particularly in technique. When one reads Freud, one can only weep about this change, one that was all too pragmatic, but apparently necessary in the course of time and its inexorable dialectical challenges.

In the small Midwestern town of my childhood, we had a general practitioner who went to Vienna to become analysed by Freud. When he returned, he told my family how happy he had been with his analysis. He also related how much Freud hated Americans, whom he believed were superficial, pragmatic, and too optimistic. Freud feared for the future of psychoanalysis in the USA, the doctor stated, because he felt Americans did not really understand the unconscious.

Notes on the origin of taboo

I shall not review Freud's work in detail, but I shall list a few of his comments about the subject of taboo. Taboo, along with totemism, seems to have been the organizing principle that governed and mediated primitive tribal cultures. The power they wielded was due to the animism (soul transfer) that characterized them. Animism, which Freud discussed at great length in *Totem and Taboo*, seems to have been neglected by modern scholars as the potent force behind primitive mental mechanisms, particularly projective identification. I must confess that I myself, who have written so extensively on that subject, never realized the importance of the ingredient of animism. Kleinians approach it with the idea of omnipotence, but animism far transcends omnipotence in its awesome, eerie, and preternatural phenomenology.

The practice of taboo originated from external sources in primitive societies so as to regulate their living arrangements. While the principal taboo had always been erected against incest (with descendants of the primordial totem), taboos also emerged against contact with tribal leaders, slain enemies, and dead relatives.

Whereas totemism emerged, according to Freud, as the social aspect of religion, taboo seems to have preceded the advent of religion to constitute the first group conscience. Freud and Wundt (whose work on taboo Freud reviewed at length) agreed that the custom of taboo is not religious; in fact, it may be pre-religious. (The non- and pre-religious nature of taboo reminds one of the premoral, autoerotic stage of infant development cited both by Abraham [1924] and Fairbairn [1940].) Taboo is older than religion and older than the gods, according to Freud. (But not according to Jaynes [1976] who, in his concept of the "bicameral mind", asserts that "gods" existed from the very beginning in human and individual histories.)

Taboo also represents the oldest penal system and,

> The strangest fact seems to be that anyone who has transgressed one of these prohibitions himself acquires the characteristic of being prohibited—as though the whole of the dangerous charge had been transferred over to him. [Freud, 1912–1913, p. 22].

Freud related the "contagious power" of taboo to the temptation to imitate others. He then stated that recollection (memory) and temptation come together. That is why, in the case of dead relatives, for example, the name of the dead one must not be enunciated, so as not to be recollected.

In these passages, which are representative of many others in Freud's text, one can see that Freud's thinking prefigured Klein's later concept of projective identification. It also strongly suggested the organizing importance of *envy*, another concept Klein was later to explicate. Freud frequently referred to Bachofen's idea of the prevalence of matriarchy before the time of patriarchy in human pre-history. Klein later took Freud's patriarchal Oedipus complex back to its matriarchal roots (Grotstein, 2000). It is of great interest to observe these, and other, prefigurations of Klein's work in Freud's essay.

Another conclusion one reaches from Freud's essay concerns *binary oppositions* (Lévi-Strauss, 1962): the idea that opposing impulses, such as love and hate, or murder and sparing, belong together. They become organized as reciprocally mutual oppositions, encountered as wishes and countermeasures. The latter are instituted in order to ward off activation of talion law.

While ascribing a demonic power to taboo, Freud cited the underlying common denominator of *ambivalence*, characterizing such opposing qualities as veneration and horror, as in the case of the taboo of touching leaders or royalty. Freud then stated,

> The most ancient and important taboo prohibitions are the two basic laws of totemism: not to kill the totem animal and to avoid sexual intercourse with members of the totem clan of the opposite sex . . . These, then, must be the oldest and most powerful of human desires. [pp. 31–32]

Thus, incest and parricide underlie taboo.

It is of some interest to review other objects of taboo in ancient cultures, e.g., childbirth, the dead, enemies, image-making, menstruation, proper names, names of the dead, pregnancy, sexual intercourse, touching, use of a god's name, and virginity. Jews are reminded of taboo in at least two areas: (a) their kosher laws which mediate between sacred (*kosher*) and unclean (*traif*), and (b) their prohibition in enunciating the name of their God.

Freud went to great length to demonstrate the intimate connection between the characteristics of taboo and the nature of obsessive–compulsive neurosis, not the least of which is ambivalence. In fact, one of the inescapable conclusions from Freud's venture into anthropology is that neuroses in general, and the obsessive–compulsive neurosis in particular, ontogenetically retrace the phylogenetic history of culture. To put it in another way, neuroses may be viewed as arrested racial memories: the phenomenon of taboo is the veritable origin of conscience and character in the individual and the code of justice in society.

Taboos in psychoanalytic practice

When Freud published *Totem and Taboo* (1912–1913), one can only wonder if an emotional subtext were operant in him in regard to another level of taboo—his belief that his followers (Jung, Rank, Adler) had committed the "taboo" of differing with him, thereby challenging his (oedipal) authority. It would be a while before Ferenczi would perform an "experiment perilous" in which he exchanged roles with one of his analysands and became an analysand himself. During these early decades of psychoanalysis, there was a lack of sanctioned opportunity to experiment, not only with changes in technique, but even with different theoretical formulations. We are all aware of what happened not only with Ferenczi, but also with Jung, Adler, Rank, Alexander, Reich, Klein, Horney, and others.

Today, it is much more permissible for analysts to expand, extend, alter, or replace aspects of psychoanalytic theories, but changes in technique are frowned upon. For his deviations from the standard procedures, Ferenczi (1920) was severely criticized by Freud and other colleagues; understandably so, but how can a profession grow without experimentation? Further, what would constitute acceptable boundaries for experimentation?

Psychoanalysis is an institution that deals with sacred (and also, paradoxically, thought-to-be profane) aspects of individuals. As such, it is subject to protective, regulative procedures reminiscent of taboos. Sexual, or even friendly, relationships with analysands are among these taboos. The sexual taboo, while certainly understandable and valid, touches on an infrequently addressed point: the tantalization that analytic technique provokes in the analysand who then, understandably, counter-tantalizes the analyst, who then may abrogate the taboo because of his/her guilt in being the "tantalizer of the first part". This is not to condone any acting-out of temptation, but to put a complex and sensitive issue in perspective.

One would hope the analyst would already have analysed his guilt about conducting the one-sided analytic procedure. In my experience, few analysts truly understand the rationale (a) of the transference regression that inescapably occurs when two individuals convene to discuss the subjectivity of only one of them, and (b) why it is necessary for the analysand to bear his/her ancient as well as current longings without being reciprocated. The goal of repeating one's past is insufficient. More airing of this problem is in order.

One of the basic taboos of psychoanalytic technique, other than the sexual, is the notion of gratifying the analysand's impulses or wishes, rather than purposely, though not sadistically, frustrating them, so that the impulse can have the opportunity to become conscious, harnessed to words. Perhaps a different perspective on this taboo is in order. Many of the rules of psychoanalytic technique can be alternatively understood to correspond to acting technique (Stanislavski, 1933), especially the idea of being disciplined in remaining in character with the role being performed. One may consider psychoanalysis as an improvizational passion play, one in which a hidden theme will emerge if the actors remain loyal to their respective roles.

Deviant psychoanalytic theories as taboo

There seems to be an evolutionary trend in the *Zeitgeist* in which developing "received wisdom" seems imperceptibly to "vote in" new ideas. Here, I refer to self psychology, intersubjectivity, the two-person relationship, alteration of our understanding about gender identification, etc. In contrast, within my lifetime, I was a participant in a "holy war" in Los Angeles in which, after a series of site visits, the American Psychoanalytic Association threatened the Los Angeles Psychoanalytic Society/Institute (LAPSI) with suspension if they did not get rid of their Kleinian training analysts! Being Kleinian, then, was taboo. I recall Bion's witty statement at the time, "Klein is like witchcraft—to be disavowed in public and practised only in privacy."

Susanna Isaacs-Elmhirst, a Fellow of the Royal College of Physicians, replaced Donald Winnicott as Chief Child Psychiatrist at Paddington Green in London. Her husband, Alec Isaacs, was a contender for the Nobel Prize for having discovered Interferon, but died before the final choices were made. Dr Isaacs-Elmhirst emigrated from London and applied for membership at LAPSI. Freud's last analysand, one of the senior members there, declared he would not want to belong to a society that included Kleinians! Her application was thereupon overwhelmingly rejected.

The Kleinian taboo at LAPSI had been exported by Anna Freud to the USA when she learnt that Wilfred Bion and Albert Mason had left London for Los Angeles, allegedly for "colonization". Yet, that taboo was in itself a red herring. The subtext for the harsh verdict of the site visits had to do, in my opinion, with what was felt to be

LAPSI's impertinence in democratizing the choices of training analysts. Hitherto, LAPSI had followed the practice then standard in all North American institutes of having a training analysts' committee that arbitrarily selected individuals whom they favoured to be training analysts. One could not apply for the position. One had to be chosen. LAPSI had also discontinued the traditional requirement of a written paper that the candidate had to present in order to graduate. The site visit committees on three separate occasions judged these innovations to be departures from acceptable standards and attributed their origin to the deterioration of LAPSI's standards occasioned by the influx of Kleinians. (One can read further about these matters in Douglas Kirsner's [2000] *Unfree Associations.*)

This experience taught me that, at any given moment, new ideas were unsafe to contemplate or put into practice. I had become more aware than ever that the teaching institutions of psychoanalysis operate all too similarly to religious institutions, like the Sanhedrin, the Holy See, the Lutheran Synod, etc. The events that took place between the American Psychoanalytic Association and LAPSI were all too reminiscent of the Councils of Nicea and Trent.

The taboo of "O" and of God in psychoanalysis

London Kleinians had their own issues in regard to taboo. When one reads their modern works, the bibliographical references reveal a remarkable absence of catholicity. Winnicott, Fairbairn, and North and South American and continental contributors are not often referenced. One gets the impression of a closed, hermetic system of thought.

Another taboo they demonstrate is quite remarkable. Wilfred Bion, Melanie Klein's most outstanding analysand and follower, seems to have achieved a position of uneasy and divisive acclaim amongst his fellow London Kleinians. His contributions to the study and treatment of psychosis are highly thought of by them, as are his later contributions about container–contained, reverie, alpha-function, beta elements, L, H, and K linkages, etc. His theory of transformations is another matter (Bion, 1965, 1970). No London Kleinian discusses "transformations in O". One of the synonyms

Bion assigned to O was "godhead". He also spoke of the "religious instinct". These ideas were taboo.

Bion became a pariah in his native land. It seems to be received wisdom there, moreover, that his sojourn in Los Angeles—where he wrote the three-part, quasi-autobiographical, quasi-imaginative *Memoirs of the Future* (1975, 1977, 1979)—was one in which he showed evidence of psychosis. Bion's later works are in a state of taboo *vis à vis* London Kleinians and the curriculum of the British Psychoanalytic Institute.

The hidden order of taboo

When Freud explicated the concept of taboo, citing especially the anthropological studies of Sir James Frazer, he found that the hidden order of taboo, in primitive as well as cultured societies, was the issue of incest. Much of the thinking that has gone into the setting up of the rules for psychoanalytic treatment derive from the incest taboo. For psychoanalytic treatment to take place, there must be a covenant between analyst and analysand to keep the frame and boundaries inviolable so that the analysand's unconscious phantasies can arise and evolve in safety, especially because the analytic atmosphere is so highly conducive to the emergence of transference and countertransference desires. Thus, the incest taboo in psychoanalysis is quite understandable.

There is, however, another problem in regard to the incest taboo that warrants discussion. By virtue of the fact that all analysts seem to respect the sanctity of the psychoanalytic process and also are so aware of temptation on both sides of the couch, it is my belief that a group process takes place in which analysts are so keen to guard the innocence of the analysand against the endangerment of temptation that they collectively project their own unresolved temptations into putatively "deviant" members of their own society, as well as more apparently deviant individuals outside the society. It is as if they are saying, "It's hard enough for me to remain pure. How then can I be sure of you?"

Behind the incest taboo in psychoanalytic practice lies a deeper stratum, the domain of the sacredness and innocence of the vulnerable infant and our need to protect it from our own sadism. Just as the analyst's silence serves as a vacuum to draw the analysand's unconscious feelings to the surface, so does the sense of innocence of the analysand-as-infant draw our worst, desecrating self (as well as our more noble self) to the surface. Here I am referring to the propensity towards child abuse to which the helpless innocence of the infant/child seems conjoined.

At base, the need for the analyst and analysand to form and adhere to a sacred *covenant* that binds both of them, particularly the former, has to do with the need for the latter to be able to experience safety in revealing feelings, unfolding their personalities, and regressing in the service of the ego. A similar covenant is needed between infants/children and their parents and their culture. Behind this need is the dark realization that when an analyst does the taboo thing, i.e., breaks technique or has loose boundaries, he exposes his fear of "O", i.e., his fear of his own experience of the Absolute Truth about Ultimate Reality. The analysand becomes demoralized by the analyst's unconscious revelation of his own dread of life. The same holds for abusive parents. When a father abuses his daughter, for instance, the latter loses a father and gains a terrified, terrifying pseudo-sibling.

The taboo of innovation

I am writing this contribution shortly after having participated in a "Conference on Buddhism and psychotherapy" sponsored by UCLA. The other speaker, a PhD in clinical psychology and an academic at UCLA, had once served for ten years as a monk in a Tibetan monastery. He was well acquainted with both Western and Eastern techniques for healing. He spoke mainly about the different techniques of meditation. The audience was impressed by what he had to say about meditation, as well as by their own experiences with it. The question emerged from many in the audience as to how legitimately to combine meditation with psychoanalysis and psychotherapy. I found myself intrigued by that innovative question, the implementation of which would be considered taboo by many of my colleagues.

The other speaker also presented a lecture in which he intriguingly integrated the contributions of Wilfred Bion with the wisdom of Tibetan Buddhism. It was quite remarkable how close they seemed to be.

It is well known that "psychoanalysis is not for everyone". That statement is undoubtedly true, and psychoanalytic institute curricula place considerable emphasis on how to choose "analysable cases". What needs to be done is for us to accept the limitations of our effectivity as a *challenge* to extend our technique.

For instance, it seems to be received wisdom that cognitive psychology and behaviour modification techniques are superior to psychoanalysis for certain conditions. Let us say that is true. How, then, can we integrate some useful aspects of their techniques for our purposes? I might also mention the technique of guided imagery in that regard.

As this contribution is being written, an innovation in technique is already being tested: telephone supervision and psychotherapy, and soon visual teleconferencing. We can all come up with a number of valid objections, but I am sure that these distribution methods are here to stay.

Another innovation in our time is the advent of neuroscience, especially psychopharmacology. I believe that now is the time for official policy directives to be issued and implemented in which psychopharmacology is formally integrated with psychoanalytic teaching.

Having come to realize that psychoanalysis can be thought of as a passion play and that many of the rules for the conduct of psycho-analysis are equally applicable to acting technique, one then wonders whatever happened to psychodrama? Could some of the aspects of psychodrama be integrated with psychoanalysis?

I supervised a recent graduate from one of the local psychoanalytic institutes who finally—and reluctantly—confessed to me that she "double-booked" her supervisory notes. She practised in her own idiosyncratic manner and wrote false notes afterwards to present to me. I became intrigued by what she really did do with her analysands. She informed me that she tells stories to them, from her own life, from the analysand's life, or from her vast storehouse of stories. The stories seem to be acceptable analogues to the analysand's feelings at the moment. What a pity that my supervisee did not feel that her novel technique was worthy of being shared. At least she and I have passed that hurdle between ourselves, but she certainly (I believe) could not present her work to her psycho-analytic society.

One of the conclusions one could draw from what I have just presented is that the understandable reasonableness that inheres in the rules that have been set down for the practice of analysis has not been sufficiently separated from the restrictive taboos that underlie them. Reasonable restrictions do not provoke temptation. Taboo does. The former is an ego quality. The latter is an archaic, superego quality. It is the difference between laws and command-ments. Taboos and commandments are inflexible and provoke rebellion because of their inflexibility; laws do not.

Splitting, projective identification, and taboo

Freud (1912–1913) implicated the defence mechanism of projection in regard to taboo:

> We have now discovered a motive which can explain the idea that the souls of those who have just died are transformed into demons and the necessity felt by survivors to protect themselves by taboos against their hostility. Let us suppose that the emotional life of primitive peoples is characterized by an amount of ambivalence as great as that which we are led by the findings of psycho-analysis to attribute to obsessional patients. It becomes easy to understand how after a painful bereavement savages should be obliged to produce a reaction against the hostility latent in their unconscious similar to that expressed as obsessive self-reproach in the case of neurotics. But this hostility, distressingly felt in the unconscious as satisfaction over the death, is differently dealt with among primi-tive peoples. The defence against it takes the form of displacing it on to the object of the hostility, on to the dead themselves. This defensive procedure, which is a common one both in normal and in pathological mental life, is known as a *"projection"*. The survivor thus denies that he has ever harboured any hostile feelings against the dead loved one; the soul of the dead harbours them instead and seeks to put them into action during the whole period of mourning. [pp. 60–61]

In deconstructing this passage, I should like to list the rele-vant signifiers. Freud was to elaborate upon the phenomenon of mourning a few years later (Freud, 1917e). Here, he deals with the *ambivalence* that characterizes the bereaved one. Actually, this is not ambivalence, but splitting of the affect. Ambivalence presupposes that hate and love are held simultaneously in consciousness and are consequently integrated. The achievement of ambivalence towards the lost object constitutes the culmination of mourning. Splitting between love and hate (without integration) predisposes the mourner to melancholia, Freud was to argue later.

In the primitive option, the equivocal (but not ambivalent) melancholic savage projects his unconscious hatred into the dead object and thereby produces a phantasmal demon. The demonic aspects represent the combination of the projected hostility plus the mourner's unconscious sense of omnipotence and intentionality (will). Against this demonically transformed object, the savage erects a taboo to protect him against the return of his projective identifications (Klein, 1946, 1955). Here we see the most primitive origins of what is later to be called repression. The taboo is instituted to protect the mourner from his own projections, which seems to be the most common usage of taboo, according to Freud.

Klein, in her conceptualization of splitting and protective identification, helped us to understand (a) splitting of the object, ego, and impulse, and (b) how talion law derives from the subject's projection of his/her own aggression into the object, which then becomes (1) damaged by the projection, and (2) identified with the aggression that then becomes aimed back towards the projecting subject, with the added load of projected intentionality and omnipotence. It is as if the subject shot the object with a gun and anticipated a demonic hydrogen bomb in retaliation.

The concept of projective identification takes on new meaning when animism is added. When the infantile aspect of the personality undergoes defensive projective identification, the content of the projection includes: (a) various aspects of the projecting subject, including, ego, id, and/or superego, (b) affects, and/or (c) impulses. It also invariably includes (d) infantile omnipotence, and (e) unconscious intentionality (will, purpose). To these we would now add (f) animism, the transfer of the projecting subject's "soul", which casts such a numinous and preternatural quality and quantity to animism when it is projected.

Conclusion

Taboo, along with the rites of totem, was the organizing principle governing societal customs and behaviour of primitive man. Antedating religion, it constituted the earliest group conscience and penal system. Taboos are principally directed against incest and against contact with tribal leaders, slain enemies, and dead relatives. The power behind taboos lay in the phenomenon of animism. Freud realized that taboos and totems bear a striking analogy to the obsessive–compulsive neurosis.

Taboos exist in muted form today in superstition, religious practice, and everyday life. They also exist in organizational structures, such as psychoanalytic institutions. Psychoanalysts have taboos about experimentation, about challenging institute authority, and about using putative "heretical" ideas. There are taboos in psychoanalytic technique that deserve to remain, but as *principles*, not *taboos*. There are others that are suspect and should be frequently reconsidered.

As the tongue alters the pronunciation of languages and creates dialects, so does psychoanalytic practice spontaneously alter over time under the mysterious forces implicit in the *Zeitgeist*. We must remain open; yet we are permitted to honour and respect those principles (aka "taboos") that we have, *at* the moment and *for* the moment, rendered obsolete.

References

Abraham, K. (1924). A short study of the development of the libido. In: *Selected Papers on Psycho-Analysis* (pp. 418–501). London: Hogarth, 1948.

Bion, W. R. (1965). *Transformations*. London: Heinemann.

Bion, W. R. (1970). *Attention and Interpretation*. London: Tavistock.

Bion, W. R. (1975). *A Memoir of the Future. Book I: The Dream*. Rio de Janeiro, Brazil: Imago Press.

Bion, W. R. (1977). *A Memoir of the Future. Book II: The Past Presented*. Brazil: Imago Editora.

Bion, W. R. (1979). *A Memoir of the Future. Book III: The Dawn of Oblivion*. Strath Tay, Perthshire: Clunie Press.

Fairbairn, W. R. D. (1940). Schizoid factors and in the personality. In: *Psychoanalytic Studies of the Personality* (pp. 3–27). London: Tavistock, 1952.

Ferenczi, S. (1920). The further development of an active therapy in psycho-analysis. In: J. Rickman (Ed.), J. Suttie (Trans.), *Further Contributions to the Theory and Practice of Psycho-analysis* (pp. 198–216). New York: Boni and Leveright, 1927.

Frazer, J. G. (1910). *Totem and Exogamy, a Treatise on Certain Early Forms of Superstition and Society.* 4 vols. London: MacMillan.

Frazer, J. (1922). *The Golden Bough: A Study in Magic and Religion.* New York: MacMillan.

Freud, S. (1912–1913). *Totem and Taboo. S.E., 13*: 1–64. London: Hogarth.

Freud, S. (1917e). Mourning and melancholia. *S.E., 14*: 237–260. London: Hogarth.

Grotstein, J. (2000). *Who Is the Dreamer Who Dreams the Dream? A Study of Psychic Presences.* Hillsdale, NJ: Analytic Press.

Jaynes, J. (1976). *The Origin of Consciousness in the Breakdown of the Bicameral Mind.* Boston, MA: Houghton Mifflin.

Kirsner, D. (2000). *Unfree Associations: Inside Psychoanalytic Institutes.* London: Process Press.

Klein, M. (1946). Notes on some schizoid mechanisms. In: M. Klein, P. Heimann, S. Isaacs, & J. Riviere (Eds.), *Developments in Psycho-Analysis* (pp. 292–320). London: Hogarth, 1952.

Klein, M. (1955). On identification. In: M. Klein, P. Heimann, S. Isaacs, & J. Riviere (Eds.), *New Directions in Psycho-Analysis* (pp. 309–345). London: Hogarth.

Lévi-Strauss, C. (1962). *Totemism.* Boston, MA: Deacon, 1963.

Poincaré, H. (1952). *Science and Method.* New York: Dover.

Stanislavski, C. (1933). *An Actor Prepares.* E. R. Hapgood (Trans.). New York: Routledge, 1989.

CHAPTER TWO

Some taboo implications of current fashions in psychoanalysis

Morris Eagle

A serious discussion of taboo and forbidden thoughts should make one at least somewhat uncomfortable in one way or another. If it does not, it suggests that we are pretending or playing at uttering taboo thoughts, much like the person who ostensibly is ready to give voice to the presumably embarrassing acknowledgments of his or her serious faults and shortcomings and then comes up with, "I admit it. I'm too good." The presumed acknowledgement of the taboo becomes a thinly disguised occasion for self-congratulation. I think there is something of this dynamic at play in some of the current literature on countertransference. Analysts are in a rush to confess their most personal and often pathologically tinged associations and reactions These confessions sometimes are subtly boastful. "Look how open, undefended, and healthy I must be to be able to so freely reveal my personal hang-ups. A less secure person could certainly not do this." So, in a truly psychoanalytic spirit, we might be sceptical of an over-eager readiness to express the presumed taboo and wonder what kind of narcissistic self-aggrandizements may be involved. My immediate concern here is that the reader will direct my prescription to my paper. That is a risk that I will have to take.

I am reminded here of an old Jewish story as well as Wittgenstein's comments about psychoanalysis. The joke goes as follows: the president of the synagogue—and one must keep in mind that in American synagogues the president is generally a well-to-do, prominent business man rather than necessarily a pious man—is rather loud and ostentatious in his prayers, intoning, "Oh God, listen to my prayers, even though I am your lowly servant, a nobody." A member of the congregation, a poor peddler, hears him and prays to God similarly. He, too, says aloud, "Oh God, listen to my prayers though I am a lowly servant, a nobody." One congregation member pokes the other and says, "Look who thinks he's nobody." So much for humility!

Upon reading Freud, Wittgenstein felt that he was a genius, but also believed that psychoanalysis was seriously misleading. Wittgenstein maintained that the psychoanalytic idea that residing deep in our unconscious are forbidden dark and powerful sexual and aggressive urges and desires is flattering, rather than taboo and disturbing, to most people. He suggested that most people react to such attributions with a sort of "Really? All that is going on in little ordinary me?" What is really threatening to most people, Wittgenstein implied, is the fear that there is really little below the surface and is captured by a *New Yorker* cartoon of some years ago in which the psychoanalyst is saying to the patient, "Deep down you're shallow."

So, returning to the original point, one measure of whether we really give voice to taboo and forbidden thought in this book is the degree to which they truly challenge accepted assumptions, modes of thought, and current fashions and make us uncomfortable. I begin by briefly describing some developments in contemporary psychoanalysis and then discuss what I think are some of their taboo implications. I do not expect that my description will be complete, but I think the following features will be recognizable to you as characteristic of what I will refer to as the new paradigm in psychoanalysis.

Transference

Special attention is given to transference (Wallerstein, 1990) and countertransference (Gabbard, 1995), which are identified as the "common ground" of contemporary psychoanalysis despite differences in theory. For some (e.g., Gill, 1994) only transference interpretations are therapeutically useful and non-transference interpretations are virtually irrelevant to the analytic process. Even when this strong claim is not explicitly made, it is implied by the insistent, at times exclusive, emphasis given to transference interpretations. One result of all this, I suspect, is that those analysts and psychodynamic therapists who do not exclusively focus on transference interpretations in their work tend to feel that they are not real analysts and not really psychoanalytic. I also strongly suspect that these analysts and therapists, especially young ones, do not feel especially free to openly and publicly question this piece of "received wisdom". The result is the unspoken development of a disjunction between public theory and writing and private practices, a kind of black market existing alongside the public economy. I cannot prove or provide evidence for the existence of this phenomenon, but I expect that my description will evoke a sense of recognition in at least some of you.

The disjunction between explicit theory and prescription and actual clinical experiences and practices often comes to the fore in training. In my experience, it is not uncommon to confront the following situation in the training of graduate students in clinical psychology, particularly in psychodynamically orientated programmes. Many students who are placed in community and hospital clinic settings work with patients who are often on welfare, are poorly educated, have very difficult lives, and are struggling simply to survive. On the one hand, the students are taught in their courses all about transference and the unique importance of transference interpretations. And on the other hand, they are working with patients for whom a focus on transference interpretations often seems grossly inappropriate and to whom such interpretations seem largely incomprehensible. The result is that they sometimes feel utterly confused and cannot apply what they have learnt to real work with real patients in particular real world settings. That is not so bad. They should feel confused. What I find more disconcerting are those students who persist in playing analyst and repeatedly making transference interpretations when such interpretations simply do not seem to fit the realities of the particular clinical situation. Understandably, they suffer through these difficult experiences so that they can earn their degree and begin a private practice with patients who are sufficiently socialized to play the game properly and accept the "rules" regarding transference interpretations, disclosure of countertransference reactions, as well as other interventions.

It should be noted that, quite remarkably, all the repeated and confident assertions about the special therapeutic role of transference interpretations are generally made without any consideration given to the question of whether there is any systematic evidence that an exclusive or near exclusive focus on transference interpretations is especially linked to positive therapeutic change. For example, Gill devoted much of his 1994 book, *Analysis in Transition*, to the thesis that analysis of the transference is the single most important activity, perhaps the only therapeutically significant activity, in analysis. However, there is not a single reference to any systematic evidence supporting that idea. Merton Gill was an old and good friend of mine and I know that, more than most analysts, he was interested in, and respectful of, research and evidence. Yet, even Gill could take a rather definite position, apparently without feeling the need to cite supporting evidence. As another example, recently I reviewed the 1999 book edited by Mitchell and Aron, entitled *Relational Psychoanalysis: The Emergence of a Tradition*. More than half of the chapters in this big, thick book are devoted to issues of transference and countertransference. However, there is not a single reference in the entire book to any systematic evidence indicating that transference interpretations are more effective than non-transference interpretations. From what I know of the limited literature in this area, there is little unmixed empirical support for the proposition that a focus on transference interpretations is especially linked to positive therapeutic outcome.

Apart from the lack of systematic evidence, my own experience—and I cannot believe that I am that different from other therapists—is that, contrary to the "received wisdom", many extra-transference interpretations and insights can have a significant impact on patients. Also, there are many occasions when transference interpretations simply do not fit, and where mechanically following the "rule" that virtually all the patient's productions should be looked at as indirect allusions to the transference (Gill, 1982) may lead to forced and heavy-handed interpretations.

Countertransference

Other pieces of "received wisdom" that have come to dominate the contemporary psychoanalytic literature have to do with counter-transference, now "totalistically" defined (Kernberg, 1965) as the sum total of the analyst's cognitive and affective reactions to the patient. There are two ideas regarding countertransference that seem to me, if not contradictory, at least incongruent with each other. One idea, dating back to Paula Heimann's (1950) influential article and most fully elaborated by Racker's important 1968 book, is that the analyst's countertransference is the most useful guide the analyst has for "reading" the patient's unconscious mental contents. As I have elaborated elsewhere (Eagle, 2000), this proposition has both a strong and weak version. Very briefly, in its strong version, the claim is that countertransference is a sure-fire guide to the patient's unconscious. The weak form is that it can, under certain circumstances, serve as a guide. However, just as bad money drives out good, despite lip service cautions, the strong version tends to predominate in the literature, both by commission and omission: that is, the citing of only positive incidences and the failure to provide instances where the analyst's countertransference reactions do not serve as a useful empathic tool; indeed, where they egregiously mislead.

What is the taboo thought here? It is, as Gill (1994) and others have noted, that, quite ironically, despite the linking of the new concept of countertransference with an interactional, two-person view of the analytic situation, there is a danger that, at least in its strong version, the current view of countertransference lends itself to a new version of the blank screen—or blank mirror—one in which the analyst who, like all good mirrors, merely reflects the object and brings nothing of his or her own to the reflected image. There is also the danger, as Melanie Klein (1946) noted a long time ago in regard to the concept of projective identification, that the patient will be "blamed" for feelings and reactions that truly belong to the analyst, or at least are the result of a complex interaction between the analyst's idiosyncratic history and personality and cues emitted by the patient. It seems to me—and there is not sufficient space to elaborate here—that just as Melanie Klein feared, confused and undisciplined use of the concept of projective identification, with its vague talk of patients putting things into the analyst, have ushered in a new one-person psychology: the one person who is now the focus of attention is the analyst, not the patient (Eagle, 2000). Pushed to the extreme, the new view of the role of countertransference suggests that the analyst need not bother listening to the patient in order to understand and decipher his or her productions. All the analyst need do is monitor his or her own countertransference reactions to learn what is going on in the patient.

Side by side with the conception of countertransference as a guide to the patient's unconscious inner world is the somewhat incongruent view that the analyst's idiosyncratic countertransference also inevitably determines, among other things, his or her selection of which material he or she will focus on, the nature of his or her understanding of that material, and the content and style of his or her interpretations. Add to this Renik's (1996) advocacy of the role of the analyst's personal values and influence on the treatment, Mitchell's (1998) claim that rather than having expert knowledge of the patient's mind, the analyst's expertise lies in meaning-making, self reflection, and organizing and reorganizing of experience, and his insistence that there is nothing corresponding to the phrase "in the patient's mind" about which either patient or analyst can be right or wrong. (See Eagle, Wolitzky, & Wakefield, 2001.) All this paints a picture which suggests that rather than serving as a reliable guide to the patient's unconscious, it is the analyst's particular countertransference that will almost completely determine how he or she understands the patient, what he or she will selectively focus on, and what interventions he or she will make. Furthermore, if, as Renik suggests, psychoanalytic treatment consists, in large part, of openly accepting the idea that one exerts one's personal influence derived from one's own personal values, and if, as Mitchell suggests, the analyst has no expert knowledge of the patient's mind, but rather offers meaning systems and new perspectives, it follows that the direction, shape, and fate of any analysis, including its success or failure, will be largely determined by the personal qualities and values of the particular analyst and by the particular analyst–patient match.

If the idiosyncratic and personal qualities of the analyst are that crucial, one might consider a number of challenging implications. One such implication is that perhaps there are more than the two possible treatment outcomes usually referred to in the literature: not only patients helped *vs.* not helped, but also a third outcome: patient iatrogenically harmed. This possibility is partly based on the idea that, given the overriding role of idiosyncratic personal factors, perhaps some analysts and therapists should not be doing treatment, or, at least, should not be doing treatment with certain patients. Of course, there is no easy way to evaluate these things. Nevertheless, the question needs to be raised and some of its possible implications discussed. Perhaps every analyst should undergo not only periodic analysis, but also periodic supervision, preferably with the use of taped sessions. Perhaps the outcome of treatment should be evaluated, on a periodic and ongoing basis, not only by patient and therapist, but also by a third, mutually agreed upon, independent party, and, of course, I do not mean HMOs and insurance companies. Perhaps analysts ought to be more ready to let go of patients when things do not seem to be working out; not an easy stance to take when one's livelihood is at stake. Perhaps Masters and Doctoral degrees and the training they entail, whether in social work, psychology, or psychiatry are not especially relevant to the kind of clinical work one does.

Training and personal qualities of therapist

I am reminded of the early National Institute of Mental Health study (Rioch et al., 1963) that showed that housewives given two years of training produced good therapeutic results. Indeed, Rioch and colleagues argued that professionals with many years of training should devote themselves to the advancement of knowledge and leave more of the practice to those with fewer years of training. In 1979, Strupp & Hadley reported that college student patients treated by college professors, chosen for their ability to form understanding relationships, showed as much improvement as those treated by highly experienced therapists who had an average of twenty-three years of experience. According to Strupp, the patients treated covered a wide range of conditions, including neurotic depression, anxiety reactions, obsessional trends, and borderline personalities. So, one could not easily say that the college professors did so well only because they were working with untroubled, non-disturbed patients. Also of interest in this study was the great variability within each group, which could suggest that among both the experienced therapists and the college professors, some got good results and some got poor results.

Needless to say, not much attention is paid in our field to these kinds of studies. If silence is one mark of a taboo, then these findings certainly have a taboo status. However, given the contemporary conceptions of the therapeutic situation, including the abiding role of countertransference, these sorts of findings should not be a great surprise. If the personal qualities of the therapist constitute a, if not the, critical factor in the outcome of treatment, then why should it not be the case that housewives, college professors, or anyone else with certain personal qualities might be at least as effective as mental health professionals? Why should it also not be the case that among everyone engaged in doing treatment, there is likely to be great variability regarding suitability for doing therapy, at least in part as a function of their personal qualities? Or at the very least, there may be great variability in suitability for doing therapy with certain patients. As long as one held to the model of the blank screen and fully objective analyst, one could cling to the idea that all well trained analysts are essentially suitable and interchangeable for all patients. And perhaps when everyone tried to be a blank screen, they were essentially interchangeable. But now the cat is out of the bag. We are now told that personal style, personal history, personal bias, and personal influence—many aspects of which we are not and cannot be aware—shape the treatment and determine whether retraumatization, with its suggestion of iatrogenic worsening, or positive change will occur.

I am aware, as are most of us, that being a therapist and taking that professional role seriously often brings out the best and healthiest in us. One reason for this may be that the therapeutic situation permits a safe and bounded intimacy or perhaps, better yet, a safe combination of disengagement, or rather limited engagement and intimacy, thus constituting an ideal compromise to the conflict between separateness and relatedness (Eagle, 1998). However, I am not sure that this is true for all people I know doing therapy. There are some colleagues about whom, I must confess, I have strong doubts regarding their ability to do constructive therapeutic work.

These doubts are based on my ordinary impression of them outside the therapeutic situation, and on the nagging feeling that they could not be that different in their consulting room from the way they are outside it: that the sleaze factor, or the true believing rigidity factor, or the materialistic greediness factor, or the crusading fanaticism factor, or the pervasive narcissism factor, or the sadism factor, or, above all, the limited ability to reflect on whatever troubling and potentially interfering personal qualities they may have factor, that all these could not simply disappear the moment they begin doing treatment.

I am sure, at least I hope, that I am not the only one to have such uncharitable thoughts. This brings to mind a number of related experiences I had in the past two or three years. One year, Charles Brenner was invited to give a talk at the Derner Institute at Adelphi University, and another year, Jacob Arlow. On both occasions I joined them and a few other people for an evening of dinner and talk after their presentation. I disagreed with many aspects of the theoretical positions taken by Brenner and Arlow. However, on a personal level, I and others found both of them to be totally charming, personable, dignified, cultured, warm, and humorous. What is my point here? I find it difficult to believe that these personal qualities would not play some positive role in their therapeutic work, despite what many take to be their presumed analytic stance.

I had a somewhat different experience when I recently attended a meeting in which Beatrice Beebe presented, as she usually does, some fascinating material on infant–mother interactions. During the discussion, a well known analyst waded in with questions and acerbic criticisms that were as unrelenting as a pit bull and were sufficiently sadistic in manner and style to make some of us at the meeting squirm with discomfort and resentment. I had been working on this paper before attending the meeting and was still thinking about it, on and off, during the meeting. The thoughts that occurred to me during the display of downright hostility and meanness that I observed were: how in the world can this man do constructive analytic work with his patients? Could he really be that transformed when he enters his consulting room? I believe that the nature of his theoretical orientation and however much he might profess the importance of, say, empathic understanding or "tact" in his writings, would have little or no effect on my judgement of him as a person and of what kind of analyst or therapist he would probably be.

The relation between the theoretical position one takes or the "school" to which one is loyal and the spirit and manner in which one conducts treatment with different patients is likely to be a complex one. I do not know, and I do not think any of us know, that an analyst who professes, say, a relational or a self psychology theoretical orientation is necessarily more related, more empathic, or affectively present than an analyst who espouses a traditional view. Indeed, it may be the case that some people are drawn to a relational or self-psychology view not because they are more related or more empathic, but because these are especial areas of difficulty and conflict for them. We just do not know. I suspect that an empirical study would show that qualities such as relatedness and empathy would cut across theoretical orientations and would be largely a matter of individual personality, although training and theoretical orientation may enhance or diminish the role of these qualities.

In writing about these matters, I am constantly reminded of Carl Rogers' emphasis on such personal qualities of the therapist as genuineness, authenticity, warmth, and unconditional positive regard. I also recall that some so-called Rogerians offered workshops in genuineness, authenticity, warmth, etc., entirely missing the point that these attributes are organic to the person rather than something that could be acquired in a one- or two-day workshop. In any case, it seems to me that implicit in the current totalistic conception of countertransference and its influence on the course of treatment is somewhat of a convergence between Rogers and contemporary psychoanalysis, perhaps itself a taboo thought.

There is little doubt, then, that one implication of the current view of the analytic situation, particularly when the blank screen role of the analyst is relinquished, is that the personal, idiosyncratic attributes of the analysts are likely to shape the course and fate of the analysis. In my view, this does not mean that there is no room for the classical conception of countertransference. For when countertransference is understood as a particularly clear barrier to the treatment due to the analyst's unresolved conflicts and blind spots, there is, at least, theoretical room provided for sensitivity to the issue of how certain personal issues and qualities of the therapist might especially interfere with, as well as facilitate, the treatment.

When, however, it is viewed either solely as something "put there" or stimulated by the patient, or solely as ubiquitous and inevitable, one can find reasons to ignore its potential interference: in the first case, because it is presumably an invaluable tool, and in the second case, because, given its inevitability and ubiquitousness, there is not much one can do about it anyway.

So, these two somewhat different contemporary views of countertransference converge to protect us from confronting the possibility that certain personal qualities, motives, unresolved conflicts, and blind spots may constitute barriers to effective therapeutic work. And we cannot easily be comforted by the thought, quite prominent in the literature, that all we need to do is scrutinize our countertransference reactions. For it may be the nature of at least certain countertransference reactions that they cannot readily be brought to awareness and scrutinized. That is what it means to have a blind spot, a consideration that is prominent in the classical conception of countertransference and easily ignored in the totalistic conception.

Money

I want to bring up another taboo issue that rarely gets mentioned in discussions of countertransference: the issue of money. I guess the totalistic conception of countertransference is not that totalistic. Clearly, making money and earning a living are important motives for practising psychotherapy. A question that does not seem to get discussed is the degree to which not wanting to reduce one's income may serve as a motive for holding on to certain patients too long. Analysts and therapists, like other people, get used to a certain standard of living and do not like having it lowered. Since analysts are not necessarily more immune to rationalization than anyone else, it is probably easy to deny to oneself, in regard to a particularly well-paying patient, that one motive, among many, for continuing treatment beyond a certain point might be one's reluctance to experience a possible drop in income. It has always been difficult to discuss this issue openly, but is especially so because of the abusive pressures of HMOs and insurance companies to radically shorten or eliminate therapeutic treatment. By even raising the issue, one appears to be siding with the enemy.

If I ever had any doubt that analysts are capable of extraordinary rationalizations and other self-deceptions when money is at stake, these doubts were removed by what I heard and observed some years ago at a couple of meetings at the Toronto Psychoanalytic Institute at the time that over-billing (that is, billing over the amount allotted and paid for by the province) was outlawed in Ontario. Some analysts who stated that they were outraged at the government's interference with the sacrosanct relationship between patient and analyst revealed in the very next breath that one way that they get past the law banning over-billing was through private collusive arrangements with patients, including the imposition of so-called "administrative fees". Some analysts reported that they gave new prospective patients the following option: either enter treatment and pay no extra fee, or pay extra for the analyst's cogitations about the patient between sessions, with the clear implication, of course left unsaid, that no such between-sessions cognitive service would be provided were the patient not to agree to the over-billing under the guise of an administrative fee.

My favorite lulu at one of these meetings was a proposal by one analyst that they all engage in "civil disobedience". I could not resist pointing out that historically, effective civil disobedience was characterized by at least three components: (1) pursuit of what is generally perceived as a noble and moral cause; (2) public support due to the perceived nobility of the cause; and (3) a willingness to endure personal sacrifice, including the sacrifice of going to jail. I remarked, with what I hope was proper irony and understatement, that I did not think any of the three components I had identified were conspicuous in the present case.

Given the depth of feelings that most of us have about money, it seems remarkable that it rarely gets discussed in the literature; and this at a time when some analysts feel free to suggest self-disclosure of sexual and aggressive thoughts and feelings, and just about all sorts of feelings. I do not recall a single instance in which anyone in the literature reported the private countertransference thought, let alone disclosed to the patient, "You know, I just felt anxious and concerned that you might leave because I need the money." Or the thought, "I was just having the greedy fantasy of doubling your fee so that I could buy that new car I want." The absence of such reports suggests to me that money is truly a taboo area in our field. I am reminded of a joke that illustrates the degree to which what constitutes a taboo varies with the times. A guy goes into a store and asks, in a loud voice, for a packet of condoms and then whispers, "and a packet of cigarettes".

The postmodern turn

Let me turn now to a final complex taboo issue, or, really, a set of taboo issues. The taboo consists, once again, in not fully spelling out the implications of a particular set of ideas in the contemporary psychoanalytic literature. The ideas, I am certain, are familiar to all of you. They reflect what Louis Sass (1992) has called the post-modernist turn in psychoanalysis. (See also Eagle, 2003.) One component of this position in contemporary psychoanalysis is the claim that the analyst does not uncover or discover unconscious mental contents, i.e., wishes, derives, defences, and schemas in the patient's mind. Indeed, in a recent paper, Mitchell (1998) argues that the analyst has no authoritative expert knowledge of the patient's mind. Rather, the contemporary analyst generates or negotiates or co-constructs—choose whichever term you prefer—new meaning systems, new perspectives, retellings, coherent and more serviceable narratives . . . again, choose whichever term you prefer. The point of view I have criminally condensed is central to the writings, among others, of Mitchell, Renik, Schafer, and in a more ambiguous way, Spence. In a rather extreme version of this point of view, Richard Geha (1984) has argued that psycho-analysis deals in, and has no choice but to deal in, what he calls "aesthetic fictions" and, indeed, accuses Spence of being a closet positivist because he believes that there is a distinction between historical and so-called narrative truth. I will not try to discuss the difficulties of this general point of view. My colleagues and I have done that elsewhere at great length (e.g., Eagle, 2003; Eagle, Wolitzky, & Wakefield, 2001). The point I want to focus on here, one that is pertinent to the theme of this conference, is the distinction between the point of view that some analysts profess in journal articles and books and what they tell and do not tell their patients, as well as what most patients assume and believe when they come for treatment.

I believe that when they enter treatment, virtually all analytic patients assume that they will gain self-knowledge and learn something more of the truth about themselves in psychoanalysis, and that, in some way, such insight will contribute to a more satisfying life. If, as is strongly suggested by the contemporary psychoanalytic writers I have mentioned, this assumption is largely illusory, one not shared by their analysts, why are patients not disabused of this notion? As Sass (1992) asks, is the presumed impossibility of determining the veridicality of interpretations a secret being kept from patients? Do patients believe, along with Mitchell (1998), that there is nothing corresponding to the phrase "in the patient's mind" about which they or the analyst can be right or wrong? Do they accept the goal articulated by Schafer (1992), that it is important that they become more "relativistic historians" of their lives? Do they accept the idea that psychoanalysis only constructs persuasive narratives, new perspectives, and new meaning systems, and does not include uncovering and working through their conscious and unconscious thoughts, feelings, conflicts, defences . . . that is, what is going on in their mind? As my colleagues and I asked in a recent paper (Eagle, Wolitzky, & Wakefield, 2001), when Renik (1996) makes the interpretation to his patient that her anger at her sister is partly a defence against feeling critical and angry towards her parents, does she interpret this intervention as merely a "new perspective" that might "work" for her, or does she understand Renik to be saying that she actually harbours angry and critical feelings towards her parents? Do patients really accept the idea that their goal in treatment is primarily to adopt new "meaning systems"?

Much is made these days of the necessity and desirability of honest and careful scrutiny of patient–analyst interactions, of the analyst's countertransference reactions, and even of the analyst's self-disclosure of these reactions. Is it not odd and somewhat anomalous in such a context to withhold and keep mum about one's basic assumptions regarding the nature and goals of treatment and the nature of the patient's mind? One wonders how long patients would remain in treatment if they were told that the analyst is not interested in uncovering and discovering anything, but rather in offering aesthetic fictions, coherent narratives, or the like. One also wonders how well analysts could conduct treatment if their general philosophical ideas that appear in journal articles and books fully infiltrated their day-to-day clinical work. To quote Friedman (1998), if one accepts the positions of the "new view" theorists, then analysis "is, indeed, an adventure of a vastly different sort than we imagined" (p. 260) and one wonders "how an analyst would work who no longer believes in hunting for something that is already there to be discovered" (p. 261).

What are the taboo thoughts here? Do not contemporary analysts who have taken the postmodern turn I have briefly described openly present their ideas? They are certainly not taboo in that sense. What then is the nature of the taboo? I think there are two kinds of taboos. One is that which I have just discussed: the taboo against sharing one's basic views of the nature of the psychoanalytic enterprise with one's patients. Indeed, it might not be possible to embark on or continue that enterprise if one did share these views, that is, if one did not treat them as a taboo topic as far as patients are concerned.

The second taboo is that one must not acknowledge, either to oneself or to others, the dissociation between one's postmodern philosophical views and one's everyday clinical work where these views play little or no role. In our 2001 paper (Eagle, Wolitzky, & Wakefield) we document the degree to which there is a marked disjunction between Mitchell's and Renik's conceptual and philosophical stance and the specific clinical material that is intended to instantiate and support that stance. There is not enough time to demonstrate this at any length. But let me provide one or two brief examples. I have already noted that, despite his insistence that he is offering new perspectives rather than attempting to uncover truths, when Renik interprets to his patient that her anger at her sister is partly a defence against feeling critical and angry towards her parents, he surely must believe that, at some level, she actually harbours such feelings towards her parents. To make such an interpretation simply because it "works", without believing that the patient has such feelings, is arbitrary and seems unethical.

As for Mitchell, although maintaining that there are no mental processes corresponding to the phrase "in the patient's mind" about which one can be right or wrong, and after arguing that there are no "preorganized" central dynamics in the patient's mind, he nevertheless proceeds to interpret the patient's dream in terms of "his struggle with his son [that] were in some measure reflective of struggles with a part of himself that had been buried" (p. 23). He also noted that the patient's father "was internalized by him in a complex fashion" (p. 23), refers to parts of the patient "that he has long since entombed and which he deeply fears" (p. 23), and notes the patient's struggle "with a sense that he has tragically mutilated his own inner resources and potentiality" (p. 24). The idea that the patient is engaged in this struggle is not presented as merely one of a number of meanings or perspectives that he might find "vitalizing and personally meaningful" (p. 24), and if the patient did find this way of looking at himself "vitalizing", etc., one assumes that he did so because it resonated with some deep feelings in himself or in his mind: that is to say, to use Freud's language, because it tallied with something real in him.

Confronting psychoanalytic taboos

Let me now bring this chapter to an end, with some final comments. I think the idea of a conference and book on taboo topics and thoughts within the discipline is an inspired one. Indeed, I think that there should be such a conference every few years. In working on this chapter, it became clear to me—and I hope I have succeeded in making it clear to you—that along with probably every other discipline, psychoanalysis, too, has its myths, self-deceptions, and taboos, which, of course, is an irony for a field such as ours and yet should be unsurprising. We are presumably experts in the taboos and self-deceptions of others, but it is always difficult to be an expert on one's own taboos and self-deceptions. The latter is virtually a contradiction.

One reason that the topic of taboos is such an appropriate one for us is that a focus on taboo thoughts and feelings and self-deceptions and defences constitutes the starting point of psychoanalysis. For at the heart of repression—the concept that marked the birth of psychoanalysis and that Freud (1914d) called the "cornerstone" (p. 16) of psychoanalysis—is the idea that certain thoughts, feelings, and desires that are "incompatible with the ego" are to be treated as taboo. That is, they are not to be consciously thought about, experienced, or acknowledged. And, as George Klein (1976) noted, repression also implies not making connections, not understanding and/or not spelling out the implications and personal significance of certain ideas and experiences. One of Freud's important insights was that in order to maintain mental contents as taboo, one must deceive oneself.

I have tried to show that taboos and their accompanying self-deceptions are not only present at the individual intrapsychic level, but are also present at the level of the discipline as a whole. I have identified a number of areas that I think are marked by taboos and self-deception: the question of individual suitability for doing treatment; the dogma pertaining to transference interpretations; the contradictory conceptions of countertransference; the failure to make fully explicit some implications of the "totalistic" conception of countertransference; the relative silence around the topic of money; and the disjunction between the analyst's conceptual stance on the one hand and his or her clinical work and what patients assume about that work on the other.

It might be the case that self-protective taboos and self-deceptions will inevitably arise, not only at the individual level, but also at the social level of the discipline and the profession. At the individual level, taboos and self-deceptions are to be dealt with by analysis and, if necessary, re-analysis. It would be interesting to think of appropriate interventions at the level of the profession as a whole. Perhaps periodic conferences and books of this type—a sort of parallel to returning to analysis—can be held in which we ask ourselves what topics, meanings, and implications we are treating as taboo and in what ways we are deceiving ourselves. We could even invite serious outside critics of psychoanalysis, where our purpose would be not to defend ourselves in reflexive defensive and indiscriminate fashion, but rather to listen in such a way that we would defend ourselves when that is warranted and acknowledge our limitations, failures, blind spots, and self-deceptions when that is warranted. The measure of success of such discussions would lie in the degree to which at least some of one's view about one's work and one's field would be altered. This is undoubtedly a quixotic idea, but that, too, is one of the purposes and prerogatives of symposia.

Epilogue

I want to add as an epilogue a brief description of the reception of this paper when it was given as a keynote talk at a joint international conference on "Taboo or not taboo? Forbidden thoughts, forbidden acts" at Niagara-on-the-Lake in Ontario, Canada in June 2000. The paper was met with a resounding silence: not a single question or comment from the audience. The paper was given in the dining room immediately before dinner and this, I was reassuringly told, could account for its apparently flat reception. Of course, it is possible, perhaps likely, that the main reason the paper did not elicit any discussion or any other reaction but silence is the usual one: not a very interesting paper. However, in the judgement of colleagues I respect and in my own judgement, I think the paper is a pretty interesting one and raises some important issues. One possibility, then, is that the reaction of silence to the paper was at least partly attributable to its taboo content; that is, to the discomfort it produced. I noted at the beginning of the paper that if we are really serious about our intention to have a discussion devoted to taboo and forbidden thoughts, then all the papers presented here should make us at least somewhat uncomfortable in one way or another. I hope the readers of this chapter and book are made somewhat uncomfortable in one way or another.

References

Eagle, M. (1998). Becoming a psychologist–clinician. In: J. Reppen (Ed.), *Why I Became A Psychotherapist* (pp. 67–76). Northvale, NJ: Jason Aronson.

Eagle, M. (2000). A critical evaluation of current conceptions of transference and countertransference. *Psychoanalytic Psychology*, 17: 24–37.

Eagle, M. (2003). The postmodern turn in psychoanalysis: A critique. *Psychoanalytic Psychology*, 20(3): 411–424.

Eagle, M., Wolitzky, D. L., & Wakefield, J. C. (2001). The analyst's knowledge and authority: a critique of the "new view" in psychoanalysis. *Journal of the American Psychoanalytic Association*, 49: 457–489.

Freud, S. (1914d). On the history of the psychoanalytic movement. *S.E.*, 14: 2–66. London: Hogarth.

Friedman, L. (1998). Overview. In: O. Renik (Ed.), *Knowledge and Authority in the Psychoanalytic Relationship* (pp. viii–xxii). Northvale, NJ: Jason Aronson.

Gabbard, G. O. (1995). Countertransference: the emerging common ground. *International Journal of Psychoanalysis, 76*: 475–485.

Geha, R. E. (1984). On psychoanalytic history and the "real" story of fictitious lives. *International Forum of Psychoanalysis, 1*: 221–229.

Gill, M. M. (1982). *The Analysis of Transference: Volume 1. Theory and Technique.* New York: International Universities Press.

Gill, M. M. (1994). *Psychoanalysis in Transition.* Hillsdale, NJ: Analytic Press.

Kernberg, O. (1965). Notes on countertransference. *Journal of the American Psychoanalytic Association, 13*: 38–56.

Klein, G. S. (1976). *Psychoanalytic Theory: An Explanation of Essentials.* New York: International Universities Press.

Klein, M. (1946). *Collected Writings.* Volume 3. London: Hogarth.

Heimann, P. (1950). On counter-transference. *International Journal of Psychoanalysis, 31*: 81–84.

Mitchell, S. A. (1998). The analyst's knowledge and authority. *Psychoanalytic Quarterly, 67*: 1–31.

Mitchell, S. A., & Aron, L. (1999). *Relational Psychoanalysis: The Emergence of a Tradition.* Hillsdale, NJ: Analytic Press.

Racker, H. (1968). *Transference and Countertransference.* Madison, CT: International Universities Press.

Renik, O. (1996). The perils of neutrality. *Psychoanalytic Quarterly, 65*: 495–517.

Rioch, M. J., Elkes, C., Flint, A. A., Usdansky, B. S., Newman, R. G., & Silber, E. (1963). National Institute of Mental Health pilot study in training mental health counselors. *American Journal of Orthopsychiatry, 33*: 678–689.

Sass, L. A. (1992). The epic of disbelief: the postmodernist turn in contemporary psychoanalysis. In: S. Kvala (Ed.), *Psychology and Postmodernism* (pp. 166–182). London: Sago.

Schafer, R. (1992). *Retelling a Life: Narration and Dialogue in Psychoanalysis.* New York: Basic Books.

Strupp, H. H., & Hadley, S. W. (1979). Specific vs. nonspecific factors in psychotherapy: a controlled study of outcome. *Archives of General Psychiatry, 36*: 1125–1136.

Wallerstein, R. (1990). Psychoanalysis: the common ground. *International Journal of Psychoanalysis, 71*: 3–19.

PART II
EXPRESSIONS OF EROS

CHAPTER THREE

Sexual excitement in the transference–countertransference situation

Charles Spezzano

P sychoanalysis, in its origins, seemed capable of opening up a radical confrontation with human sexuality; radical not only in the sense of the analyst and patient noticing together and talking together about all aspects of the patient's sexual feelings, fantasies, and conflicts, but radical also in the sense of analyst and patient allowing themselves to know and discuss the infusion of sexuality into their ways of relating to each other. It is not clear, however, that individual psychoanalyses are generally able to catalyse such confrontations.

In this chapter, I want to explore the notion that there remains (perhaps inevitably) a taboo on such confrontations, which psychoanalysis also intrinsically intends to confront. We appear able to disrupt, but not destroy, this taboo, in part because, as Freud suggested, it is a key thread in the social fabric that contains us. So, in each psychoanalysis there ought to be an intense clash between, on one hand, the anxiety-laden pressure to maintain the socially structuring (and ethically and legally enforced) taboo on a full confrontation with human sexuality and, on the other hand, the pressure (and commitment) to offer each patient the opportunity for (and to analyse the obstacles to) such a full, radical confrontation.

This is not to say that psychoanalysis has completely lost interest in the ubiquity of sexual excitement and its widespread intrusion into human cultural, interpersonal, and clinical encounters. My impression is that so-called classical and modern Freudian analysts, in the USA, have maintained a relatively unique focus on the vicissitudes of sexual excitement and the anxiety, guilt, and conflicts associated with it. In 1972, Dewald reported this interpretation: "I'll be automatically seduced by you and a whole hurricane of feelings will be loosed and we will both be destroyed" (p. 306). In 1987, *Psychoanalytic Inquiry* devoted an issue to a discussion of a week of analytic sessions conducted by New York "classical" analyst Martin Silverman (1987). His focus on the patient's sexual fantasies was the source of most of the controversy in the discussions of his work by other analysts.

By contrast, in a volume of papers from a British conference on sexuality, there is a chapter by Budd (2000) titled "No sex please— we're British", in which the author points to "a British attitude to the erotic life which assumes that if we have good object relations our sexual lives will not trouble us" (p. 54). Similarly, in the British Kleinian object relational literature, libidinal excitement mainly fuels reparative gestures for damage to objects done by hate and envy. Even perversions are not mainly fuelled by sexual excitement or the wish to feel sexually excited, as can be seen if one follows the writings on the subject by Betty Joseph, where sexual excitement is a supporting actor to the leading role assigned to aggression and the death instinct. Similarly, in France, Green (1995) was led, by the marginalizing of sexuality, to ask, "Has sex anything to do with psychoanalysis?"

Even in the USA, however, manifestations of a continued taboo on fully unmasking the clandestine workings of sexuality intrapsychically and in the transference–countertransference situation have led to essays calling for a correction. Bader (2002) offers an extensive account of unearthing and analysing (towards the goal of reducing anxiety and guilt associated with) sexual fantasies. Similarly, Celenza (2000), reversing the British trend described above, argued that sexuality is the driving force behind sadomasochistic interplay, while aggression serves defensive, concealing purposes.

Celenza's point seems to me to be well taken, considering the extent to which contemporary psychoanalysis, on balance, has become more of a confrontation with destructiveness and narcissism. Even perversion, a phenomenon about which Freud offered one of his most radical theories, has become a site of investigation into sex taken over by aggression (the prevailing London Kleinian position), or sex, even the quintessentially Freudian oedipal-conflict variety, redescribed as mostly a narcissistically driven human agenda (as in French psychoanalysis, especially the work of Chasseguet-Smirgel).

This, of course, might simply be a correct evolution in psychoanalytic understanding. It may be that destructiveness and narcissism are the primary sources of anxiety, conflict, and even apparent sexual phenomena, such as what we call the perversions. It might also be, however, that the affect of sexual excitement makes us anxious—in our lives, in our clinical work, and in our theorizing—because, as Phillip Roth has put it: "No matter how much you know, no matter how much you think, no matter how much you plot and you connive and you plan, you're not superior to sex" (2001, p. 33).

It is the latter possibility that I explore in this chapter. I suggest that we have a taboo about too radically confronting sexuality in clinical work and in theorizing, because sex is too hot to handle. Freud, as we all do, succumbed to the powerful taboo against fully pulling the curtain back on sexual excitement when he undermined his own brilliant uncoupling of the sexual drive from any specific aim or object. This uncoupling effectively meant rendering the word "perversion" meaningless, but, as the historian of psychoanalysis Arnold Davidson (1987) captures it, "Even if Freud's conclusions in effect overturn the conceptual apparatus of perversion, it is well known that he did not embrace these conclusions unambiguously or unhesitatingly" (p. 271). Freud continues to write about certain versions of sex as appropriate and others as deviations, while "the notion of appropriateness has lost all of its conceptual plausibility" (*ibid.*). So, Arnold concludes, we might well "wonder about the accessibility of Freud's achievement to Freud himself" (*ibid.*, p. 275).

The direction of Arnold's speculations—about why Freud might not have been able to remain fully consistent, in his thinking and writing, with one of his own breakthroughs in understanding human sexuality—is that conceptual innovators cannot always escape the gravitational pull of the concept with which they grew up, even if they have overturned it. In addition, from inside psycho-analysis rather than from inside history, my attention is drawn more to the very last lines of Arnold's essay: "Whether Freud went too far or not far enough, this is exactly the right range of question. How far can you go? How far will you go?" (*ibid.*, p. 277). The same question is relevant for us.

An example of what I mean is the well-established social psychology finding that people rated high in physical attractiveness are, illogically and irrationally (given the data presented to experimental judges), rated high in all sorts of other categories. Analysts and patients are probably affected by physical attractiveness in their unconscious reactions to each other. For many years, there were few reports of analysts becoming aware that they caught themselves relating to some patients in a certain way because they found those patients attractive. About ten years ago, this began to change, with reports on erotic countertransference such as those by Hirsch (1993) and Gabbard (1994).

To us, as analysts, the variable of physical attractiveness ought be seen as mediated by sexual excitement. It is a fundamental premise (implicitly or explicitly) of most—if not all—psychoanalytic theories, that affects, arising out of unconscious mental activity, are powerful forces in how we represent people in our minds. Sexual excitement was, for Freud, at least as powerful as any affect in determining the formation of object representations. Analysands, like people-raters in social psychology experiments, will only occasionally be conscious of the ways in which finding someone physically attractive is having an impact on us, but we know, in our theories, that "physically attractive" is not simply a cognitive–aesthetic reaction. It is also, if not mostly, a libidinal reaction. A mediating affect is sexual excitement. This "physical attraction and sexual excitement effect" can hardly be imagined to invade the psychoanalytic situation only rarely. Yet, the kind of comments John Steiner made (1996), as just one example, in a matter of fact way, about moments of anger infusing the analytic work ("I was aware of my irritation" [p. 1080]; "I found myself adopting a somewhat condescending tone" [*ibid.*]; ". . . led both of us to express our irritation with each other and to become aware of it" [*ibid.*], are not made in anything like that matter of fact way, if they are made at all (which, to me, seems rare), about feelings of sexual excitement or attraction, as might take the form of "I was aware of my excitement about his or her face/body/outfit/fantasy", or "I found myself talking excitedly", or ". . . led both of us to express our sexual excitement about each other".

In addition, even though we have long recognized the efficacy of observing when patients get excited and then anxious, there are times when patients point to their anxiety themselves but do not realize the implications. Sometimes, in consultations, clinicians have described situations in which patients say, "I don't like focusing on the idea of me having sexual feelings about you. It's pointless. Nothing can happen. It makes me anxious." The patient presents this as self-evident: sexual desire towards an unobtainable object catalyses anxiety. Manifestly, however, it ought to catalyse frustration or disappointment. The anxiety has to be explained. Its presence is not self-evident. Yet, often, clinicians presenting this material have found themselves agreeing with the patient's manifest claim. This precludes consideration of the anxiety. What are the dangerous aspects of the idea of sexual involvement with the analyst? When this issue has been attended to in certain analyses, I have observed patients becoming aware that they would be willing to forgo whatever healing they have fantasized happening in their analysis for the imagined fulfilment of their excited ideas about a sexual relationship with the analyst. In turn, they then became aware that they were frightened by the power of their desires. I think that the therapists who brought the cases for consultation had overlooked this edge of their patients' fantasies about sex with the analyst, in part, defensively. They realized that they were made anxious by awareness of the relatively ubiquitous temptation to risk ruining their life and career for sexual desire. The unconscious taboo against a full confrontation with sexuality here takes the form of a mutual agreement to avoid the realization that everyone (including the analyst) is vulnerable to a train of thought in which awareness of likely consequences of acting on sexual excitement become muted enough to make the fantasy of doing so seem momentarily possible.

Similarly, some analysands (I think these all have been male) were surprised to realize that one ingredient in their anger at their wives was their sexual attraction to these women. Imagining that they had overlooked problematic aspects of teaming up with their particular spouse because they had been blinded by sexual excitement made them angry, first at themselves, and then defensively at their wives. The fantasy of "you made me love you" became a source of anger. This, too, I believe, is a type of fantasy representation of the power of one's sexuality that can be marginalized in favour of seeing the anxiety of the patient as mainly, if not only, about the anger itself.

This favouring of seeing the anxiety as about anger rather than wild desire is also part of the continuing taboo about sex because it rests, in part (in each case where it is overlooked), on the individual clinician, supported by a community-wide looking the other way (towards anger), anxiously avoiding the bringing out into the open of the commonness of sexual fantasies blinding us to other aspects of many situations. If the potential for this is ubiquitous, then, as I believe Freud feared, there is always a reasonable possibility that unconscious defences will leave either or both members of the analytic pair more aware of anger or boredom than of sexual excitement, even if, perhaps especially when, the latter is a prime motivational force in the immediate transference–countertransference situation.

To go a bit further with this observation of blinding by sexuality, its relevance runs directly into the taboo against a full confrontation with sexuality, but it can easily be kept marginal by a sort of winking acknowledgment of people letting their sexual excitement steer the ship. This does not emphasize the anxiety involved in a constantly threatening awareness of how much this is so at any given moment. As one example, we devote a significant amount of cultural and economic time, space, and energy into the staging and costuming of the female body. Whatever the ultimate origins of this socially central practice, it emphasizes our awareness of the power of sex, as does a prose poem written by Evan Connell, who is best known for the novels about Mr and Mrs Bridge. In *Notes from a Bottle Found on a Beach at Carmel* (1962), he wrote about one panel of a medieval triptych somewhere in Europe that depicts a woman from whose vulva radiates a profusion of luminous xanthic lines. He then links this image to a child's painting of the sun. He suggests that in the imagining of these radiating lines the child has represented the inconceivable power of the object. The inconceivable power of the object is what I am addressing here. A clinical example will help to illustrate.

A man who was referred to me because the woman with whom he had begun therapy had felt disturbed by his repeatedly, over a long period of time, treating her understanding him as her seducing and exciting him. She experienced this eventually as an impasse that they could not resolve, and he became confused and dropped out of treatment. When he contacted her to consider restarting the treatment, she suggested he see someone else and my name was among those she gave him.

He mostly wanted to talk about the hurt and upset he felt about this unsuccessful attempt at therapy, and we floundered in this for a while until he came into an analytic hour complaining that a woman he glanced at on the street in front of my office had seemed annoyed, despite her being dressed, as he saw it, seductively. Several times previously he had mentioned these kinds of encounters, which he sarcastically called close encounters, and he always complained in the same way. This time I said that he seemed to think of the woman as having dressed to excite him. He somewhat reluctantly played with the idea that even a woman who hoped her outfit would excite might not be interested in exciting him, or might not want him to use her to excite himself. He described, as if becoming aware of it in a new way, how he carefully tried to keep looking at certain women he found excitingly dressed and often crossed over some line that he felt existed in the woman's mind. I wondered to him if this line was crossed in a woman's mind when an admiring glance turned into an unwelcome using of her to excite him. I interpreted that he was trying to find a way to be sexually excited in a situation where the other has not agreed to be a source of sexual excitement. He does this because he has come to require some measure of this feeling state to keep from lapsing into a state of futility, as Fairbairn called it. To do this without feeling the terror of rejection and humiliation, he must believe unconsciously that the woman wants him to be sexually excited.

At another point, the interpretive emphasis in this case was on his anxiety about the woman not only wanting him to be excited, but also having complete control over when and whether he did. Both anxieties were related to his sense of sexual excitement being a necessary ingredient for an overall sense of aliveness, while, at the same time, experiencing his sexual excitement as out of his control once it got going inside him. That is why he required the fantasy of the woman being in control of it.

Similarly, a female analysand frequently, during the first few years of analysis, implied or said explicitly that the level of sexual excitement in the room and in me was virtually up to her. She kept the flame low, but could turn it up at will. This both reassured and frightened her. It meant she did not have to trust me, but it also meant she had to trust herself (the latter internal demand being addressed by a fantasy that men would not notice her sexual attractiveness unless she wanted them too).

I think that, in both cases, the emergence of these fantasies and the anxiety associated with them was facilitated by my clearly being interested in where and how sexuality caused anxiety. In analyses, where, for any number of reasons, I might lapse in attentiveness to this aspect of a patient's unconscious psychology, we do not get to it much at all unless I can catch my own defensive distraction from it and not be afraid to be obviously curious about their experience of sexuality.

To some extent, I am describing a clinical situation that has an analogue in the varying readiness any of us has to be aware of someone flirting with us and, conversely, to catch ourselves being flirtatious. In some analyses, pointing out that a story about some type of relational event or breakdown seemed to have a moment of sexual tension that went unrecognized by the analysand (and so he or she cannot make sense of the scene or conjures a paranoid fantasy about it) helps to clarify a key developmental conflict. One familiar example that has occurred in several analyses involves a comment by a father about the way the daughter (the analysand) was dressed. It might have been a complaint about a short skirt or more than the normal amount of noticing a blouse that happened also to be lower cut than usual. When such events are reported with no awareness on the part of the analysand that the event might have included sexual tension between father and daughter, the analyst has to be comfortable about taking the risk of being the one who says "sex" first: "You haven't indicated any awareness that the story about you and your father might easily be heard as a story about a man experiencing some anxiety and conflict when his daughter has dressed in a way intended to draw the attention of her boyfriend but also catches the father's attention."

None of what I have drawn attention to in this essay is offered as profound or cutting edge theorizing. My aim is quite the opposite. One of the original ideas of psychoanalysis—that, in colloquial terms, sex can be mind-blowing—can easily be marginalized into an "of course, we all know that" by patient and analyst. This marginalizing—supported by an implicit trend in theorizing that emphasizes aggressive, destructive, and narcissistic sources of anxiety and relational disturbance—is one manifestation of a perpetual conflict in psychoanalysis: our constant awareness of sex and our constant apprehension that we may be able to warp our minds around its origins and vicissitudes.

References

Bader, M. (2002). *Arousal.* New York: Thomas Dunne.

Budd, S. (2000). No sex please—we're British. In: C. Harding (Ed.), *Sexuality: Psychoanalytic Perspectives* (pp. 52–68). Philadelphia, PA: Brunner-Routledge.

Celenza, A. (2000). Sadomasochistic relating: what's *sex* got to do with it? *Psychoanalytic Quarterly, 69*: 527–544.

Connell, E. (1962). *Notes from a Bottle Found on the Beach at Carmel.* New York: Random House.

Davidson, A. (1987). How to do the history of psychoanalysis: a reading of Freud's *Three Essays on the Theory of Sexuality. Critical Inquiry, 13*: 252–277.

Dewald, P. A. (1972). *The Psychoanalytic Process.* New York: Basic Books.

Gabbard, G. (1994). Sexual excitement and countertransference love in the analyst. *Journal of the American Psychoanalytic Association, 42*: 1083–1106.

Green, A. (1995). Has sex anything to do with psychoanalysis? *International Journal of Psychoanalysis, 76*: 871–883.

Hirsch, I. (1993). Countertransference enactments and some issues related to external factors in the analyst's life. *Psychoanalytic Dialogues, 3*: 343–366.

Psychoanalytic Inquiry (1987). 7(2).

Roth, P. (2001). *The Dying Animal.* New York: Random House.

CHAPTER FOUR

Sexual taboo in the analyst: yes or no?

Ronald Ruskin

Introduction

S exual taboo violations have occurred since the inception of psychoanalytic treatment, but have only recently come under scrutiny. The author poses the question: given the relaxed moral standards in contemporary life, is the retention of sexual taboo for analysts a necessary, absolute condition of practice? Can there be positive outcomes when sexual boundary violations occur? Might there be mitigating circumstances or therapeutic benefits to such violations?

The most powerful learning experience for a future analyst is arguably his or her analysis. Analytic institutes are based on the centrality of expertise and power of the analyst in the analytic dyad. Functioning as leaders, teachers, and supervisors, senior analysts attain a pre-eminent position by virtue of psychoanalytic knowledge, clinical practice, and probity of character. In a training hierarchy, experienced practitioners are responsible for candidates, providing academic and ethical guidance, and models with which younger analysts and students of psychotherapy may identify. For these reasons, this chapter discusses sexual violations with particular reference to senior analysts and training analysts, although some case examples are taken from psychiatric training programmes.

The influence of contemporary society

Contemporary society and mass media have blurred distinctions between erotic fantasy and consensual reality, between psychotherapy as romantic love/rescue *vs.* psychotherapy as treatment. For example, Dr Susan Lowenstein, the psychotherapist in the film, *The Prince of Tides* (1992), had a sexual liaison with her patient's brother, Tom Wingo (Nick Nolte). Her love was seen as a facilitating, pivotal influence in Tom Wingo's recovery.

Barbara Streisand, who played Dr Lowenstein, said,

> I chose to play the character of Lowenstein because she is a wounded healer. I know she exists, this woman capable of healing others yet needing help herself. Imperfect, human, like the rest of us. Where is it written that doctors have to be perfect, have to be gods? [quoted in Strean, 1993, p.100]

This theme of the fallen, wounded, yet accepted healer is prevalent in popular culture.

Is it time, as popular films suggest, to relax the lofty expectations of the therapist–healer? Or are social expectations of therapists already too relaxed? Is the very nature of societal and personal sexual expectation increasingly ambivalent, containing both urgent expression of erotic desire and compelling interdiction against such action? In the context of a postmodern age where categorical, moral imperatives are necessarily subverted, precise professional, technical, moral codes are viewed as essentially relativistic. Should this apply to the taboo against sexual activity between analyst and patient as well?

The central question: the nature of the sexual taboo

What is the nature of the sexual taboo in the analyst and its position in psychoanalytic treatment, training, and the development of psychoanalytic institutes? This chapter will explore this question and the consequences and impact for training programmes and analytic societies once the taboo has been broken. I will share cases of such violations, and openly discuss this difficult, troubling area.

Sexual contact between a psychiatrist and a patient is directly prohibited by the Ontario College of Physicians and Surgeons, the American Psychiatric Association, and the Codes of Ethics of various psychoanalytic societies. Two thousand five hundred years ago, the Hippocratic Oath referred to this interdiction:

> I swear by Apollo the physician, and by Aesculapius to keep the following oath: I will prescribe for the good of my patients and never do harm to anyone. In every house where I come I will enter only for the good of my patients, keeping myself far from all intentional ill-doing and all seduction, and especially from the pleasures of love with women or men, be they free or slaves. [Hippocrates, in Bartlett, 1955]

Despite Hippocratic prohibitions against sexual contact between physicians and patients, sexual violations seem all too evident in the narratives of patients and colleagues. The impact of such violations is often traumatic for the individual victim. Intrusive affects (unresolved shame, betrayal, guilt, rage, depression, anxiety), social isolation, and avoidance are commonly reported. While such patients, their friends, and family bear directly the traumatic stigma, the impact spreads through academic and therapeutic communities to include colleagues, teachers, supervisors, trainees, and other mental health professionals.

No clinical study has demonstrated positive analytic outcome after patient–therapist sex; yet the absence of reported positive outcome does not disprove its possible existence. Clinicians whisper anecdotally that some patients view their sexual relationships with therapists as positive. If this is, in fact, true, such anecdotes require description, verification, and follow-up. One senior analyst claimed that his female patient desperately wanted his love and refused to accept no. While this appeared to be true initially, soon after the analyst consummated the relationship, the patient complained to the licensing body. This is often cited as a predictable outcome. Nevertheless, such pertinent clinical situations are valuable to explore. Another analysand insistently demanded that the analyst have sex with her during analysis, stating she had benefited from a sexual experience with her former therapist, who subsequently had moved away. The analyst explored the analysand's sexual longings in the transference, and her chaotic and traumatic childhood, whereupon she became more openly hostile and sad.

It is relevant to question whether intense sexual longing in therapeutic experience may obscure disturbed mental states such as psychic fragmentation and early trauma or loss. Indeed, detailed clinical evaluations of therapist–patient dyads in which there have been sexual boundary violations often reveal childhood incest and sexual abuse in patients (Kluft, 1990), and unresolved, narcissistic and sadomasochistic conflicts in the therapists (Gabbard & Lester, 1995; Strean, 1993; Twemlow, 1997). Another sub-group of analysts and analysands who have sexual contact are those who eventually marry each other, but of this there is little written. Systematic studies of patient–analyst sexual contact do not exist, probably because of analysts' fear of state/provincial revocation of licensure, as well as civil and criminal prosecution (personal communications: Gabbard, 1999; Gutheil, 2000).

The taboo against seeing, talking, feeling

It is difficult for analysts to openly describe their cognitive and affective states in psychoanalytic work. "While all analysts struggle with loving and sexual feelings towards patients, until recently the psychoanalytic literature was with few exceptions . . . surprisingly silent on the subject" (Gabbard, 1994, p. 1084). In a recent paper, "Love in the therapeutic alliance," Novick and Novick (2000) described the earlier, classical view of countertransference, which suggested an internal closure on affective states within the analyst so that, unequivocally, no form of erotic reaction was to be tolerated. Open reports of erotic and hostile transference and countertransference, debates about therapist use of self-disclosure and enactments, and discussion about touch between analyst and patient have been absent in the literature and clinical case discussions until the past decade.

Shortly after Simon (1991) explored the psychopolitics of oedipal concepts, Green (1995) pointed out a twofold repudiation of genital sexuality and the Oedipus complex:

It is no longer considered to be a major factor in child development nor an etiological determinant for the understanding of clinical psychopathology ... [I]n clinical presentations [there is] a neglect and ... absence of sexuality in conceptual tools which were supposed to enlighten our ideas. [p. 871]

Interestingly, sexual violations within psychoanalysis have been increasingly reported in the past decade. It seems plausible to hypothesize that the decline in the centrality of the Oedipus complex in contemporary psychoanalysis may be related to the apparent increase in sexual boundary violations.

Now, with tolerance for paradigmatic shifts toward exploring the subjective contributions of analyst and analysand in the analytic process, may we include open discussion of the taboo against sexual activity in the analytic situation, examining carefully the positive and negative consequences of such incidents? Have academic training programmes and analytic societies been receptive to such exploration and discussion? The general consensus is that there is a code of secrecy in psychotherapeutic work and a culture of silence in analytic societies. In particular, there is a taboo against the explicit discussion of sex and sexual feelings between training analysts and candidates.

Training programmes: open discussion or secret societies?

Frosch (1991) referred to ruling cliques and tensions in training, while Kernberg (1986) asserted that:

Psychoanalytic education today is all too often conducted in an atmosphere of indoctrination rather than open scientific exploration. Candidates as well as graduates and even faculty are prone to study and quote their teachers, often ignoring alternate psychoanalytic approaches. ... Candidates are systematically prevented from knowing the details of their faculty's analytic work ... The more senior the analyst, the less he shares his analytic experience with students. [pp. 799–800]

Kernberg continued this argument in a recent article stating: "The results have been an active isolation, throughout the world of self-contained psychoanalytic institutes from their academic and cultural environments" (2000, p. 99).

Scharff and Scharff (1999) drew attention to "organizational problems of elitism, political influence, and ignorance of group dynamics . . . as inhibitors of change and innovation" (p.1). They offered a Group Affective Model for teaching psychoanalytic concepts based on the "assumption that affects are the motivating and integrating engine of self-organization at all levels—in the mind, in the neuropsychological functioning of the brain, in relationships, and in groups" (p. 10). They added that: "Present methods of instruction have involved splits between education and training analysis, between cognition and affect, and between concepts of individual and group unconscious processes" (p. 34).

These splits militate against open discussion of disruptive events in training programmes, particularly when rumours and knowledge of sexual contact between an analyst and patient occur. Powerful, conflictual responses in the analytic group lead towards closure, and what Bion (1961) referred to as a non-working group. Addressing such disruptive events is not only crucial in each psychoanalytic dyad, but is also necessary for group process and conflict resolution in the academic and analytic societies.

Totem and taboo

Freud (1912–1913) wrote of the difficulty translating a definition for the Polynesian word "taboo". He referred to the Latin *sacer*, the Hebrew *kadesh*, and the Greek *ayos* (sacred, holy, saint). "Why", Freud asked, "should we concern ourselves at all with this riddle of taboo (p. 22)?" He replied,

> Taboos of the savage Polynesians are after all not as remote from us as we were inclined to think at first . . . The moral and conventional prohibitions by which we ourselves are governed may have some essential relationship with these primitive taboos . . . An explanation of taboo might throw a light upon the obscure origin of our own "categorical imperative". [*ibid.*, p. 22]

Freud later described the two basic laws of totemism: "not to kill the totem animal and to avoid sexual intercourse with members of the totem class of the opposite sex" (*ibid.*, p. 32). This quality of social isolation for fear of moral/physical contagion was an important theme in Freud's description of taboo. It is also instructive, for our purposes, as a type of group split in action and reaction following taboo violation in societies. Writing of the implicit and explicit consequences for the taboo violator, Freud stated:

> Anyone who has violated a taboo becomes taboo himself because he possessed the dangerous quality of tempting others to follow his example: why should he be allowed to do what is forbidden to others? Thus he is truly contagious in that every example encourages imitation, and for that reason, he himself must be shunned. [p. 33]

Underscoring the ambivalent nature of emotional life, Freud added that: "In this respect taboo observances, like neurotic symptoms, have a double sense" (*ibid.*).

Freud suggested that the prohibition, which becomes internalized, is motivated by erotic desire or hostility towards one's closest kin: "Conscience is the internal perception of the rejection of a particular wish operating within us" (*ibid.*, p. 68). Conscience operates in groups and individuals. Injunctions are transmitted from one generation to another in the form of ethical and moral codes of behaviour. Freud (1912–1913), citing Wundt, described taboo "as the oldest human unwritten code of laws" (*ibid.*, p. 18). Certain individuals and groups may attempt to revise or rebel against such codes.

The sexual taboo in analytic societies

In 1911, Freud wrote to Carl Jung, who had transgressed sexual boundaries with his patient, Sabina Spielrein, "I myself have never been taken in so badly, but I have come very close to it a number of times and had a narrow escape" (McGuire, 1974, p. 230). Freud was relatively candid about his own erotic countertransference, advised against sexual relations with patients, and was deeply concerned about the analyst's moral character. Yet, he was ambivalent about Jung's relationship with Spielrein, and analysed his own daughter, Anna.

Reflecting on the growing awareness of sexual abuse in our patients, Person and Klarm (1994) admitted that analysts were slow to acknowledge the central role of trauma, citing the relative absence of articles mentioning incest or seduction in English language psychoanalytic journals from 1920 to 1985. Margolis (1994) likewise noted:

> The universality of incestuous fantasies was acknowledged but we doubted the veridicality of memories of actual incest . . . [and later found that] . . . many patients who, as children were sexually abused by their parents are especially vulnerable to becoming sexually involved in adulthood with their therapists . . . In recent years a number of societies have been wracked by disclosures that prominent colleagues had been involved sexually with their patients. [p. 986]

Paul Dewald (1996) also drew attention to such broken taboos:

> For many years it was assumed that psychoanalysts adhered universally to a high standard of ethical behavior, both professional and personal . . . Any deviations that came to light were considered anomalies, aberrations attributed to sociopathic bad apples. Only the grossest conduct disturbances seemed to count as violations . . . In response to a number of nationally publicized cases in which psychoanalysts were accused of violating ethical standards—similar violations had occurred locally—the St. Louis Institute undertook to evaluate its curriculum . . . Analysts are inherently neither more nor less ethical than other professionals. [p. 23]

Dewald (1996) became aware of a significant, worrisome trend in most institutes: the topic of sexual taboos had never been addressed. In the St Louis community, instances of flagrant violations of ethical standards were widely known. It had taken years of expensive legal manoeuvring to correct individual cases. In other instances, no adequate resolution was ever reached. The Institute's approach became that prevention through education would be more effective than dealing with violations once they had occurred.

In response to an APA ethics subcommittee survey sent to forty societies and twenty-eight institutes in the USA, Ralph Engle (1996) reported that only six institutes offered a course on ethics. Of the fifty-four cases brought before the committee for review, the majority (81%) were boundary violations, mostly sexual. Thirty-seven per cent involved intercourse between male analyst and female patient. In Canada, we do not have comparable data, though in the past decade, six analysts, mostly male, were expelled or resigned from analytic societies; of these more than 50% were for sexual violations (R. Freebury, personal communication, 2000).

The following three cases have been selected from my personal experience.

Case A

Dr A, a respected professor in a Canadian department of psychiatry, worked with young female patients. As it became known that Dr A was having sexual contact with patients, he left academia and moved out of the province before disciplinary action could be taken. At a Grand Rounds on boundary violations several years later, Dr Jay Black, a former associate of Dr A, expressed the shock, dismay, and horror of colleagues at such unprofessional conduct. Dr Black openly described his own passive helplessness and self-recrimination. Ten years after the fact, Dr Black admitted publicly that he had been so upset by Dr A's betrayal of his ideals, the abuse of women, and the inadequacy of his department, that he returned to psychoanalysis. Visibly moved, concerned about the tragic ubiquity of such events, Dr Black urged heightened awareness and expressed continued remorse and distress for what had transpired. As I listened that day, I found myself profoundly moved. I reflected on the impact of such violations in my earlier professional experience and how it had taken me years to work through such difficult events.

Case B

In his late forties, Dr B had the image of an altruistic, dedicated psychiatrist. He was a distinguished and genial polyglot, a training analyst interested in psychosomatic research and great literature. I considered myself fortunate to work at the same Quebec hospital as Dr B, and selected him as my psychotherapy supervisor. He had an immense, receptive energy that made him available to junior residents as well as patients. Dr B's public persona as devoted therapist and inspiring psychotherapy teacher stimulated in many students the sense of a physician admirably uniting hospital psychiatry and psychoanalytic therapy. Many attractive women consulted Dr B. I found myself struggling not to stare as I walked past the waiting-room. I envied his knowledge and old-world charm.

Later, I heard rumours that Dr B was having sexual relationships with his female patients. I put the idea out of my mind. Many years passed. I moved to another province. Subsequently, I heard from colleagues that Dr B had indeed committed boundary violations.

Rutter (1989) encapsulated a similar experience about a revered mentor:

> I distinctly remember watching a nearly impenetrable wall of denial go up inside my mind. The notion of Dr. Reynolds having sex with patients was completely preposterous. He was a man who articulated for the rest of us the most humane values of our profession . . . He would never betray his values and all he had taught us about the art of healing. But along with my disbelief . . . I discovered a simultaneous certainty . . . that what I was hearing had to be true . . . and there finally came a time when I said . . . "Of course he's sleeping with his patients; I have no doubt about it . . . It explains how I've felt around him at times . . . Unfortunately, as is characteristic of the way in which we deny when faced with issues of forbidden sexuality, it took me and most of my colleagues years to absorb the truth. In the meantime, tacitly protected by our silence, Dr. Reynolds continued having sex with more patients, creating more damage. [pp. 10–11]

Case C

Dr C, a senior psychoanalyst, was a highly regarded therapist and teacher. He published many articles and was instrumental in promoting analysis in a major academic and analytic centre in eastern Canada. I remember first hearing him speak and being drawn to the clarity, depth, and wisdom of his knowledge. Unlike my father, whom I considered sensitive, lovable, yet physically weak and temperamental, Dr C impressed me with his academic rigour, personal charm, and physical and intellectual strength. I consulted him about analytic training. Eventually he became one of my analysts.

I believe I had a reasonably good analysis with Dr C, as did many colleagues. We compared notes of our positive experiences. One evening, I joined colleagues and former analysands in celebration of Dr C. Moved by the presence of devoted students and family members, I wrote him a fond letter, admiring his capacity to be a "good father" to others. Subsequently, I grew more distant from Dr C, associating with other study groups, and utilizing different theoretical perspectives.

There was a private and troubling side to Dr C which, years later, I came to know. An analysand told me she had been seeing a patient who was sexually abused by Dr C. Incensed, she demanded to know if I had ever been in treatment with Dr C. I tried to calmly sit this one out in my analytic chair, breathing, and reflecting back to her how distressed and enraged she sounded. We attempted to process the meaning of this to her in analytic work with her own patient as well as in our transference–countertransference experience. She described incestuous fantasies towards her father, saying I looked like him when he was younger. She brought photos. There was a resemblance. She expressed erotic and troubling desires towards me. About Dr C, I was silent.

What was I to make of the apparently real event? I confess I was shaken, split, perhaps shattered, into different experiencing elements: one part completely disbelieving what my analysand told me; a second part considering it to be a distortion, yet possibly based on a real fragment; then, at another level, something disturbing trembled in me: I felt horror and imagined the event was absolutely true. That night I told my wife and called a trusted colleague, who said he heard similar rumours, but nothing substantial. Over the course of that year, rumours continued to grow. What does one do with rumours?

These events occurred over a decade ago. Each time I reflect on them, I am filled with a sinking, sad, unsettling, at times morbidly exciting, feeling. I have never publicly described these events—I felt ashamed and enraged, at other times complacent and indifferent.

At that point in the early 1990s, I had been elected chair of Public Relations for our local psychoanalytic society. I reflected that if the rumours were even partly true, or became public, the analytic community would be required to explore ways of dealing with Dr C's behaviour. I contacted the Ethics Committee and was told that this matter was confidential and that such information could not be communicated. Furthermore, there was a threat that legal action would be directed to anyone who openly discussed it. I asked for a yes/no answer from the Chair. Were there complaints before the Ethics Committee on Dr C? If so, how many? The Chair paused, then told me he was in an untenable situation: he could not speak openly, but yes, there were complaints of a sexual nature, more than one, and the Committee was hamstrung by threats from Dr C's team of lawyers.

Dedicated analysts worked diligently to expedite this matter and bring Dr C's case to an end. Eventually, he lost his licence and was expelled from the analytic community. Years later, there are many unanswered questions, splits in the society, and unsettling feelings.

I had not known there had been rumours about Dr C years before. Why had nothing been done? What about the impact on his analysands who had been abused? What moral and ethical responsibility did the analytic society bear? What about practising analysts who may have been abused by Dr C, but were too fearful or ashamed to report their experience or obtain help? How about conscious or unconscious complicity of senior colleagues who did, or could do, nothing? What could be done to reduce (a) the incidence of such tragic events and (b) the affective consequences and impairment following such taboo violations? Do analytic societies have a categorical imperative that such unfortunate behaviour be immediately addressed? What about treatment and rehabilitation for Dr C and others like him who run the risk of violating sexual taboos with patients?

Discussion

In the material presented, apart from the undeniably tragic consequences for patients, there is a common and significant subjective response to sexual taboo violation within myself and among colleagues. Conscious affects of denial, shock, disbelief, rage, betrayal, horror, shame, and guilt are directed to the taboo action, the violated object, and the violator. Depending on subjective experience and organizing principles, different affects are directed to the taboo violations within the analytic society and can cause major group splits. Some colleagues strove to squelch discussion of Dr C's behaviour. Others were silent. Some were so enraged that reasonable discussion became difficult.

In the cited cases, affective reactions to sexual violations needed to be processed and worked through in academic communities as well as the analytic society. New learning occurs through process-ing group affective experience (Scharff & Scharff, 1999). Profound cognitive–affective states are stimulated when analysts learn of violation of the sexual taboo by colleagues. In each case, an extended period of time (years) was required for working through conflictual material and containing traumatic disillusionment. Self-reflection, group work, individual analysis and / or supervision may facilitate the working-through process. When Dr C's violations came to light, I returned to weekly supervision for two years to evaluate my capacities as an analyst and to reassure myself that I was not contaminated by faulty technique or unconscious identifi-cations with Dr C.

Distressing in these events is our degree of vulnerability to secret influence by the multi-faceted nature of taboo. Not only must we encounter conscious feelings of revulsion and moral discomfort, but also the darker, forbidden envy, excitement, desire, and clan-destine omnipotent wishes to be similar to the taboo violator. "Whenever I thought about his forbidden liaisons, beneath my outrage lurked a secret envy, I wish I could do what he had done" (Rutter, 1989, p. 12).

Analytic societies and mental health groups are vulnerable to such behaviour. What makes taboo violators difficult to address is our reluctance to accept that the taboo against sexual action between analyst and patient should be absolute and universally applicable. Endorsement without reservation is hard because of differing standards in the wider culture and the bivalent nature of taboo.

Once this taboo has been broken, how do we respond to the many anxieties aroused by abused patients, fallen colleagues, and the need to protect ourselves? Attempts to logically resolve this issue within analytic societies are problematic because of the inten-sity of subjective experience, non-disclosure, transferential issues, and failure of large groups to resolve conflict. This may be particu-larly true when perpetrators are revered and powerful senior ana-lysts who at one time represented the ego-ideal of the group. Small groups (Scharff & Scharff, 1999) may facilitate discussion of the intense, external and internal conflict generated by taboo violations. Systematic research on analyst–analysand sexual relationships and therapeutic outcome is at present lacking, and might be difficult or impossible to obtain. None the less, the difficult, yet fundamental notion of taboo is well worth exploring.

Conclusion

In our attempts to move forward in practice and in our creative elaboration of theory, we have moved away from Freud's concept of taboo and the inevitable unconscious emotional ambivalence of its thought and action. In postmodern society, we have repudiated our hard won oedipal knowledge in order to accommodate to a seductive merger with practices that neglect our analytic origins. We must keep in mind Freud's insight that taboo represents, on one level, the fear or interdiction of violation, and yet, on another level, the wish to commit similar action, to imitate the taboo violator.

Sexual taboo violations by analysts have devastating effects on all levels of psychoanalytic activity. They must be openly discussed and dealt with at the earliest possible opportunity. The most damaging response to violations of sexual taboo is neglectful silence. As is evident from the popularity of films such as *The Prince of Tides*, the public has a perverse fascination for fallen healers, a potential that lives in us all. Our experiences to date require us to maintain the taboo barrier as a service to ourselves, and our patients. There appears to be no middle ground or scientific revision at this stage of our knowledge.

References

Bartlett, J. (1955). *Quotations* (abridged). Boston, MA: Little, Brown.

Bion, W. R. (1961). *Experience in Groups*. London: Tavistock.

Dewald, P. (1996). In St. Louis a gateway to ethics teaching. *American Psychoanalyst, 30*(2).

Engle, R. (1996). Ethics revision, now under way, requires both words and deeds. *American Psychoanalyst, 30*(2).

Freud, S. (1912–1913). *Totem and Taboo. S.E., 13*. London: Hogarth.

Frosch, J. (1991). The New York psychoanalytic civil war. *Journal of the American Psychoanalytic Association, 39*: 1032–1062.

Gabbard, G. O. (1994). Sexual excitement and countertransference love in the analyst. *Journal of the American Psychoanalytic Association, 42*: 1083–1106.

Gabbard, G. O., & Lester, E. P. (1995). *Boundaries and Boundary Violations in Psychoanalysis*. New York: Basic Books.

Green, A. (1995). Has sexuality anything to do with psychoanalysis? *International Journal of Psychoanalysis, 76*: 871–884.

Kernberg, O. (1986). Institutional problems of psychoanalytic education. *Journal of the American Psychoanalytic Association, 34*: 799–834.

Kernberg, O. (2000). A concerned critique of psychoanalytic education. *International Journal of Psychoanalysis, 81*: 97–120.

Kluft, R. (1990). *Incest-Related Syndromes of Adult Psychopathology*. Washington DC: American Psychiatric Press.

Margolis, M. (1994). Incest, erotic countertransference, and analyst–analysand boundary violations. (Editorial). *Journal of the American Psychoanalytic Association, 42*: 983–989.

McGuire, W. (1974). *The Freud–Jung Letters: The Correspondence between Sigmund Freud and C. G. Jung*. R. Manheim & R. F. C. Hull (Trans.). Princeton, NJ: Princeton University Press.

Novick, J., & Novick, K. K. (2000). Love in the therapeutic alliance. *Journal of the American Psychoanalytic Association, 48*: 189–218.

Person, E. S., & Klarm, E. (1994). Establishing trauma. *Journal of the American Psychoanalytic Association, 42*: 1055–1081.

Rutter, P. (1989). *Sex in the Forbidden Zone*. New York: Fawcett Crest.

Scharff, J. S., & Scharff, D. E. (1999). The affective learning of psychotherapy. Paper presented at the Fall Meeting of the American Psychoanalytic Association, December.

Simon, B. (1991). Is the Oedipus complex still the cornerstone of psychoanalysis? Three obstacles to answering the question. *Journal of the American Psychoanalytic Association, 39*: 641–668.

Strean, H. S. (1993). *Therapists Who Have Sex with their Patients: Treatment and Recovery*. New York: Brunner Mazel.

Twemlow, S. (1997). Exploitation of patients: themes in psychopathology of their therapists. *American Journal of Psychotherapy, 53*: 357–375.

CHAPTER FIVE

Grappling with tenderness in psychoanalysis

Janet McCulloch

Introduction

C ontroversy surrounds the image of tenderness in psychoanalysis. This conflict has persisted from the time of Freud
and Ferenczi through to modern theorists and clinicians.
Still, awareness and expression of tenderness are necessary in an
analysis that seeks to explore and understand the depths of life
experience. Intrapsychic, interpersonal, and institutional barriers
that interfere with acknowledging tenderness as an authentic therapeutic agent are present in abundance. Where these barriers are
high in all three spheres, tenderness becomes taboo and the result
is disuse, misuse, or abuse of this potential.

Everyone begins life in a state that includes tenderness, a state
characterized by softness, vulnerability, sensitivity, and fragility. The
response evoked in the care-giving environment by the infant's tenderness, and the infant's experience of his or her tenderness within
this environment, contributes to the development of unconscious
fantasy and patterns of experience in relationships. In patients who
have suffered severe developmental trauma, deprivation, or privation, the state of fragility has not evoked an attuned responsiveness.

Correspondingly, the associated affect states of warmth, softness, affection, and kindness are absent. Here, the analyst's understanding, interpretation, and containment of the patient's hostility and rage is essential for the survival of the analysis.

It is, however, the repeated experience of the analyst's "soft spot" for the patient and the softness of the analysis that is mutative and allows for real character change in these individuals. The amalgamation of these elements provides the simultaneous experience of hard and soft, strength and tenderness. This is possible only where the analyst, or the analysis itself, has resolved the conflict between these two polarities and arrived at a place where there is no taboo.

As an analyst, I was raised in a Contemporary Institute where Freud and Kohut were introduced together and the many languages of psychoanalysis were mixed into a vibrant cacophony spoken by eager polyglots. My views on technique were further shaped by the concomitant study of the martial arts during my analytic training. Out of this background came an interest in the controversial image of tenderness within the discipline of psychoanalysis. This essay traces the controversy from its origin in the Freud–Ferenczi conflict and explores tenderness as a necessary therapeutic agent. Case material is used to illustrate the powerful therapeutic action of tenderness. Drawing on the martial arts, I suggest a framework for the clinical use of tenderness in psychoanalysis.

The philosopher, Roland Barthes (1978), refers to tenderness as "the root of all relations, where need and desire join, that infinite, insatiable metonymy, the other embrace, the return to the mother" (p. 224). It is fitting, then, that the controversy concerning tenderness in psychoanalysis begins with Freud and Ferenczi: respectively, the father and the mother of psychoanalysis.

Freud (1915a) viewed tenderness as originating in the sexual drive, a drive which is split into two parts, with the sensuous repressed and the tender remaining conscious. With respect to technique, Freud's fundamental principle is hard: abstinence and privation. The patient's need and longing should be allowed to persist as a force that impels work.

Ferenczi, on the other hand, viewed tenderness as primary. On the spectrum from frustration to gratification, his technique is soft, with relaxation, elasticity, indulgence, and warmth. The work of interpretation is suspended during states of regression. Ferenczi (1988) warned that if we keep our "cool attitude even vis-à-vis an opisthotonic patient, we tear to shreds the last thread that connects" (p. 79). He speaks of the state of tenderness in the child in which softness and sensitivity predominate. He differentiates tenderness or passive object love from the violent ebullition of passion. He sees the response of the care-giver to the child's tenderness as pivotal, with the needed response being tenderness. If passionate love of a different kind is forced upon the child, it may lead to the pathological consequences described as the confusion of tongues, with guilt, sadomasochism, and a precocious maturity (Ferenczi, 1955).

Ian Suttie (1935) further explores tenderness in *The Origins of Love and Hate*. For Suttie, tenderness is based not on sexual desire, but on the pre-oedipal, emotional, fondling relationship between mother and child. Weaning or psychic parturition deprives the child of something it has enjoyed. If the parturition is abrupt, it may lead to distress, anger, and insecurity. Suttie describes the ways in which a child may respond: developing friendly, tender sociability with others; fighting for its rights by finding surreptitious regressions; or submitting and repressing with the subsequent development of a defensive taboo on tenderness where the longing for it is painful and forced out of the consciousness. Anything that tends to re-arouse it is hated. He sees the taboo as separating men from women, parent from child, analyst from analysand, with the parent (analyst) unconsciously resisting regressive longings and forcing the child to grow into a hard cynicism with a core of anxiety and anger.

In writing about work with patients at the level of the "basic fault", Michael Balint (1968) describes pre-oedipal, pathological configurations arising out of a significant discrepancy between the particular needs of an infant and the capacity of the environment to respond to these needs. These individuals describe a feeling of emptiness, or sense of futility. Balint speaks here of the use of a more elastic technique and the need for deep involvement by the analyst. He describes a type of regression—for the sake of recognition—that requires an environment (analyst) that accepts and consents to sustain and carry the patient as the earth or the water sustains and carries. The analyst must not resist, give rise to too much friction, insist on harsh boundaries, but must consent. The image of tenderness is readily evoked in this description of an analyst who yields, softens, and gives way.

The following vignettes from a control case are purposefully brief, with little detail, as they are intended to illustrate the general principle of the clinical use of tenderness. This is a patient like many others, where the approach of tenderness has proved essential and has brought us to pivotal moments in the analysis.

Ms A is an intelligent woman, a lawyer, and divorced mother of three grown children. She was raised in post-war Europe, the only child of an obsessional father and a rigid, critical mother. She learned early to hide her feelings: "The pain goes in . . . It must not been seen." To illustrate, Ms A talks of running for the phone, breaking her toe in the process. On the couch, she recounts looking down at her foot to see the baby toe sticking out perpendicularly from the others. She goes on with her narrative. After briefly reflecting on similar experiences, I ask, "What language do you swear in?" Ms A pauses briefly then replies, "You know, no one even noticed that anything had happened. I didn't make a sound, didn't say a word." As this would suggest, Ms A is extremely well-defended and resists much of the affective experience of her inner life. She brings cognitive strengths to the analysis, preparing for each session, thinking and working hard in her analysis.

The following exchange illustrates the manner in which tenderness is utilized in the service of the analytic process. On a Friday afternoon, prior to a three-day break, Ms A gives a long, uninterrupted monologue with no trace of emotion. My mind wanders. I feel bored and ask myself why. The answer is simple. It is easy for me to distance myself because behind the monotone mask, her story and life are full of pain, loss, and disappointment. If I listen, I come close and feel the pain. So, I come back and involve myself in her story. As the session draws to a close, she asks, "I wonder what you are thinking?" I reply, slowly, "I am thinking that you have had a lonely life." She is silent for a moment, then brushes me off with, "It wasn't so bad. At least I am very independent."

On Monday, however, she returns and I hear, "That sentence kept ringing in my ears. She thought I had a lonely life. I felt. And I don't like to feel . . . stranded and lonely." Ms A continues with affectively charged material about a childhood spent drawing pictures of empty houses, no one inside.

Another illustration drawn from a long week of struggle. Ms A is ill. At sessions, she seems silent and withdrawn, critical of the family who tries unsuccessfully to care for her in a manner that she can accept. She picks up her belongings at the end of the session, wipes off my coffee table with a Kleenex, and puts an empty paper cup in the garbage can. I am feeling resentful and rejected as I wonder why she is so demanding and unable to accept care, theirs or mine.

Stepping back from the session, I ask the same questions of myself. Why am I so demanding of her? She did come to sessions despite her illness. Why am I unable to accept care from her? As I recognize the answer and my own resistance to the regressive longings for care, my feelings soften. The next day, she returns, stating, "I imagined that you would think that was just crass, cleaning up like that. You would think if I felt at home here I would have just left it." I answer honestly, "I saw you were cleaning up. I think that was your way of taking care of me."

There is a long silence, then quiet tears, then, "I do care for you. I didn't think you would see it." Ms A proceeds with a moving account of her unsuccessful, childlike attempts to care for parents whom she saw as fragile and damaged and who rejected and rebuffed her sincere, but sometimes clumsy, efforts.

These two vignettes contain moments in which tenderness is experienced by the analyst and communicated to the analysand. In his text, *Modernity and Self-Identity*, Anthony Giddens (1991) refers to "fateful moments" (p. 5) in which, no matter how reflexive an individual may be in the shaping of experience, he or she has to sit up and take notice of new possibilities. These moments have profound repercussions. Western Buddhism has related the "fateful moment" to the process of rebirth or enlightenment (Smith, 1996). Similarly, the new, unexpected experience of the analyst's tenderness may provide a "violation of the expected" (Stern, 1998, p. 905) and a new form of object relatedness.

These simple moments provide a qualitative change in atmosphere and have the capacity to turn the world upside down, to rearrange the inner landscape. Preceding the fateful moment is a period of heightened defensiveness on both sides of the dyad. Both have hardened: the analyst into boredom or resentment, the analysand into isolation and intellectualization. Early life experience has taught the analysand to anticipate rejection, criticism, and cold from the other at such moments. Here, it does not happen.

The vignettes exemplify the "now moment" and the "moment of meeting" (*ibid.*, p. 911) in the analytic dyad as described by Stern and co-workers in "the process of change study group". Stern describes "now moments" that are lit up, affectively charged, not part of the usual way of being in the dyad. The instant and form of their appearance remains unpredictable. The most intriguing "now moments" arise when the patient does something unexpected. He sees the therapist responding as a person, relatively denuded of the trappings of the role. This is the soft, elastic, consenting analyst.

To premeditate and set out to create a "now moment" is contra-dictory to the concept and could lead to loss of authenticity. But, given the powerful impact of such moments, an analyst may theo-rize as to when the now moment is most likely to occur. This will enhance recognition of the moment of possibility where the analyst may do or say the unexpected and the patient responds as a person, for a moment denuded and undefended. How can this instant be created, and when is it most effective? Here, I turn to the martial arts for understanding.

The many forms of martial arts exist along a continuum from the soft, "internal" styles such as Tai Chi, emphasizing meditation and philosophy, to the hard, "external" styles emphasizing combat and competition. Shotokan Karate is known as a hard style. These martial artists are the Kleinians of the martial arts world. Their hard, one-stroke techniques have a lethal capability. As training progresses to higher belt levels, soft techniques are incorporated. Practitioners at the brown and black ranking learn the value of con-trasting soft, flowing moves with the hard and fast techniques. With a soft technique, as in aikido or judo, the opponent's own energy is used to propel the throw. A crucial factor is the sudden, unexpected nature and timing of the practitioner's move. It is softening, or giving way at the height of a mutual resistance, or at the moment of the opponent's attack, which will lead to the opponent's collapse. Once the opponent is off balance, an opening is created.

In his classic guide to strategy entitled *The Book of Five Rings*, the fifteenth century Japanese swordsman, Mushasi (1933), speaks of knowing collapse:

In single combat, the enemy sometimes loses timing and collapses. If you let the opportunity pass, he may recover and not be so

negligent thereafter. Take advantage of the enemy's collapse. It is
essential to follow-up firmly on any loss of poise. The follow-up
calls for directness and power. [p. 39]

The analyst may take advantage of openings in a similar way,
moving in with an interpretation that further clarifies and exposes
a split-off affect state.

In the vignettes presented, I would see the enemy or opponent
as the resistance, or the hard, rational side that defends against feeling. Ms A's early environment had not responded with attunement
to her infantile state of softness and vulnerability. Correspondingly,
the associated affect states of warmth, softness, affection, and kindness were absent. These parts were split off and devalued, needing
to be reintegrated to restore balance and integrity. Ms A often
wished to feel, or decided to, but could not really feel.

For Ms A, tenderness was an unknown, dangerous entity,
warded off whenever she could see it coming. Within the session,
the opening is created by the analyst's soft acknowledgement of
loneliness at the conclusion of Ms A's lengthy monologue and was
made all the more powerful by the isolating effect of the monologue
itself. Similarly, the analyst's acknowledgement and appreciation of
care stood in stark contrast to the analysand's off-hand, callous self-
deprecation in the second vignette. The strength of the defence
itself was a force used to overcome Ms A's resistance. Here, the
swordsman, Mushasi, would move in with a hard interpretation
aimed directly towards either the defence or the affect state, clari-
fying, articulating, and exposing.

A further image with respect to timing comes from Mushasi's
writing. In the sessions described, the analytic dyad was dead-
locked in mutual resistance to painful, unwelcome affect states.
Mushasi suggests a technique called Letting Go Four Hands, used
where a stalemate has been reached. The essence of Letting Go Four
Hands is to stop immediately the approach being used to move
suddenly and completely into a different tactic. Letting go in the
context of analysis implies relaxing within discipline in order to
experience and communicate tenderness or softness, a move that is
both powerful and unexpected.

Essential in the application of tenderness is the quality of
authenticity. Authentic tenderness might or might not be available.

In the novel *Immortality*, Milan Kundera (1990) writes: "For as soon as we want to feel or decide to feel, feeling is no longer feeling, but an imitation of feeling, a show of feeling" (p. 195). So, then, how do we come to allow ourselves to feel tenderness?

In both the vignettes presented, the development of the feeling of tenderness arose consequent to a "turning on myself"; that is, after turning the inquiry back towards myself. "Why are you so distant?" became "Why am I so distant?"; "Why are you so demanding?" became "Why am I so demanding?" Turning on myself in the service of the analysis was the necessary ingredient in changing hard into soft and creating the now moment. Here, I would reference Bruce Lee (1975), the Ferenczi of the martial arts world, whose revolutionary system Jeet Kune Do teaches: "The true opponent to be overcome is oneself" (p. 9).

A prerequisite for the analyst's experience of tenderness is that the analyst has achieved an inner assurance that allows for participation in a deeply felt relationship. With this, the analyst may contact, yet contain, the longings for tenderness in the countertransference. Without it, the analyst might be unable to allow the necessary lowering of resistance. Searles (1959) vividly describes the "time-honored horror of such countertransference", which necessitates the relegation of the deepest intensity of feeling into the analyst's unconscious (p. 299). Such banishment would produce an analyst unable to relax at the crucial moment, forced to rely on rigid technique that crystallizes, rather than flows.

The achievement of inner assurance through study and practice allows for forgetting learning and more spontaneous, less self-conscious technique. Then, the greatest emergence of tenderness becomes possible. In martial arts, this is known as the point of No Sword; here, the opponent's sword is your sword. In other words, the analysand's defence, a hard shell of isolation, creates the force necessary to overcome the resistance. This requires an accurate sensing of the energy, feeling, and mood of the other.

Tenderness or softness is most likely to be helpful in the analysis of patients who are cognitive and rational, aggressive and controlling. As with Ms A, affect states of softness and warmth are split off and defended against. These individuals have tremendous resistance to experiencing tenderness and pain. These affects may be inaccessible within the invalidated unconscious. The analyst's tenderness, coming at the height of resistance, moves the patient to a new space that is otherwise unreachable. These patients would otherwise return, again and again, to the area of Balint's "basic fault". Instead, the analyst's softness moves the analysand into both recognition and symbolic expression of painful affects.

As with anything else, the analyst's tenderness can be misused. This is illustrated by Ferenczi's patient who was reported as boasting, "I can kiss Papa Ferenczi whenever I want" (1988, p. 45). To avoid misuse by either partner, the selection of an adequate balance between hard and soft is essential. This balance could be informed or guided by the Samurai saying regarding Bushi no Nasaki, the tenderness of the warrior: "Rectitude carried to excess hardens into stiffness. Benevolence indulged beyond measure sinks into weakness" (Nitobe, 1979, p. 32).

Within the framework of martial arts, the soft, gentle, yielding forms have the intent to grasp, hold, and draw the opponent closer. This is useful with patients who remain distant and avoid intimacy. The analysand who keeps the analyst at arm's length may be brought within reach, or disarmed by an interpretation delivered softly. The analyst who is able to move in close with tenderness or gentleness will be able to bring the analysand into areas of painful affect that would otherwise be resisted.

Most martial arts systems recognize that moving in close to the opponent will both invalidate most defences and allow for the use of greater leverage in techniques. In analytic work, as in martial arts, it is important to remember that a hard strike directed at a nerve centre may be counterproductive if it totally disables or incapacitates the analysand. In contrast, gentle pressure on a nerve centre or joint creates pain and awareness that may provide direction and motivation for change.

A closely related framework that provides a guide for the effective use of tenderness is the principle of complementarity embodied in the concepts of yin and yang. Yang, with its aggressive, controlling character, or yin with its soft, yielding character, may appear in either analyst or analysand. When the analyst comes to recognize the analysand in a state of yang, the analyst's unexpected move into yin may destabilize the analysand and overcome resistance. This principle of complementarity allows the analyst to avoid the trap of over-reaction or counter-reaction and to retain or restore a balance within. An analysand whose energy has been expended in yang may be drawn easily into yin by the softness or gentleness of the analyst. (Both vignettes illustrate this principle.) At that moment, the analyst follows through with the focus and concentration of the hard interpretation that represents the return to yang for the acquisition of insight and consolidation of new learning.

In the ongoing, dynamic process of analysis, the analyst's deepest aim is to restore the patient's flow, complementarity, and harmony. In time, this allows the analysand to regain contact with the central self, to heal the split between hard and soft, and become a resilient adult, grounded and living in the present. For those whose life experiences have created hard, tough exteriors, it is the analyst's tenderness that allows the experience of softness to re-emerge and fosters the integration of the elements.

References

Balint, M. (1968). *The Basic Fault*. London: Tavistock.

Barthes, R. (1978). *A Lover's Discourse*. New York: Hill & Wang.

Ferenczi, S. (1955). *Final Contributions to the Problems and Methods of Psychoanalysis*. London: Hogarth.

Ferenczi, S. (1988). *The Clinical Diary of Sandor Ferenczi*. Cambridge: Harvard University Press.

Freud, S. (1915a). Observations on transference love. *S.E.*, *12*: 159–171. London: Hogarth.

Giddens, A. (1991). *Modernity and Self-Identity*. Cambridge: Polity Press.

Kundera, M. (1990). *Immortality*. New York: HarperCollins.

Lee, B. (1975). *Tao of Jeet Kune Do*. Santa Clarita: Ohara.

Mushasi, M. (1933). *The Book of Five Rings*. T. Cleary (Trans.). Boston, MA: Shambhala.

Nitobe, I. (1979). *Bushido: The Warriors Code*. New York: Ohara.

Searles, H. (1959). Oedipal love in the countertransference. In: *Collected Papers on Schizophrenia and Related Subjects* (pp. 284–303). New York: International Universities Press.

Smith, S. (1996). Western Buddhism: tradition and modernity. *Religion*, *26*: 311–321.

Stern, D. (1998). Non-interpretive mechanisms in psychoanalytic therapy. *International Journal of Psychoanalysis, 79*: 903–921.

Suttie, I. (1935). *The Origins of Love and Hate*. London: Kegan, Paul, Teuch & Truber.

PART III

TRANSCENDING TRADITIONAL THOUGHT: BUDDHISM AND SPIRITUALITY

Self or no self: psychoanalytic and Buddhist perspectives on neuroendocrine events and subjective experience[1]

Robert Besner

Introduction

This chapter examines the convergence of psychoanalysis, Buddhism, and biology in two essential human domains: the body, and the construction of subjective experience. It outlines a model of functioning in which our cognitive activity and our moment-to-moment sensation of physiological arousal have such an intimate reciprocal relationship that they are woven into a total fabric of subjective experience, with the two factors at different times pushing and pulling each other. In effect, our experience oscillates between these two modes of being, at times with cognitive contents eliciting physiological states, and at times with physiological states driving cognition. This oscillation tends to occur largely outside of our awareness and tends to be excluded from consideration in the psychoanalytic process.

A mounting body of evidence in neuroscience and infant research is establishing the centrality of physiological arousal states to subjective experience. Yet, curiously, this area of inquiry remains largely outside of psychoanalytic investigation. The sources of information from which we typically derive psychoanalytic understanding are narrative contents of a person's self-report, taken together with its affective colouration, and the therapist's perception of his or her own internal experience in this dyad. But our failure to engage, with awareness, in the complementary mode of experience driven by physiological arousal states deprives us of information essential to understanding a person's subjective experience.

This chapter raises the question of including, in the scope of psychoanalytic investigation into human experience, our physiological arousal states as a complement to the narrative presentation. The object of understanding is not the specific contents of the myriad self states described in psychoanalysis. Rather, it is to explore, through examining the process of construction of the self and the subjective narrative, how the dynamic relationship between narrative contents and the sensation of physiological arousal expresses itself in the experience of the self at each instant.

The relevance of Buddhism to a psychoanalytic investigation of the self

The models of mind of psychoanalysis and Buddhism hold in common several propositions that provide a basis for this discussion. They share the essential developmental notion that psychological life follows a course progressing from lower to higher function, a path of increasing differentiation. They both subscribe to the understanding that behind manifest content lie meaningful processes that are in themselves developmental, and have some degree of variability and plasticity. Both systems acknowledge the permeating effects of narcissism.

For both, the self can be seen as a rapid succession of instantaneous mental events (Besner, 1989). Kernberg (1975, 1978) described these as self–affect–object (S–A–O) units. Daniel Stern (1986) called them RIGS (Representations of Interactions that have been Generalized). Through these emergent representations, with their related affects, we are always in the process of creating our "selves" in a specific moment. Upon this activity, we tend to impose an overlay of self-conscious elaborations and justifications, or narcissistic privilege.

Contradictions between the two systems also exist (Welwood, 1987). Among them, psychoanalysis and Buddhism diverge in their understandings of this overlay (Applebaum, 1979). Unlike psycho-analysis, Buddhism fundamentally questions the privileging of the self and its consequent influence on all functioning. It has developed techniques to cultivate the cognitive skills necessary to interrupt the process of recreating the world in the shadow of the self (Lacan, 1978) at each instant. It offers an understanding of the process of coming-into-being of each moment of experience from an initial sensory impact to a full-blown, self-centred conceptualization (Narada, 1975).

Three ideas from Buddhism recur implicitly throughout this chapter and illustrate the ease of fit between Buddhism, psycho-analysis, and biology. The first idea is karma, which is essentially the law of cause and effect. The second is the notion of a "store-house consciousness" in which the residue of past experience lingers, with the potential to be realized in the future (Wei-Tat, 1973, pp. lx–lxxv). This construct is analogous to the associational matrix of cortical and other neurons, and to the phenomenological uncon-scious of psychoanalysis. The third idea is a central theme in the *Tibetan Book of the Dead*: characteristics of mind, conditioned by the residue of past experience, at the moment of death transition through an intermediary space, then reappear in the next rebirth (Evans-Wentz, 1957). Consider this as a metaphor for what occurs at each moment of subjective experience. For example, an internal or external event activates sensory receptors, which activate a corti-cal associational matrix, which sends processes down to the limbic system, which signals the endocrine glands to release hormones into the bloodstream. A multiple feedback loop is established in which factors like projections from the limbic system to the cortex, and hormones in the blood, affect the brain. These material traces of subjective/neuroendocrine activity then condition thoughts and feelings of the subsequent moment of experience (Panksepp, Siviy, & Normansell, 1985; Spyer, 1989). We do not have to die for this to happen, and we do not have to mystify it. Our past actions condi-tion our subsequent ones. This is instant karma.

Physiological arousal states

Freud (1885) first developed a neurological model to account for drive, or neuroendocrine discharge, but, without the work of the next 100 years at his disposal, he could not use this model to account for the construction of subjective meanings (Pribram & Gill, 1976). For a while, he preserved his interest in the neurological substrate of mental functioning by studying the effects of traumatic events, but he finally came to focus on subjective meaning as the basis for understanding human experience (Freud, 1900a, 1905d; Masson, 1984). Psychoanalysts since then have pursued this as their subject matter and have created a treasure of understanding of the human condition. We have devoted little attention, however, to the neurological substrate of behaviour for most of the century, until recent developments in infant research and neuroscience opened a window on events underlying subjective experience.

Today we know we are all, at each moment, in a state of physiological arousal in which neuroendocrine and other regulatory factors produce particular biochemical states in our bodies. These states are constantly in flux, surging in response to internal and external stimulation, and subject to minute, regulatory processes (Schore, 1994; Taylor, 1992).

Neuroendocrine conditions have *systemic* effects on us. Consider the consequences of varying amounts of serotonin available for synaptic transmission (Malone & Mann, 1993), or of activation of the amygdala, with cortisol being dumped into the bloodstream in a stressful moment (Johnson, Kamilaris, Chrousos, & Gold, 1992). These events are encompassing for the person. They produce a total moment of involvement with this arising state, including cognitive content, a feeling state, autonomic arousal, and neuromuscular activity (Bakal, 1999), sometimes as subtle as a change in facial expression, or perhaps clenching of the thoracic, abdominal, or perianal musculature, or curling of the toes.

These states, while detectable, generally remain below our threshold of awareness (*ibid.*). Except for particularly potent eruptions, they operate constantly, but quietly, in the background of our subjective experience, like the hum of fluorescent lighting, or the lapping of waves at the shore.

Perception of these internal events *is nothing other than* the experience of the changes in neuroendocrine and exogenous factors (e.g., caffeine) that are bathing our tissues. We can feel it. This is the stuff of non-verbal experience.

Often, we consider these events as remote from our subjective experience, as the "machine" in which the "ghost " of subjective self resides (Damasio, 1994). From our point of view, however, the ghost is the machine: the detection of these internal events is synonymous, even identical, with our experience of our "selves". Even when considering external events, once they reach our sensory–perceptual apparatus, they become internal events subject to all the same influences.

Infant research has been helpful in illuminating this substrate of our subjective experience. The preverbal infant, with its subjective self of memory traces and cortical associations still unformed, none the less communicates its internal state of physiological arousal in mutually regulating interactions with care-takers (Beebe & Lachman, 1988; Hofer, 1984; Schore, 1994; Trevarthen, 1989; 1997). Physiological arousal states transmit affect and contain meaningful communication regarding subtle changes of state. Furthermore, and quite remarkably, they actually evoke patterns of neuroendocrine responsiveness in relationship. Characteristic tendencies for physiological arousal patterns endure throughout one's lifetime (Schore, 1994; Sroufe & Rutter, 1994). This research suggests that while a state of physiological arousal is an internal event, its transmission indicates that these physiological eruptions account not only for our individual experience, but also for our very embeddedness in relational life.

As the infant matures and the capacity for representational activity develops (Piaget, 1978), memories and associational patterns appear in the context of both internal states and interactions with others (Stern, 1986). These can be seen as the contents of Kernberg's self–affect–object units. We do not usually think of these self–object–affect units as physiological events, but they are (Modell, 1993). They are alterations of neuroendocrine conditions because they are laid down as memory traces, networks of cortical neurons with specific projections to one another and to the limbic system and hence to endocrine glands (Schore, 1994). All such cognitive content comes packaged as a physiological event. Conversely, any physiological arousal is liable to activate a network of memory traces, affects, and conceptualization expressed in a self state or relational posture (Levin, 1991; Schore, 1994).

From this point of view, the self and the body, the psyche and soma, are inseparable. To remove the self from its place in the body would be invalid. There can be no disembodied self, or psyche, since this entity is only the reified compilation of self-representations, composed of cognitive associations and emotional tendencies, which ultimately are neuroendocrine events.

Parallel to, and underlying our subjective lives, we are riding a biochemical tide of neurotransmitter and hormonal surges, of successive waves coursing through our tissues. Underneath it all, we are the same bubbling cauldrons of juices and gases as the infant, except, perhaps, with less gas.

Biological imperatives

What are the motivating factors driving our subjective experience and behaviour? In addition to psychodynamic factors and endogenous biological conditions, there are what I call ethological or biological imperatives. These are hard-wired capacities and tendencies related to the adaptive functioning and survival of the individual, present across species (Bowlby, 1969).

The principle biological imperative is to preserve the organism which, when organized at a subjective level, appears to be about preserving the self. Consider the example of separation and attachment. What begins as an adaptive, biological survival strategy (for example, anxiety generated in the infant by actual or imagined separation) later may be paired with stimuli that do not represent realistic threats of the same magnitude. Depending on the individual's native and learned capacities for modulation of his or her physiological arousal state, the intensity of the threat to self can feel the same, such that the person feels flooded with, and probably convinced of, anxious impressions and interpretations of events, with corresponding behavioural results (Dozier, Stovall, & Albus, 1999).

Such ethological factors—nodal points of organization of human behaviour—underlie all psychoanalytic theories. Behaviour under the rubric of sex and aggression is the object of understanding of classical analysis. The vicissitudes of the imperative for attachment are described by object relations and attachment theory. The imperative towards organizing and sustaining the self is explored in self psychology. What are all these schools examining but variations of specific, prewired channels of neuroendocrine arousal?

So, what is the problem? It lies in the natural channelling of these biological imperatives for sexual and aggressive expression, relatedness, and regulation of self states through such psychological processes as accumulated self and object representations (Jacobson, 1964), identificatory processes (Freud, 1923b), and defensive operations (A. Freud, 1966). This is, of course, a spectacular achievement of human evolution. Yet, just because in this process of the construction of the self the emergent physiological processes and psychological operations reciprocally influence each other, subjective experience becomes vulnerable to its own creative influences.

In this dialectic, these naturally occurring modes of organizing human experience tend to overshoot their mark, so that the biological imperatives that favour survival of the organism are amplified. They are co-opted into the service of preserving the primacy of the self, and translate themselves into subjective imperatives (Besner, 1989). Through this process, the self becomes reified and privileged. Our very human capacities for cognition and reflection serve not only adaptive needs, but, analogous to the secondary autonomous processes outlined by Hartmann (1964), tend to take on a momentum of their own. Through failures of modulation, they may become obstacles to adaptation themselves as they foreclose on possibilities not determined by compulsive self-interest.

The construction of the subjective narrative

Consider two conditions of our subjective lives. First, our preverbal, neuroendocrine activity persists as the substrate of subjective experience (Schore, 1994). Second, our conceptual activity is gestalt-seeking (Kohler, 1970): it attempts to organize our perceptual and somatic arousal states through myriad attributions, projections, and insinuations. Upon the flux of instantaneous internal events (Hume, 1739), we impose a conception of continuity and causality, an overlay of narrative dramatic fabric. In our efforts to organize the field of experience, we build up a narrative momentum that tends towards appropriation of what it perceives. The physiological arousal state that serves as wellspring to the conception of its own meaning is soon, itself, lost in the sea of subsequent layering of arousal states and conceptions of them.

The nature of associational sequences is such that, once activated, neuroendocrine circuits in turn trigger other neural networks of related content and emotional quality. This means that in a sequence of associations, these further emotionally-tinged thoughts, elaborations of the initial thought, are liable to be artefacts of the initial physiological eruption. Yet, most of the time, we do not question their validity. Insidiously, the verbal–conceptual components of psychological functioning achieve apparent primacy in our subjective experience. This is for a good reason: we represent them to ourselves verbally, so they are easily accessible. The attributions upon which they are based are, however, unreliable (Mitchell, Johnson, Raye, Mather, & D'Esposito, 2000; Nesbitt & Wilson, 1977). That we live in a constructed narrative means we live in an echo chamber of attributions, bouncing and ricocheting off one another, occurring so quickly as to be difficult to detect. From this point of view, we are living a highly articulated, elaborate fantasy (Lacan, 1978; Loftus, Feldman, & Dashiell, 1995; Richardson, 1985; Roediger, 1996).

This self-scripted narrative assumes compelling, quasi-imperative proportions. Each instantaneous occurrence of it (the initial sensation of the physiological arousal state flowering into a full-blown conception associated with affect) is an overwhelming event, analogous in its effect on a person to a tidal wave. At every moment we are "swept away" by this torrent of internal events, by an overwhelming cascade of activity.

The potential for difficulty in this process lies in people's belief in the veracity of their associative process, of their internal reality, which can come to supersede external reality (Spence, 1982). The surge of affects and associations is more compelling than logic and empirical evidence, and supplants it. Belief in one's associations is less demanding than tolerance for ambiguity and ambivalence in life. It becomes easier to search out justifications for the associations.

In this way, our functioning slips insidiously from a range in which perception serves the sensitive discernment of a situation to one in which it is distorted by a fundamental narcissistic imperative. This shift is synonymous with personalizing the activation of associational networks and emotion centres in the brain and the discharge of hormones into the bloodstream, whether it happens to oneself or to someone else. Even our most closely held personal meanings are subject to this process.

The defining effect of this narcissistic imperative is the belief in a self, or psyche, at the centre of all experience. While they are functional constructs in various contexts, for the purposes of this discussion it is more useful to consider the terms self and psyche as reifications, and to examine their underlying constituent processes. What is being reified is a range of biological, functional capacities necessary for survival. These include capacities for a sense of continuity and cohesiveness (agency), as well as an observing capacity. Each one of these may be viewed without reference to a supraordinate construct such as self or psyche. Instead, the subject of these capacities would be direct, or actual, experience.

In the process of narrative construction, such functional capacities tend to be incorporated into the experience of a self. Correspondingly, in psychoanalysis, the very process of experiencing is transformed into an anthropomorphized agency or structure. This might be useful in providing, for example, continuity of experience in space and time (Grossman, 1982). For all its lyrical richness and poetry, however, it has several limitations. The primacy of the self-referenced narrative tends to distort perception, self-experience, and behaviour in self-serving ways. It ignores the ongoing process of its own construction, which is necessarily in flux. It minimizes the actual physiological antecedents that the narrative is attempting to transmit. Lost are the relative contributions of physiological arousal and verbal representation to any moment of experience, as well as the very process of developing the narrative from incipient arousal state to full-blown moment of subjective experience.

Implications for psychoanalysis

From a psychoanalytic approach, this process of narrative construction is not particularly problematic. On the contrary, understanding the act of rationalization, or justification of subjective experience is a prime feature of psychoanalysis (Freud, 1923b). For Buddhism, these justifications are secondary to the underlying process of self-reification. This process itself is the problem, in as much as it links impersonal biological activity to a self-interested imperative (Besner, 1989).

Psychoanalysis and Buddhism address themselves to two different orders of functioning, so their mandates are not identical (Welwood, 1987). Psychoanalysis is often concerned with consolidating self-structures and reinforcing selected aspects of the narrative, while Buddhism tends to be concerned with articulating the experiential qualities of the present moment, including, but independent of, the narrative layering. Such a focus on direct, immediate experience in the present moment necessarily produces a different set of constructs than the psychoanalytic ones that account for continuities in human experience.

Despite this difference in focus, there still is overlap between the two systems in the area of deconstruction of subjective experience and the self (Besner, 1989). A central mandate of psychoanalysis is the deconstruction of the narrative in order to allow insight, new relational and self-experience, and behaviour change. In pursuing this project faithfully, we are confronted with the question of the substantiality of the self. This is so because the deconstruction reveals the self as an illusory icon, elements of continuity notwithstanding, a convenient compilation of instantaneous and fleeting self and object representations which are nothing other than the experience of the activation of neuronal traces and accompanying endocrine discharge. The same can be said in general for the other projections, concretizations, and unfounded inferences that constitute the self and which characterize much of our mental production.

While psychoanalysis is attuned to affect (by definition a somatic experience) as primary in treatment and theory, still the narrative content that frames the affect easily becomes the primary focus of attention. This chapter poses a question to psychoanalysis: at what point should it limit its investigation of human experience? As empirical evidence mounts in support of the subtle, yet profound and pervasive, influence of physiological regulation in our internal and interpersonal experience, the scope of analysis is being inevitably expanded.

The difference between the systems is that the threshold for what is a problem is lower in Buddhism. It challenges the conventional state of affairs in which self-interest remains unquestioned as a prime motivator. Buddhism also presents an alternative to the process of biological imperatives translating themselves into subjective imperatives with their concomitant urgency of self-interest: this is to attend to the process earlier, say, at the stage of awareness of the initial sensation of the arousal. This is hard to do, though, and, invariably, another surge will occur, accompanied by the same problem.

The process of self-construction, fuelled by the interplay between cognitive and physiological factors, becomes hardened by the felt urgency of the narcissistic imperative. This development predisposes us to become preoccupied with ourselves beyond adaptive goals, and has a questionable, determining effect on subjective experience and behaviour. In Buddhism, this process is described as follows: "Mind, hardened by its experience potentialities, assumes the appearance of an object" (Guenther, 1977, p. 167). The process of experiencing becomes obscured in narcissistic preoccupations by those functions through which it is organized.

In order to meet the challenge, Buddhism has developed techniques to help cut this explosion of imperative narrative construction. Meditation and other practices are techniques of developing the capacity to observe mental and other internal events (Brown, 1977; Engler, 1984). Through this regulation of attention, it becomes possible to detect arousal states, including their cognitive contents, affective flavour, and somatic experience, earlier in their emergence (Sheikh, Kunzendorf, & Sheikh, 1996). The effects of the initial eruption tend to become more subtle, physiologically and behaviourally. This reduces the subjective urgency attached to arousal states, so that the person is less compelled by each passing momentary configuration of sensation, affect, cognition, and conception. Such a process might lead to the relinquishment of many fictive layers and narcissistic elaborations of the narrative self.

Conclusion

That the self is a compilation of a fleeting series of affectively-laden self-representations is well established in psychoanalysis. This formulation has been verified by studies identifying neurological events with such representations. While the neuroendocrine factor implicitly underlies all psychoanalytic theories, in both our theoretical and clinical work we continue to split off subjective experience from its location in the human body. Despite empirical evidence to the contrary, we tend to ignore this failure of integration. Instead, we collude in the process of reifying the narrative, excluding from consideration the physiological undercurrents driving our momentary, subjective experience.

But what is it that people struggle with subjectively, other than the effects of arousal patterns coursing through their bodies in the form of impersonal impulses, affects, visceral changes, and so on? A thought is a body action. It is a change in physiological arousal state.

The variable we are looking at is the threshold of detection of arousal. Typically, in clinical practice and in general human experience, this awareness occurs only dimly, and late in the process of arousal, if at all. There has been little psychoanalytic investigation into such fundamental questions as: what is the nature and quality of the moment of experience of a S–A–O unit; how does the arousal of a specific S–A–O unit translate into the impulse or intention to act; how accessible to consciousness are such mental contents and their vicissitudes? Learning to recognize these emergent states could be an important tool in understanding and modulating the regulatory processes determining human subjective experience and behaviour, whether we are acting as clinicians, theoreticians, or citizens.

Although psychology has the technology to detect subtle changes (Sheikh, Kunzendorf, & Sheikh, 1996), it has yet to fully integrate this phenomenon with its understanding of subjectivity. Still, we are gaining the knowledge to recognize the salience of the physiological substrate of our subjective experience. We can now ask if there is a method of relating with this immediate experience underlying the flood of cognitive representations and fully developed affect states that constitute our subjective worlds. Insights from Buddhist meditation might assist us in answering this question.

To dwell on the cognitive–affective torrent of narrative associations is to reinforce the neuro-endocrine circuitry that accompanies it. Conversely, to observe the underlying state of physiological arousal itself, and its imminent dissolution at each instant, results in a relative diminution of the centrality of the narrative contents, along with their unconscious and inexorable role in driving the physiological arousal state. There is no end to the chain of associations, except for cessation of the compulsion to construct a narrative self at each instant. The questioning of the privileged status of this activity would allow us to discover what might be there in the absence of our compulsive self-referencing.

We live in biology, but we represent it to ourselves lyrically. Biology impels us in the service of adaptation, but the act of construction of the self compels us in the service of its own edification. We are always engaged in a process of self-construction, using as raw material the ongoing process of physiological arousal and the concomitant emergence of momentary states of subjective experience. This chapter is a call to integrate established psychoanalytic understandings of narrative presentation with the oscillation between cognitively and physiologically driven modes of experience in which we dwell.

Summary

This chapter challenges two closely held and related assumptions of psychoanalysis: the dichotomization of mind and body, and the virtually complete reliance on personal meanings to the exclusion of attending to other features of our actual experience. It outlines how central elements in Buddhist thought can be demonstrated in both established and evolving notions in psychoanalysis and western psychological science. Psychoanalysis can be seen as working to integrate or synthesize conflicts, divergences, and disruptions in a person's system of personal meanings. The present work is based on the growing body of evidence that demonstrates that our personal meanings arise from, contribute to, and fundamentally are carried along by, our states of physiological arousal. From this point of view personal meanings, while salient, are insubstantial. They have long been recognized in psychoanalysis as superficial, requiring exploration in terms of manifest content. Even deeper meanings are similarly transparent and evanescent, as they, too, can be deconstructed, ultimately to the experience of physiological arousal, or sensation. Yet, the role of sensation in constructing our subjective experience remains unexplored in psychoanalysis. How we can continue to fail to integrate this feature of the situation?

To raise these questions is not to devalue the formidable contribution of the exploration of personal meanings to the alleviation of human suffering. Through psychoanalysis, someone well might process and relinquish progressive layers of personal meaning, and thereby achieve personal development. But this quality of subjective experience, however richly articulated, shares an essential similarity with unanalysed life: they both hold tight to a reified narrative construction of subjective experience, thereby privileging this construction over other possibilities. To question this notion is not typically within the analyst's scope of practice or expertise.

These conditions foreclose on areas of human potential so far unexplored in psychoanalysis. The taboos here are that, in the psychoanalytic devotion to pursuit of the narrative, we tend not to attend to our actual experience, or to acknowledge this shortcoming. This paper suggests a shift in emphasis allowing for greater integration of the mind and body components of subjective experience.

Note

1.   Paper delivered at "Taboo or Not Taboo" Conference, Niagara-on-the-Lake, Ontario, Canada, 1 July 2000. I would like to acknowledge research assistance from James Steiben and editorial comments from Brent Willock, PhD.

References

Applebaum, S. (1979). Go east, young robot. In: S. Appelbaum (Ed.), *Out in the Inner Space: A Psychoanalyst Explores the New Therapies* (pp. 267–288). New York: Anchor Press/Doubleday.

Bakal, D. (1999). *Minding the Body: Clinical Uses of Somatic Awareness*. New York: Guilford.

Beebe, B., & Lachman, F. M. (1988). The contribution of mother–infant mutual influence to the origins of self and object relationships. *Psychoanalytic Psychology*, 5: 305–337.

Besner, R. (1989). The self and beyond: conceptions of psychological functioning in psychoanalysis and Buddhism. Unpublished Doctoral Dissertation, University of Denver, Colorado.

Bowlby, J. (1969). *Attachment and Loss: Volume 1. Attachment*. New York: Basic Books.

Brown, D. (1977). A model for levels of concentrative meditation. *International Journal of Clinical and Experimental Hypnosis, 25*: 236–273.

Damasio, A. (1994). *Decartes' Error: Emotion, Reason, and the Human Brain*. New York: Putnam.

Dozier, M., Stovall, K. C., & Albus, K. (1999). Attachment and psychopathology in adulthood. In: J. Cassidy & P. R. Shaver (Eds.), *Handbook of Attachment Theory and Research* (pp. 497–519). New York: Guilford.

Engler, J. (1984). Theraputic aims in psychotherapy and meditation: developmental stages in the representation of the self. *Journal of Transpersonal Psychology, 16*: 25–61.

Evans-Wentz, W. Y. (1957). *The Tibetan Book of the Dead Or The After-Death Experiences on the Bardo Plane, according to Lama Kazi Dawa-Samdup's English Rendering*. London: Oxford University Press.

Freud, A. (1966). *The Ego and the Mechanisms of Defence*. New York: International Universities Press.

Freud, S. (1885). Project for a scientific psychology. *S.E., 1*: 295–397. London: Hogarth.

Freud, S. (1900a). *The Interpretation of Dreams*. *S.E., 4 & 5*. London: Hogarth.

Freud, S. (1905d). *Three Essays on the Theory of Sexuality*. *S.E., 7*: 135–243. London: Hogarth.

Freud, S. (1923b). *The Ego and the Id*. *S.E., 19*: 12–59. London: Hogarth.

Guenther, H. V. (1977). Mentalism and beyond in Buddhist philosophy. In: *Tibetan Buddhism in Western Perspective* (pp. 162–177). Emeryville, CA: Dharma Publishing.

Grossman, W. I. (1982). The self as fantasy: fantasy as theory. *Journal of the American Psychoanalytic Association, 30*: 919–937.

Hartmann, H. (1964). *Essays on Ego Psychology: Selected Problems in Psychoanalytic Theory*. D. Rapaport (Trans.). New York: International Universities Press.

Hofer, M. (1984). Relationships as regulators: a psychobiologic perspective on bereavement. *Psychosomatic Medicine, 46*: 183–197.

Hume, D. (1739). *A Treatise of Human Nature*. 2 Volumes. London: Dent, 1911.

Jacobson, E. (1964). *The Self and Object World*. New York: International Universities Press.

Johnson, E., Kamilaris, T., Chrousos, G., & Gold, P. W. (1992). Mechanisms of stress: a dynamic overview of hormonal and behavioural homeostasis. *Neuroscience and Biobehavioural Review, 16*: 115–130.

Kernberg, O. (1975). *Borderline Conditions and Pathological Narcissism*. New York: Jason Aronson.

Kernberg, O. (1978). *Object-Relations Theory and Clinical Psychoanalysis*. New York: Jason Aronson.

Kohler, W. (1970). *Gestalt Psychology: An Introduction to New Concepts in Modern Psychology*. New York: Liveright.

Lacan, J. (1978). *The Seminars of Jacques Lacan, Book 2, The Ego in Freud's Theory and in the Technique of Psychoanalysis (1954–1955)*. J. A. Miller (Ed.), S. Tomaselli (Trans.). New York: Norton, 1988.

Levin, F. M. (1991). *Mapping the Mind: The Intersection of Psychoanalysis and Neuroscience*. Hillsdale, NJ: Analytic Press.

Loftus, E., Feldman, J., & Dashiell, R. (1995). The reality of illusory memories. In: D. Schacter, J. Coyle, G. Fischbach, M. Mesulam, & L. Sullivan (Eds.), *Memory Distortion: How Minds, Brains and Societies Reconstruct the Past* (pp. 47–68). Cambridge, MA: Harvard University Press.

Malone, K., & Mann, J. (1993). Serotonin and major depression. In: J. Mann & D. J. Kupfer (Eds.), *Biology of Depressive Disorders, Part A: A Systems Perspective*. New York: Plenum.

Masson, J. (1984). *The Assault on Truth: Freud's Suppression of the Seduction Theory*. New York: Kropt.

Mitchell, K., Johnson, M., Raye, C., Mather, M., & D'Esposito, M. (2000). Aging and reflective processes of working memory: binding and test load deficits. *Psychology and Aging, 15*: 527–541.

Modell, A. H. (1993). *The Private Self*. Cambridge, MA: Harvard University Press.

Narada, M. (1975). *A Manual of Abhidharma*. Kandy, Sri Lanka: Hudhist Publication Society.

Nesbitt, R. E., & Wilson, T. D. (1977). Telling more than we can know: verbal reports on mental processes. *Psychological Review, 84*: 231–259.

Panksepp, J., Siviy, S. M., & Normansell, L. A. (1985). Brain opioids and social emotions. In: M. Reite & T. Field (Eds.), *The Psychobiology of Attachment and Separation* (pp. 3–49). Orlando, FL: Academic Press.

Piaget, J. (1978). *The Development of Thought: Equilibration of Cognitive Structures*. Oxford: Blackwell.

Pribram, K., & Gill, M. (1976). *Freud's "Project" Re-Assessed*. New York: Basic Books.

Richardson, W. J. (1985). Lacanian theory. In: A. Rothstein (Ed.), *Models of the Mind: Their Relationship to Clinical Work* (pp. 101–117). New York: International Universities Press.

Roediger, H. L. (1996). Memory illusions. *Journal of Memory and Language, 35*: 76–100.

Schore, A. (1994). *Affect Regulation and the Origin of the Self: The Neurobiology of Emotional Development*. Hillsdale, NJ: Lawrence Erlbaum.

Sheikh, A., Kunzendorf, R., & Sheikh, K. S. (1996). Somatic consequences of consciousness. In: M. Velmans (Ed.), *The Science of Consciousness: Psychological, Neuropsychological and Clinical Reviews* (pp. 140–161). London: Routledge.

Spence, D. P. (1982). *Narrative Truth and Historical Truth: Meaning and Interpretation in Psychoanalysis*. New York: Norton.

Spyer, K. M. (1989). Neural mechanisms involved in cardiovascular control during affective behaviour. *Trends In Neuroscience, 12*: 506–513.

Sroufe, A., & Rutter, M. (1984). The domain of psychopathology. *Child Development, 54*: 1615–1627.

Stern, D. (1986). *The Interpersonal World of the Infant*. New York: Basic Books.

Taylor, G. (1992). Psychosomatics and self-regulation. In: J. W. Barron, M. N. Eagle, & D. L. Wolitzky (Eds.), *The Interface of Psychoanalysis and Psychology*. Washington, DC: American Psychological Association.

Trevarthen, C. (1989). Development of early social interactions and the affective regulations of brain growth. In: C. von Euler & H. Forssberg (Eds.), *The Neurobiology of Early Infant Behavior* (pp. 195–215). New York: MacMillan.

Trevarthen, C. (1997). Communication in infancy. In: G. Bremner & A. Slater (Eds.), *Infant Development: Recent Advances* (pp. 247–273). London: Erlbaum.

Wei-Tat (1973). *Cheng Wei-shih Lun: Doctrine of Mere Consciousness*. Hong Kong: Cheng Wei-shih Lun Publication Committee.

Welwood, J. (1987). Reflections on psychotherapy and spiritual practice. *Vajradhatu Sun, 24*: 11.

CHAPTER SEVEN

There is more than meets the I: psychoanalytic reflections on spirituality[1]

Jeffrey B. Rubin

S everal times in the past year prospective patients have indicated in the initial consultation with me that they were seeking a "spiritually-oriented" therapist. One patient, whom I shall call Joan, informed me she wanted to encourage her "spiritual side" to emerge. "Spiritual", for her, referred to an outlook on the universe that was not materialistic and valued the uniqueness of the individual and greater authenticity, personal centredness, balance, and wisdom.

The word "spirituality" arises with greater frequency in the past few years in psychoanalytic articles, conferences, and books (Eigen, 1998, 2001; Grotstein, 2000; Marcus, 2003; Roland, 1996; Rubin, 1996, 1998, 1999, 2004; Spezzano & Garguilo, 1997; Symington, 1994; Ulanov, 1985). These writings have not been integrated into psychoanalysis. They are more like stray notes than a central motif.

Even though I have practised meditation and yoga for over thirty years and written a book on psychoanalysis and Buddhism (which Joan apparently did not know about), I was taken by surprise by the spirituality she sought. The surprise was not because psychoanalytic treatment cannot aid contemplative pursuits—I have personally and professionally witnessed the way that it can—but because her quest to experience spiritual facets of herself was so incongruent with the pervasive pathologizing of religion and shunning of spirituality in the first one hundred years of psychoanalysis. Ever since Freud (1927c), drawing on a secular, Enlightenment agenda underwritten by the privileging of reason and science, critiqued religion as an illusion designed to allay one's vulnerability and helplessness in the face of the terrors of the universe, psychoanalysts have neglected or pathologized religion and spiritual experience (Rubin, 1996, 1999, 2004). We are usually anti (or un) spiritual, unreflectively approaching spiritual matters with antipathy, naïveté or scepticism (Barbre, 1998, p. 176). We assume spirituality is delusive or misguided; a regressive urge for unity with the preoedipal mother, a woolly search for false, illusory salvations, a self-centred withdrawal from the world, or voluntary self-hypnosis (Alexander, 1931). Helene Deutsch considered her treatment of a nun less than a complete cure because she could not convert her. Otto Fenichel maintained that every successful psychoanalysis results in the termination of religious belief.

Not all psychoanalysts have pathologized spiritual experiences—witness the work of Fromm, Horney, Kelman, Milner, Ulanov, Bion, Kovel, Ghent, Symington, Roland, Grotstein, Eigen, Jones, Sorenson, Cooper, Finn, Magid, Marcus, and myself—but most have. Jung (1933) went so far as to claim that the absence of a "religious outlook", which includes spiritual experiences, leads to neurosis, which flies in the face of the positivistic epistemology and the Enlightenment distrust of religion that has deeply shaped psychoanalysis. Spirituality, not sexuality, aggression, gender, or even race, might thus be the unconscious of psychoanalysis.

In this chapter, I shall reflect upon how spiritual experiences might enrich psychoanalysis and how psychoanalysis might enlighten spiritual seekers. My thesis is two-fold: (1) both psychoanalysis and the spiritual quest have been impoverished by the lack of contact between them, and (2) both could be enriched by a dialogue in which there is mutual respect, recognition of differences, and willingness to learn from each other (Rubin, 2004). Insights from spiritual experiences could expand psychoanalytic conceptions of the nature of self-experience, empathy, and compassion. Experiencing spirituality can lead to an enlargement of consciousness and an enrichment of one's world (Milner, 1973).

There is a tendency outside psychoanalysis to idealize spiritual experiences as blissful and inherently positive. Psychoanalysis reveals the fallacy of romanticizing these experiences and can elucidate pathologies of spirit.

My strategy is first to explore psychoanalysis' neglect of the spiritual and the cost to psychoanalysis. Then I examine pathologies of spirit. Next, I consider some clinical implications of valuing spiritual experiences. In the concluding section, I point towards some ingredients of a contemplative psychoanalysis, a psychoanalysis that would be receptive to, yet properly critical of, spirituality.

Defining and explaining what we mean by "spirituality" is difficult. The dictionary defines it as "not tangible or material", that is, beyond sense impressions, perhaps ineffable. "Spiritual" is often contrasted with the psychological as well as the material, the mundane, and the flesh.

Spiritual writing has taken numerous forms, including Attic Greek dialogues, Biblical texts, poetry, metaphysical tracts, memoirs, and psycho-spiritual self-help manuals. Whether these writings are confessional, prescriptive, satirical, or polemical, they often share at least some interest in questions of ultimate meaning and concern—who we are, why we are here, and how we should live—that are often not addressed in the research laboratory, the opinion poll, and sometimes even on the analytic couch.

The meaning of a word, Wittgenstein (1953) reminds us, is its "use in the language". Several years ago, curious about the meaning of spirituality, I jotted down the ways patients used the word. There was a cluster of overlapping meanings and uses. It always referred to something positive: for example, Martin Luther King Jr, Mother Theresa, or the Dalai Lama, who were presumed to exhibit unusual compassion or wisdom. It never connoted anything negative. The word was used in five different ways. It expressed a deeply felt sense of unity and connection with the universe: one surrenders control and self-interest and opens to the world; the gap between self and universe lessens and one experiences the divineness of life and a serenity of being. The second use of the word depicted deeper, more sustaining values guiding one's life—higher meaning and purpose than self-actualization or self-fulfilment—and a more balanced, flexible, tolerant attitude towards life. The cultivation of particular qualities and virtues ordinarily neglected in daily life in Western secular culture, such as awe, wonder, humility, resilience, forgiveness, joyousness, love, wisdom, and compassion, were closely linked to the third use of the word. Spirituality was also used to refer to a better, more humble, alive, contented, and loving self, or an unconditioned, uncorrupted, pure, authentic core of one's being and a natural, organic way of living, devoid of artifice and dissembling. Finally, spiritual paths referred to practices designed to foster any of the first four experiences.

Despite the salutary facets of spirituality, it has been pathologized or neglected in much of psychoanalysis for a variety of reasons. Religion, according to Freud, offers illusory consolations. It has also been guilty of numerous "crimes" and "misdemeanours," (Freud, 1927c, p. 27) including acts of intolerance, violence, and oppression towards dissenting viewpoints and alternative religions. There are also personal reasons why Freud dismissed religion. He had a deeply problematic relationship with his mother that he completely denied and disavowed (Breger, 2000; Rubin, 1999; Stolorow & Atwood, 1979). He consciously idealized her, describing the mother–son relationship (in a strikingly un/pre-Freudian formulation) as completely free of conflict and ambivalence. Disavowed dimensions of his struggles with his mother shaped and skewed his views on women. There is evidence that he unconsciously connected and conflated religion and the feminine (Rubin, 1999). His dismissal of the former was, I believe, deeply influenced by his negative, mystifying experiences with the latter.

The third reason for spirituality's dismissal in psychoanalysis was that James Strachey's English translation of Freud's German was shaped and confined by positivistic assumptions, which gave a scientized sense to Freud's humanistic insights and made the spirit seem even less germane to psychoanalysis (Bettelheim, 1982). A soulless version of Freud's work could not address nor illuminate the spiritual.

Exploring the domain of spirituality foregrounds the question Winnicott (1971) recognized that psychoanalysis—with its essentially "tragic" world view (Schafer, 1976), its acknowledgment of the inescapable mysteries, afflictions and losses permeating human existence—has rarely addressed: "What is life about, apart from illness?" (p. 98). This may be changing slowly. Analysts are beginning to write about hope and ecstasy as well as spirituality and mysticism.

Psychoanalysis has suffered because of its neglect of spirituality. The cost of a psychoanalysis that ignores or eclipses the sacred is that it embraces a secular modernist/postmodernist world view in which the individual is disconnected from larger sources of meaning and solace. Individuals are left unmoored and disconnected when they are not embedded in something beyond the isolated, unencumbered self.

Freud (1927c) claimed that to question the meaning of life is a sign of emotional illness. The search for meaning—a central (though not exclusive) property of the spiritual life—might, however, enrich one's life and be life-affirming rather than defensive (Corbett, 1996, p. 168). To not question the meaning of life can lead to being attached to meaninglessness, fostering alienation and anomie, compromising emotional health. From such a secular perspective, life is disenchanted, emptied of wonder, mystery, awe, sublimity, and sacredness. The alienation of many patients (and therapists) may not be unrelated to such a disconnection from the world. Substitutes are then consciously or unconsciously recruited to ground the disconnected individual. The self and the theories and organizations we are affiliated with, for example, may be treated as idols, which theologian Reinhold Niebuhr defines as "absolutizing the relative", by which he means making a particular, local, partial truth into a universally valid one. There is greater attachment to our theories and a lack of tolerance and civility in psychoanalytic institutions, especially toward those with differing points of view. Making the individual the ground of being leads to an excessively egocentric conception of self-experience. When the isolated individual is the ultimate source of meaning, altruism and self-centredness are seen as dichotomized rather than intimately interpenetrating.

To see the self-centred psychoanalytic view of self, reflect for a moment upon the differences between Martin Buber's view of relationships and those of many relational thinkers (Benjamin is a notable exception). The latter view the other in terms of what it did or did not provide the self. The other is seen not as a subject with its own unique needs but, to use the language of Klein, as a need-gratifying object. The relationship between self and other is reduced to an instrumental one with the crucial question being: "What did I get (or not get) from the other?" Buber, on the other hand, stresses a *moral* relation with the other, asking what can I give to the other, not simply what the other can do for me. The other is seen in Buber as a subject, or a thou, with his or her own needs and ideals.

With the notion of the depressive position, Kleinian thought offers a vision of self-experience that goes beyond the egocentric version that permeates many psychoanalytic conceptualizations of self. In the depressive position, the other is experienced as a whole and separate person. One experiences guilt and the urge for reparation towards others because of the damage or hurt one has inflicted.

Reflect for a moment upon mundane or extraordinary experiences you might have had playing a musical instrument, painting, solving a scientific conundrum, communing with nature, whitewater rafting, or making love . . . As barriers between self and notself erode in the "non-self-centered subjectivity" (Rubin, 1996, 1998) one experiences in such spiritual moments, one feels aligned with the universe: a self-expansive, self-enriching connectedness with the world characterized by a sense of engagement, not escape or detachment. In this being-at-oneness, one experiences the world from a more inclusive perspective in which self and other are seen as mutually interpenetrating facets of the universe rather than as polar oppositions. Experiencing the world and one's self from this perspective casts a different, more benign light on such perennial human struggles as anxiety, guilt, fear, and the possibility for happiness and inner peace.

Spiritual experiences suggest there is more to life than the depressive position. Non-self-centred subjectivity, experiences of spirituality, are a fourth state of being that is different from and transcends the autistic–contiguous, paranoid–schizoid, and depressive positions that Klein and Ogden elucidate. (I read Grotstein's [2000] writings on a fourth position characterized by serenity and reconciliation with the universe as I was preparing to submit this manuscript.) Spirituality is, for Grotstein, the "latent capacity within imperfect subjects for attaining full development" (p. xxvi). He terms the "state of serenity" in which one becomes "reconciled to the experience of pure, unadulterated Being and Happening"— with an obvious nod to Melanie Klein and the post-Kleinian revisions of Thomas Ogden—the "transcendent position" (p. 282). One is not at war with oneself or the other. Self and other exist in a non-dualistic relationship that might be devoid of conflict, guilt, and fear. One is in a philia, or friendship, rather than adversarial relationship with oneself in most spiritual experiences. While afflictive states of mind such as strife and trepidation are often absent in moments of spiritual experience, negative experiences such as self-nullifying fusion with, and compliance to, another may be present. More on this later.

The profusion of analysands and analysts exploring spiritual practice, and the increasing number of conferences and articles on psychoanalysis and spirituality, suggest we may be witnessing a hunger for, and a return of, the spiritually repressed (Rubin, 1998). More than five hundred therapists and spiritual seekers attended a conference in 1994 in New York City on "Healing the Suffering Self: A Dialogue among Psychoanalysts and Buddhists", sponsored by two psychoanalytic institutes. One reason increasing numbers of people are turning away from psychoanalysis might be its secular psychology, not simply managed care or the anti-analytic contemporary cultural climate. Might many analysands and analysts turn to the meditative cushion or the yoga ashram because psychoanalysis does not fully nurture their spiritual needs or hunger?

The psychoanalysis of spirit: psychopathology of spirituality in everyday life

Even of Holiness / there is offal: / Just as there is sweat / and hair and excrement, / So Holiness too / has its offal. [Nachman of Bratzlav, 1996, p. 270)

Spirituality is usually presented as an antidote to the rampant narcissism in personal, corporate and political relations that permeates and plagues our world. Going "beyond narcissism" is unreflectively accepted by many people as a feasible solution to the egocentricity that afflicts us individually and as a culture (Epstein, 1995). The plethora of scandals in spiritual communities in recent years involving esteemed "masters" illegally expropriating funds and sexually exploiting students (Boucher, 1988) suggests, however, that the idealization of spirituality can be harmful because there are sometimes hidden dangers (Rubin, 1996, 1998, 2004).

There are illusions, obsessions, and pitfalls on the spiritual path. The pursuit of spirituality rarely stands up to the pure image we have of an individual attempting to reach a higher plane of awareness and understanding. Instead, it may be used to bypass, circumvent, or attempt to heal emotional trauma. It can allow us to avoid conflict that we would be better off dealing with directly, forestalling growth by masking developmental lacunas or arrests.

Spiritual literature acknowledges hazards on the spiritual path ranging from sloth and torpor to pride and anger. Buddhism terms these afflictive energies the ten "impediments" (Buddhaghosa, 1976), the ten "fetters"(Narada, 1975), and the six "hindrances" (*ibid.*). Learning to skillfully manage these obstacles is a crucial facet of Buddhist practice (Rubin, 1996, p. 130). Despite the fact that interferences play an indispensable role in the meditative process, they have been neglected and incompletely understood in the meditative literature. Classical (Buddhaghosa, 1976; Narada, 1975) and contemporary Buddhist literature (Goldstein, 1976; Goleman, 1977; Kornfield, 1977; Walsh, 1981) delineate many conscious personal and environmental interferences to meditation: "hindrances" (such as sense desire, anger, restlessness, sloth, and doubt); "impediments" (e.g., excessive involvement with projects and theoretical studies divorced from practice); and "fetters" (including attachment to blissful, non-ordinary states of consciousness, adherence to [wrongful] rites and ceremonies, ignorance, and self-centred thinking). Unconscious psychological and interpersonal obstacles to meditative practice, however, have not been systematically elaborated (Rubin, 1996).

There is a complex relationship between spirituality and psychopathology that psychoanalysts have tended to reduce and flatten, conceiving of the two in singular, narrow ways. Within psychological circles, the psychological is traditionally treated as superior to the spiritual. The latter is then viewed as pathological. In religious literature and communities, spiritual experiences are presumed superior to psychological ones.

Roland (1996) challenges and expands traditional psychoanalytic conceptions when he suggests that the "spiritual and normality / psychopathology" are "on two separate continua, intersecting and interacting in various ways" (p. xvi). The relationship between psychology and spirituality is multi-dimensional, depending on changing contexts. At moments, it is separate and distinct. For example, there are therapists and patients who are self-aware, psychologically healthy, and not orientated towards the spiritual, and there are genuine spiritual seekers who are not interested in psychological matters (*ibid.*). At other times, the relationship between spirituality and psychology/psychopathology is overlapping, complementary, even synergistic. A double or triple helix might give a sense of what I am pointing towards.

There are situations where the psychological and the spiritual dovetail and cross-pollinate. Some analysands suffer from neglecting the spiritual. Spiritual practice could aid their psychological development. Meditation can help patients and therapists attend with greater clarity and depth to their experience. It can also cultivate affect tolerance and a more fluid, multi-dimensional, less narcissistic experience of self (Rubin, 1996, 1998, 1999). Psychological conflicts sometimes impede the spiritual quest. Psychoanalysis could aid spiritual seekers in resolving inner psychological issues and developmental arrests and to gain insight into troubling transferences with spiritual teachers. Resolving emotional struggles could deepen spiritual practice. Psychoanalytic understandings of the dynamics of interpersonal relationships could elucidate psychopathology in spiritual communities. Psychoanalytic and spiritual traditions are both necessary for the art of living.

A psychoanalysis of spirit would attend to the hidden motivations and secondary gains of the spiritual quest, as well as its exalted dimensions. Psychoanalysis could show that spirituality, like all human experience, has multiple meanings and functions, ranging from the adaptive and transformative to the defensive and pathological. Psychoanalytically-informed reflections on spirituality could offer tools to de-idealize spiritual experiences and elucidate pathologies and illusions of spirit. In working psychoanalytically with several Buddhists, students of yoga, a rabbi, nondenominational spiritual seekers, and spiritually-inclined artists, I have observed a variety of pathologies of spirit including using the spiritual quest or spiritual experiences to narcissistically inflate oneself, evade subjectivity, deny emotional losses, shield oneself from the painful vicissitudes of everyday experience, and neglect ethical responsibility. The spiritual path has allowed its devotees to engage in masochistic surrender, schizoid detachment, obsessional self-anesthetization, and to pathologically mourn traumatic experiences. I will discuss several of these, providing illustrative examples rather than fully fleshed out clinical vignettes.

As a jumping-off point for considering pathologies of spirit, consider a poem by Jane Kenyon (1996):

> Once in my early thirties I saw
> that I was a speck of light in the great
> river of light that undulates through time.
> I was floating with the whole
> human family. We were all colors—those
> who are living now, those who have died,
> those who are not yet born. [p. 191]

The last six words of her concluding line awakened me out of the blessed, unitive tranquillity the poem induced:

> "For a few
> moments I floated, completely calm,
> and I no longer hated having to exist" (*ibid.*).

Narcissism haunts our culture, generating self-inflation, ruthless self-centeredness, intolerance and hard-heartedness toward those who suffer or are less fortunate. I have observed great narcissism in people on the spiritual quest. Buddhism offers a powerful critique of narcissism, as well as strategies for addressing it, but may sometimes inadvertently foster rather than resolve self-disorders and egocentricity.

In *Psychotherapy and Buddhism*, I discussed the attraction for one Buddhist, whom I called Albert, of the no-self doctrine. An affable humanities professor in his late twenties, Albert suffered from conflicts over individuation and success, excessive self-judgment, diminished self-esteem, inauthenticity, compliance, and a pervasive sense of directionlessness and meaninglessness. He was an only child raised as an agnostic. In the beginning of treatment, he described his mother as caring and devoted. As treatment proceeded, other images of her emerged. He then saw her as rigid, concerned that everyone should conform to her view of reality, which included how her son should act and be. She was scared of feelings, committed to banishing all aspects of internal, subjective life. She demanded that everyone around her should live in accordance with her narrow view. Albert felt she lived in a "fortune cookie" universe in which her "shoulds" were idealized. Clichéd responses ("You must have felt badly when you got that rejection") replaced genuine emotional engagement. Albert felt powerless and non-existent in her presence. She was a "fencer who parries everything I say". Instead of being affirmed and validated by her, he felt invisible.

Albert had a distant relationship with his father, whom he experienced as intelligent, critical, and passive. He submitted to his wife and never sustained interest in his son. Albert never felt understood or supported by him.

Albert described a pervasive pattern with his parents of their laundering communication of all subjective meaning, trivializing his feelings and nullifying his authentic subjectivity, while appearing to exude empathy and concern. In Albert's view, his parents did not see themselves or him as subjects capable of introspecting, feeling, desiring, or playing. Rather, he was coerced into accommodating their pre-existing viewpoint. To stay connected to them he had to hide his subjective life. He "harmonized" with his parents' view of reality so as to not feel "like an astronaut cut off from home base" because that was the only hope of being emotionally related to them. His parents were sorely unresponsive to his inner reality and failed to encourage his uniqueness from emerging or flourishing. They encouraged compliance with their narrow mode of being by rewarding submissiveness and conventionality, discouraging authenticity and individuation.

Albert developed a private world of depth and richness, but had great difficulty believing in its validity and sustaining his commitment to it. The price of conforming to his parents' wishes was to bury his sense of how he should live. He kept alive the tenuous hope of being accepted by them by banishing huge parts of his self, subverting and obscuring his "voice". This led to a limited view of himself and his capabilities. What *he* wanted lacked significance to him; he felt his life was not his own. This left him feeling directionless.

Because his subjectivity had been so profoundly erased, he felt he had no subjective existence. He felt invisible in his family, with no voice and no impact. He was attracted to the no-self doctrine because it resonated with his experience of nullification in his family. The self-evasion and nullification that Buddhism fostered for Albert was a defence against his own sense of non-being. Believing in no-self rationalized and artificially disavowed his sadness and grief about an unlived life. It is not that he did not live, or missed out on life; there was no subject to experience subjective existence. (A patient of mine, a student of Zen said, "Psychoanalytic treatment helped me with *self*-realization, not *non-self* derealization".)

Self-emptiness is often masked by idealization of spiritual teachers, the divine, and the spiritual idea of the voidness of reality. From self psychology, we learn that one momentarily derives strength by identification with, and submission to, an idealized spiritual teacher who is presumed to be unconditionally accepting and loving, never harsh, judgemental, or abandoning. The teacher, cause, ideology, or experience provides vital, missing functions to the self, such as guidance, direction, identification with idealized strength, calmness, or wisdom that one lacked from parents or surrogate caregivers. Personal deprivation and bereftness is thus denied and avoided.

In its most extreme versions, such surrender can take the form of masochistic submission in which one becomes pathologically deferential towards a spiritual teacher or community. Initially, uncritical devotion may feel relieving, as it offers connectedness and direction about how to live. One observes over a longer period of time that the person does not think for him/herself, denies signs of group think, and rationalizes disturbing behaviour of teachers or community members. Individuality is obliterated, not enriched. When the teacher is immune to feedback and the student has no impact, authoritarianism is operative (Kramer & Alstad, 1993). Questions that cannot be asked about the teacher, spiritual experiences, or doctrines that are supposed to be taken on faith might signal the presence of a teacher or community that is autocratic rather than liberational.

Sometimes spiritual *experiences* are idealized. Experiences of oneness and bliss offered one meditator—a highly competent, successful, middle-aged professional—a way of avoiding, rather than confronting and coping with, the excruciating pain and sadness of his divorce. Ron initiated therapy after his wife of twenty years announced she wanted a divorce. He was stunned and felt he was falling apart. Intelligent and articulate, Ron was highly regarded in the legal field. He was intense, with a commanding presence and incisive intellect. I felt there was little margin for error in our interactions. He treated me as a hostile witness in court whenever I attempted to explore his feelings.

Ron experienced severe stress, feeling "out of control" since his wife's sudden announcement, which he tried to handle by meditation. He had developed an unusual facility for cultivating states of deep focus and prolonged concentration, feeling peace, rather than sorrow, in these states. While this translated into a feeling of confidence and detachment from stressful emotions, the underlying issues that contributed to his wife's decision to end their relationship, and his inability to cope with it, remained untouched. Feelings of fragmentation escalated, and Ron could no longer escape by meditating.

Ron grew up in a home in which there was a facade of "love". His parents, highly preoccupied academics with demanding careers, provided for his physical and educational needs but were detached from his emotional ones. They were more comfortable with logical thought than feeling. Ron's emotions were rarely engaged and never validated. He learned he would have to take care of himself because his parents were not available for emotional support. Logical thought became a kind of "foster parent". Ron lived in a realm of pure thought, viewing the world through the prism of his intellect. Emotional conflicts became problems to solve with logic.

The onslaught of feelings unleashed by his impending divorce overwhelmed Ron's highly developed capacity for rational thought. Meditation gave him a concrete strategy for attempting to manage his emotional life. In therapy, he realized that meditation anaesthetized powerful feelings of loneliness and grief, resulting in his avoiding and prolonging the necessary process of mourning and healing.

Experiences of oneness offered another patient, a depressed woman in her late forties, a way of avoiding the agony of her life. At the beginning of our first session, Eileen launched into a recitation of her spiritual insights. A highly successful entrepreneur, she nevertheless felt she was a failure, that life had passed her by. She had no children or husband and was involved in an on-again, off-again relationship with a married man. She renounced normal emotional attachments, claiming ordinary relationships were unnecessary evils, obstacles to more important, selfless, spiritual love for humanity. "Real love is not possessive," she informed me, with a coercive tone. "We are one. Fear is an illusion. We are God. We are Love. We are Sacred. If everyone felt the way I feel, there would be peace on earth." Unfortunately, there was not much peace in her soul.

Eileen was disconnected from colleagues, therapists, friends, acquaintances, and the world. Her contacts with others usually devolved into battles. Her assertion of boundless love and freedom was belied by the acrimony and distance that characterized her relationships. It also enabled her to keep at bay profound, shattering loss: the death of her parents when she was a young adult, and the disappointment of not getting married or having a child. Feeling connected with the sacred allowed Eileen to believe her life was not a failure, that it had deep, even transcendental, significance. It provided her with an opportunity to feel she was special and had not missed out on any vital experiences. It was not that she was abandoned, betrayed, and might never love or be loved: in "cosmic consciousness" she had the greatest and only really substantial love, and a glimpse of something visionary—the interconnection of people, the power of love, and the holiness of daily life. Since her spiritual experiences were utilized in the service of defensive self-protection, however, they never led to a genuinely self-transformative experience.

In my work with Ron and Eileen I saw how spiritual experiences can all too often be a form of pathological mourning in which traumatic or disturbing experiences of loss, abuse, or neglect are sealed off and the person's current life is endlessly shaped and delimited by these disavowed, unconscious experiences. Mourning is arrested as one enacts rather than remembers, experiences, integrates, and works through the past.

The spiritual quest, no less than making money or achieving fame, can be recruited to enhance stature or self-esteem. Many spiritual aspirants fall victim to what the Tibetan Buddhist teacher Chogyam Trungpa termed "spiritual materialism". "Spirituality" becomes, for many seekers, a badge of specialness in two ways: (1) spiritual experiences or attainments lead to self-inflation, and (2) what Nietzsche (1887) might term spiritual asceticism is utilized

to make one feel more pious or evolved than those less self-deny-
ing. "I am better than you because I have less than you."

My patients emphasized five aspects of healthy spirituality.
Drawing on Winnicott's view of transitional experiencing, Grotstein's transcendent position, Eigen's reflections on spirituality, and
my own experiences, I will extend these reflections. When you least
expect it—walking on a country road, meditating, making love,
grappling with a work of art, playing sports—it happens. You did
not cause it, though you were open to it. If you were looking for it,
it could not happen. At least, not then. You are taken by surprise.
When it first happened to me in a basketball game when I was eigh-
teen, I did not even know it existed.

Sometimes it is spawned by pain; other times, by silence or
beauty. It is usually unusually intense and compelling, featuring
heightened awareness and aliveness. You see glory in the flower,
grace in the slithering animal in the grass, wonder in the starry
skies. Time may elongate. You feel the luminous embedded in the
ordinary. You feel centred and balanced, intimate with the universe.
Self and the universe are sacred. You are catapulted out of (or into)
your self. Your sense of self expands—at least momentarily—
beyond a cohesive, integrated self to a communion and homecom-
ing with the universe. Life feels more alive, wondrous, less (or non-)
conflictual, and has deeper meaning. Happiness and peace are
bleached-out ways of expressing what you feel. It is Radiant and
Luminous; suffused with aliveness; life being Alive. Spiritual experiences give Life to life. It is good to be alive. Radiant aliveness.
Luminous aliveness. Bliss. Aliveness and joy show you that your
self is wider and the universe richer than you knew. (Eigen's [2001]
poetic expression of spirituality and mysticism aided me in articulating my sense of these experiences, particularly their bliss and
radiance.)

Spiritual experiences, from my Winnicottian-inspired perspective, are not possessions we have/own, or ends to which we strive,
or even facets of our personalities, but ever-present possibilities
of being involving the intersection of self and the larger world
in which we are embedded. (Winnicott's [1951] reflections on transitional objects and phenomena played a seminal role in my
conception of spiritual experience. Creativity, not spirituality,
was emphasized by Winnicott in his reflections on transitional

experiencing. My work could be viewed as spiritualizing Winnicott's.) We must embody spiritual insights in how we live, how we treat ourselves and others. Are we becoming more connected to life? Is our empathy and compassion deepening and expanding? Do we feel more joy and meaning?

The sacred is all around us. We can experience it in daily activities, work, our homes and relationships, as well as in altered states. In such moments—that arise in the moment, yet often feel timeless—there is an intersection of human beings and the world leading to a sense that there is more than meets the I. The individual feels graced by something larger than the self that touches and flows through the self. These moments represent an opportunity for expanding our sense of identity and overcoming our separateness.

Psychoanalysis and spirituality: clinical considerations

It remains to be considered whether analysis in itself must really lead to the giving up of religion. [Gay, 1987, p. 12 (Freud to Eitingon, June 20, 1927)]

In itself psycho-analysis is neither religious nor nonreligious. [Freud, 1963, p. 16 (Freud to Pfister, Feb 9, 1909)]

An increasing number of patients seek a life of greater spirituality. Where does this leave the psychoanalyst trained in an analytic culture that valued the clear-eyed reason of science and overwhelmingly pathologized and marginalized religious and spiritual concerns? Freud's undogmatic agnosticism about his atheism in *Future of an Illusion* (1927c) serves as a suggestive reminder: "If experience should show—not to me—but to others after me, who think as I do—that we have been mistaken [in our critique of religion] we will renounce our expectations" (p. 53).

Traditionally, the spiritual path and psychoanalysis have been segregated. There needs to be a rapprochement in which each is more receptive to what light the other might shed on the art of living. A *contemplative psychoanalysis* would appreciate the constructive as well as the pathological facets of spiritual experiences. If it is anti-analytic to treat spiritual experiences as inherently psychopathological, as the majority of psychoanalysts have done, it is unanalytic to take spiritual claims at face value, without enquiring into the complex, multi-dimensional meanings and functions they possess in the mind and heart of a particular person. There needs to be a close encounter of a new kind between psychoanalysis and the spiritual quest, in which neither discipline is presumed to have unique access to the sovereign truth and they are neither segregated from each other nor assimilated into one another. Psychoanalytic imperialism emerges when it tries to conquer spiritual experiences; when it has a "nothing but" attitude towards them; when everything spiritual is explained by, and reduced to, psychoanalytic categories. Spiritual traditions need to avoid their own brand of intellectual (or spiritual) imperialism in which a spiritual text or meditational practice is treated as if it is the final truth about reality. Psychoanalysis and the spiritual quest have different, although at times overlapping, concerns. If they are too separate and autonomous, then fruitful contact is precluded; no meaningful cross-pollination is possible. If they are too merged, then important differences are eclipsed. The task for psychoanalysis and spiritual disciplines, like the challenge for individuals in a committed relationship, is to balance autonomy and connectedness (Jones, 1996) achieving intimacy that preserves and enriches the autonomy of each.

Therapists rarely talk about their spiritual life and its impact on treatment. There are sound, time-tested reasons for this, ranging from not wishing to shape the transference to not wanting to infringe upon the patient's autonomy. The dearth of discussions of spirituality and psychoanalytic treatment seems to make it a *taboo topic* in psychoanalysis. The impact of an analyst's spiritual views and spiritual life—including his or her atheism—is then rendered unconscious. In the spirit of bringing to consciousness something that could enrich psychoanalysis, I shall offer tentative reflections on this subject.

Spirituality affects my theory and practice of therapy in explicit and implicit ways. It is rarely a topic of explicit discussion, unless brought up by the patient. My experiences have influenced my view of the world as well as my conception of human nature and relationships. This affects how I think of the therapeutic relationship and the possibilities of treatment to generate change in implicit and explicit ways. Ever since I had spiritual experiences, I have experienced the truth of the French surrealist poet Paul Eluard's remark, "There is another world and it is in this one." There is more to life than is dreamt of in our psychoanalytic psychologies. While psychoanalysis is skilled at exploring and revealing the fallaciousness of vacuous, illusory hopes, there is a mirror opposite danger that, like Freud, we will normalize a tragic, melancholic view of the universe. I see life as a dialogic movement of change and stasis, with personal evolution an ever-present possibility. Patients have biological, existential, and psychological constraints. They also have undreamt of creative potentials. This gives me more hope than I might have if I subscribed to the tragic view of the universe that permeates psychoanalysis.

Psychoanalysis lacks compelling visions of the self after analysis, as Bollas (1997, pp. 48–49) notes. Psychoanalytic conceptions of health are too limited and dispirited. There is more to life than achieving common human unhappiness or the depressive position. Spiritual experiences give me a different—I believe fuller—sense of human possibilities. There may be capacities for empathy and compassion that psychoanalysis has not yet mapped. A story about Gandhi is illustrative. A man attended one of Gandhi's spiritual talks with the goal of assassinating him. He was so moved by the power of Gandhi's teachings that he scrapped his plan. After Gandhi's talk, the assassin prostrated himself in front of Gandhi and tearfully informed him that he had been hired to kill him. (Imagine that someone told you that. How would you feel?) Gandhi looked him in the eyes with deep compassion and said, "How are you going to explain to the people who hired you about your failure to carry out the plan?" Gandhi empathized with the assassin's plight even when his own life had been threatened.

"It is impossible to escape the impression", notes Freud in the opening sentence of *Civilization and Its Discontents* (1930a), "that people commonly use false standards of measurement—that they seek power, success and wealth for themselves and admire them in others, and that they underestimate what is of true value in life." While spiritual traditions have their own world view, beliefs, and practices, they tend, like Freud, to critique conventional societal values. Not only do they critique the egocentricity and materialism of secular world views, they also offer an alternative system of values based on selflessness, compassion, altruism, and wisdom. My values have been affected by spiritual experiences. Many people in our culture—even those who scoff at the vacuousness of conspicuous consumption—live as if wealth directly correlates with happiness. Expanded material comforts have not necessarily deepened our individual or collective peace of mind. While there is no inherent virtue in poverty, and financial struggles obviously do not foster inner peace and contentment, economic prosperity does not resolve our fundamental psychological and spiritual questions or problems. What I have observed clinically—partially as a result of already believing it and thus looking for it—is that people often suffer because of the search for fame and material goods, as well as the panoply of causes psychoanalysts have so ably elucidated. My spiritual background has led me to question patients' values such as consumerism, especially the correlation between wealth and happiness.

My spiritual experiences have led to a less dualistic view of the relationship between people. I see self and other as deeply connected, irreducibly interrelated. I have a deep, abiding sense that patient and analyst are not two; we are in the treatment together. While I am not responsible for their life, their choices, even for how they use the treatment, I feel a deep responsibility for fully engaging the process.

The spiritual experiences I have had affect who I *am* in the treatment: my *being*, the quality of my presence. I have periodically been told by certain patients that something healing is transmitted in the treatment, especially a quality of deep stillness and attentiveness, non-judgementality and flexibility. Immersion in meditation practice over three decades has heightened my attentiveness in the treatment, including my receptivity to countertransference, creative imagination, and intuition.

Spiritual experiences have fostered in me a deeper sense of the mystery of the universe, human development, and treatment. This has encouraged more receptivity to the unknown in therapy. Aware of the *more* than what I currently know and believe, I am more able and willing to surrender to the therapeutic process and let go of beliefs of how human development and treatment should unfold. I feel my patients are potential supervisors, as Langs & Searles (1980) have so ably written, which breeds a less defensive attitude about my theories or the correctness of my insights or interpretations. It makes me hold my theories lightly rather than tightly.

Hope, connectedness, and non-defensiveness may create a different kind of intersubjective space between me and the patient, infused with a spirit of safety, curiosity, and respect. Therapy then has the potential to be a "sacred space" in which shame may be decreased and openness fostered. Patients are encouraged to say and experience what they had not been able to before, and to be heard in ways they did not expect and had not previously known.

Spirituality and wholeness

In this chapter, I have attempted to depict what spirituality is, how it might enrich psychoanalysis, and how psychoanalytic understandings might aid spiritual seekers in avoiding a variety of potential pitfalls. Spirituality plays an incredibly vital role in our culture: expanding and enriching human subjectivity; connecting us to a larger reality in which we are all embedded; re-enchanting the world; disclosing undreamt-of dimensions of being; infusing our lives with mystery, vitality, awe, and wonder. A world without spirit is impoverished. Life without a larger purpose than individual fulfilment is alienating and lacks meaning. Narcissism reigns. Value and wonder are eclipsed. A universe that values spiritual experiences is deeply enriched.

Repression of spirituality in psychoanalysis and the culture contributes to the enormous alienation, anomie, and melancholy that permeates people's lives. Psychoanalysis, like the larger culture in which it is embedded, suffers because it only intermittently realizes that there is more than meets the I. Fullness or wholeness of being necessitates openness to, and experiencing of, broader dimensions of being that can be revealed in spiritual experiences.

Psychoanalysis could benefit from retrieving spiritual experiences split off in the modern age when the self became separate and isolated. Spiritual experiences extend relational thinking, suggesting that it is not simply the self in relation to a care-giving (or therapeutic) matrix, but a self in relation to a larger life-world in which analyst and analysand are embedded.

Psychoanalysis is traditionally viewed as an atheistic science of human subjectivity, or, more recently, intersubjectivity. The atheism is often taken for granted and unconscious, a silent backdrop, part of an invisible, unacknowledged assumptive framework for viewing the world and conducting treatment. It tends only to emerge when religiously committed patients are in treatment. It then generates a great deal of countertransference, as many analysts view religion and spiritual experiences through the distorting lens of knee-jerk pathologizing.

Psychoanalysis can appreciate spiritual experience without accepting the mystifications of organized religion. The notion of spirituality has become, in our culture, what the literary critic Kenneth Burke (1950) termed a "god-term", a universal category beyond examination. It is central to our existence, but also the site of numerous illusions and abuses. Psychoanalysis offers tools to elucidate pathologies and pitfalls on the spiritual path. If contemplative traditions temper the egocentricity of psychoanalytic accounts of self-experience, and thereby prevent absolutizing of the self-centred self, then psychoanalytic attention to psychological complexity and the shaping role of unconsciousness in human thought and action might expand the domain of the non-self-centred, contemplative self (Rubin, 1996, 1998).

There is no guarantee that blissful, absorptive union leads to intimacy, self-understanding, or moral action. Fusion experiences are no guarantee of goodness, as survivors of sexual abuse know. Since spirituality can lead to self-evasion or even immorality, it needs to be integrated with psychological wisdom and moral sensitivity.

Spirituality lives in the everyday, where there is no separation between sacred and profane, and where the profane (including otherness and self-care, imminence as well as transcendence, carnality no less than compassion) is sacred and the sacred is profane. Spiritual seekers often desanctify and devalue ordinary existence when they segregate the sacred and the profane. Imminence, passion, intimacy, and carnality can get eclipsed. Because of its attention to the moment and to mundane, embodied existence, as opposed to other-worldly disembodied transcendence, psychoanalysis can sanctify the ordinary, reveal the imminence of the divine, and foster spirituality and morality in this world.

Karl Marx revealed our social unconscious; Sigmund Freud illuminated our personal unconscious. In the twenty-first century we need to become aware of the "sacred unconscious" (Smith, 1982, p. 178). If we get in touch with the personal unconscious, we are less driven and imprisoned by the past, more liberated from demons that have haunted us. If we get in touch with the social unconscious, we are aware of social conditioning and exploitation and are more individuated from our culture and its values. If we got in touch with the sacred unconscious, we would see the world as more holy, as whole. The world would be experienced as more magical and enchanted. We would celebrate life in all its inexhaustible vibrancy and diversity. We would feel more serenity and joy. There would be less distance between people. We would feel more compassion towards nature and other beings.

Psychoanalysis at its best can demystify spiritual abuses without eclipsing the possibility of spiritual experiences. A non-reductionistic, contemplative psychoanalysis of the future, in which spiritual experiences were valued as well as critically examined, could foster a civilization with greater meaning and sacredness and less discontent.

Note

1. This chapter was inspired by Mark Finn and benefited from discussions with Diana Alstad, Neil Altman, Emma Anderson, Jim Barron, Claude Barbre, Mark Branitsky, Lou Breger, Peter Carnochan, Paul Cooper, Doris Dlugacz, Mark Finn, Jerry Garguilo, Jim Jones, Don Kalsched, Joel Kramer, Barry Magid, Esther Menaker, Louise Reiner, Alan Roland, Tony Schwartz, Mary Traina, Ann and Barry Ulanov, Brent Willock, and Avi Winokur. I am especially grateful to Neil Altman and Barry Magid, whose feedback on a penultimate draft greatly enriched this chapter.

References

Alexander, F. (1931). Buddhistic training as an artificial catatonia. *Psychoanalytic Review, 18*: 129–145.

Barbre, C. (1998). Review of psychotherapy and the sacred: religious experience and religious resources in psychotherapy. *Journal of Religion and Health, 37*: 176–177.

Bettelheim, B. (1982). *Freud and Man's Soul*. New York: Random House.

Bollas, C. (1997). Interview with Anthony Molino. In: *Freely Associated: Encounters in Psychoanalysis with Christopher Bollas, Joyce McDougall, Michael Eigen, Adam Phillips, and Nina Coltart* (pp. 5–51). London: Free Association.

Boucher, S. (1988). *Turning the Wheel: American Women Creating the New Buddhism*. San Francisco, CA: Harper and Row.

Bratzlav, N. (1996). The Torah of the void. In: *A Book of Luminous Things*. C. Milosz (Ed.). New York: Harcourt Brace.

Breger, L. (2000). *Freud: Darkness in the Midst of Vision-An Analytical Biography*. New York: Wiley.

Buddhaghosa, B. (1976). *The Path of Purification*. B. Nyanamoli (Trans.). Berkeley, CA: Shambhala.

Burke, K. (1950). *A Rhetoric of Motives*. Berkeley, CA: University of California Press.

Corbett, L. (1996). *The Religious Function of the Psyche*. New York: Routledge.

Eigen, M. (1998). *The Psychoanalytic Mystic*. Binghamton, NY: ESF.

Eigen, M. (2001). *Ecstasy*. Middletown, CT: Wesleyan University Press.

Epstein, M. (1995). *Thoughts without a Thinker: Psychotherapy from a Buddhist Perspective*. New York: Basic Books.

Freud, S. (1927c). *The Future of an Illusion*. S.E., *21*. London: Hogarth.

Freud, S. (1930a). *Civilization and Its Discontents*. S.E., *21*. London: Hogarth.

Freud, S. (1960). *The Letters of Sigmund Freud*. E. Freud (Ed.), T. Stern & J. Stern (Trans.). New York: Basic Books.

Freud, S. (1963). *Psychoanalysis and Faith: Dialogues with the Reverend Oskar Pfister*. H. Meng & E. Freud (Eds.). New York: Basic Books.

Gay, P. (1987). *A Godless Jew: Freud, Atheism and the Making of Psychoanalysis*. New Haven, CT: Yale University Press.

Goldstein, J. (1976). *The Experience of Insight: A Natural Unfolding*. Santa Cruz, CA: Unity Press.

Goleman, D. (1977). *The Varieties of the Meditative Experience*. New York: Dutton.

Grotstein, J. (2000). *Who Is the Dreamer Who Dreams the Dream?: A Study of Psychic Presences*. Hillsdale, NJ: Analytic Press.

Jones, J. (1996). *Religion and Psychology in Transition: Psychoanalysis, Feminism, and Theology*. New Haven, CT.: Yale University Press.

Jung, C. G. (1933). *Modern Man in Search of a Soul*. New York: Harcourt, Brace & World.

Kenyon, J. (1996). Having it out with melancholy. In: *Otherwise: New and Selected Poems*. Saint Paul, MN: Graywolf Press.

Kornfield, J. (1977). *Living Buddhist Masters*. Santa Cruz, CA: Unity Press.

Kramer, J., & Alstad, D. (1993). *The Guru Papers: Masks of Authoritarian Power*. Berkeley, CA: North Atlantic Press.

Langs, R., & Searles, H. (1980). *Intrapsychic and Interpersonal Dimensions of Treatment*. New York: Jason Aronson.

Marcus, P. (2003). *Ancient Religious Wisdom, Spirituality, and Psychoanalysis*. Westport, CT: Praeger.

Milner, M. (1973). Some notes on psychoanalytic ideas about mysticism. In: *The Suppressed Madness of Sane Men: Forty Four Years of Exploring Psychoanalysis* (pp. 258–274). London: Tavistock, 1987.

Narada, T. (1975). *A Manual of Abhidhamma*. Columbo, Sri Lanka: Buddhist Publication Society.

Nietzsche, F. (1887). *On the Genealogy of Morals*. W. Kaufmann (Trans.). New York: Random House, 1967.

Roland, A. (1996). *Cultural Pluralism and Psychoanalysis: The Asian-American Experience*. New York: Routledge.

Rubin, J. B. (1996). *Psychotherapy and Buddhism: Toward an Integration*. New York: Plenum Press.

Rubin, J. B. (1998). *A Psychoanalysis for Our Time: Exploring the Blindness of the Seeing I*. New York: New York University Press.

Rubin, J. B. (1999). Religion, Freud, and women. *Gender and Psychoanalysis*, 4:333–366.

Rubin, J. B. (2004). *The Good Life: Psychoanalytic Reflections on Love, Ethics, Creativity and Spirituality*. Albany, NY: State University of New York Press.

Schafer, R. (1976). *A New Language for Psychoanalysis*. New Haven, CT: Yale University Press.

Smith, H. (1982). The sacred unconscious. In: *Beyond the Postmodern Mind* (pp. 177–185). Wheaton, IL: Theosophical Publishing House.

Spezzano, C., & Garguilo, J. (Eds.) (1997). *Soul on the Couch: Spirituality, Religion, and Morality in Psychoanalysis*. Hillsdale, NJ: Analytic Press.

Stolorow, R., & Atwood, G. (1979). *Faces in a Cloud: Subjectivity in Personality Theory*. New York: Jason Aronson.

Symington, N. (1994). *Emotion and Spirit: Questioning the Claims of Psychoanalysis and Religion*. New York: St Martin's Press.

Ulanov, A. (1985). A shared space. *Quadrant, 18*: 65–80.

Walsh, R. (1981). Speedy Western minds slow slowly. *Revision, 4*: 75–77.

Winnicott, D. W. (1951). Transitional objects and transitional phenomena. In: *Through Paediatrics to Psycho-Analysis* (pp. 229–242). London: Hogarth, 1978.

Winnicott, D. W. (1971). *Playing and Reality*. London: Tavistock.

Wittgenstein, L. (1953). *Philosophical Investigations*. New York: Macmillan.

PART IV
FINANCIAL AFFAIRS

Down low and dirty: talking about how money matters, especially on a sliding scale

Janet Tintner

Almost across the board, I tend towards self-deprecation around money. I slide my fee too easily and too fast. I am not rigorous enough in charging for missed sessions. These tendencies are manifestations of my mixed feelings around entitlement and self-esteem. None the less, I charge a range of fees, including a full fee, which I usually stick to, so this laxity is not universal.

A question addressed in this chapter is how my pecuniary propensities interact with a patient's life circumstances and personality. Aron and Hirsch (1992), from an interpersonal perspective, indicate that, in dealing with money, the analyst engages in a delicate balancing act due to the realistic impact of finances on the analyst:

> The analyst is always maintaining some balance between participating and observing the interaction. When it comes to the monetary transactions between analyst and patient, the analyst is a very real participant and this puts additional strain on his or her capacity as observer. [*ibid.*, p. 252]

This paper illustrates twists and turns in that balancing act. Via the presentation of a patient I will call Rita, I will illustrate an enactment of transferential and countertransferential issues around a low fee. Ostensibly, I chose to present Rita because I charged her a lower fee than I have charged anyone else. On reflection, she is also someone towards whom I feel tender and with whom I experience relative freedom to play and get dirty, and feel tender towards.

A second question to be explored concerns the taboo aspect of money. Money, like sex, Freud (1913c) averred, is taboo, and like sex, should be taken on directly. In part, this taboo can be addressed by talking specific figures, but what about if the emotions or interpersonal interactions evoked are so powerful that one wants to avoid them or feels ashamed talking about them? Various writers have focused on specific emotions analysts dodge in dealing with money, one being anger. In her erudite paper, Dimen (1994) notes that there is a contradiction between love and money in the therapeutic relationship. Monetary transactions evoke the hating components in this care-taking relationship. From her perspective, the failure to set monetary limits might be an avoidance of the rage financial issues can evoke, which contradict or clash with the nurturing aspect of the therapist. To keep fees too low might deprive patients of the opportunity of expressing and working through the hate that coexists alongside the love.

Aron and Hirsch (1992) note that fee setting can reveal the analyst's greed, neediness, and dependency. On the other hand, if analysts charge too little, they may be imprisoned in a diminished view of their patient's, as well as their own, possibilities. Symington (1983), for instance, describes his "act of freedom" in questioning why he was charging one patient less than others. He thought poor so-and-so just could not afford more, then decided this did not have to be so. Raising her fee opened up the treatment, acting as "an agent of therapeutic change".

I found Symington's (1983) paper liberating, and Dimen's (1994) thought provoking and challenging. I am, however, left feeling that there is definitively something wrong with a low fee. This chapter will question that notion. I will suggest, like Symington, that what is "wrong" is for the analyst to lose the freedom to explore his or her own difficulties in coming to his/her sense of the particular details of the analytic frame. That freedom may include questioning, within limits, current analytic ground rules concerning fees. As well as illustrating problematic aspects of my charging a low fee, I will suggest the enactment also benefited our work. The issue is therefore not simply how low the fee is, but how it is addressed and gets worked out.

Case presentation

Rita is a stylish, sexy, forty-something twin, born towards the middle of eight children in a working-class family. Her mother focused on appearances, wanting to present an idyllic familial face to the world. Behind closed doors, both parents beat their children. Maybe because of her feistiness, Rita got more than her fair share of mother's, but never father's, physical wrath. She remembers being unable to go to church because her white dress was so badly blood-stained after mother's beating. Rita's clothes were hand-me-downs. Money was short, so one could not ask for anything new. Rita recalls her delight when father, a more benign figure in her inner world, bought her a T-shirt she requested. This event was exceptional for two reasons: it was new clothing and father risked doing something his wife might not agree with. He was usually unable to stand up to her.

Rita came to New York alone, with no money, few acquaintances, and few qualifications. By the time I saw her, a decade later, she had a challenging, low-paying job. Even though she is very social, she was depressed and withdrawn. She was successful at her job, but so conscientious she felt like "an indentured servant". She wanted to finish her BA, but had been unable to complete the relatively few credits. Her last long-term relationship was with a man she knew from home who joined her here. Her anger with him was intense. At times she hit him, which frightened her. She had a strong support network of friends, but did not have energy to look for a relationship.

I started seeing Rita while I was training at the William Alanson White Clinic where fees ranged from thirty to fifty dollars a session. Rita's was $40. When she became my own, as opposed to a clinic, patient, I raised her fee $5 dollars. During this time Rita returned to school, taking night classes toward her BA. She eventually quit her job to do school full-time and apply for an MA. She planned to work part time and use $10,000 she had saved to survive. When she moved into a shared apartment on a less than desirable block on the outskirts of Harlem, she said she had to stop seeing me. She wanted to come, but could not afford it.

I felt this was partly resistance but said, "OK, how low a fee do you need?" She or I said $25. That was it—the fee, without negotiation.

I slowly became aware that, while Rita was engaging, she did not carry our connection in any sustaining way between sessions. What looked like lively relatedness at times obscured fenced off impenetrability. In periods of need or crisis, she grew distant and shut down. With ostensibly ferocious independence, she declared she did not need me. Then she contemplated moving to obscure locations for equally obscure reasons. She contemplated moving to South Carolina because rural scenery would calm her. I angrily asked, "What do you think I am? How could you be so flippant about the treatment? How come it did not figure in your considerations about moving?" I would not have stated this to a full fee patient because I would have feared losing the money. Not the anger, but the entitlement of emphasizing the importance of the relationship would have been different.

My insistence on the importance of our relationship—my attempt to get through the fence—opened up discussion of her threats to move as her way of expressing hostility. Direct expression of anger is still difficult. She does get angry when I question her distancing herself, telling me I am too pushy. Once she stormed out when things got too hot because, as she later told me, this was the best way to torture me. I also think it is too hard for her to remain in the room when she is that angry.

Nine months later, I received mail from Rita's insurance company indicating that a small portion of her fee was covered. I had not been aware of this. I was furious. She knew I felt used and duped. I raised the fee to $40. She said she had forgotten she had insurance. Since she had been submitting bills to this company, I suggested there were aspects of herself, and our interaction, that were getting played out. I suggested there was a more manipulative side to her than she liked to acknowledge, that while she was comfortable emphasizing her independence, there were other wishes—to be taken care of—of which she was less aware. In retrospect, I wonder if the low fee, or my difficulty in asking for myself made it harder for Rita to ask directly. Her subterfuge may have been a way of bringing these aspects of herself to the surface.

Fast forwarding, several years ago, Rita met the man to whom she is now married. She is pleased with their communication, conflict resolution, and feels safe. She graduated with an MA, with huge loans. The fee, which, problematically, her husband pays, was $75 until she started working, and is now full fee.

The sessions I will focus on show how we talked about money. They occurred shortly after I received, Rita's permission to discuss our work in this presentation. She was planning her wedding, which her husband was paying for. We discussed instances when Rita fights her husband, such as when purchasing joint items he ignores her wishes and taste. She does not feel entitled to get equally angry when her wishes are not met, expressing that anger by emotional withdrawal or sexual reticence/witholding.

Difficulty in being taking care of financially, then tolerating ensuing feelings of guilt, shame, need, and being beholden, became clear. Speaking of her husband and me, she said it made her uncomfortable to talk about the intertwining of the personal and the monetary. A professional relationship involves money, she said, whereas a personal relationship does not. "Not both?" I asked, adding that we have a personal relationship, which, as with her husband, includes money. She responded, "I want to keep that out. I see the financial component as external, not intimately involved. On an intellectual level, I know it's a part of it. I have to deal with it. On an emotional level, I absolutely don't want to deal with it. It's a grey area. It's dirty."

The conflict between wanting to have and feeling she was not allowed to—that had been played out with me when she felt she had to stop—crystallized when Rita found a wedding dress she loved. Her husband balked at the price, suggesting she call the designer to see if she could get it cheaper. If she could only find the dress at a bargain price, she said, then it would be all right. She would not be torn between her wish to have and her feeling that she could not. A bargain price would solve the problem. I suggested maybe I had been a bargain.

I asked what the dress was like and how it looked on her. She replied, "I wanted something simple. The dress was stunning—contemporary but classic—ivory white, simple on top, with a wide, cut out skirt. I looked gorgeous, but didn't know what to do. I went back and forth. It was $3,000—extravagant, unnecessary—but then, I thought, I've waited thirty-eight years to get married. I've always bought things on sale. I've never spent a lot of money on anything." Crying, she continued, "I wish my parents would buy it for me. Even my sister offered to help me pay." I asked what made her cry. She replied, "It's a conflict. I want to look gorgeous in this stunning dress, but then I think, am I being shallow, like mother, wanting to show off too much? Is this a natural wish or my dark side?"

Discussion

An overview of the treatment suggests a trend from surreptitious grabbing toward more open asking. Rita remembered father buying a T-shirt as special because she could not remember any other instance of asking for something and getting it. She never directly asked me for such a low fee. She said she would have to leave because of money. One level of enactment, therefore, was repeating with me what she has always done: avoiding asking directly, but attempting to get some of what she needs, concretely and emotionally. The enactment is complex, because even though I do give, or maybe give in to her, she needs an element of subterfuge. She was afraid of mother's beatings that could occur at any time. With me, she created a situation (unconsciously, she protests) where she could be caught and become the object of my wrath. Even though I charged this fee, Rita got and kept it by hiding the insurance dollars, which were an aspect of her circumstances, and also represented an unconscious piece of self. She prides herself on independence, hating to think of needing anything from anyone, yet these are the very aspects of self that were enacted between us.

Although I centre this discussion on entitlement, I am not suggesting this is the specific issue evoked around money. My focus is on conflictual issues around taking and giving. What is most important is the analyst's awareness of his or her particular conflicts around how the fee is set and how money gets dealt with during therapy.

Aron and Hirsch (1992) comment on the impact of reality on the analyst's role as participant–observer because of the analyst's financial needs. If the analyst has a sliding scale, the patient's reality is also a factor, as is the patient's perception of the analyst's reality. In terms of my assessment of Rita's reality, a clinic patient is asked details of their finances up front, whereas one might otherwise allow these details to unfold. When she started seeing me, Rita knew I was in training, starting a practice, and it was a low fee clinic. She knew I was getting something for myself in working at this fee, not solely acting out my issues with self-esteem.

This case is an interesting, maybe contradictory, illustration of how the patient's reality matters. When I met Rita, she was in a low-paying job. It was hard for her to go back to school, keep her job, and have to move. Even though she lied about her insurance, she was struggling financially, even with the insurance company's $10 or $15. I was furious about her deception that distorted her reality. None the less, especially with some distance, her circumstances still seem real to me. The deception had to be analysed, but I do not feel duped in terms of the global picture.

On what may be termed the negative side of my dealing with money, Rita continues to find it hard to ask for what she wants. As with her wedding dress, she can become withdrawn and fearful with her, at times, vociferous husband. She fears the attack she anticipates will follow her request and fears the volatility of her own aggression. When she became angry with me, she walked out of the session. We worked this through, but we have not verbally dealt with the intensity of her anger. She has been hugely angry with her husband, as has he with her, and the marriage survives. She still experiences a level of toxicity around expressing anger. In so far as expressing anger around money helps a patient work through their hate, this has not occurred. Any typical anger toward an analyst asking for money, such as anger at the analyst's greed, has been avoided.

An additional, possibly more egregiously, problematic result of my pliability around money is in the area of Rita's remuneration. She is not being optimally rewarded professionally, despite retraining. She raises these issues with me, albeit often obliquely, yet refuses to analyse the feelings or explore her resistance to remedying this problem. There is a clear confluence of issues between us in this realm. Even though I now charge my full fee, her difficulty remains so far untouchable. I have suggested to her that seeing my struggle in this area makes it more complicated for her. Consciously, she does not feel this is the case, but in this murky territory the answer is still obscured.

On the positive side, Rita is feisty and determined to build for herself. She now has an MA, husband, child, and a potential career. It seems in some way I buttressed Rita's attempts to feel more entitled. Lowering the fee, then not retaliating when she lied, might have given her a sense that I saw her as entitled to treatment and, implicitly, a more expansive view of life. This aspect of our interaction spoke to her buried yearning. It might have been easier for me to be tender around money than in other ways (cf. Chapter

Five). Like Rita, I had the urge to get away from my country of origin to build a different life in New York, though I was well financed in my escape. While not my conscious intent, in my actions I gave Rita what had been withheld from her by her mother, both in the low fee and in the ensuing discussions about the meaning of these transactions (cf. Chapter Nineteen).

I am not suggesting that charging a low fee is anything like what has been termed "a corrective emotional experience". Nor am I suggesting that my motives were altruistic. Charging a low fee was safe (in terms of its psychic familiarity) for both Rita and me. The freedom for Rita lay in the enactment of my being a bargain. She has shopped on sale all her life, priding herself on her capacity to spot bargains and put clothes together with taste and flair. Acquiring me was an enactment in that, like her acquisition of clothes, she could allow herself to get and stay, with increasing closeness, if she had a bargain. Sliding to such an extent gave me a perverse sense of freedom, allowing me to put my difficulties with entitlement out of the picture. Paradoxically, this also allowed me to assert myself and take a stand about the importance of our relationship as a factor to be considered if she was thinking of moving.

Returning to the delicate, participant–observer balancing act, a sliding scale is obviously complicated. What may be most important is that these matters get talked about. The problem might have been not so much my low fee, but my failure to negotiate when I set it and then, when I further lowered it, avoiding negotiation again. A request for $5 or $10 more would have forced us to struggle with the resistance. It would have been a way of keeping my needs alive and giving Rita a way to be more in touch with her wish for treatment, which was tenuous at a certain point. If one is sliding a fee, specific dollar amounts matter, as does the subsequent freedom to move, both lower and higher.

Finally and speculatively, in reaching decisions with a sliding scale, an additional taboo might be the area of giving. There is a grey zone going from attending patient's real life events (such as shows or weddings, which may be more discussed) to actually giving to a patient, in thought or action, which I view as taboo. For instance, when one sees a magazine article that directly pertains to what a patient is discussing, does one use that with the patient? Does one save the article and bring it in? Does one mention it or just note the thought and keep it mind? If boundaries are clearly in place, is there room for experimentation (cf. Chapter One)? The potential for acting out is great in these murky areas, yet one wonders why such issues are not more openly discussed.

References

Aron, L., & Hirsch, I. (1992). Money matters in psychoanalysis: a relational approach In: *Relational Perspectives in Psychoanalysis* (pp. 239–256). Hillsdale, NJ: Analytic Press.

Dimen, M. (1994). Money, love and hate: contradiction and paradox in psychoanalysis. *Psychoanalytic Dialogues, 4*: 69–100.

Freud, S. (1913c). On beginning the treatment. *S.E., 12*: 123–144. London: Hogarth.

Symington, N. (1983). The analyst's act of freedom as agent of therapeutic change. *International Review of Psycho-Analysis, 10*: 283–291.

CHAPTER NINE

For a fistful of dollars: psychoanalytic issues in handling cash payments

Mark V. Mellinger

C onducting psychoanalytic treatment in exchange for cash, though rarely discussed, is often viewed with doubt and suspicion. Langs (1982) was unequivocal about this when he instructed psychoanalysts to refuse cash payments and to stamp the cheque for deposit only, so that the patient might be given proof of the analyst's law-abiding ways. In their book on the vicissitudes of the fee, Herron and Welt (1992) devote only a few lines to cash:

> It is a popular conception (we hope, misconception) that therapists hide some of their income and that cash payments help them do this and will generally be so used. Again the issue of interest is the patient's motivation in making a cash payment. [p. 94]

Training supervisors sometimes pass on this caution and it has gained the status of a dictum in some quarters. In our field, it is not uncommon for seasoned clinicians to express their views with a sense of authority, and for trainees to suppress their doubts in the face of such certainty. There is more to this subject, however, than has been conveyed by recent cautionary advice. The status of cash in the treatment contract might unveil rich complexities to be utilized in understanding and affecting the patient.

Cash transactions are readily understood as falling into the "taboo" realm because they are associated with the small commerce of the street and with illegal or embarrassing purchases. It is conventionally understood that respectable purchases are to be made in a manner that leaves a permanent record. Perhaps our doing this work for money (in any form) evokes guilt, defensiveness, and aggression. To make cash the medium of exchange simply lays this aspect out too bluntly. If we are inclined to feel sullied by the fee, a cheque can make it more antiseptic.

This was not always the prevailing view on psychoanalytic payments. Dimen (1994), in her penetrating work on the functions served in psychoanalysis through money, refers to: "[Karl] Abraham's (1921) certainly accurate diagnosis of severe anality in people who insist on paying not only analyst's bills but even the smallest sums by check" (p. 70).

Payment, in whatever form, has been an assumed or stated part of psychoanalytic work from the beginning. Indeed, it is a central factor differentiating psychoanalysis and psychotherapy from their more commonplace counterparts: friendly advice, religious guidance, psychic reading, and chat-room keyboarding. Of course, treatment is often done without charge to the patient. In clinics and private practices, people are sometimes seen for free. Herron and Welt (1992) point out that:

> There are a variety of motives . . . However therapists expect something for such service . . . It is still a transaction, only the currency has changed. A "fee" is still being charged, such as patient gratitude, recognition . . . as a good and giving person . . . or experience. [p. 5]

Dimen goes beyond the usual rationales for the centrality of payment to argue that it serves as a vehicle for the hatred that, in dialectical relationship with the loving intimacy of the treatment, generates the transcendent experience of analytic work. Indeed, as she shows, the interdependency of the two lives in analytic relationship is proved real and palpable through the intercession of the fee.

There are far worse reasons to be doing this work than for the money. We might do it to cement an identity within a cultural and economic elite, to further our philosophies, reassure ourselves of our intellectual, moral, or interpersonal superiority, or, like Lucy in the *Peanuts'* comic strip, because we are just nosy. There is probably no reason that should not arouse some suspicion.

So, if we are going to value payment, why not be more neutral about its being in the form of cash? One explanation is that we are more embarrassed than other professionals about our love of money. The biblical caution, "Love of money is the root of all Evil" (I Timothy, 6: 10) exerts a subtle influence on many of us. Aron and Hirsch (1992) present Ferenczi's sensuous delineation of this love.

Ferenczi (1914) described the development of the interest in money in terms of libido theory. Children show a natural interest and pleasure in defecating and in holding back their stool. The retained faeces are the first savings and the first toys. In moving towards an interest in mud, the child gives up the anal–erotic pleasure in the smell of the faeces. "Street-mud is, so to speak, deodorised dejecta" (*ibid.*, p. 322).

Next the child gives up the pleasure in the moisture and interest shifts to sand. Later interest shifts to pebbles and stones, and later to marbles and buttons. "The attributes of evil odour, moisture, and softness are represented by those of absence of odour, dryness, and now also hardness" (*ibid.*, p. 325). Finally, interest is shown in coins, and, as cognitive development proceeds, coins are replaced by stocks, bonds, and abstract figures. "Pleasure in the intestinal contents becomes enjoyment of money, which, however, after what has been said is seen to be nothing other than odourless, dehydrated filth that has been made to shine" (*ibid.*, p. 327).

Cash is the original money object, stealing cathexis from the first loves of breast, faeces, and genitals. As children, we received thrilling coins, given by loving adults, imparting precious bits of the allure and mystery of adulthood. Its uniformity and elaborate design conveyed the presence of an immense and powerful society. Possession of money made us a part of that power. Soon, we witnessed the power of money to excite and induce rage and anxiety in adults. Popular culture augmented our growing visceral appreciation of money as a universal good, prayed for, worked for, even killed for. Alongside this message there remained the caution: the pursuit of money will cost you your soul!

Rothstein (1991) describes how patients test and seduce us with money. He cautions analysts to treat such seduction in the same way as sexual seduction and to observe celibacy past termination, for all time. It is in matters relating to payment that we may find analysts showing the least flexibility. Attitudes towards money often reflect blind adherence to those of our analytic role models (Tulipan, 1986). We feel more secure taking risks in technique than in our fee policy.

Dimen (1994) describes how Freud's passion to free psychoanalysis from Victorian shame and moralizing about money is revealed in his work. Also revealed, however, is his captivation with his wealthy "goldfish" patients in his personal letters and also with the cautionary tale of "the Devil's Gold" (Freud, 1908b, p. 174). This German folktale describes the seduction of women by the Devil and his giving them gold in return. When the Devil leaves, the gold turns to excrement.

The socio-economic status of Freud's family is clouded in mystery. His youth is sometimes referred to as marked by poverty (Jones, 1953), but other accounts hint at wealth (Warner, 1991). Perhaps Freud's ambivalent statements about money reflect a wish to distinguish his frank approach to discussing money from the prevalent stereotype of the money-loving Jew. Another factor influencing Freud's ambivalence regarding money was the arrest of his Uncle Josef Freud for selling counterfeit fifty rouble notes, possibly with the collaboration of Sigmund's half-brothers. This occurred when Sigmund was nine years old, and resulted in torment from his schoolmates (Krull, 1986).

In Freud's recounting of the Devil's tale, and to some extent in Dimen's paper and in her citations from Karl Marx, we might read a hint of piety: "You cannot serve God and mammon". Piety is not, however, the message Dimen is putting forth. Money, she argues, is a force that, by its function as a universal standard of value, degrades that which is beyond price or unique unto itself. How, then, can it not also degrade psychoanalysis? Well, in a way it does, and in so doing, saves it from its own great potential for piety and self-aggrandizement. Our fees enrich and also humble us. The payment of them both empowers and impoverishes our patients. The transaction insults both parties to it, yet clarifies and relieves both from obligations and wishfulness.

This impious humanism is present as well when patients are treated at public expense, without cost to them. It is present in the experience of the therapist as an employee, civil servant, or actor in a complex system of reward management.

The case of Ms Washington may exemplify the effect of non-standard "currency" on the treatment of someone with no money. Living on welfare and struggling mightily with both her inner and outer torments, Ms Washington and her therapist, a colleague of mine, worked out a way for her to pay for treatment with half her monthly allotment of USDA surplus cheese. Both parties spoke to each other with mouths that had shared that block of yellow sustenance. The same transference manifestations were in evidence as with conventional fees: did the therapist really need/appreciate/value the substance that Ms Washington might have put to her own use? The same resentments, and shame over resentments, coloured the countertransference, but also contributed to a shared awareness of the precariousness of human interdependence. This sense became a lens, which, in the course of treatment, brought Ms Washington's life into clearer focus.

Most of us can see in our choice of careers some effort to resolve the seeming dichotomy of feeding our souls *vs.* feeding our faces. We take some pride in a profession that balances the two goals handsomely. At any given moment, one or the other might enthrall us, but it is their interplay that gives psychoanalysis its peculiar efficacy.

In the consulting room, money functions as a pipeline for symbols and fantasies between the personal and the mundane, the inner and outer realities. It opposes idealization and other illusions, including those of an eternal connectedness. Payment indicates that there is a job to be done, hence, a time within which to accomplish it. The hateful and hated tyranny of the clock is mirrored by the hateful fixity of the fee; the unfeeling charge for sessions missed through the intercession of cruel chance. Settling accounts in cash reveals this (necessary) hatefulness in the relationship in a harsh light. Analyst and analysand witness wallets and purses opening, careful fingers and eyes counting bills.

Dimen (1994) concludes:

> Psychoanalysis is not revolution, and it doesn't make the contradiction between money and love go away. But for a brief, utopian moment, it permits transcendence. In the psychoanalytic contact, the contradiction between money and love, a relation between contraries that can be transformed, finds a temporary, reparative resolution in the paradox between love and hate, a relation between contraries that never changes. . . . The lesson of contradiction is . . .

[t]hat money negates love, this we know preconsciously ... But paradox is different; it is relearned each time it is lived. [pp. 97–98]

The repetitive act of paying the analyst becomes a rhythmic beat, a sacred rite of witnessing the paradoxical relationship become flesh.

My intent is to put cash payment in the limelight so as to grant it some semblance of equality. The conventional system of payment by cheque is, in contrast, shown in a sceptical light. This is not to try to establish any superiority for cash, only to offer it some much-needed affirmative action.

Let us examine the situation that arises when an analyst states her refusal of cash as a means of payment. US Federal Reserve Notes bear the inscription: "This note is legal tender for all debts public and private". It would appear from this inscription that we are not in a legally defensible position if we refuse cash. While an analyst's active solicitation of cash payment would taint the treatment with the analyst's personal needs, so, too, would an announced refusal to accept cash.

Holding cash payment as a taboo necessitates a deviation from a traditional understanding of transference analysis and counter-transference disclosure; specifically, it generates a moralistic disclosure. An argument often made is that by accepting cash we imply to our patient that we are interested in evading income tax. Let us disregard for the moment that this implication is often quite accurate. If this is a serious concern, it can be remedied through the simple and charmingly Victorian expedient of providing a cash receipt. I would suggest use of carbon paper or another method that provides a duplicate for the therapist's own records. Cash payments are devilishly hard to recall accurately.

A patient who asks for a reduced fee because of paying in cash is asking us to collude in a deception. Such a deal can be refused without prejudice regarding the form of payment. But, the automatic refusal of cash as payment, just like the request for cash, clouds the transference with unwanted information about the analyst's relationship to money, authority, and morality.

Psychoanalysts generally do not deviate from their prime method (the elucidation of transference) merely to prevent a patient from getting the wrong idea about us? Our work depends on the patient's transferential interest in what we are up to. The negative transference usually has greater utility than the positive component for advancing the treatment (Epstein, 1991, personal communication). Fantasies about the analysts' relationship to the greater authority of the Internal Revenue Service are tools for understanding much about the patient's place within the societal sphere. The fantasy of the analyst paying taxes on cash receipts would be as interesting as the fantasy of the analyst dodging those taxes. Again, Aron and Hirsch:

> The reality of the analyst's attitudes and behavior concerning money inevitably comes across to patients. It is not just a matter of their affecting the "working alliance". We are arguing that whether or not the analyst reports all of his or her income may very well affect the development of the transference. [p. 253]

The patient has a clear legal right to pay for services with cash, cheque, or, I suppose, even credit card, should the analyst offer this option (I do not know of anyone who does). Where sufficient trust exists, payment by cheque is a privilege that is generally offered. It does, however, seem legitimate to revoke such a privilege from a patient who regularly abuses it. Some patients bounce cheques in an effort to engage their analyst in an intense, mutually hostile relationship that re-enacts a struggle for survival with an ambivalently loved object. "Cash on the barrelhead" can be a powerful tool to engage a sociopathic patient in a muscular embrace sufficient to prevent the therapeutic connection from exploding.

One growing use of cash payment is the managed care co-pay. While some patients cover this with a monthly cheque, many are in the habit of paying the $10, $15 or $25 in cash, per session. The temptation is to stick it in a pocket, since it occurs in the last seconds of a session and the next patient is waiting. Inevitably, there will come a day when neither party has the right combination of bills to close the transaction. A patient will either owe or have credit for $5, which will be remembered by one or the other. The monthly cheque certainly solves these problems, but the cash exchange may be fraught with meaning that, if short-circuited by a cheque, might not reappear in as clear a context.

Let us consider further the use of cheques for payment. While it is almost universal, and therefore rarely examined for its impact on psychoanalytic work, it is far from ideal. The principal problem posed by cheques is not a clinical or theoretical one. The depositing of cheques is a public act, one that leaves a record, and often now a digital image, and thus constitutes a threat to the patient's confidentiality. This is particularly true outside of urban centres or with well-known patients, but can be risky anywhere and with any patient. I am more aware of this when depositing the cheques from my suburban practice in the local bank branch than I am in dealing with cheques from my city office. Anonymous bank tellers are, in reality, my patients' neighbours. I have no doubt that sometimes a name is recognized. Tellers take some interest in the transactions they process, thus it is preferable to bank and practice in different locations, if possible. Even with this precaution, there is some risk, particularly for any publicly known patient, but probably no more than the risk of being seen entering our doors. Still, for some patients, it might be more protective of their privacy, and of the unique isolation of psychoanalytic space from the comings and goings of the ordinary world, to abstain from the more public cheque.

I wonder if the act of leaving a record of one's treatment counters the unsettling sense of the evanescence of the work itself. Sessions are unwitnessed, forgotten by both parties, and seem to vanish without a trace. So does the patient's hard-earned money. The processed cheque with the analyst's signature or stamp is proof that one was there.

Cash is a medium rich in potent symbolism. Fenichel (1938) observed that money stands not only for faeces, as Abraham and Ferenczi had described, but can substitute for any substance, or even insubstantial quality, that is exchanged between people, such as milk, sperm, protection, power, or anger. The actual handling of the cash evokes fantasies, often including sexual symbolism. Does the patient pay with freshly dispensed twenties or reach for a pocketful of rumpled bills? Does she show off a purse full of big bills? Is change needed? Is he down to his last dollar? Money comes with its own history. Where did these particular bills come from? Is this money "clean" or "dirty"? Should the analyst enquire? Or care?

Mr Jackson, an accountant to some questionable clients, paid with bills that bore the dank smell of a cellar, or a grave. He took visible delight in the transfer, which made me a third party to a chain of *sub rosa* trans-actions. Although none was asked for, I gave a written receipt for the cash, both to keep alive the possibility in the transference that I was not myself a criminal, and because he was uncharacteristically poor at counting the money and remembering what he had paid. His errors, interestingly, were always in my favour, requiring me to point out his overpayment. Analysis eventually uncovered early and persistent sexual threats from a respected family member, and his parents' failure to notice. The anxiously exciting secrecy surrounding the forbidden desires of a generally respected citizen was mirrored both in his work and our transactions. As Mr Jackson became more able to believe his own story, and even risk referring to his experiences in his parents' presence, he began to find it inconvenient to dig up cash with which to pay me. Cheques became a simpler way to settle accounts with me. My willingness to enter into an arrangement with Mr Jackson that he had tainted with the fruits of his shady dealings allowed us to work our way out of the dank pit he had been living in all his life. I am not sure he could have owned up to his deeper shame had I been unwilling to handle his lesser shame.

Handling patients' cash raises primeval fantasies. How does accepting the patient's cash contaminate or impregnate the analyst? In accepting a patient's cash we may be seen, or see ourselves, as accomplices in the patient's life and livelihood. There may be a fantasy in the analyst's mind that now a Godfather-like favour can be demanded of us. At other times, cash might have an emotionally moving effect. The analyst might feel, through the notes them-selves, the value of the treatment to this patient. Tens and twenties bring a host of associations to the many other things this person could have bought.

In handling and exchanging cash, the spectre of greed, fanta-sized and actual, is sure to be present in the room. As analysts, we may feel that our greed will suddenly become visible and palpable as we touch the money. Herron and Welt (1992) also describe how a therapist's early experience of being the parentified child provid-ing care for a parent who is unable to care for them might be enacted in the treatment of patients. The patient might be cast in the role of the parent who should, but cannot, take care of us. So we take care of the patient, arousing unconscious resentment and greed. Payment becomes symbolic resolution and triumph over this desperate dynamic.

Greed is what the therapist feels but cannot be aware of because of
a sense of unworthiness. It is difficult to be aware of feeling greed,
as well, when one has been trained from infancy to be a selfless
helper. [*ibid.*, p. 40]

When this dynamic is out of awareness for the analyst, it may
achieve awareness in the patient. Indeed, the corresponding satisfaction of seeing the analyst's longing to be taken care of might
itself be worth the price. How then do we distinguish the analyst's
longing for an undoing of an old and tragic deprivation, from a
healthy acceptance and enjoyment of being paid for one's work?
Where does a fair exchange turn into a sense of entitlement and,
from that, to a hateful clutching at another's wealth? The medium
of cash itself plays a part in this transformation. Its antiquity as an
object plunges the transaction into a transferential netherworld.
Scarcely was the meaning of money internalized in us than the
vision of boundless quantities of it sprang to mind in a perfect
recreation of the pre-linguistic experience of the boundless generos-
ity of the breast. The excitement of the arrival of the wealthy patient
is one that we might be prepared to manage. Here, the intercession
of the insulating bank cheque lowers the affective temperature. A
few twenties from a more middle class patient might catch us more
off guard.

Mr Lincoln arrived for a first consultation. He spoke of his critical wife
and daughter and his escape from them into his work. "What work do
you do?" I asked (for whatever reason). "I manage a $2 billion mutual
fund," he replied. Although for the most part I was able to attend to his
worries and resentments after that, some of my attention was on what
now seemed like my modest $150 top fee. We agreed that a twice-
weekly schedule would work. At the end of the consultation he pulled
out a cheque book and asked what the charge would be. I told him my
(new) fee of $165. With a trace of a smile he said, "I don't want to tell
you how to run your business doctor, but I expected something beginning at least with a two."

Low fees may be a response to an unconscious struggle with
greed as much as high fees are. Herron and Welt again: "Greed
defended against by reaction formation is a problem for those therapists who run from the recognition . . . that money obligates the

therapist to the patient" (p. 40). They see the roots of this reaction formation in a dynamic they imply is commonplace in those who become therapists: the transformation of the need to be cared for into the caring for the depriving parent. They continue, "It is not that such therapists are not greedy . . . Their heritage of privation has taught them that the object's actual greed and their own projection of greed onto the object are dangerous" (pp. 40–41).

Klein (1952) says, "The bad breast will devour him in the same greedy way as he desires to devour it" (p. 64). Herron and Welt extend Klein's idea to the undercharging therapist:

> Such a therapist backs away from those symbols signifying needs, thus backing away from her own privation . . . The passive–aggressive stance binds the therapist to the patient and thereby to his or her own parent. Healthy aggression is therefore not freely available to the therapist for taking care of herself by . . . adequate fees. [pp. 40–41]

So, does consciousness of one's greed make it any better? It might make it easier to work within the transference–countertransference tango/tangle. Would adding a cash dimension to an already supercharged monetary relationship further complicate it? Of course! As analysts we seek to clarify, not to simplify, what goes on. We strive to limit the introduction of our own needs and desires into the analytic process, but accept that we will inevitably fail at this, and that when we do fail, we will probably not see it. One way to counter this inevitability is to regard our every move with the same curiosity that we have towards our patient's acts and statements. In taking this stance, we consider that what seems to us like a healthy and forthright attitude towards being paid probably has more basic urges and needs hiding under its skirts.

In this era of diminished valuation of all psychotherapeutic work, and particularly of our model, psychoanalysts sometimes are inclined to see themselves in a somewhat holy light for continuing their principled work with little reward. This is a lovely little conceit that is usually harmless. If it becomes too central a part of our mythology, a little cash can balance the saintliness with the spectre of the whore. Perhaps psychoanalytic practitioners are already too uncomfortable with the comparisons made to prostitution. This comparison need not be insulting to either profession.

Although both psychoanalysis and prostitution subject their practitioners to a level of use and abuse that most people would not tolerate in a work setting, they have more positive similarities as well. Both endeavours seem to provide, within a business relationship, something usually considered part of a personal relationship. In fact, by virtue of the absence of a conventional personal connection, they provide something impossible to obtain elsewhere.

We can take some satisfaction in two essential differences from prostitutes. We do not leave the customer satisfied, and we do not (ordinarily) risk our health and life in our work. In granting a sense of personal safety and distance, the analyst's cheque may be equivalent to the prostitute's condom.

We withhold a great deal of our everyday selves from our patients in the interest of allowing a broader transitional space to develop between us. Desire for money is among the things we try to keep from sharing. We might even keep it out of our own awareness. The fee prevents this fact of life from being totally submerged, but it is sometimes handled in a brief, minimized, and ritualistic fashion. The cheque allows the ritual to be more removed from the truth of the economic intercourse. The analyst's comfort with payment by cheque need not necessarily deny the analyst's desire for the cash that it represents, but obvious discomfort with or refusal of cash is more likely to be perceived by the patient as an area of conflict for the analyst than as good citizenship.

The cash taboo has the power to cloud our analytic judgment. Rather than advocating for or against cash, we need to clarify its uses and risks. It is an element of the analytic setting, like the physical environment or the time frame. Like these other parameters, our different attitudes towards payment contribute to our most valuable asset as an institution: our diversity and continued struggle to free our work from dogma.

References

Abraham, K. (1921). Contributions to the theory of the anal character. In: D. Bryan & A. Strachey (Trans.), *Selected Papers of Karl Abraham, MD* (pp. 370–392). New York: Basic Books, 1953.

Aron, L. & Hirsch, I. (1992). Money matters in psychoanalysis: a relational approach. In: N. Skolnick & S. Warshaw (Eds.), *Relational Perspectives in Psychoanalysis* (pp. 239–256). Hillsdale, NJ: Analytic Press.

Dimen, M. (1994). Money, love and hate: contradiction and paradox in psychoanalysis. *Psychoanalytic Dialogues*, 4: pp. 69–100.

Fenichel, O. (1938). The drive to amass wealth. *Psychoanalytic Quarterly*, 7: pp. 69–95.

Ferenczi, S. (1914). The ontogenesis of the interest in money. In: *First Contributions to Psycho-Analysis* (pp. 319–331). New York: Brunner/Mazel, 1952.

Freud, S. (1908b). Character and anal eroticism. *S.E.*, 9: 167–195. London: Hogarth.

Herron, W., & Welt, S. (1992). *Money Matters: The Fee in Psychotherapy and Psychoanalysis*. New York: Guilford.

Jones, E. (1953). *The Life and Work of Sigmund Freud*. New York: Basic Books.

Klein, M. (1952). Some theoretical conclusions regarding the life of the infant. In: *Envy &, Gratitude & Other Works 1946–1963* (pp. 176–235). New York: Free Press, 1975.

Krull, M. (1986). *Freud and his Father*. New York: W. W. Norton.

Langs, R. (1982). *Psychotherapy: A Basic Text*. Northvale, NJ: Jason Aronson.

Rothstein, A. (1991). The seduction of money. In: S. Klebanow & E. Lowenkopf (Eds.), *Money and Mind* (pp. 149–152). New York: Plenum Press.

Tulipan, A. (1986). Fee policy as an extension of the therapist's style and orientation. In: D. Krueger (Ed.), *The Last Taboo: Money as Symbol & Reality in Psychotherapy & Psychoanalysis* (pp. 79–87). New York: Brunner/Mazel.

Warner, S. (1991). Sigmund Freud and money. In: S. Klebanow & E. Lowenkopf (Eds.), *Money and Mind* (pp. 121–132). New York: Plenum.

CHAPTER TEN

When the patient has more real world power than the analyst

Jill Howard

E ver since Freud's (1913c) observation that "Money matters are treated by civilized people in the same way as sexual matters—with the same inconsistency, prudishness, and hypocrisy" (p. 131), psychoanalysts have been invited to treat the subject of money directly and frankly. This goal is, I believe, for most of us, easier said than done.

The treatment of a truly powerful and wealthy patient is likely to evoke intense feelings of envy and greed in most of us who lead lives not so privileged. Rothstein (1991) wrote of the countertransference longings and greed he experienced with a patient who wanted to leave him money in his will. Long after the treatment ended, he experienced fantasies of this phantom wealth. This observation also supported his feeling that, because the unconscious is timeless, transferences and countertransferences might be analysed, but they are never entirely worked through.

Two years ago, when the lease to my office was seriously threatened, I recalled my earlier work with Diana, a wealthy, powerful woman who regularly spoke of buying me a brownstone in which to practice. Her foundation was always looking for places to donate money and what better way could she find to say thank you than that. I never quite saw myself as a charitable cause, but the brownstone fantasy, as well as many others, has lingered long beyond the termination of Diana's treatment.

Diana's therapy was consistent with many of Silas Warner's (1991) observations of the treatment of the very rich. The most frequent cause for the problems of "affluenza", wrote Warner, stems from a deprived childhood. A surplus of money often substitutes for close empathic relationships (especially with mother), and results in a home environment he called "a golden ghetto without walls" (p. 183). He also noted that all of the specialized services offered by family servants, teachers, and coaches might lead to true respect for their special instructors or they may experience contempt for them and treat them like servants. Both are experiences I had in my treatment with Diana.

> When I first met Diana in the waiting room in April of 1988, I was unprepared to find a statuesque, thirty-eight-year-old blonde beauty who, in her simple, elegant, pink dress and pearls, was the epitome of old WASP society. She waltzed into my office and settled into the chair in a way that took over the room (something the referring physician had alerted me to). I was, much to my analytic chagrin, immediately aware of her beauty and of the wealth and power her demeanour bespoke. When I asked her what had brought her to treatment, she stated, "I have been married to three men who all tell me I'm crazy. I have come to find out if that is true."

> Ten minutes into the hour, she got up out of her chair and started wandering around my office. In much the same way as young children explore the consulting room, she wandered around, picking things up, then carefully put them back. Her eyes and body posture clearly stated that this was hardly someone taking over my office. Only much later in the treatment did I realize that Diana was a young child in an elegant woman's body, immediately announcing her developmental stage through re-enactment. I said nothing (not by virtue of adopting an analytic attitude, but because her behaviour left me feeling confused). This pattern went on for three or four sessions. At times she joked and I laughed. At other times, she wandered and I watched. Years later, she would tell me that she stayed because I had a sense of humour and patience, which she knew would someday be necessary if we were going to make it through the work ahead.

The enactment was so powerful that I did not realize we were immediately in the throes of an intense transference–countertransference interaction. Specifically, she was the lonely, helpless child in search of guidance and protection. I stood by feeling bewildered, confused, and unhelpful, just like her mentally ill mother and her weak, amoral, alcoholic father. Given the intensity of this early exchange, I was quite surprised to discover three years later, when she really did take over my office, that she had no memory of any of these events.

Diana was out of the consulting room as much as she was in it during the first four months of treatment. She jetted to Palm Beach, London, Paris, and Aspen. When I questioned her flight, she informed me that if I was to have a patient like her, I would have to be comfortable accepting a fee whether or not she was there. It was, after all, her life. When I told her my concerns were less about her fee (though I wonder) and more about our ability to develop a relationship, she assured me it would work out. I also felt I had been put on notice, just as if I was one of her servants.

Four months into treatment, Diana fell down the stairs and broke her ankle. She made it to her session, on crutches, straight from the hospital. For one moment, she was grounded.

Despite Diana's demands that I be omnipotent and powerful, I was again helpless to protect her in November when she was diagnosed with breast cancer. A lumpectomy was performed in December. The next night, she had a Christmas party for fifty people. In addition to her obvious state of denial, I learned that Christmas was magical to her. She used it to be utterly expansive and all-giving to everyone she knew. Later in the treatment, we talked about what this meant to her, but in December 1988, I simply suggested she was not dealing with her loss and that I suspected jetting off to Vail to ski might not be the answer.

The mourning process began. For the next six months, Diana's life consisted solely of radiation treatments and our work. Just prior to the diagnosis, Diana stated, "If I have to come to the West Side two times a week, I'd like to have a double session to make it worth the trip." In her own arrogant, condescending way, she had let me know how important I was to her while simultaneously devaluing me, my office, and the whole West Side. However, it also meant that we had four hours a week together to work through her issues around her illness, fears, and manic defences. (Later, these sessions would occur across four days.) It is at this point that I see our more serious work beginning.

Power and control

At that point, I had not yet entered formal psychoanalytic training at the William Alanson White Institute. As a result, our work was fraught with many technical decisions which, for better or worse, had an impact on the analysis. I have selected one of the more technically controversial aspects of this treatment to capture how giving and receiving can be used in the service of power, control, and seduction.

The subject of gift giving and receiving in analysis is undoubtedly one which is bound to raise some discussion. I made the choice to accept all that was offered, verbally and otherwise, until such point that I became uncomfortable. It is not surprising that this is the patient who made me reconsider this position.

In January of 1989 (the first year of treatment), Diana looked up my birthday in the American Psychological Association Directory. She arrived at my office with birthday presents for me. I was taken aback. While I stated that analysis was a place to speak about the wish to give, I sent a mixed message by accepting the gifts. They included *The Washington Post* from the day I was born, bound in a leather case with my initials, and a book entitled, *All I Ever Needed to Know I Learned in Kindergarten*.

One month later, Diana again arrived with gifts for me on the day I was leaving for vacation. The gifts, a royal blue cashmere sweater, scarf, and gloves were, she said, "Because that is your favourite colour and I think you are going skiing, so they will come in handy." Diana chirped on blithely through the session until I stated that it was intolerable to her that I was leaving and she could only be sure I would think of her if I wore her gifts. Without the gifts, she would no longer exist for me. Diane crumbled in front of my face, sobbing uncontrollably for ten minutes. At the end of the hour, I suggested that she would never know what I really felt for her if she kept giving me gifts and, though I would accept them, I hoped that she would someday choose to articulate her positive and negative feelings for me without such a concrete expression.

In June 1989, the gift came in an altogether different package. After much work and recovery from her illness, Diana and her husband adopted a baby girl, Karen. Six days later, Diana arrived in my office with Karen, placed her in my arms, and stated, "Don't worry if she cries. She cries with strangers." Karen immediately fell asleep in my arms and remained asleep for the double session. When I offered Diana the idea that she was bringing her baby to me because she was estranged from her mother, she replied, "You're not really going to interpret this. I just wanted you to see her." "What else would I do?" I asked. It was not long before she accepted the notion that it was she who longed to be held in my arms.

In December 1989, Diana arrived with a Christmas present from Tiffany's. It was a crystal star. "You can save the interpretation," she stated. "Clearly it is a sign of my idealized transference." While she was saved that interpretation, I did point out that the extravagant parties, gifts, and celebration could not conceal her dreaded holiday depression.

This was, for me, a countertransference nightmare. How could I continue to accept these gifts? How, on the other hand, could I justify a change of stance? I could not resolve these questions at the time. Instead, I stuck with the issue of giving gifts that would not be reciprocated. She flatly stated, "There are other gifts around this office. That Freud doll, this dragonfly, that planter. All of them were gifts." When I asked how she knew that, she said, "They are not your style. You would not have bought them." She was, of course, correct. Then she stated in a way you can probably imagine by now, "I think you are bothered by the value of my gifts. However, the amount of money I spent on the sweater, or this crystal, is of no more significance to me than the cost of that Freud doll might be to someone else." While it was true, it did not ease my growing discomfort.

For Christmas 1990, Diana brought me her seven favourite books of all time. She chirped her way through the session until I asked her to tell me why she had picked each book and what she wanted me to understand about her from her selections. The stories of lost, alienated adolescents, or difficult childhoods, were each explained in a subdued tone. This was the Christmas without excess. She stated that I would be relieved to know that the books were all paperbacks and not expensive. At this point, I offered Diana what has come to be known between us as the "bank account" theory. This theory emerged from examples in Diana's life, as well as the treatment, where she bought herself protection from others in anticipation of some future debt. I suggested she was giving gifts to build up her bank account with me so that, when the bad times came, she could draw on her account.

In December 1991 (four years into treatment), Diana and I worked extensively, in advance of Christmas, on her wish to continue buying affection. While she understood she was depriving herself, and me, of a more authentic encounter, she was not sure it was worth the trade-off. She struggled through the Christmas season with the most moderation she had yet shown, but arrived at her last session with another box from Tiffany's. In one of the most poignant moments of her treatment, she placed the box on the ottoman, half way between the couch and my chair. She stated, "I do not know if you will accept this gift, and, if you choose not to, I will not be devastated. I bought it for you long ago and it has been in my closet. I was not going to bring it, but I decided analysis is about feeling freer to be who you really are and this is who I really am. I will not keep putting you in such a difficult position. It is clear to me that you enjoy the gifts I choose, but that it goes against your analytic grain. Whether or not you take it, I am convinced my bank account is full enough. Truly it is the best expression in a gift I have yet found." The gift was a crystal heart.

I was quite moved. Because I was at this point in supervision with Dr Robert Shapiro, I decided to buy time until our next meeting. I stated that I did not know what I wanted to do and that I needed time to think about it. I said I would keep the gift in my office until she returned.

Dr Shapiro and I discussed the power of the interaction. Noting my conflict, he asked what was disturbing me. I stated that I did not wish to refuse the gift, but that it was not the analytic way. He suggested that Diana was clearly considering what needed to be considered and was exploring it in a way that left me free to do as I chose. When she returned, we opened the gift together, placed it on my table, and I stated that it was the last gift I would accept.

It was, therefore, without guilt, that I refused to keep the book that was delivered by messenger to my door on Valentine's Day, 1992. I opened the package, took notes from the jacket cover, and gave the book to Diana when she returned ten days later. I summarized what I had written and told her I had never opened the book. The book, *Griffen and Sabine*, is a story about a correspondence and romance which began from a small postcard. The notes I read to Diana described the characters as "inextricably linked strangers". It was the tale of a man's "logical, methodical world" being turned upside down by a "strangely exotic woman". He wondered if she were "a twin? a clairvoyant? a malevolent angel?" and whether this would be "the flowering of a magical relationship or a descent into madness?" These jacket notes seemed to capture Diana's conflict in the treatment with me at that time.

Diana responded, "I missed the madness and malevolence part. It was stubborn of you not to read it." "Who is being stubborn?" I retorted. We explored the darker images of the book, and I simply commented that she had a way of being *present* even when she was not here.

In my mind, the last, and most powerful instance of gift-giving came in an entirely verbal form. In June 1992, I discovered a song by Garth Brooks that moved me deeply. I spent an entire weekend playing the song and discussed it in my own treatment the following Monday. On Tuesday, Diana came to session and stated that she had discovered the most amazing song, *The River*, by Garth Brooks. She thought of me all weekend as she played it. The words that had captured her and the analytic struggle were, "So don't you sit upon the shoreline and say you're satisfied. / Choose to dance the rapids and dare to dance the tides". I thought to myself, if she could not be with me, she would become me.

I had long since concluded that Diana's uncanny ability to know what someone wanted and to give it to them was a source of much of her power and control. I also understood, however, that it was only possible because of the fragility of her boundaries. What had once been a powerful mechanism for survival was now occurring at the expense of her authenticity. The pseudo-intimacy created by her ability to penetrate another's boundaries was aiding and abetting her fear of craziness.

Conclusion

Diana, like many other people of her social strata, is not someone who is used to hearing the word no. Intuitively, I understood that if I rejected her first gift, it might well cause a narcissistic injury sufficient for her to flee treatment. My lack of experience did not provide me with an alternative. In accepting the gift, I set a drama in place that would take many years of analysis to understand.

In retrospect, I think my inexperience also resulted in less of an "analytic superego" than I now have and, therefore, we experienced a more authentic, albeit difficult, encounter. Diana seemed too fragile at the time to accept the idea of no. It was only after years of difficult enactments and analysis that she understood what was bothering me with the gift giving and could consider the reasons I ultimately did say no.

This material is consistent with Muriel Dimen's (1994) discussion of the contradiction between money and love that is part of our culture. She argued that:

> A money relation is thought not to be a love relation. Money appears to negate love, producing the hate that signs their contradiction but the psychoanalytic situation is a case where money permits love . . . where you would not get to love unless money was exchanged, where money in fact guarantees the possibility of love and where, therefore, the contradiction between money and love, and the hate it generates becomes safe. [p. 96]

The wealthy, powerful patient seems to me to have even more confusion around love, money, and hate than the patient with less real-world status. There is always a question of whether the person or the money is sought out in friendships and intimate relationships. There is often deep damage from the "affluenza" syndrome, and a cynicism that can easily turn into the enemy of analysis, if not analysed.

It was my hope, in accepting all of Diana's productions, concrete and verbal, libidinal and aggressive, that we could, together, help her understand and temper her grandiosity and help her to realize and accept her genuine abilities. By both accepting and highlighting the fragmented nature of her experience, and setting the limits she longed for, I hoped to aid her in containing her feelings. This containment seems to have improved her boundaries and allowed her to do much of the integrative work to mend the rampant splits.

This treatment has certainly raised many questions for me as to the interaction of the analyst and analysand's personal styles. What would a treatment with Diana have looked like with an analyst who maintained a tighter frame? How would she have responded to an analyst with tighter boundaries, or one who placed greater emphasis on anonymity? How would she have expressed her conflicts with an analyst who was not Jewish and who was not as intrigued as I know I was by the issues her background offered?

Diana and I held a shared fantasy through many phases of the treatment that, had we met elsewhere, we might have been good friends. When I extricated myself from the intensity of our interaction, it was clear to me that this was part of the seduction that had been at the centre of the treatment from the beginning. After all, our lives and backgrounds are as different as two lives can be. Either we would never have crossed each other's path or, if we had, neither of us would have noticed the other in any serious way.

Because we, as analysts, feel unbelievably fortunate in this day and age to be referred a wealthy patient who will make a wonderful analysand, I think we may underestimate how worried the patient, who is fundamentally still a patient like every other, is of being rejected. Long ago, Diana reminded me of this issue, and of the difference between real world power and the power of psychoanalysis. She said, "I realized yesterday that I not only stayed with you because of your sense of humour but also because you are Jewish. There is something I want for myself that you have and it is something I associate with being Jewish—a warmth and straightforwardness. It occurred to me that, similarly, you may be interested in me because of what I am and you are not. Is that why you picked me as a patient? It is far more reciprocal than I ever thought. I have been so interested in myself that it just never occurred to me before."

References

Dimen, M. (1994). Money, love, and hate: contradiction and paradox in psychoanalysis. *Psychoanalytic Dialogues*, 4: 69–100.

Freud, S. (1913c). On beginning the treatment. *S.E.*, 12: 123–144. London: Hogarth.

Rothstein, A. (1991). The seduction of money. In: S. Klebanow & E. Lowenkopf (Eds.), *Money and Mind*. New York: Plenum.

Warner, S. (1991). Psychoanalytic understanding and treatment of the very rich. In: S. Klebanow & E. Lowenkopf (Eds.), *Money and Mind*. New York: Plenum.

CHAPTER ELEVEN

The analyst and the bribe

Adam Phillips

"What has he done, if no one can name it?"
"He has done everything."
"Oh—everything! Everything's nothing"

(Henry James, *The Wings of the Dove*, Book Second)

I n her book *Lacanian Psychotherapy With Children*, Catherine Mathelin (1999) described a child analyst who had been seen in consultation by a father who said to her, while taking out his cheque book with an expansive gesture, "Ask any price you want. My son doesn't talk. So do whatever you want as long as you make him talk, and then let's not talk about it any more" (p. 11). This apparently absurd vignette is used by Mathelin to illustrate the way in which contemporary analysts can "find parents handing over to them responsibility for their children's upbringing" (*ibid.*). "In former times," she writes ruefully, "patients were caught off guard at the first meeting with an analyst. Today they think they know what they are getting into" (p. 17). Money, I want to suggest, is, from a psychoanalytic point of view, a way of thinking that we know what we are getting into and, of course, a way of knowing what we are getting. We know what money is by what we think we know it can do for us.

So what, then, is absurd about the man with the cheque book? What is so ridiculous, so patently misguided, about his flaunted cheque book? If we are amused, Freud would say, we are also somewhere troubled. There is what he calls "the laughter of unease" if not also "the narcissism of minor differences" in our reaction to the spectacle this man makes of himself, but also of the analyst. After all, what is the analyst supposed to know about children that can be bought; and what must this knowledge, this skill be like, if the more you pay the more you get?

The man seems to have made a category mistake, treating psychoanalysis as though it were a service in which if the analyst gets the amount of money she wants, the client/father will get more of what he wants: his son talking, and no more talking about the problem. His money will instrumentalize his wish. It is sensible to assume that if you pay for psychoanalysis, it must be like other things you pay for, and unlike things you do not pay for. The more you pay a prostitute, a car dealer, a hotel, the more you get; you do not, in the ordinary way of things, pay your friends money to get more friendship from them.

What might amuse and disturb us about this man with his cheque book is that he assumes his money—"Ask any price you want"—permits him to disregard the wishes of the analyst, and, indeed, of his son. Money, he assumes, can make his wishes the wishes of everyone involved. His money is a solvent of difference. It makes whatever is taboo accessible. This father at least behaves as if he knows exactly what he is getting into. And he is being staged, if not actually set up, as an example by the analyst, to reveal something about the nature of psychoanalysis, of just what it involves. If the man with the cheque book has got it wrong, what would it be to get it right? The father said to the analyst, "Ask any price you want. My son doesn't talk. So do whatever you want as long as you make him talk, and then let's not talk about it any more." It is implied he should have said something like, "I can pay your fee. My son doesn't talk. And I want you to use the skills you have (by virtue of your qualification) to enable him, if possible, to talk, and so that we can understand our part in his symptom." We are being told, in other words, that psychoanalysis is different—has even, perhaps, been able to exempt itself—from most other services in the culture, and its difference, at least in this example, resides in its attitudes to, in its assumptions about, money.

I imagine the analyst balked at three of this father's assumptions: first, that the analyst wanted as much money as possible from the father; second, that the more money she got, the more successful she would be in the father's terms; and third, that the amount of money asked for would permit her to, as the father said, "Do whatever you want as long as you make him talk." In other words it was, above all, the father's money that the analyst wanted (i.e., the father already knew, without asking, what the analyst wanted); the amount of money invested would dictate the success of the venture (which the father also already knew: success would be the son talking, and no more talking about the son not having talked); and it would be money alone that would free the analyst to do what she wanted (which was, in fact, to do what the father wanted).

The analyst seems to be saying that there are some things money cannot buy; there are some things money cannot do. These, one might say, are at once banal and novel suggestions. It is as though psychoanalysis knows something (perhaps new) about money that can show us where money does not work. You can, to put it crudely, buy a psychoanalysis, but you cannot, in the same sense, buy something that the analyst or the patient consider to be a successful psychoanalytic treatment (just like you cannot bribe someone to have a dream or to be cured).

Money, in this culture, seems to guarantee our expectations. (If I pay this much for a car, it entitles me to expect, to look forward to, certain things.) Money can seem to turn us into knowing predictors of at least bits of our future. When we pay money for something, we are making a (secular) prophecy.

If the analyst is the one who is supposed to know, so, too, is the consumer. He may not know exactly what he is getting for his money, but he has some idea. The person who goes to an analyst comes to get something for their suffering. From their past, and from their culture, they have ideas about what transforms suffering. They have what Peter Reder and Glenda Fredman (1996) call a (long) relationship to help. They did not, of course, begin as children by paying for what they needed. They might, however, find themselves, as adults, paying for something akin to this earlier concern, and interest.

When Freud said the reason no adult is really satisfied by money is because it is not something that satisfies young children, is not something that children want, he was alerting us to the idea of money as a substitute-satisfaction; money as a derivative as opposed to an original (or ordinary) satisfaction (as, say, being stroked, fed, caressed, and cuddled are). In so-called growing up, there is the elaboration, the sophistication of forms of exchange: food, excrement, smiles, sounds, caresses, words, and eventually money. The currencies multiply—both the objects exchanged and the ways of exchanging them—and then, we might feel, they narrow. Freud was also making us wonder, from a psychoanalytic point of view, just what it might be that is added to the nature (and experience) of exchange by money. In what sense are the original pleasures of childhood better (and in what sense are there original pleasures)? If we do not pay our parents for their love, even though we may find ourselves paying them back for their love, what do we then make of the things we do have to actually pay for, with money?

When the father with the magic cheque book and the dumb son meet the psychoanalyst, at least two languages collide. For the father, money as the measure of all things makes all things possible. For the analyst in this allegory, how money is assumed by this man to work is taken to be a misleading description of things. It might, indeed, be, as they say, symptomatic: the father believes that it is money that talks, and that talking money is the best way of talking about talking; and his son does not speak. In the example as given, it is as though we are waiting to hear what the analyst might say, might reply to all this omnipotent magical money-talk.

What the father seems to want, above all, is that his money will work. It is as though he knows what he wants—that is, has no wants of which he is unconscious, in relation to his son, and the analyst—and that money makes such wanting efficient. After all, if money cannot literally, as it were, get his son to speak, what can?

What makes this scenario so resonant—that gives such a new twist to old clichés (every man has his price, money can't buy you love, and so on)—is that it is a psychoanalyst who is being addressed, and a child who is being bargained over; a son who cannot or will not speak to his father.

Is not everyone struck dumb now by belief in money? To put it another way, can anyone think of anything else to talk about? Are there now any alternatives? Is there anything more persuasive than the money-cult? Like any fetishistic object used in the way this father uses his cheque book, it makes it very difficult for everyone, including him, to work out just what we are valuing when we value money? If money talks, persuades, moves, in the way his father seems to believe, then what, the son might wonder, is the relationship between money and words, between money and desire?

The father's very insistence on money as the key, as the prime mover in his son's treatment, both conceals his doubts about money and narrows the repertoire of what else could be of use or significance. If money will not work, this frantic representative man seems to be saying, what will? (The father says to the son, my money will make you talk; but what if it doesn't?) What the analyst's presence in this drama of exchange and its refusal makes us wonder is whether we can recognize any more the areas of our lives in which money will not do the trick; in which the belief that money is the answer is a misrecognition of the question.

The psychoanalyst is being offered up here as someone who speaks a rather different language, or another language within the current language. After all, the psychoanalyst must be in an extraordinary, extraterritorial, if not culturally privileged position, if she has something that a cheque book cannot reach. It would be to misunderstand the nature of psychoanalysis to believe that if you paid your analyst more then his fee, you would get a better session. To understand why that should be so would be to say something about the nature of analysis, and the significance of money. What the analyst has to offer is paid for, but more money does not buy you more of it. More money can buy you more of the analyst's time, but not more of this other thing that is being sold. The analyst, in other words, is selling something only some of which can be bought.

Perhaps one of the reasons—one of the poorer reasons—that psychoanalysis is under attack is that it is a service, a commodity, that exposes, or puts into question, our fantasies about monetary value. The analyst is a charlatan because he cannot tell you what it would be to get your money's worth from an analysis. That is because the phrase "getting your money's worth" implies an omniscience that can be part of the problem; it is, as it were, a misplaced know-ingness. To talk of having got one's money's worth can be to betray an uncertainty about how to value one's experience (what something is worth to me may be incommensurate with what it cost me in money). The father will get his money's worth if the son speaks; but it would not make sense to ask what would it be for the boy, or indeed the analyst, to get their money's worth in this situation.

The analyst, it is assumed, makes a minimal, market-based self-evaluation and establishes with some flexibility—a minimum and a maximum charge—her fee. If the patient negotiates with the analyst about the fee, it is not assumed that the quality of the treatment is being negotiated by the same token. If the analyst works in good faith, the quality of her attention and intervention will not vary according to fee. (When so-called better analysts—those who are apparently more senior, more experienced, more talented, more famous—charge more money than the rest, they compromise the principle I am describing.) The way psychoanalysis is managed—both arranged, and practiced—sets it against, or at odds with, the father waving his cheque book.

If the analyst here cannot be bribed, not because she is so morally scrupulous, but simply because more money is in some way irrelevant to the enterprise, is actually a misunderstanding of what goes on in psychoanalysis, of what it is, what, then, is money, from a psychoanalytic point of view, such that it cannot be so much resisted but rendered impotent? When it comes to psychoanalysis, the wish to pay more (or less) for what you are getting would, itself, be psychoanalysed, deemed symptomatic of something. Money is a different currency in the context, within the setting, of a psycho-analytic treatment.

A psychoanalyst is someone you pay to not tell you what you will get. Not because she will not tell you, but because she cannot tell you. She does not know quite what will happen when she and the so-called patient start talking and listening to each other. The patient is paying for something, but he can never know what the product will be. He pays for a means, but not an end. The analyst will reliably provide him with time, space, attention, and skills, but the net result is not definable beforehand, and may never be.

"In former times," Mathelin wrote, "patients were caught off guard at the first meeting with an analyst. Today they think they know what they are getting into." They think they know, in her view, because there is so much psychobabble—so much spurious psychological knowingness—circulating in the culture.

Psychoanalysis has entered, or begun to acknowledge that it is competing in a marketplace of therapies in which people are wanting, in the homogenizing language of that marketplace, to get their money's worth. When the analyst is asked the standard question, what will my money be buying me, he cannot, by the lights of his own profession, either answer this question at all, or answer it simply or easily. Indeed, the psychoanalyst is one of the few people left in the culture who might interpret rather than straightforwardly answer that question. Once this traditional question is not straightforwardly answered, the patient cannot know—or cannot know very much about—what he is getting into. The use value of an analysis is indeterminate, and bears a peculiarly mystifying relationship to its exchange value, to use the old language.

It is not, I want to make it clear, that psychoanalysts, by virtue of their profession, are somehow more morally upright, than any other profession. It is just that it is at least possible to bribe, say, a judge, or a doctor, or a politician with money, money over and above what they would ordinarily be paid. If you bribe a policeman he might be able to do something for you, to arrange something you want. What can you bribe a psychoanalyst to do? What would more money be exchanged for? If a patient (or a patient's relative) were to attempt to bribe (or just offer more money to the analyst), the analyst would not treat it, in the ordinary way, as a bribe. She would respond quite differently to the judge, or the policeman, or the doctor. The offer of money would not be received, either positively or negatively. It would not be treated as though it were a breach of decorum, or an affront to civilization as we know it. In exchange for the offer, the patient would be given an interpretation that would also be a refusal of the money. The patient would find his money, and his words about his money, taken in an unexpected direction. He thought he would be able to buy more of something, or a better version of something, but what he has been given back has cost him the original price. When it comes to the ordinary bribery of everyday life, the patient will be caught off guard; he will be getting into something that his offer of money probably has not prepared him for. He will find himself paying money in order, among other things, to have the meaning of his money shown to him (cash for questions). This is not usually what his money does for him; this is not how it is supposed to work.

It is, of course, hardly news that when you go to an analyst your words will not be treated at so-called face value. That is what psychoanalysts do; they interpret. Yet, there is something peculiarly paradoxical about paying for the meaning, for oneself, of paying for things, about a professional practice that puts into question what, from one's own point of view, one's money entitles one to.

As we imagine the analyst and the son (as nominated patient) listening to the father's words, "Ask any price you want. My son doesn't talk. So do whatever you want as long as you make him talk, and then let's not talk about it any more", perhaps it should be stated baldly: can the unconscious be bribed with money? To put the question at a different angle, what do we want when we want money? That means not only, of course, when we want more money, but also when we want less. Is there a part of ourselves for which money is not, indeed never can be, the currency? Is this part of ourselves, however described, progressively silenced in a culture that speaks in money and is therefore progressively driven to distraction?

In Rome, in 1869, the young Henry James wrote to his friend, Grace Norton:

> I have seen today one really great picture—one of those works which draw heavily on your respect, & make you feel the richer for the loss: the portrait of Innocent X, by Velasquez at the Doria Palace. [1999, p. 30].

James has been describing the wealth of the Vatican: "To the Vatican I have paid of course many visits . . . Its richness & interest are even greater than I supposed". Rome—or rather the wealth, in both senses, of its art and its visible, suggested histories—has made him money-minded. It is as though writing in Rome, about Rome, has invested his sentences with what Melville calls, in *Bartleby*, a "paramount consideration." It makes him write in the language of profit and loss. "It is," as he says in the letter, "poor work writing from Rome."

It is not strange that writing about money would be, for James, a way of writing about aesthetic experience. There is what he describes as an exchange going on between himself and the sights the city has to offer, and he cannot help but wonder, as a young American in Europe, just what is to be gained from all this accumulating history, all the artistic riches that are everywhere to be found.

"It doesn't do to stand too much alone," he writes to Grace Norton, "among all these swarming ghosts of the past, and there can be no better antidote to their funereal contagion than a charming modern living feminine letter." The past is also like an illness, even a plague is suggested by the swarming ghosts and the funereal contagion, though quite what James is fearful of catching, apart from his death, is not clear; but it is something to which a "charming modern living feminine letter" is an antidote; not a charming modern living woman, it should be noted, but her letter, her writing. The feminine letter, he jokes, will protect him from something fatal; he feels, however whimsically, endangered in Rome, at some kind of loss.

There is, among so many riches, the one really great picture, the Velasquez Pope. With this painting, paradoxically, James' loss of something is his gain. His lessness in front of this painting does not diminish him, but the way he puts the experience is characteristically contrived. There is, as it were, a sting (and a surprise) in the tail. "It is," he writes, "one of those works which draws heavily on your respect, & makes you feel richer for the loss."

On the one hand, James is simply saying that this painting makes you respect it a great deal. On the other hand, he is saying that this painting draws so much respect out of you—like money out of a bank account—that you have very little left (for anything else). It actually depletes you of the thing you want to give it, AND you feel all the richer. Not, presumably, for now having less respect. James is saying here that he is, in a certain sense, all the richer for having spent so much respect on this painting. How, we may reasonably wonder, does this work if we do not take it in the more obvious sense intended?

Perhaps respect gets in the way of the exchange, of the appreciation, of these works of art; so, by drawing heavily on James' respect—like drawing out a sting—James is freer to do something else with the Velasquez that makes him feel richer. It might all be reminiscent, for example, of what Freud (1912c) writes about in "On the universal tendency to debasement in the sphere of love", the way in which, for some men having a high regard, too much respect for the woman is counter-erotic; indeed renders them impotent. "As soon as the condition of debasement is fulfilled," Freud writes, "sensuality can be freely expressed, and important sexual capacities and a high degree of pleasure can develop" (p. 183). There is no plausible evidence that this is what James is somehow describing, and a lot of inferential evidence that he would have found such a parallel unlikely, but James is saying that he is all the richer when his funds of respect are so drawn on (and therefore depleted). He spends a lot of respect on the Velasquez, and gets a greater sense of its greatness.

Foreshadowing Frost's remark that strongly given is kept, the more respect James is able to give, the more appreciation he gets back. He feels the richer for the loss, as he says, because he is losing something in order to gain something else. The noble word for such a transaction is sacrifice; the other word for it is a bribe. You give up something, you hand over something you value, for a greater good. It is what we have come to think of as the obvious good deal. It is part of the deal, as it were, that it reveals to us what it is supposedly that we most want. If we can bear to have less of one thing, we might have more of something else. So, investment is a wonderful notion because, if you are lucky and shrewd, you can have more of the thing you have less of by making the investment. James, of course, does not say anything as vulgar as that he has invested in, or even spent his respect on, the painting; he just says he has drawn heavily on his respect. Where the funds come from, and what they are now doing, is omitted from the description.

I have taken this detour via James in Italy in 1869 just to say something rather obvious; which is that money enters the verbal equation, enters the exchange—as analogy in James, or, starkly, in the patient's father's attempt to bribe the analyst—as a way of describing a wish to get more, licitly or illicitly. Like Viagra, money is the means to what is deemed to be the pleasure we seek. Clearly, in this culture, more life is associated with more money. It is, however, of necessity—or in so far as it is a means and not an end— what Freud calls a fore-pleasure. The pleasure is the route to the object of desire. "You cannot give money," John Forrester writes in *Truth Games* (1997), "in the gratuitous sense of giving, because money is pure exchange" (p. 152). Even if you hoard it, even if it is never used, in fantasy it is buying you a future good. Money, that is to say, is something we cannot help but do something with. It is the material of (and for) our most compulsive dream-work. It is our ultimate, inert transformational object: it can make us feel better. Money has become one of the best ways of describing the more that we apparently want, and the lack we most apparently feel. It is instrumental in the acquiring of objects.

James gets more aesthetic pleasure by drawing on his funds of respect, as though respect, like money, can be successfully invested. He will also, paradoxically, be richer for the loss of respect entailed. James' figure of speech is characteristically resonant; it makes one wonder about the ways in which he is wondering what is going on when he looks at this painting. He is finding ways of describing a peculiar kind of exchange that has happened. He is describing not so much an intention as an effect. If anything, it is as though the painting has an intention, "one of those works which draw heavily on your respect"; as though something about the picture has made him invest attention in it, just as something in any object of desire calls something up in us; indeed, that is how one recognizes an object of desire. It draws one out (even if one's response to being so drawn out is to draw in). James, involuntarily, is drawn on by the Velasquez.

The patient's father is involved in a quite different kind of exchange. He invites the analyst to draw on his fund of money. He believes that by investing more money in the situation he can get a more favourable (favourable to him) result, and this is what he intends to do. He has to make the analyst the accomplice of his intention. By definition, she cannot be his accomplice.

This chapter is about whether the fact that you cannot bribe an analyst tells us anything new about money, and anything new about psychoanalysis. To put it another way (more modestly), it is notes towards the definition of the word "more". Clearly, the word money has a complicated and necessary relationship with the word more. Money can only give us more of certain things, while wanting to persuade us that it can give us more of everything. The analyst with whom I started—the analyst who, of necessity refuses her patient's father's bribe—is setting a limit. The more of something the father wants to buy is not available, is not commensurate with more money. The treatment may not be available for less money, but it is not more available, more effective, for more money. So what does the analyst have to sell that more money will not buy?

Given the culture that the analyst and her client—as they are sometimes called—live in, the father's bribe and his exasperation at its refusal are entirely understandable. Is this some kind of joke? It is in talking about jokes that Freud (1905c) talks about bribery. The joke, he says, "the major purposes and instincts of mental life employ ... for their own ends" (p. 133), is itself a kind of bribe. Indeed, we are bribable, Freud believes, because we are ineluctably in search of pleasure, however self-compromising and compromised our quests for pleasure are. The joke bribes us with pleasure in order to allow us to experience a further pleasure that is impermissible. So, for example, jokes free us, in Freud's view, to enjoy what he, or Strachey, calls, in an odd phrase, "our hostile aggressiveness". "A joke will allow us to exploit something ridiculous in our enemy which we could not, on account of obstacles in the way, bring forward openly or consciously," Freud writes.

> Once again then the joke will evade restrictions and open sources of pleasure that have become inaccessible. It will further bribe the hearer with its yield of pleasure into taking sides with us without any very close investigation, just as on other occasions we ourselves have often been bribed by an innocent joke into overestimating the substance of a statement expressed jokingly. [*ibid.*, p. 103]

Jokes are the black-market of pleasure. They seduce us through pleasure into taking pleasures that would otherwise be forbidden us. The paradox that Freud adds to our moral life is that the sanctioned good is never sufficiently desirable because it is not forbidden. We have to be very clever animals in desiring what we must not have, or in pursuing what we must not be seen—by ourselves or others—to be pursuing. We dress to hide our motives from ourselves. The joke bribes us, in part by saying it is only a joke, when, in fact, we are indulging our most transgressive desires. Without what he calls "any very close investigation", we get something we are not supposed to want. The joke disarms criticism; the implication is that what we might once have called our critical faculties, or even our minds, are, by definition, the enemies of the forbidden pleasures we seek, the furtive sovereign good that is our secret heart's desire.

The important point here—and six of the eleven references to bribery in Freud are in the joke book—is that Freud begins to realize in this book that, in so far as desire is forbidden, we have to be, as it were, bribed into taking pleasure, and the only bribery that works is pleasure itself. Although he never returns to it as a topic in its own right, this "wrapping" that the joke does, and that Freud says, "bribes our powers of criticism" (*ibid.*, p. 132), is essential to Freud's picture of the way the mind works. We have to bribe ourselves; we have to be bribed into pleasure, by pleasure. Jokes, like dreams, wrap our pleasures up—wrap our desires up, as though they were presents—so we can acknowledge them without having knowledge of them. Desire is only bearable in disguise; for disguise to be effective it has to take on the nature of a bribe. We steal our pleasure rather than take it. We dress it up, and dress up for it.

A bribe, the *Oxford English Dictionary* says, is: "1. to take dishonestly; to extort. 2. to influence corruptly, by a consideration, the action of . . . 4. to gain over by some influence . . . a thing stolen, robbery, plunder." A bribe, in short, is a way of getting what one wants despite moral principle, not because of it. What Freud refers to as "powers of criticism", or "close investigation", or, in other contexts, as the censor, the super-ego, the conscience, all these seats of virtue and discrimination have to be lured, persuaded, seduced, or cajoled into blindness, surrender, or merely consent.

The joke is exemplary because it appears to be that impossible thing—an innocent bribe. If it works, however, it gets you to abrogate your principles, to see, without seeing, that your preferences do not always accord with your standards. The racist or sexist joke amuses you despite yourself. You have been tricked into a pleasure that you would rather not be having. It is only through bribery, Freud is saying, that unconscious desire, forbidden pleasures, are at all possible for us. Pleasure requires permission, for Freud, from the requisite internal agencies, and because the pleasures are forbidden the permission is immoral. In Freud's view, we cannot agree to such pleasures; we have to be bribed.

The writer, Freud (1908c) writes, in "Creative writers and daydreaming", softens the character of his egoistic daydreams by altering and disguising it, and he bribes us by the purely formal—that is, aesthetic—yield of pleasure which he offers us in the presentation of his fantasies. We give the name of an incentive bonus, or a fore-pleasure to a yield of pleasure such as this, which is offered to us so as to make possible the release of still greater pleasure arising from deeper psychical sources. In my opinion all the aesthetic plea-sure which a creative writer affords us has the character of a fore-pleasure of this kind, and our actual enjoyment of an imaginative work proceeds from a liberation of tensions in our minds . . . It may even be that not a little of this effect is due to the writer's enabling us thence forward to enjoy our own daydreams without self-reproach or shame. [*ibid*., p. 153]

What Freud calls the formal, aesthetic pleasures of a piece of writ-ing are a bribe—what he calls tellingly an incentive bonus—synonymous with fore-pleasure. We are deceived into a relatively shameless enjoyment of the "still greater pleasure arising from deeper psychical sources". Without the bribe, that in the analogy with the incentive bonus is explicitly linked to money, this greater pleasure would be neither available nor possible. Unconscious desire requires a bribe in order to be gratified. The bribe is the wrapping the joke does, the bizarre representational form the dream takes, or the aesthetic form the writer uses to make known what Freud calls his egotistical daydreams. All these things, Freud suggests, as bribes are like incentive bonuses: money given to improve performance, money as a lure.

In what sense does money work like a joke, or indeed like the aesthetic formalism of the writer? The answer might be: by giving you one seemingly innocent good, it gratifies something in oneself less innocent, but more desired. It is, at least in following the logic of the link Freud makes, a cover story. It offers you one thing, a bank note, a joke, a piece of writing, but it promises you another.

A bribe is also different from an incentive bonus because a bribe, in the words of the *OED*, corrupts you; it compromises you morally. It is more about getting away with something, then getting some-thing. It speaks of the illicit, the underhand, and the unofficial. It privileges, explicitly and implicitly, desire over scruple. Whatever it conceals, it makes it clear that what someone wants is more impor-tant to them than the reason they cannot or should not have it.

Bribery, one might say as a crude Freudian, is the financial form incestuous desire takes. You only bribe somebody for something when you know that for some reason, which you may not know—that there is a reason why you should not have it or, which perhaps comes to the same thing, when you want more of something you have already got. Enough is morally acceptable; more is too much. It is the difference between being dressed and undressed.

When the boy's analyst is offered more money by the father, he is asking for more of something that cannot be given. An analyst is a person who cannot be given an incentive bonus. Or, to put it the other way round, were the analyst to accept an incentive bonus, she would implicitly be giving the so-called patient a misleading description of what she did.

Unconscious desire, Freud suggested, requires something akin to an incentive bonus for its gratification to be possible. Why does money not do the trick with the analyst, or indeed with the patient? Why did the father not offer his son money to talk, and then to shut up about it all? Money as a lure, as an object of desire, supposedly improves all kinds of performance, and yet, of course, there are areas of our lives, social practices, in which money does not work either as an incentive or a bribe. Money can get you the clothes, but not the passionate erotic experience.

Writing to his friend and collaborator, Fleiss, in 1898, Freud made a startling, albeit Freudian, point that I referred to earlier. "Happiness'" he wrote, "is the belated fulfilment of a prehistoric wish. For this reason wealth brings so little happiness. Money was not a childhood wish" (Freud, 1887–1902). Freud seems to be saying something simple here, whether or not we believe it to be true. We are only really happy when we satisfy a childhood wish. No child has ever wanted money; therefore, money does not really satisfy adults when they acquire it. By now, of course, there are plenty of children who want money, so it might be better to go back a bit and say no baby has ever wanted money, which might even be marginally more interesting.

Despite the, to me, obvious interest of Freud's point here, it is also as though, at this moment, Freud has either forgotten himself, or rather his ideas, or it is too early in his project for him to quite see what he might be saying. What always was and will be, for Freud, THE childhood wish is the incestuous one (or ones). Because

these are forbidden, the child can only develop by finding disguised alternatives, substitutes, or sublimations of these desires.
Any object of desire, by virtue of being one for Freud, has an echo
of the forbidden, links us with our losses and our most fervent
anticipations. In the Freudian schema, it would be easy to see
money as the ideal, that is to say, perfectly disguised or displaced
incestuous object. Everybody wants as much of it as they can get.
Everyone feels profoundly ambivalent about this desire. It is called
greed, which is perhaps a more manageable word than violation, or
transgression. Everyone organizes themselves around money: its
acquisition, its distribution, its repudiation. It is that which can
never be ignored, either positively or negatively, and so on. And
it is, therefore, ripe for metaphorical elaboration; without the
money economy James lived in, he would not have been able—like
Freud—to write in those terms about his aesthetic experience. So,
talking about money in this quasi-Freudian romance, talking in
terms of money, of profit and loss, of wealth and poverty, is the best
way modern people have of talking about incest.

It may be worth noting—though it is solely my impression—
that it is often far easier for people to talk about their sexuality now
than about their money. When people come for psychoanalysis
nowadays their resistance to talking about money, their inability to
speak freely, is patent. It is as though when people are talking (and
not talking) about money, they are always talking about, or gestur-
ing towards something else. Money buys you the clothes that get
you the life dreamed up through the clothes. Talking about money
is talking about the dressing-up box.

There is something also poignant about the father trying to bribe
his son's analyst. If we do not bother to attribute a poor motive to
the father, we can see that at that moment he believes there is something—something in the culture—that can get him what he wants.
Money can get him what he wants, and what he might want is his
son's well being. If money cannot get us what we want—and it can
only get us what we want by telling us that what we want money
can buy—how can we get what we want, or even discover what
that might be?

Whether or not what we want is for our childhood wishes to be
fulfilled, whatever those might be, whatever we construe those as
being, what is unavoidably true is that infancy and childhood are

where wanting starts. By linking the child with money as a way of linking the child with the adult he will become, and with the adults that look after him, and by linking money with wishing, Freud gives us something to go on from. Money as a material object the child might not want (the child would surely prefer affection), but money as the hard currency of wishing—money as the wish given, as it were, material form—would surely be something irresistible, once it was intelligible. Money becomes the adult medium for wishing; money is good to wish with (though whether and how it is better than bodies to wish with would be the question). Part of the pleasure of its acquisition is its promise of further pleasure to come (as though one could buy the body one desires). Like the wish it is promising, by formulating a future it makes a future. One of the aims of psychoanalysis might be to make wishing itself pleasurable again, rather than merely persecutory, or suggestive of disappointment.

A person bribing an analyst is someone willing what cannot be willed, arranging something that cannot be arranged. The analyst clearly wants to earn her living, and may even really like money, but more money cannot buy a better promise of cure. Nor, more absurdly, would the patient be more likely to get better if the analyst paid them. The patient and analyst are assumed to want something other than, or as well as, money. The money buys the conditions for a possible cure, but not the cure itself (just as a luxurious hotel bedroom may provide the conditions for a wonderful erotic experience, but it could not guarantee it). The initial money exchanged is like a legitimate bribe; it gives the pleasure that might make possible a further pleasure, the pleasure of alleviated suffering, of becoming more the subject (less the victimized victim) of one's own desire.

The bribe of the agreed upon fee might work, but more bribe will not make a difference. What is curbed by the analytic contract is the power of the bribe. It is as though the analyst says to the patient, your bribe here goes so far and no further; I will give you my time, attention, skill, and the personal history I have, but more money, more bribery will not get you more of these things, because these things are not like that. Money does not seem to work on them, or indeed, in and of itself, to make them work. (You can, as it were, buy the analyst's bodily presence, but not her responsive receptivity.)

Unsurprisingly, perhaps, given his time and place, Freud tended to describe attention, attraction, the influence people have over each other, as forms of investment. The pleasure-seeking self, the libidinal body, gets and spends. It manages through distribution the excesses it is heir to, transforming daunting quantities of desire into rather more reassuring pieces of meaning.

In its push for language, its always ambivalent desire for the forbidden object of desire, the person Freud described courts and confounds her own intelligibility. Like James in Rome, like a father with a cheque book, he is fabulously impressed—informed and over-awed—by fantasies of wealth, by what money can be used to do and say, by the language of accumulation and purchase, but also, more paradoxically, in how we use money as a way of talking about what cannot be bought. More of the analyst's skill, more of the father's wishes, cannot be bought with more money. The riches of Rome, the Velasquez, cannot be bought, and it is not exactly acquisition of a material object that James is after, and children do not buy their parents, and cannot buy their parents' love.

Using money as linguistic currency shows us what is unlike money (just as speaking about clothes is a way of endlessly rediscovering what our bodies are not like). We keep coming up against, we are continually caught out by, where the analogy breaks down. More money will not buy us more love (which lets us wonder what love or desire might be like if they cannot be bought). I may describe my attention as invested, but the consequences of my investment are unpredictable in ways in which my financial investments are not. (I may be uncertain what is profit and what is loss.) My so-called dream-work rewards me with a dream, whether or not the dream is rewarding to the person I think of as myself.

Perhaps it is necessary—or at least useful—to have a group of people in a culture who, by virtue of their profession, but not by virtue of their moral rectitude, are not fashion victims. The psycho-analyst, like everyone else in the culture, can be bribed by pleasure; indeed, in Freud's terms, has to be bribed in order to get pleasure. The psychoanalyst cannot, however, be bribed with money. She cannot help practising something that more money cannot buy more of. In a culture bewitched by the language of money she, of course, finds it very difficult to describe what she does. People tend, therefore, to be suspicious about her motives.

Summary

This chapter described the senses in which it is impossible to bribe a psychoanalyst with money (or anything else). It then discussed Freud's account of the joke as a bribe, and the ways in which pleasure is bound up with the whole notion of bribery, because pleasure, in Freud's sense, is always driven by the forbidden, by the taboo. Money was understood in this paper as a wishful solvent for the problem of taboo.

References

Forrester, J. (1997). *Truth Games: Lies, Money and Psychoanalysis.* Cambridge, MA: Harvard University Press.

Freud, S. (1887–1902). *The Origins of Psychoanalysis: Letters to Wilhelm Fliess, Drafts and Notes: 1887–1902.* M. Bonaparte, A. Freud, E. Kris (Eds.). London: Imago, 1954.

Freud, S. (1905c). *Jokes and their Relation to the Unconscious. S.E., 8:* 1–258. London: Hogarth.

Freud, S. (1908c). Creative writers and daydreaming. *S.E., 9:* 141–154. London: Hogarth.

Freud, S. (1912d). On the universal tendency to debasement in the sphere of love. *S.E., 11:* 177–190. London: Hogarth.

James, H. (1999). *A Life In Letters.* P. Horne (Ed.). London: Penguin.

Mathelin, C. (1999). *Lacanian Psychotherapy with Children.* S. Fairfield (Trans.). New York: Other Press.

Reder, P., & Fredman, G. (1996). The relationship to help. *Clinical Child Psychology and Psychiatry, 1:* 457–467.

PART V

CONFIDENTIALITY:
TOO MUCH OR TOO LITTLE?

CHAPTER TWELVE

Confidentiality in the public realm: what and whose is it?[1]

Harriette Kaley

The freedom of psychoanalysts to formulate psychoanalytic questions is fundamental to the entire enterprise. Can that freedom be appropriately exercised on material that is in the public realm? Are there some things we cannot say in our attempts to improve our work? Those are the issues addressed in this chapter.

Public material does not, of course, usually need our insights; obviously, the bulk of what appears in our daily newspapers and other media manages without us. But there is a vast and increasing amount of material available outside our professional world that deals with people's inner lives, indeed, often refers, glancingly or not, to their psychotherapeutic and psychoanalytic treatments. The confessional trend that has grown so markedly in the past century and the increasingly intense gaze turned upon every aspect of the lives of public figures assure us of a seemingly unending stream of information, misinformation, and rumour about all sorts of people, but especially the famous. Intimate matters about celebrities, other well-known people, and figures in public life are regularly revealed publicly. The late Princess Diana is a prime example. Even where she herself was reticent, there is no dearth of others to fill us in; much of what is known or believed known about her romantic relationships comes from others in her circle. Where the people involved do not themselves explicitly tell all, news reports of their activities are informative. For example, when recording or movie stars wind up in court, as celebrities Sean (Puff Daddy) Combs and Winona Ryder recently did, and as innumerable others do in the course of divorces, the public record forms the basis for speculation. The recent revelations concerning sexually abusive priests in the Catholic church is another case in point.

Speculations made by psychoanalysts among themselves about such material rarely come to public attention, but that is not because they are not made. Is there any doubt that psychoanalysts, concerned with people's dynamics and the interplay between individual psyches and the world in which we live, formulate questions and theories about incidents like these? Professional ethics limit us in commenting for the mass media about people we have not seen clinically, but certainly that does not stop us from wondering among ourselves about what was going on. Recently, however, our freedom to do even that has collided with concerns about privacy.

The problem arises when a particular kind of information enters the public realm. It happens sometimes that information about psychoanalytic treatment becomes known, perhaps as a result of the analysand speaking openly about it, sometimes in more circuitous ways. It might, for example, be discussed by family members or other intimates, or reported, usually posthumously, by biographers or historians. Marilyn Monroe's well-known psychoanalytic vicissitudes are a highly visible example.

Some have averred that such knowledge should not be the basis for psychoanalytic commentary; the reason given is that our professional commitment to privacy and confidentiality becomes operative and demands our silence (Bollas & Sundelson, 1995). The implications of that position are serious. When psychoanalytic or psychoanalytically-relevant data—or even the kind of information that is just plain provocative to people thinking psychoanalytically—comes from outside the consulting room, from some sort of public realm, are we then proscribed from using that data to formulate psychoanalytic questions, or to examine the psychoanalytic process? No one has yet suggested that we are not to think whatever we think in the face of such revelations, but are we to refrain from any professionally responsible comment?

The question arose for me in particularly salient form after a presentation I gave in 1995 at a professional meeting. I had had in mind for quite a while a panel on issues in treating the famous patient, and had been talking to colleagues about the widely discussed problems in treating such people. Recently, there had been great controversy over Woody Allen's well-publicized psychoanalytic ventures. The poet Anne Sexton's analyst had made tapes of sessions available to her biographer. And, of course, the memory of Marilyn Monroe's death, possibly by suicide, almost certainly by some sort of acting out, had created open season on comment about her well-publicized work with Ralph Greenson. I, for my part, had for a long time been interested in the failed analysis of a famous movie star of the 1950s and 1960s, instigated by reading a biography of him written by an acquaintance. To my initial surprise and enduring concern, it turned out that a major issue in the actor's life was a fourteen-year analysis with a well-known, well-published, highly regarded, and highly influential analyst.

For this chapter, I will refer to the star as X. In the presentation, X was named, but the purpose of this chapter is different. The reference for the biography is not given here because the title includes X's name, and the star's identity is not relevant to this chapter (although the situation was different in the original presentation). Given the present focus, I am, with editorial agreement, omitting references that might reveal who X is. It should be noted, however, that the references include biographies, magazine articles, and psychoanalytic publications. It is probably not possible to conceal identifying information completely, since the various presentations and publications could be searched out by a determined reader, but there is no reason for this chapter to facilitate that. Here, the issues do not depend on the details of the particular case. They are, instead, about whether psychoanalysis may turn to the widely available data about the star's life and the somewhat less available data about the analyst in the service of the understanding the tumultuous psychoanalytic process. For that, specific names are irrelevant.

Those close to X had always had grave and open reservations about the analysis that presided over a tortuous decline, addled with drugs, alcohol, and closeted homosexual acting out, and ended with X's premature death under questionable circumstances, much like Monroe's. At the 1995 panel about "Issues in the treatment of the famous patient" (Kaley, Kaplan, & Spezzano, 1995), Louise Kaplan spoke critically about Greenson's understanding of the "real relationship" in connection with his treatment of Munroe. I spoke about transference and countertransference issues that I believed had torpedoed X's analysis. Charles Spezzano was the thoughtful discussant.

X's analysis had by that time been amply documented in many published sources. It was generally understood that his analyst, a leader in the profession at the time, had refused to acknowledge the patient's quite visible addictions. Widespread published rumour had it that the reasons for this had to do with an unwholesome bond between them and, especially, the analyst's own hidden homosexuality. (Remember this was the 1950s. As Spezzano noted in his panel discussion, "Hell, we were just out of the McCarthy era.") Determined to separate rumour from fact, I read virtually all of the analyst's professional writings, interviewed many of X's surviving friends and colleagues, and spoke and met with many students, patients, colleagues, and immediate family of his analyst. What emerged, to my surprise and that of many others, made it certain that the analyst had indeed been a closeted homosexual, and, furthermore, that the rumours were true that he had had an alcoholic partner. I had been so sure we would never know about those persistent rumours that I literally had to rewrite the paper at the last minute when the facts became abundantly clear. Documenting those conclusions finally and unambiguously, as well as the obfuscation with which the analyst's partisans had surrounded it, made it inevitable that any consideration of X's analysis must examine the transference–countertransference interactions. That is what my paper sought to do. It was presented as a sad case study illustrating the dangers of unexamined countertransference, noting what the analyst might himself have recognized as warning signs, and the importance of consultation when one's relations to a patient become markedly entangled.

Spezzano's discussion exemplified what I had hoped the paper would provoke. It was a thoughtful consideration of the question of specialness in an analysis. The analyst was reliably reported (in the biography of X referred to earlier) to have said, "If that man gets out of my control, he'll die within three months", and to have rejected the pleas of X's advisers to send him to Menninger's to treat the alcoholism. Spezzano asked what it does in an analysis when the analyst develops a fantasy that the patient is better off with us, no matter how badly he is doing in that relationship, than without us. He suggested that, at the time of X's analysis, something blinded the analyst from telling the patient that things were terribly amiss in the treatment. These days, Spezzano offered, it might be imaginable to say, "I am concerned that we have constructed together a sense that you can only live inside this treatment and that us together watching you destroy yourself is somehow an improved state of affairs over you falling apart on your own." Spezzano had more to say on this theme, all of which I welcomed as precisely the kind of clinically meaningful assessment I had hoped would follow from the clinical material.

In the discussion period that followed, virtually the only comment came from a lawyer, trained also in psychoanalysis and literature. He took me to task not only for having named the patient, but also, to my greater surprise, for having named the analyst. His argument, as I understood it, was that confidentiality for both patient *and* analyst was "timeless". The fact that I was not the analyst did not absolve me, and neither did the fact that I was revealing nothing not already available in published materials about two public figures. Later, he co-authored a book on confidentiality that, on its flap copy and in the book, identifiably and sarcastically referred to my presentation. It could not fail to escape me that another presentation at the same meeting about Marilyn Monroe, which referred to her several experiences with analysis, elicited no such remarks from the audience.

Afterwards, in light of the contentious discussion and the possibility of publishing the paper, I sought comment from the American Psychological Association Directors of Ethics and of Publications. Neither of them saw ethical problems with it (though, not surprisingly, the Director of Publications suggested how I should rework the paper).[2] The experience had been so unsettling that I put the paper away. Recently, though, I began to reconsider.

I had heard from a colleague who was writing about Masud Khan (with whom I had been in supervision at one point) and his ultimately failed analytic work with D. W. Winnicott (Hopkins, 1998, 2000). She reported pressures to not use certain available information about clinical and personal matters. Her work, as far as I can tell, had two major goals: to examine clinical material for the light it might in itself throw on analytic process, and to explore how the clinical work illuminates and is illuminated by the lives as well as the writings and works of both analysts. Not, I think, very different from my own purpose. The difficulties encountered by the Khan–Winnicott project made it seem once again that the issue was very much alive and in need of consideration.

Case material comes in many forms. When it is one's own analytic patients, of course one is bound by confidentiality. But what about when it comes in other forms? Other people's clinical materials, in the formal and informal shape of case reports, presentations, supervision, and the myriad exchanges we have among ourselves as we train and mature professionally, are ubiquitous. We all use them as reference points. What would happen if we failed to do so because the material is not gathered in our own consulting rooms? Of course, we accept the responsibility of confidentiality when we listen to case material in clinical presentations or supervision, but what happens when there are other contexts? What happens when, as analysts, we recognize in publicly available reports information that is psychoanalytically relevant? Is an analyst obligated to be reticent or even silent about such material in the public realm if the identities of the parties are possibly recognizable, perhaps even relevant? When Bill Clinton's relationship with Monica Lewinsky burst into public awareness, every analyst I spoke to had something interesting and often illuminating to say, usually based on his or her understanding of transference and countertransference and the complications of political and erotic power.

What I am examining here is my experience and the questions it raises about the proprieties of examining comparable, though less politically explosive, material within our professional circles. Is there, indeed, as my lawyer–interrogator implied, an unbridgeable gap between the confidentiality requirements of clinical work and our efforts to improve that work through continuous theoretical and technical examination? Is there a permanent interdiction on examining possible delicate issues in the treatment of the famous because it might lead to identification? Or is there, in the end, a worthwhile difference between gossip and the intrinsic information gained by knowing who the people in a case study are? Between what is taboo and what is politically correct? Is there a difference between breaking confidences and reinterpreting what are already matters of public record? Is the reframing of existing narratives a respect-worthy part of the analytic endeavour? Should we remain silent in the name of professional respectability and leave the field to uninformed media speculation? Is confidentiality timeless? Whose confidentiality? And who is the keeper of the confidence, especially once it has already been spilled? Is every analyst responsible for the confidentiality of all analytic work? The argument that we are all our brothers' keepers is enticing, but does it override our communal commitment to oversee and improve our work by reporting and reviewing case studies? And what does confidentiality mean for analytic material, or psychoanalytically relevant material, that has been already made public knowledge by non-psychoanalytic parties? Even if the people involved are public figures?[3] Even if none is alive?

I have argued elsewhere (Kaley, 1997) that censoring informed comment about such material would eliminate not only much of Freud scholarship but also psychobiography and psychohistory. The understandings that we owe to Freud scholarship would be impermissible, because much of it is based on identifying his patients. The analyst co-author of the book on confidentiality has produced work about serial killers that draws on published accounts as well as on his own clinical experiences (Bollas, 1995). It appears that it is possible for significant psychoanalytic insights to emerge from non-confidential sources.

Ultimately, can there be taboos in work like ours? Especially under circumstances such as I have described, can there be taboos in our professional discussions? Obviously, it is important that as psychoanalysts we operate with professional propriety and discretion. In the end, however, we need to recall that psychoanalysis came into being by breaking taboos, and has advanced through continuing to break them. In this kind of situation, I am inclined to believe that there is a difference between protecting confidentiality and indirectly helping to cover up failures—whether our own or others—out of a misguided conviction that we must not talk even among ourselves about how we and our colleagues are with our patients. Clinical work profits from close examination by others.

The evolution of clinical technique and the theoretical structures that support our clinical practices demand such close examination of actual cases, our own and those of others.

Like all thoughtful people, analysts are opposed to gossip and breaches in confidentiality and, of course, we favour candour and responsible discussion of the foibles and failures of even the most recognizable among us. This essay, however, is about more than issues like apple pie and motherhood. It is about what it would do to the profession if the historical record were constricted; if, under the banner of protecting confidentiality, we were prevented from having full and accurate knowledge as the basis for refining our work.

It is outside the scope of this chapter to discuss what is gained in terms of specifically psychoanalytic understanding from the story of X. It may, however, be noted that the story has much to offer to the literature about boundary violations (adding yet another "good" analyst to those who have tripped at such borders), and about the way in which new information creates new narratives about patients' lives, the full truth being forever inaccessible.

An underlying problem seems to be whether a psychoanalytic form of political correctness is afoot. The premise of the meeting which the present volume documents is that politically correct positions—which include, after all, a group's acknowledged taboos—warrant examination rather than unquestioned acceptance. As the meeting progressed, it became evident that, for the growth of the profession, many taboos are better honoured in the breach than the observance. The history of psychoanalysis demonstrates that many things considered incorrect, to the point of being taboo, become less so—become, even, the approved cutting edge of our work—as we live with them and explore their operation. An illustration is the shift in the place of countertransference. Once taboo by virtue of being understood as an obstacle to treatment, it is now widely, if not universally, believed to be one of the analyst's subtlest psychoanalytic tools. The contemporary focus on the interaction within the psychoanalytic setting that has so significantly enlarged our sense of the usable data is an outgrowth of the movement of countertransference from taboo to centrality. Other taboos successfully broken include such innovations as group treatment, treatment of psychotics, use of the chair rather than the couch, vacation periods interrupting treatment, and the like. Different analysts undoubtedly have different lists, since taboos tend to be connected to schools of psychoanalytic thought.

One of the problems is that desanctifying sacred cows—and that is what breaking taboos is—is inevitably initially disturbing. For example, in 2002, in a special issue entitled "Ernest Jones revisited: a symposium", *Studies in Gender and Sexuality* (3[4]) published Philip Kuhn's inquiry into Jones' 1906 trial for indecent assault, together with critical commentaries. As the man who virtually shaped the canonical view of Freud and of the early history of psychoanalysis, Jones is a person whose probity has rarely been called into question. Kuhn provides considerable enrichment of the previously sparse historical and biographical record based on assiduous research into contemporaneous newspaper and institutional reports. Jones' own glossing over the incident and similar ones in his memoirs is also examined in light of other material. Although commentators in the issue differ in their degree of support for Kuhn's findings, or for his style of reporting them, it is clear that his work fills in details that enlarge the background against which we understand our early professional history, however humbling it then is to contemplate. It is chilling to think that such inquiries might halt.

History reminds us that what is politically correct changes with time. We see that in, for example, the current re-evaluation in the USA of affirmative action initiatives. For that matter, the entire swing here back towards political conservatism after liberalism held sway for many years illustrates the changeability of belief systems. If our fundamental convictions and values are to avoid the fickleness that can result, we need to understand that it is not the content of the belief that is important; it is the freedom to examine it.

In recent years, we have come to take somewhat for granted something that not long ago was a matter for argument: these days there seems something more compelling about the position that confidentiality and privacy need protection from the depredations of detached, scientific-minded colleagues than with the opposite. We need to remember that there was a time, not so long ago, when psychoanalysis was younger, when the more compelling position was the right to be scientific-minded about our work, to be seen as earnest investigators not merely exercising our prurient interests.

The point here is that what is politically correct or what is an appealing slogan changes with the political, scientific, cultural, and social climates. We need to protect our processes of investigation from such shifts in the wind that are likely to shift again with time. If we do not, the cost will be that, when the winds shift once more, what we will have lost in the interim will be impossible to reclaim.

In the end, it seems more censorship than psychoanalytic rectitude to deny us the right, even the responsibility, to comment among ourselves about psychoanalytically relevant material. Doing so is part of our ongoing effort to understand the process and the theory supporting it. Psychoanalytic reticence among colleagues on matters of public record may be as egregious a shortcoming as any.

Notes

1. A version of this chapter was originally presented at the conference, "Taboo or Not Taboo", Niagara-on-the-Lake, Canada, 2001.
2. In his e-mail of Wednesday June 27, 2001 (Re: Ethics question), Dr S. Behnke also made a noteworthy distinction between personal and confidential information. Personal information may be learnt in a variety of ways and from a variety of sources. While it might call for discretion, it differs from confidential information, which is gathered under a promise of confidentiality. Material that is in the public domain may be personal but it is not confidential.
3. At a meeting of the Toronto Society for Contemporary Psychoanalysis in 2001, a member raised a concern about whether a famous patient could ever be unguarded in psychoanalysis if there were a fear of being exposed in the future, a legitimate concern, given the intrusions into the lives of celebrities by the media. But, for our purposes, what matters is that the analyst, as the analyst of the famous patient—indeed, as the analyst of any patient—is committed to confidentiality. The patient might have the problems of the famous in terms of protecting his or her privacy, but that is another issue, and perhaps one to be explored in the analysis.

References

Bollas, C. (1995). The structure of evil. In: C. Bollas (Ed.), *Cracking Up* (pp. 180–220). New York: Hill and Wang.

Bollas, C., & Sundelson, D. (1995). *The New Informants: The Betrayal of Confidentiality in Psychoanalysis and Psychotherapy*. Northvale, NJ: Aronson.

Hopkins, L. (1998). D. W. Winnicott's analysis of Masud Khan: a preliminary study of failures of object usage. *Contemporary Psychoanalysis, 34*: 5–47.

Hopkins, L. (2000). Masud Khan's application of Winnicott's "play" techniques to analytic consultation and treatment of adults. *Contemporary Psychoanalysis, 36*: 639–663.

Kaley, H. (1997). Book review. *Contemporary Psychoanalysis, 33*: 161–165.

Kaley, H., Kaplan, L., & Spezzano, C. (1995). Issues in the treatment of the famous patient. Panel presentation at the 1995 Spring Meeting of the Division of Psychoanalysis, American Psychological Association, Santa Monica.

PART VI
FACING REAL WORLD ISSUES

CHAPTER THIRTEEN

Can psychoanalysis exist outside the consulting room?

Mark B. Borg, Jr, Emily Garrod, Michael Dalla, Jr, and Jennifer McCarroll

The purpose of this paper is to challenge the pervading conventional wisdom of two divergent approaches to psychological intervention by highlighting the intersecting aspects of interpersonal psychoanalysis and community psychology. In doing so, we challenge many of the common taboos of contemporary psychoanalytic theory regarding the activity of the practitioner. Such activities include that, in community practice, the practitioner is often the initiator of treatment (intervention), the practitioner participates in the daily life of the patient (community resident), and the practitioner has an explicitly didactic, educational role in addition to maintaining a traditional psychoanalytic role as facilitator of exploration.

With these kinds of changes in the activity of the practitioner as compared to the activity of the analyst doing individual work, why should community work of this sort still be considered psychoanalytic? We propose a model that answers this question by retaining a strong notion of the unconscious and the use of transference–countertransference enactments in the community to inform practitioners. Our focus is an intensive, four-year community intervention conducted in a housing project in an impoverished, underserved area of South Central Los Angeles, and the community changes which occurred as a result of this intervention.

Reverberations between the individual and the community

We have previously noted a significant absence of psychoanalytic thinking in contemporary community research and action (Borg, Garrod, & Dalla, 2001), yet we have also found that psychoanalysts have made significant contributions to social and community theory (e.g., Altman, 1995; Fromm, 1955; Jones, 1964; Milman & Goldman, 1979; Smelser, 1998, Sullivan, 1964, among others). Although psychoanalysts have generally shied away from direct community intervention, Freud (1921c) himself posited a clear link between individual and community concerns and processes:

> The contrast between individual psychology and social or group psychology, which at first glance might seem full of significance, loses a great deal of its sharpness when it is examined more closely. It is true that individual psychology is concerned with the individual man and explores the paths by which he seeks to find satisfaction for his instinctual impulses; but only rarely and under certain exceptional conditions is individual psychology in a position to disregard the relations of this individual to others. In the individual's mental life someone else is invariably involved, as a model, as an object, as a helper, as an opponent; and so from the very first individual psychology, in this extended but entirely justified sense of the words, is at the same time social psychology as well. [p. 69]

One important intersection between psychoanalysis and community psychology comes into focus by a common concern about the effect of trauma. In his development of the drive model, and abandonment of the seduction theory, Freud emphasized internal conflict, rather than interpersonal trauma and hardship, as the immediate basis for psychopathological processes and symptomatology. According to the drive model, it is the patient, motivated by the increasingly ego-dystonic experience of his or her neurotic symptoms, who seeks psychoanalytic treatment. Had Freud not abandoned his original seduction theory to such an extent, the notion of actual trauma as the progenitor of psychopathological

processes and symptoms would have remained more in the foreground of theory and practice.

Greater emphasis on the role of trauma in personality development, an emphasis which informs the work of many contemporary
theorists and practitioners (e.g., Bose, 1998; Bromberg, 1998; Coates
& Moore, 1997; Davies, 1998; Davies & Frawley, 1994; Gartner, 1999),
and the shifting view of causality which this emphasis creates,
encourages the clinician to pay greater attention to real aspects of
the interpersonal environment, rather than to attend solely to the
individual's internalization and elaboration of interpersonal events.
We suggest that this broadening of attentional focus signals a need
for psychoanalytic theory to perceive and understand environmental conditions which, by their deeply embedded and pervasive
nature, can often impede the individual, or the community as a
whole, from identifying a need for treatment. Rather than the individual's ability to distinguish specific, ego-dystonic symptoms that
signal a need for treatment, the presence of trauma itself, within
specific, targeted communities, may prove a potent indicator of the
need for psychoanalytic intervention.

Entering the real world of community work

In response to the Los Angeles riots of 1992, the city hired a community psychology consulting organization to plan a community treatment intervention for South Central Los Angeles. The intervention
in South Central initially targeted community leaders, members of
the Resident Advisory Council, teachers, and other people in the
community who were involved in the political and educational
lives of a targeted community within South Central consisting of
about 500 residents. Over the course of the project, forty community leaders completed a year-long "Train the Trainer" programme.
These community leaders, after completing their own training, then
provided training in the programme model, and consultation to the
majority of other community members in the general area.

Statistical measures and group and individual interviews conducted during the course of the intervention, from 1993 to 1997,
indicated that members of the community had begun the process of
working through the trauma (Borg, 1997). The outcome data

suggested that people were able: (1) to increase their sense of security within their community; (2) to form and utilize social support;
(3) to feel more in control of their social, environmental and political lives; and (4) to improve their physical health in numerous,
significant ways (Borg, 2002).

Bringing community residents and service providers together to
address chronic and acute trauma was an essential element in the
intervention (Mills, 1995). Participants were taught how rigid, conditioned patterns of thinking and feeling work to maintain biases,
prejudice, and negative assumptions about other individuals
within the community. After training, residents reported increased
ability to communicate needs to each other. Residents also felt more
respected and understood by community leaders and service
providers, including the practitioners, building maintenance work-
ers, teachers, police officers, politicians, and rent collection staff.
Residents felt a sense of increased trust in the community, which, in
turn, enabled them to maintain a sense of responsibility towards the
community and, hence, towards their individual lives.

While the programme model was primarily cognitive–behavioural, the assessment indicated that it was increased interpersonal
functioning, resulting from new modes of interpersonal interaction,
that was the cornerstone of ongoing change. For example, we documented that it was actually the relationships that formed within the
programme that had lasting results in increasing the community's
ability to empower itself (Borg, 1997; Borg, Garrod, & Dalla, 2001).
Conversely, changes in the community were directly related to the
increased interpersonal functioning of individuals, supporting the
interpersonal psychoanalytic notion that personality and character
structure are dynamic formations that are impacted by changes in
the environment (Fromm, 1947, 1970).

Intersecting aspects of interpersonal psychoanalysis and community psychology: community character

Similar to individual character, communities also develop their
own unique character (Borg, 2001). In the case of traumatized
communities, they can develop a character comprising rigidified,
repetitive modes of interacting. In order to more fully understand

how community character forms, we must first consider some inter-personal psychoanalytic notions about moderating anxiety.

Interpersonal psychoanalytic theory describes the processes by which conditioned beliefs are created and maintained through avoidance of anxiety. The social environment influences one's expe-rience of anxiety (Sullivan, 1956). Therefore, an individual's percep-tion of reality, and awareness of his or her own potential for new experiences of self, be those affective, cognitive, or interpersonal, will be limited to the degree that his or her community provokes or soothes anxiety. A community characterized by fear, distrust, secrecy, hostility, and competition will engender chronic anxiety, calling for defensive manoeuvres.

Community character is the community's (and individual's) adherence to the implicit, unstated, but ever-present laws that govern and limit interactive patterns within a community (Borg, Garrod, & Dalla, 2001). It is through the concept of community character that community practitioners can view community inter-vention from an interpersonally-orientated psychoanalytic van-tage point. From this perspective, character is seen to be the repeti-tive interpersonal behaviours or interactive patterns that charac-terize a person's life (Cooper, 1987, 1991; Fromm, 1947). At its most basic level, these adaptive/defensive interactive patterns form a stable personality structure that is utilized to address needs for satisfaction and security in the face of experiences of anxiety (Sullivan, 1953, 1956). It is then reinforced and rigidified, accord-ing to the degree that these needs are threatened in a given rela-tionship (e.g., parent–child relationships), in a specific community (e.g., taboos, local beliefs, and prejudices), or within societies (e.g., formal laws, sanctioned rules of conduct, and cultural norms).

According to interpersonal theory, individuals will protect themselves from anxiety through the use of selective inattention, or, in cases of trauma (such as the South Central community had clearly experienced), through dissociation (Sullivan, 1953). Self-protection from anxiety can, however, also create and maintain the conditioned beliefs that divide community members, hindering mutual understanding and effective collaboration. This defensive experience also keeps community members from actively identify-ing problems and seeking help.

Significant, self-sustaining community change requires intervention that addresses the functioning of problematic aspects of the community character. Changes in this character are reflected in open, mutually supportive interpersonal exchanges, which, over time, reduce the anxiety associated with assuming new beliefs, roles, and communication strategies.

Crisis, experienced at the community level, is often the impetus to loosening the community character in ways that include structural change. Communities have a tendency toward stasis. Crisis and intervention can create new movement (Lundberg, 1998). Change is reflected in new, more flexible and communicative patterns of interaction.

Breaking taboos: the active practitioner

Community interventions challenge many of the taboos and practices of contemporary psychoanalytic theories regarding the activity of the practitioner. Yet, as conceived here, community work can still retain a strong psychoanalytic sensibility.

Trauma was the factor initiating the South Central intervention, not the community members themselves. In response to the riots of the South Central Los Angeles community, city officials sought community-based approaches to address the manifestations of both acute and chronic trauma in the community. A community mental health organization was contracted to implement an intervention that would address such chronic issues as impoverishment, intra-racial violence, racism, unemployment, drug/alcohol abuse, and academic failure, and acute problems, related to the crisis itself, such as rioting, looting, arson, and inter-racial violence. As compared to individual psychoanalytic work in which the patient nearly always initiates treatment, community work conceived through a psychoanalytic lens typically breaks this proviso.

As compared to individual psychoanalytic work which happens only in the consulting room at pre-specified times, community work requires the practitioner to actively participate in the daily life of community members. This pushes even progressive understandings of the involvement of the practitioner's personality in the treatment to its uppermost limits. Community interventions often require that practitioners be extremely flexible, in terms of their roles, throughout the intervention. Interventions included participation in family dinners, weddings, graduations, funerals, and numerous daily activities. While the dramatic departure from traditional boundaries of analytic work required by community intervention might initially appear taboo in its radical deviance from standard analytic practice, we argue that the multiple and intimate contacts between practitioners and community members fall within the bounds of a contemporary, interactive view of psychoanalytic community work as conceived here.

Although traditional psychoanalysis has eschewed didactic or psychoeducational approaches to individual or group problems as forms of non-analytic engagement or "acting out", community work often involves teaching. For example, the intervention in South Central was designed as a series of workshops to teach residents how to advocate for themselves and their community. At first blush, it may seem as though this greatly increased activity of the practitioner is incompatible with a psychoanalytic approach to treatment. In the sections that follow, we challenge this assumption.

A psychoanalytic approach to community work

We believe in the viability of doing psychoanalytic community work based on the retention of a strong working notion of the unconscious and the use of transference–countertransference enactments in the community to inform practitioners. For example, Freud's (1930a) injunction, "Where id was, there shall ego be" (p. 80), speaks directly to the educative process underlying psychoanalytic practice. What distinguishes psychoanalysis from other educational experiences is its emphasis on bringing heretofore unconscious aspects of experience into conscious awareness, primarily through the process of transference. Likewise, a psychoanalytic approach to community work emphasizes making the unconscious conscious. Community interventions that, particularly in their early stages, emphasize more didactic approaches to group interaction might still, in later stages, facilitate opportunities for unconscious experiences to become manifest through transferential processes. In the Los Angeles intervention, for example, an initial didactic focus on interactive processes between group members facilitated participants' ability to become increasingly aware of their engagement in transferential distortions with one another, and of the underlying motives that fuelled these distortions.

In another instance, it was the examination and working-through of unconscious experience that later allowed for more effective psychoeducation. Community members were initially drawn to the intervention by curiosity about the political endorsement that surrounded it. Soon it became apparent that many people attending the workshops were actually the unacknowledged leaders of the community, though they overtly disavowed this. These apparent leaders, through their endorsement, increased other members' receptivity to the programme. It became evident that these members, despite their disavowals, were the "gatekeepers" of the community and that they were, at best, deeply ambivalent about the intervention itself.

Practitioners began to notice that unconscious efforts to sabotage the programme were being enacted by these "leaders". At one point, an important meeting had been scheduled and one of the perceived leaders had agreed to pass out flyers for the meeting. On the day of the meeting, no one showed up. Upon exploration, it was discovered that, somehow, the resident had "forgotten" to hand out the flyers. When questioned, the resident expressed anger that he had been "chosen" (even though he had volunteered) to deliver the flyers.

When this was explored in the group setting, other leaders supported the resident in his anger. Previously unexpressed emotions began to surface. This led to a powerful experience wherein community members described their shared experience of hope and disappointment in previous community interventions.

Although not overtly articulated in the group process, it became apparent that residents had unconscious wishes to be passively gratified, and fears of abandonment and disillusionment of these wishes. These phenomena were revealed through an increase in concrete demands for tangible services from the practitioners (such as building repairs, salaried positions, and cable TV), with expressions of anger and disappointment when these demands went unfulfilled.

Residents also voiced clear expressions of distrust and hostility towards programme practitioners as outsiders who, like all previous outsiders, would tantalize community members with hope that, ultimately, would lead to disappointment. (Altman [1995] found similar ways of relating prevalent in his exploration of the dynamics of community mental health centres in New York.) The airing of these emotions provided the first opportunity for community members and practitioners to have a real dialogue with each other about their respective hopes, plans, resources, and limitations. Community members experienced themselves and the practitioners in a new way when, upon voicing anger and fear, rather than expressing it through sabotaging behaviour, their feelings were met with attention, interest, and respect. For the first time, when practitioners began to explain their roles in the intervention as facilitators rather than "fixers", community members began to have some genuine, experiential understanding of what was actually being offered. Didactic informational offerings that became embroiled in enacted modes of interaction between practitioners and residents ultimately loosened the defensive character of the community.

In another example of a psychoanalytic approach to community work, practitioners enacted conflicts within the community in their professional relationships with each other in a way that ultimately resulted in improved communication among community members. As mentioned previously, practitioners often assumed a participatory role in the daily life of the community. These interactions provided a fertile ground for enactment of unconscious conflict.

Interpersonal ideas about transference–countertransference dimensions of psychoanalytic treatment address enactment as an ever-present dimension of the process. Levenson (1983) stated that, "The transference becomes a highly intensified replay of the material under discussion" (p. 11). As a part of the intervention, long-standing conflicts among members of the community were highlighted, and, through their enactment in the transference–countertransference matrix, were made amenable to intervention.

For instance, a small group of men formed an organization to represent the community's needs to their political representatives. The women in the community felt that this was a good idea, and decided to form an organization of their own. Emotionally heated debates ensued over which group would be recognized by community practitioners as the community's primary and legitimate representative body. In discussion among themselves, a male prac-titioner involved with the men's group and a female practitioner involved with the women's group began to enact a long-standing community conflict. The male practitioner argued that the men in the community had historically experienced a heightened sense of disenfranchisement in the community due to overshadowing and marginalization by the women. The female practitioner argued that the men were not able to follow through with their commitments in their personal lives and that there was no reason for the women to expect them to be responsible within this context.

In allowing themselves to identify with the parties in conflict, to the degree of affectively embodying their respective positions, the community practitioners were able to empathize with community members' feelings of anger at their being misunderstood, their efforts thwarted, and their motivations maligned. Gradually, the practitioners, from their respective positions of gender-based iden-tification, were able to work through initial reactions of denial and projection and, through identifying mutual underlying feelings of helplessness and sorrow, to form a common bond.

What creates change, according to Levenson (1972), is the prac-titioner's "ability to be trapped, immersed, and participating in the system and then work his way out" (p. 174). The experience of becoming embedded and gradually emerging from this enactment enabled the community practitioners to articulate the depth and nature of one significant, long-standing area of community conflict. They were then better able to help community members' increase their awareness of and communication about this conflict. Enact-ment became the means of deepening awareness of pervasive community interactions and patterns of thinking, feeling, relating, and behaving.

Interpersonal empowerment

The intervention in South Central turned on a notion of empower-ing community members. Empowerment theory describes the process whereby people in communities develop collaborative solutions that work for them (Bloom, 1996; Fawcett, Seekins, Whang, Muiu, & Suarez de Balcazar, 1984; Rappaport & Hess, 1984; Rappaport & Seidman, 2000; Warren, 2001).

Using the South Central intervention as a model, an interpersonal psychoanalytic approach to community treatment begins as a psycho-educational intervention where the practitioners take on the dual roles of being both observers and participants in the process of change (Sullivan, 1953, 1954). This experiential model provides a focus on what happens within and between individuals and groups at the time that it is occurring through increasing explorations of the transference–countertransference dimensions of these interactions. Group members work within a supportive, makeshift community, exploring the complex and often covert processes of community systems as they experience them directly, in ways that have been usually unattended in "real life" circumstances in their community.

The participant–observer status serves as an entry point into the process of collaboration. In turn, the collaboration supports the process wherein change and growth are initiated and increasingly sustained from inside the community (Bright, 2000; Perkins & Zimmerman, 1995). The process of collaboration, therefore, serves as the most general framework of the community intervention. Ultimately, collaboration forms a base of support wherein residents are able to mutually develop hypotheses about past, current, and future community functioning and implement their own ideas and strategies accordingly.

It was only by acknowledging that the residents were the "experts" on this community's needs that the community was willing and able to open what had traditionally been a closed system. In the spirit of collaboration, educational processes eventually reverberate between practitioners and residents. The knowledge and awareness of daily living within this community was taught by the residents, while it was more general and conceptual ideas that were taught by practitioners in the workshops. By explicitly focusing on the a bi-directional educational practice, the residents and practitioners were able to establish a collaborative learning loop that supported the idea that everyone involved in the project was both a teacher and a student.

In this process, traditional notions around learning and education could at times set up important challenges to the process of collaboration. There was an inherent tendency in residents and practitioners to slip into the traditional "medical model" default mode: practitioner = expert, resident = patient (Albee, 1996; Rappaport, 1981). In such re-enactments of traditional roles, a collaborative framework was utilized to challenge the typical "expert patient" roles and to reframe the working relationships that were being created within the project. Without such collaborative reframing (Watzlawick, Weakland, & Fisch, 1974), the practitioners ran the risk of imposing their own goals for the community instead of facilitating a process whereby the community could determine what it needed on its own terms.

The intervention targeted characterological defensive patterns of interaction manifest in the community character through analysis and working through of historical patterns as they were experienced in the here and now of transference–countertransference enactments. The intervention targeted the community character as it had been internalized, responded and reacted to, and maintained in the community as a shared and mutually created reality. The details of the community character structure were collaboratively brought to light. This was accomplished by honing in on, and working through, characterological defences (against the pain, anxiety, and environmental forces) that had intergenerationally protected the community through the use of rigid, inflexible patterns of interaction that were highly resistant to change.

In recognizing the emotional contours of the community character, residents were able not only to consciously change it, but also to experience a great appreciation of their community for the adaptive aspects of its character in the face of historical trauma. In the course of recovery and empowerment, the community exhibited a gradual shift from patterns of reacting to an internalized and perpetual sense of unpredictable danger to an internalized sense of community-supported safety. This shift included moving from a history of dissociated trauma to conscious recognition of trauma, and from a sense of entrenched and oppressed isolation to increased social connections among community members as well as to the outside world.

Conclusion

For a community practitioner dealing with crisis, being an observer is not enough. In order to experience the fullness of an interaction, we must understand the significance of what we see, hear, feel, and touch. This requires active participation in the interactive process as the community develops its own empowering strategies for dealing with trauma and crisis. The practice of actively seeking expansion of self-experience seems to be in synchrony with the goals of community psychologists and interpersonally-orientated psycho-analytic practitioners.

If we, as analysts and community practitioners, keep in mind that our roles intersect upon the ground of meeting the needs of our shared communities, we may be able to find ways of increasing our ability to work together with diverse populations within numerous settings. The intersection between these apparently divergent fields occurs when community psychologists and psychoanalysts are able to openly acknowledge a commitment to meeting the perceived needs of our clients and to utilizing the strengths of communities and their members as a guiding force to develop and support ongoing approaches to health and empowerment.

References

Albee, G. W. (1996). Revolutions and counterrevolutions in prevention. *American Psychologist, 51*: 1130–1133.

Altman, N. (1995). *The Analyst in the Inner City*. Hillsdale, NJ: Analytic Press.

Bloom, M. (1996). *Primary Prevention Practices*. Thousand Oaks, CA: Sage.

Bright, E. M. (2000). *Reviving America's Forgotten Neighborhoods: An Investigation of Inner City Revitalization Efforts*. New York: Garland.

Borg, M. B. (1997). *The Impact of Health Realization Training on Affective States of Psychological Distress and Well-Being*. Ann Arbor, MI: University Microfilms International.

Borg, M. B. (2001). Community psychology in Chile. *The Community Psychologist, 34*(4): 12–17.

Borg, M. B. (2002). The Avalon Gardens Men's Association: a community health psychology case study. *Journal of Health Psychology, 7*(3): 345–357.

Borg, M. B., Garrod, E., & Dalla, M. R. (2001). Intersecting "real worlds": community psychology and psychoanalysis. *The Community Psychologist, 34*(3): 16–19.

Bose, J. (1998). The inhumanity of the other: treating trauma and depression. *The Review of Interpersonal Psychoanalysis*, 3: 1–4.

Bromberg, P. M. (1998). *Standing in the Spaces: Essays on Clinical Process, Trauma and Dissociation*. Hillsdale, NJ: The Analytic Press.

Coates, S. W., & Moore, M. S. (1997). The complexity of early trauma: Representation and transformation. *Psychoanalytic Inquiry*, 17: 286–311.

Cooper, A. (1987). Transference and character. *Contemporary Psychoanalysis*, 23: 502–513.

Cooper, A. (1991). Character and resistance. *Contemporary Psychoanalysis*, 27: 721–731.

Davies, J. M. (1998). Multiple perspectives on multiplicity. *Psychoanalytic Dialogues*, 8(2): 195–206.

Davies, J. M., & Frawley, M. G. (1994). *Treating the Adult Survivor of Childhood Sexual Abuse: A Psychoanalytic Perspective*. New York: Basic Books.

Fawcett, S. B., Seekins, T., Whang, P. L., Muiu, C., & Suarez de Balcazar, Y. (1984). Creating and using social technologies for community empowerment. In: J. Rappaport & R. Hess (Eds.), *Studies in Empowerment*. New York: Haworth.

Freud, S. (1921c). *Group Psychology and the Analysis of the Ego. S.E.*, 18: 69–143. London: Hogarth.

Freud, S. (1930a). *Civilization and Its Discontents. S.E.*, 21: 59–145. London: Hogarth.

Fromm, E. (1947). *Man for Himself*. New York: Rinehart.

Fromm, E. (1955). *The Sane Society*. New York: Rinehart & Winston.

Fromm, E. (1970). *The Crisis of Psychoanalysis*. New York: Fawcett Cress.

Gartner, R. (1999). *Betrayed as Boys: Psychodynamic Treatment of Sexually Abused Men*. New York: Guilford.

Jones, E. (1964). *Essays in Applied Psycho-Analysis*. New York: International Universities Press.

Levenson, E. (1972). *The Fallacy of Understanding*. New York: Basic Books.

Levenson, E. (1983). *The Ambiguity of Change*. New York: Basic Books

Lundberg, A. (Ed) (1998). *The Environment and Mental Health*. Mahwah, NJ: Erlbaum.

Mills, R. C. (1995). *Realizing Mental Health*. New York: Sulzburger & Graham.

Milman, D., & Goldman, G. (Eds.) (1979). *Psychoanalytic Contributions to Community Psychology*. Dubuque, IA: Kendall-Hunt.

Perkins, D. D., & Zimmerman, M. A. (1995). Empowerment theory, research, and application. *American Journal of Community Psychology*, 23: 569–579.

Rappaport, J. (1981). In praise of paradox: a social policy of empowerment over prevention. *American Journal of Community Psychology*, 9: 1–25.

Rappaport, J., & Hess, R. (1984). *Studies in Empowerment: Steps Toward Understanding and Action*. New York: Haworth.

Rappaport, J., & Seidman, E. (Eds.) (2000). *Handbook of Community Psychology*. New York: Kluwer Academic/Plenum.

Smelser, N. J. (1998). *The Social Edges of Psychoanalysis*. Los Angeles, CA: University of California Press.

Sullivan, H. S. (1953). *The Interpersonal Theory of Psychiatry*. New York: Norton.

Sullivan, H. S. (1954). *The Psychiatric Interview*. New York: Norton.

Sullivan, H. S. (1956). *Clinical Studies in Psychiatry*. New York: Norton.

Sullivan, H. S. (1964). *The Fusion of Psychiatry and Social Science*. New York: Norton.

Warren, M. R. (2001). *Dry Bones Rattling: Community Building to Revitalize American Democracy*. Princeton, NJ: Princeton University Press.

Watzlawick, P., Weakland, J. H., & Fisch, R. (1974). *Change: Principles of Problem Formation and Problem Resolution*. New York: Norton.

CHAPTER FOURTEEN

When analysts need to retire: the taboo of ageing in psychoanalysis

Peter Fonagy

A clinical illustration

I t was a grey morning. London specializes in days like this. The hope of ever seeing the sun in the next twelve hours is up there with cacti blooming, pigs flying, and winning the lottery jackpot. None the less, the patient on the analyst's couch was somewhat energized by his exploration of his own dream.

He was in his twenties, training as a clinical psychologist. He experienced a self-imposed pressure to pursue his self-analysis without compromise, "taking no hostages", as he often thought about it. The analyst showed more equanimity, and was equivocal. He was all too aware of the narcissistic roots of his patient's urge for self-discovery. When faced with such exuberant displays from his patient he tended to remind him of his child-like wish to show off, to provide a display of his intellectual excitement, to reassure himself in the midst of constant self doubt. Perhaps it was a continuation of the pattern he had established with his mother, practising his homework assignment and doing gymnastic displays while answering her gentle quizzing.

But this morning a sense of unease was building up in the patient. His analyst, quiet at the best of times, had been silent for most of the second half of the session. He was anxiously listening for the normally unwelcome rustling of paper that sometimes punctuated his experience on the couch. He had complained often enough to his analyst that he showed more interest in the dictionaries he studied during the session than in the psychic turmoil excitedly displayed by his young patient. "Have you not heard of free-floating attention?" was the uncommitted reply. But there was no noise this time, just the steady breathing of his beloved transference figure.

The patient went through several iterations of attempting to elicit an analytic response. Over the years he had learnt the phrases and ideas that were likely to provoke comment: homosexual anxiety in the transference; using Kleinian metaphors and ideas (talking of body parts with attributions of mental states—breasts, penises, devouring and conquering); childhood memories of sadness and depression in his mother. No, this was not free association, but somehow he felt desperate. Could it be that his analyst had fallen asleep?

For a while he tried to keep the thought at the back of his mind. But then, as if it was somehow a taboo subject, like masturbation and sex had been at the beginning of his analysis, he felt a surge of adrenalin linked to the profanity of the idea. So, anxiously, he was determined not to think the "pink elephant thought" of his analyst being asleep. He said anything and everything else, talking quite fast, but all the while found his mind focusing and refocusing indirectly on the subject, on a sense of abandonment, on despair at failing to elicit the object's interest. Linking it to well-tested Oedipal associations, he pathetically tried to weave his associations around to the analyst's non-responsiveness; he talked of his terror that his analyst had abandoned him, perhaps he was unwell, perhaps he had had a heart attack? His mother had been ill not long before, so perhaps the association was not surprising.

Again there was no response. And now thoughts about time began to intrude. It seemed like such a long session. Surely it should have been over by now? But the sometimes ever-so-painful "It is time" was not forthcoming. This time it would have been such a relief to hear those three words. Yet all that he could detect was the steady monotonous breathing from the body behind his head.

For some reason he did not dare to look at his watch at first. It was another one of those analytic taboos. Timekeeping was the analyst's prerogative, not the patient's. He felt pathetic, both in his wish and in his reluctance. But how long can this go on? He began to worry about the tight schedule he was on. He had a long drive and was expected to see a client as soon as he got into work.

Thinking of his responsibility to others helped him decide, and he looked at his watch. It was eleven minutes after the end of the session. Such a thing had never happened before. He was confused, but raised his voice and exclaimed, "You are asleep!" He still did not dare turn around. "No I am not!" came the muffled reply. "But it is ten minutes after the end of the session." "So it is." And then, "It is time."

The patient got up, confused, and muttered something about the analyst making him late. The analyst stuck to his guns and said, "Well, you had an extra ten minutes," as if saying that the patient should stop complaining. The patient left, distraught, less by the analyst's apparent lack of interest and more by his insistence on denying reality. He felt sorry for himself, for being "stuck" in a relationship where such things could happen.

Later that evening the analyst phoned him at home and started the conversation by saying, "I owe you an apology." And so the analysis continued along the same rocky road that all intense relationships are conducted. A road with potholes of misapprehensions, disappointments, overblown crises, catastrophic disillusionments, all coupled with elation and overwhelming delight, intense mutuality, and deep understanding. This painful sleep episode receded in importance even if never properly dealt with or worked through. This is hardly surprising, given how deeply it touched the narcissistic vulnerabilities of both participants. It wounded both patient and analyst that this ordinary human thing could happen to them. Challenged by the idealization of the process they were both part of, they could not face the simple reality that people get older and with time are unable to keep to the schedule that they might have found easy in the past, that sleep architecture changes with age and it becomes harder and harder to maintain alertness. In reality, there was no shame in this experience for either party. Yet, as with all taboos, the shame was too real, humiliation was felt to permanently eclipse pride, and could not be entertained.

Psychoanalytic writings on ageing

Psychoanalysts took their time to catch on to ageing. The 1979 International Congress in New York was the first to include a panel on ageing (King, 1980). There had been psychoanalytic writings on the subject before, but only a handful that may be considered systematic treatment (Abraham, Kocher, & Goda, 1980). Freud, as is well known, was pessimistic about treating older patients (Freud, 1905a). In his paper on Femininity, he appears to consider even women of thirty to be "past it":

> A man of about thirty strikes us as a youthful, somewhat unformed individual, whom we expect to make powerful use of the possibilities for development opened up to him by analysis. A woman of the same age, however, often frightens us by her psychical rigidity and unchangeability. [Freud, 1933a, p. 134]

More recent means more optimistic as far as contributions to the subject of ageing are concerned. In part, the optimism concerns the likely response to treatment (Cohen, 1982; Coltart, 1991; King, 1980; Pollock, 1982; Wylie & Wylie, 1987). Calvin F. Settlage (1996), who reported on the "successful" treatment of a patient in the tenth and eleventh decade of her life, put it at its most definitive: "The myth of the unsuitability of middle-aged and elderly individuals for psychoanalytic treatment has been dispelled" (p. 549).

Another aspect of this optimism appears to embrace the entire process of ageing as seen through psychoanalytic eyes. This is exemplified by Adam Limentani's (1995) paper on "Creativity and the third age" that focuses on creativity in the elderly and uses examples of creative function in old age to oppose simplistic models of creativity based around libidinal sublimation. "My own view is that we should regard old age as the fruit of our own creative actions" (p. 832). It should be noted that there is something extravagantly hopeful about these statements that were never delivered to the meeting for which they were written, but were published a year after his death.

Limentani is not alone in presenting a surprisingly optimistic psychoanalytic view about the representation of old age. Hildebrand (1982), for example, claims that in old age "genitality and pre-genitality merge to form a dialectic exchange, more productive than in young people" (see also Hildebrand, 1990). Other psycho-analytic writers on old age have written about the need for the mobilization of constructive aggressive energy to make life more gratifying (Pollock, 1982):

> Energy is released for new investments in life, in the inner as well as in the outer social ambience in which one lives alone and with others. This can occur in individuals who are middle aged, older aged, or in the younger group of analysands. [p. 279]

Cohen (1982) addressed the loneliness of the elderly, not as inherent to the cultural and sociological constraints upon older adults, but as associated with narcissistic psychopathology, the consequence of intense shame that may be associated with seeking psychotherapeutic and other help, that nevertheless can respond to treatment.

Even when developmental losses associated with old age are mentioned by psychoanalytic writers, there is a curious omission in most of these lists (see, for example, Crusey, 1985; Goin, 1990; Hildebrand, 1985; Sandler, 1984). Settlage (1996) gives us a striking example:

> Old age is indeed fraught with loss—the loss of physical characteristics and capacities, of usual activities, and of loved ones. When combined with the awareness that time to live is running out, these losses alter the elderly individual's relationship to self, to others, to the larger world and to time. Responses to loss and its effects include creativity and development in the service of coping and adaptation and disturbance in psychological functioning. I offer a view of these losses and responses from the perspective of the psychoanalytic relationship. [pp. 549–550]

The loss of mental capacities, perhaps the most striking and undoubtedly the most psychologically devastating aspect of ageing (Lindenberger, Mayr, & Kliegl, 1993) appear not to rate as psychoanalytically important considerations. For example, while a loss of physical strength is not considered by Balint (1957) to play an important part, in his opinion the impact of the loss of sexual potency is the central concern of ageing. He writes of the revisiting of infantile sexuality, pornography, voyeurism, exhibitionism, masturbation, but is silent about the loss of memories, inability to concentrate, disruptions of sleep patterns, word finding difficulties, circumlocutions, perseverations, and repetitions.

Some have written about the countertransference aspects of working with elderly patients and identified some special problems that younger therapists may have with older patients (e.g., Hinze, 1987). Interestingly, the cognitive disintegration associated with ageing is not identified as a problem in any of these papers either. Pearl King (1980) noted the analyst's tendency to equate the older patient with a parent, while Abraham, Kocher, and Goda (1980) pointed to the patient being perceived as a weakened parent in relation to whom the analyst's unresolved aggression might generate particularly strong anxieties. The analyst needs to overcome his or her conflicted feelings about parents. Wylie and Wylie (1987) point specifically to the difficulties in dealing with the sexuality of the older patient because of the parental countertransference and the wish to intervene to rescue the patient from physical symptoms and illness. While the papers on special problems of elderly patients and relatively young analysts are few enough in number, the researcher would have to struggle even harder to find writings on the far more common situation of the problems posed by an elderly analyst treating a young patient.

Psychoanalysis: the octogenarian profession

The impact of ageing on Freud is quite widely acknowledged (Thompson, 1991). Freud's (1937c) pessimism in "Analysis terminable and interminable" is well known and specifically includes doubts about the therapeutic efficacy of psychoanalysis and, especially, doubts about the preventative aspects of psychoanalytic treatment: prevention of recurrence as well as prevention of the presentation of disorder in the first place. His pessimistic views have been attributed in part to the circumstances of his life at the time, which include personal conditions such as Freud's advancing cancer, his ageing, the rise of Nazism, deaths of colleagues, relatives, and friends, and disappointments with colleagues (Berenstein, 1987; Blum, 1987; Leupold-Löwenthal, 1988; Loewenberg, 1988). Mahony (1989) provided a moving account of the role of the exacerbation of Freud's illness and his difficult life circumstances around the time that he wrote "Analysis terminable and inter-minable". He points out that Freud had recently heard the disturb-ing news that his correspondence with Fliess had not been destroyed, and that Freud's dog died twelve days before the final version of the essay was completed. It is clear that Freud's enhanced awareness of his own gradual and irreversible decline influenced his views of the therapeutic value of psychoanalysis.

The curious aspect of these discussions might be summarized as follows: psychoanalysts are acutely aware, at least in their writings, of the impact that ageing and associated loss of function might have had on the writings of the originator of the discipline, yet they appear curiously unconcerned about the potential impact of the same sources of influence on those currently practising.

But psychoanalysis is an ageing profession. The average age of the membership of psychoanalytic societies worldwide has increased by a decade over the last twenty years. This is the prod-uct of the increasing age of candidates entering training, increased longevity of psychoanalysts along with the rest of the population—although there might be evidence that analysts actually do live longer than might be expected on purely actuarial grounds (Jeffery, 2001)—and the relatively low number of individuals joining the profession relative to the number of survivors. Over one third of the members of the British Psychoanalytic Society are over seventy years old. Fifty-four per cent of British psychoanalysts are between the ages of fifty and seventy. At a specially convened meeting of the Society a year ago, there was agreement that the Society should approach the problem of an ageing and declining membership by making efforts to grow.

The expected impact of ageing on mental function

Much is known about the impact of ageing on mental function, and much of this information highlights the dynamic interplay between biological and cultural factors that ultimately define multiple trajec-tories of growth and decline, gains and losses (Baltes, 1997). While some resources may increase through the lifespan (e.g., life experi-ence), internal and external resources are inherently limited. By resources, we mean characteristics of both a person and his or her environment that facilitate an individual's existence. Early life is characterized by increasing resources, for example, the acquisition of new skills, although young people also suffer from loss of resources, for example, boys lose their capacity to sing treble after puberty. The ratio of gains to losses becomes progressively less positive with age (Baltes, 1997). To put it simply, resources are not replenished as the individual grows old. This happens for good reasons: most probably, the benefits of evolutionary selection decrease with age, leading to less effective functioning.

Many studies have demonstrated that cognitive change with age is not unitary and some abilities decline more rapidly than others (Schaie, 1996). So-called crystallized intelligence, assumed to be the cumulative end-product of information acquired by an individual and demonstrated on tests of vocabulary, information accumulation, and other knowledge-based activities, declines only in late old age (Salthouse, 1982). In contrast, memory (conscious recollection and recall of an experience) and cognitive speed (performance on timed tasks in intelligence tests) decline significantly during adulthood with further acceleration in decline in late old age (Christensen, 2001). For example, cognitive speed has dropped 20% at age forty, and as much as 50% by age seventy. The reduction in performance on memory tasks between seventy and eighty is nearly 20% (Korten et al., 1997).

The most common problem associated with ageing is memory impairment. There is increasing difficulty in remembering most kinds of new information. Age differences are most marked for free recall of new information or cued recall and are far less readily observable in picture recognition or implicit memory (Park & Shaw, 1992; Park et al., 1996). Recognition memory and spatial memory is similarly vulnerable to ageing (Park, Cherry, Smith, & Lafronza, 1990; Park, Hertzog, Kidder, Morrell, & Mayhorn, 1997). The best account of these memory differences is in terms of the mental effort or processing resource required to encode and retrieve information. Thus, we might expect that older analysts will experience no difficulty retrieving familiar or readily accessible past experience, but will experience difficulty making links between things they heard in the past from a patient and what they are listening to at the moment, or between yesterday's session and today's, or even the first half of the session to the second half.

The majority of individuals show increasing problems with word finding and a tendency to remember things that happened longer ago rather than more recently. Speed of information processing slows (Salthouse, 1996). As a consequence, there is less time to perform the more complex cognitive operations that would normally come towards the end of a processing sequence, so more errors are made. Furthermore, the results of earlier processing that are required for later stages might dissipate because of the slow rate. This causes processing errors, particularly discontinuities, as information evidently available earlier is not taken into account in the final response. This can sometimes make the reactions of older adults somewhat difficult to follow, leaving the listener puzzled as to how they arrived at the conclusion.

Inhibitory functions are also less efficient in older adults (Hasher & Zacks, 1988; Hasher, Stoltzfus, Zacks, & Rypma, 1991). They experience declining capacities in maintaining attention and appear less efficient in blocking out irrelevant thoughts or activations from memory to focus only on a relevant channel of information. While in some ways this might be considered almost an ideal state for the analyst's ideal of free-floating attention (Freud, 1923, p. 235), in reality, alternating focused and diffuse attention is required (Spence, 1984). Thus, the limited capacity for effortful control of attention is likely to undermine the analyst's capacity to listen.

Some have suggested that the degeneration of cognitive function associated with age is a direct consequence of the ageing of the brain, the decline of neuro-biological integrity (Baltes & Lindenberger, 1997; Lindenberger & Baltes, 1994, 1997). There is fairly good evidence to suggest that cognitive deterioration is highly correlated with simple measures of sensory function, balance, and gait. These measures "explain" essentially all age effects on cognitive functioning, because the decrements observed are due to a common cause, decreasing neurological integrity. With the advent of neuro-imaging techniques, we have been able to find evidence for differential patterns of brain activation between old and young adults, suggesting that older adults need to recruit more brain areas to perform the same cognitive operations as young adults (e.g., Cabeza et al., 1997).

These changes are very well documented, but variability between individuals is enormous (Morse, 1993). There is no simple way based on chronological age or physical health of identifying the individuals who have significant functional deficits, although those with lower education, poor health, and high blood pressure are more likely to show cognitive decline (e.g., Hultsch, Hertzog, Small, & Dixon, 1999). Objective measures of health status, including glucose tolerance, cardiovascular disease, and lung function tend to be associated with cognitive decline, but only account for it in part. Of course, professional psychological testing of older professionals would confront us with legal as well as practical challenges.

Are these changes inevitable? Experts find the question difficult to answer conclusively. The changes in cognitive functioning described above are gradual and develop from early adulthood. It is likely that they are part of a normal developmental process. This implies that cognitive decline is unavoidable. There are studies of highly educated academics in good health with a lifetime's exposure to intellectually highly complex, challenging, stimulating environments who, none the less, demonstrate marked changes in late adulthood without the diagnosis of a dementia (Christensen, Henderson, Griffiths, & Levings, 1997; Shimamura, Berry, Mangels, Rusting, & Jurica, 1985). Most agree that decline is inevitable; it is the age at onset that varies.

The probable impact of ageing on psychoanalytic practice

In an unusual book, titled *How Psychiatrists Look at Aging*, edited by George H. Pollock (1992) Marianne Horney Eckardt sums up the whole issue of the ageing process as it affects the clinician in one pithy paragraph:

> The period of becoming old or elderly is (1) a period which is not short but long, encompassing a quarter to a fifth of our life span, and which deserves our caring attention; (2) a period which demands many profound adjustments due to losses and fundamental changes in life's habitat; (3) a period which releases us to some extent from the demands of society—the tasks of forming a family, raising children, earning a living, achieving status, success, all of these milestones are behind us; (4) a period which opens up personal time; (5) a period where the future dimension of hope and possibilities shrinks progressively; (6) a period with a future of

certainty of death but total unpredictability and the potential of many a very bleak scenario; (7) a period of confrontation which may initiate inner transformations; and (8) a period which brings us closer to spiritual values. [p. 89]

The book includes numerous accounts of clinicians struggling with the ageing process, including severe degenerative disease (written by Sam Atkin and his son Adam), enforced retirement, and the analyst's attempts to cope with the narcissistic blow and sense of loss encountered, for which his efforts at self-analysis, though valiant, did not suffice. Virginia Clower provided a frank account of the symptoms she observed in herself, along with the perspectival changes wrought by ageing in her work with patients. Martha Kilpatrick was similarly elegant and personal in her self-observations on ageing in the female analyst. Such accounts, however, are both rare and explicitly written as "curiosities" rather than as attempts to address a genuine problem of controlling the adequacy of professionalism in an ageing profession.

The British analyst, Pearl King, in writing about the identity of a psychoanalyst (at the age of fifty-eight) considered "becoming an ageing psychoanalyst as the fifth stage of the development of psychoanalytic identity" (King, 1983). She notes, in line with the data on cognitive decline, that becoming an ageing psychoanalyst is a gradual process. We only become slowly aware of what we can do satisfactorily to ourselves or to others. In a later contribution (King, 1989), she is unusual in pointing to the analyst becoming aware of "his own ageing, the depletion of his skills, capacities and abilities". Nevertheless, King, like most of us, takes refuge behind the variability of the process of ageing. She suggests that while one can take the advice of colleagues and close collaborators about realistic expectations about one's own abilities, ultimately the decision to retire is for the individual. She holds that the clue is the discrepancy between our ego ideal of how we expect ourselves to function and to be responded to by others and what is actually the case. She wisely identifies an adaptive and a maladaptive path for the ageing analyst to follow: the adaptive one of creative ageing and the maladaptive one of ignoring problems and denying the reality of declining capacities, missing the opportunity for identifying creative choices. She describes how her personal choice was to give up clinical work and start a new career doing research and writing. King's (2002) discussion is refreshing for its straightforward way of dealing with the subject and its honesty.

It seems that, more than other professions, psychoanalysts are over-dependent on their role as therapists and teachers. The experience of being the focus of parental transference for a good portion of one's professional life is likely to alter one's unconscious sense of self in the direction of believing oneself to be the omnipotent, fantasied, immortal, parental figure. Patients, candidates, and the entire social culture of psychoanalysis—the innumerable committees, political infighting etc.—begin unconsciously to represent extensions of the self. These structures embody a sense of immortality and create a sense of identity. This is a different level of investment to that which we are likely to observe in other professions. A withdrawal from professional activity implied by retirement becomes intolerable, as this would threaten a sense of professional identity (King, 2002).

It should be recognized that the profession is now fully engaged with the issue of ageing in psychoanalysts, but largely from a demographic rather than a cognitive standpoint. For example, the recruitment of younger candidates has become a priority across the IPA and a number of psychoanalytic societies. Of course, expectations about standards of living have changed, and few young people consider it possible to undertake psychoanalytic training until they feel reasonably established professionally, at least in the UK (for an intelligent discussion of this issue, see Target, 2002).

However, the demography of the profession is not the taboo issue. What is rarely talked about publicly by psychoanalysts is the impact of age on the clinical skills of an analyst. Appropriately, given the tremendous variability in the mental capacities of older adults, there is no compulsory retirement age for psychoanalysts. Yet, anecdotally, we hear from candidates on the couch about supervisors who fall asleep during supervision, who forget key details of cases presented to them. We witness how some of our colleagues become increasingly rigid in their thinking with age. I have also noticed how pseudo-concern about colleagues being "too young" can, at times, serve as a mask for the envy of youth. Similarly, the wish to progress rapidly to complete analytic training and become a Member of the "clan" is often defensively interpreted as a character weakness and an indicator of a wish to avoid serious engagement with one's own problems and deep, but slow, analytical clinical work. Yet, we also know that such signs of narcissism are merely desirable hallmarks of youth. We observe our older colleagues as their capacities deteriorate, yet they retain positions of responsibility and respect, made unassailable by unresolved transference. We collude in overlooking the transparently semi-delusional wish of some colleagues to ensure their personal continuity through exerting undue control over the younger generation, blatantly favouring those who modify their belief systems to be closest to their own.

Of course, none of this is unique to psychoanalysis. The conservatism of older colleagues pervades most professions. Yet, in other professions, this is easier to discuss and explore. Ageing is the prototypical taboo for psychoanalysts. We can readily talk about that which most of our non-analytic colleagues find hideously shameful: bisexuality, masturbation, our own narcissistic vulnerabilities, even profound destructiveness in ourselves and in our patients. But a profession that has at its core the legend of Oedipus is condemned forever to idealize seniority and experience. It is all too easy to see the actions of young colleagues as derivative of a poorly analysed wish to displace the parent and, of course, such feelings probably do feed into criticisms of the older generation. Yet, as Freud (1912–1913) so clearly described in *Totem and Taboo*, veneration of elders is a reaction formation against unconscious patricidal and matricidal wishes. The failure of the profession to develop appropriate systems to deal with incompetence associated with ageing might be directly linked with our clinical immersion with intergenerational hostility and an understandable reluctance to confront it outside the consulting room.

Is the taboo of the ageing analyst an issue of concern, or one that we can afford to relegate to the status of "expectable human imperfection" and benevolently overlook as we do the many eccentricities associated with our profession? I would not be writing in this vein if I thought the problem to be benign and without consequence. Many writing about psychoanalytic training have commented on the gerontocracy of many training institutes. The conservatism of the training structure designed in Berlin before the war and maintained almost unchanged worldwide is a monument to our inability to deal with intergenerational ambivalence.

A dramatic example of the depth of the problem comes from a study of the Swedish Psychoanalytic Society, reported by Imre Szecsody at the Joseph Sandler Research Conference earlier this year. An independent review of the training undertaken by non-analytic researchers at the University of Stockholm identified a remarkably high level of complacency on the part of candidates of the Swedish Institute. There was an apparent idealization of the training and a complete abhorrence at the thought of the mere possibility of improvement. I have had a similar experience in the British Society, when the mere possibility of the Society changing its procedures from being a reporting society (the candidate's analyst reports on the progress of the candidate) to a non-reporting society (where the confidentiality of the analytic relationship is sacrosanct) was considered. It was the candidates and the senior training analysts who, in the main, opposed the change. The identification of young people with the concerns of their elders is quite remarkable and surely unusual for an educational programme. The taboo of the cognitive decline linked with ageing and its complement, "filial piety", infect us from the beginnings of our association with institutional psychoanalysis.

Looking to the future

The inevitability of cognitive decline, our investment in our professional activity as a source of our sense of identity, and the emotional conflict experienced by our junior colleagues in confronting us with our growing inadequacies because of the filial piety that evolves as a consequence of the subject matter combine to make for a toxic mixture. We have no mechanisms for ensuring that our older colleagues offer a clinical service of adequate quality. Quality assurance will increasingly be a communal responsibility for psychoanalytic societies, and therefore the taboo of ageing analysts risking bringing the profession into disrepute has to be confronted. Medical revalidation is now generally recognized as essential to safeguard the public interest. A fair and transparent procedure for revalidating psychoanalysts should perhaps be developed by the International Psychoanalytic Association. All agree that age by itself is a poor indicator of ageing, or, at least, its cognitive aspects. It is quite conceivable to organize clinical presentations and clinical discussions of other people's material that would indicate the level of a person's clinical work. It would be essential that such records are assessed by anonymous peer reviewers in the light of our difficulty in being identified as critics of older analysts. Similar procedures need to be put in place for qualifying an individual to supervise. Of course, all this is just an aspect of what ought to be a move to address the far broader issue of general lack of transparency in our profession that pervades our training and advancement within the professional organization. Clear criteria, rather than idealized intuition, which we know to be vulnerable to distortion by unconscious fantasy, will eventually have to dominate our procedures if these are to withstand increasingly common ethical and legal challenges. Dealing with the taboo of the analyst's cognitive decline is a small step along this long, hard, and somewhat barren road.

References

Abraham, G., Kocher, P., & Goda, G. (1980). Psychoanalysis and ageing. *International Review of Psychoanalysis, 7*: 147–155.

Balint, M. (1957). *The Doctor, His Patient and the Illness*. London: Pitman Medical.

Baltes, P. B. (1997). On the incomplete architecture of human ontogeny. Selection, optimization, and compensation as foundation of developmental theory. *American Psychology, 52*(4): 366–380.

Baltes, P. B., & Lindenberger, U. (1997). Emergence of a powerful connection between sensory and cognitive functions across the adult life span: a new window to the study of cognitive aging? *Psychology and Aging, 12*(1): 12–21.

Berenstein, I. (1987). Analysis terminable and interminable, fifty years on. *International Journal of Psychoanalysis, 68*: 21–35.

Blum, H. (1987). Analysis terminable and interminable: a half century retrospective. *International Journal of Psychoanalysis, 68*: 37–47.

Cabeza, R., Grady, C. L., Nyberg, L., McIntosh, A. R., Tulving, E., Kapur, S., Jennings, J. M., Houle, S., & Craik, F. I. (1997). Age-related differences in neural activity during memory encoding and retrieval: a positron emission tomography study. *Journal of Neuroscience, 17*(1): 391–400.

Christensen, H. (2001). What cognitive changes can be expected with normal ageing? *Australian & New Zealand Journal of Psychiatry, 35*(6): 768–775.

Christensen, H., Henderson, A. S., Griffiths, K., & Levings, C. (1997). Does aging inevitably lead to declines in cognitive performance? A longitudinal study of elite academics. *Personality and Individual Differences*, 23: 67–78.

Cohen, N. (1982). On loneliness and the ageing process. *International Journal of Psychoanalysis*, 63: 149–155.

Coltart, N. (1991). The analysis of an elderly patient. *International Journal of Psychoanalysis*, 72: 209–219.

Crusey, J. E. (1985). Short-term psychodynamic psychotherapy with a sixty-two-year-old man. In: R. A. Nemiroff & C. A. Colarusso (Eds.), *The Race Against Time: Psychotherapy and Psychoanalysis in the Second Half of Life* (pp. 147–166). New York: Plenum.

Freud, S. (1905a). On psychotherapy. *S.E.*, 7: 255–268. London: Hogarth.

Freud, S. (1912–1913). *Totem and Taboo. S.E.*, 13: 1–162. London: Hogarth.

Freud, S. (1923a). Two encyclopaedia articles. *S.E.*, 18: 235–262. London: Hogarth.

Freud, S. (1933a). *New Introductory Lectures on Psycho-Analysis. S.E.*, 22: 112–135. London: Hogarth.

Freud, S. (1937c). Analysis terminable and interminable. *S.E.*, 23: 209–253. London: Hogarth.

Goin, M. K. (1990). Emotional survival and the aging body. In: R. A. Nemiroff & C. A. Colarusso (Eds.), *New Dimensions in Adult Development* (pp. 518–529). New York: Basic Books.

Hasher, L., & Zacks, R. (1988). Working memory, comprehension and aging: a review and a new view. *The Psychology of Learning and Motivation*, 22: 193–225.

Hasher, L., Stoltzfus, E. R., Zacks, R. T., & Rypma, B. (1991). Age and inhibition. *Journal of Experimental Psychology: Learning, Memory, and Cognition*, 17: 163–169.

Hildebrand, H. P. (1982). Psychotherapy with older patients. *British Journal of Medical Psychology*, 55: 19–25.

Hildebrand, H. P. (1985). Object loss and development in the second half of life. In: R. A. Nemiroff & C. A. Colarusso (Eds.), *The Race Against Time: Psychotherapy and Psychoanalysis in the Second Half of Life* (pp. 211–227). New York: Plenum.

Hildebrand, H. P. (1990). The other side of the wall: a psychoanalytic study of creativity in later life. In: R. A. Nemiroff & C. A. Colarusso (Eds.), *New Dimensions in Adult Development* (pp. 467–484). New York: Basic Books.

Hinze, E. (1987). Transference and countertransference in the psycho-analytic treatment of older patients. *International Review of Psycho-analysis, 14*: 465–474.

Hultsch, D. F., Hertzog, C., Small, B. J., & Dixon, R. A. (1999). Use it or lose it: engaged lifestyle as a buffer of cognitive decline in aging? *Psychology and Aging, 14*(2): 245–263.

Jeffery, E. H. (2001). The mortality of psychoanalysts. *Journal of the American Psychoanalytic Association, 49*: 103–111.

King, P. (1980). The life cycle as indicated by the nature of the transfer-ence in the psychoanalysis of the middle-aged and elderly. *Inter-national Journal of Psychoanalysis, 61*: 153–160.

King, P. (1983). Identity crises: splits and compromise—adaptive or maladaptive. In: E. D. Joseph & D. Widlochers (Eds.), *The Identity of the Psychoanalyst*. New York: International Universities Press.

King, P. (1989). On being a psychoanalyst: integrity and vulnerability in psychoanalytic organisation. In: H. P. Blum, E. M. Weinshel, & F. R. Rodman (Eds.), *The Psychoanalytic Core*. Madison, CT: Inter-national Universities Press.

King, P. (2002). On becoming an ageing psychoanalyst. *Bulletin of the British Psychoanalytical Society, 38*: 34–37.

Korten, A. E., Henderson, A. S., Christensen, H., Jorm, A. F., Rodgers, B., Jacomb, P., & Mackinnon, A. J. (1997). A prospective study of cognitive function in the elderly. *Psychological Medicine, 27*(4): 919–930.

Leupold-Löwenthal, H. (1988). Notes on Sigmund Freud's '"Analysis terminable and interminable". *International Journal of Psychoanalysis, 69*: 261–271.

Limentani, A. (1995). Creativity and the third age. *International Journal of Psychoanalysis, 76*: 825–833.

Lindenberger, U., & Baltes, P. B. (1994). Sensory functioning and intel-ligence in old age: a strong connection. *Psychology and Aging, 9*(3): 339–355.

Lindenberger, U., & Baltes, P. B. (1997). Intellectual functioning in old and very old age: cross-sectional results from the Berlin Aging Study. *Psychology and Aging, 12*(3): 410–432.

Lindenberger, U., Mayr, U., & Kliegl, R. (1993). Speed and intelligence in old age. *Psychology and Aging, 8*(2): 207–220.

Loewenberg, P. (1988). An historical, biographical, literary, and clinical consideration of Freud's "Analysis terminable and interminable" on its fiftieth birthday. *International Journal of Psychoanalysis, 69*: 273–281.

Mahony, P. (1989). *On Defining Freud's Discourse*. New Haven, CT: Yale University Press.

Morse, C. K. (1993). Does variability increase with age? An archival study of cognitive measures. *Psychology and Aging, 8*(2): 156–164.

Park, D. C., & Shaw, R. J. (1992). Effect of environmental support on implicit and explicit memory in younger and older adults. *Psychology and Aging, 7*(4): 632–642.

Park, D. C., Cherry, K. E., Smith, A. D., & Lafronza, V. N. (1990). Effects of distinctive context on memory for objects and their locations in young and elderly adults. *Psychology and Aging, 5*(2): 250–255.

Park, D. C., Hertzog, C., Kidder, D. P., Morrell, R. W., & Mayhorn, C. B. (1997). Effect of age on event-based and time-based prospective memory. *Psychology and Aging, 12*(2): 314–327.

Park, D. C., Smith, A. D., Lautenschlager, G., Earles, J. L., Frieske, D., Zwahr, M., & Gaines, C. L. (1996). Mediators of long-term memory performance across the life span. *Psychology and Aging, 11*(4): 621–637.

Pollock, G. (1982). On ageing and psychopathology—discussion of Dr Norman A. Cohen's Paper "On loneliness and the ageing process". *International Journal of Psychoanalysis, 63*: 275–281.

Pollock, G. (Ed.) (1992). *How Psychiatrists Look at Aging*. Madison, CT: International Universities Press.

Salthouse, T. A. (1982). *Adult Cognition*. New York: Springer-Verlag.

Salthouse, T. A. (1996). The processing-speed theory of adult age differences in cognition. *Psychological Review, 103*(3): 403–428.

Sandler, A. (1984). Problems of development and adaptation in an elderly patient. *Psychoanalytic Study of the Child, 39*: 471–489.

Schaie, K. W. (1996). *Intellectual Development in Adulthood. The Seattle Longitudinal Study*. Cambridge: Cambridge University Press.

Settlage, C. F. (1996). Transcending old age: creativity, development and psychoanalysis in the life of a centenarian. *International Journal of Psychoanalysis, 77*: 549–564.

Shimamura, A. P., Berry, J. M., Mangels, J. A., Rusting, D. L., & Jurica, P. J. (1985). Memory and cognitive abilities of university professors: evidence of successful aging. *Psychological Science, 6*: 271–277.

Spence, D. P. (1984). Perils and pitfalls of free floating attention. *Contemporary Psychoanalysis, 20*: 37–58.

Target, M. (2002). The ageing membership. *Bulletin of the British Psychoanalytical Society, 38*: 38–41.

Thompson, A. (1991). Freud's pessimism, the death instinct, and the theme of disintegration in "Analysis terminable and interminable". *International Review of Psychoanalysis, 18*: 165–179.

Wylie, H., & Wylie, M. (1987). The older analysand: countertransference issues in psychoanalysis. *International Journal of Psychoanalysis, 68*: 343–352.

CHAPTER FIFTEEN

Behind closed doors: what analysts say to one another about the practice of psychoanalysis

Richard R. Hansen

lthough I am a psychologist, my primary professional identity is that of a psychoanalyst. As a psychoanalyst, I limit
my practice to working with patients whom I see three or
more times per week. Only one of the above statements is true.

Your nervous laughter reveals your anxious relief that you are
not alone in your concern that you are seeing more and more
patients that, for a variety of reasons, cannot or will not, engage in
the session frequency that has been fundamental to our training and
practice as psychoanalysts. Your laughter also reflects, as Freud
(1905c) was first to note in *Jokes and their Relation to the Unconscious*,
the spontaneous release associated with the rapid lifting of a repression. I tickled your unconscious when I barged past your defences
and said something publicly that we may rarely acknowledge, even
in our private moments, something that may even be considered
taboo. The fact is that few, if any, of us practice psychoanalysis in the
way in which we were trained, and in the way in which we prefer to
work. This has serious consequences for our perception of ourselves
as psychoanalysts, for our patients, and for our theory building.

The idea for the title of my chapter was stimulated by the
confluence of two, seemingly unrelated, series of events. The first

was a number of casual comments made to me over the course of the past year or two by senior training analysts from various parts of the country. Their comments were as follows: Analyst A: "At my current fee, I couldn't afford to see myself in analysis." Analyst B: "For many of these candidates, the only patients that they will ever see for real analyses (three or for times weekly) will be the control cases at their training institutes." Analyst C: "Psychoanalysis is like a fine painting; it's nice to look at, but who can afford it?" Analyst D: "Most analysts are lucky if they have one or two patients in three times weekly psychoanalysis, let alone four times per week."

Although they were intended as "inside jokes", these statements reflect analysts' deep frustration in practising psychoanalysis in the current climate. The ideas expressed are not for public consumption. They are analytic secrets that may be the source of self-conscious jokes, but even these jokes are spoken in hushed tones. By virtue of their secret nature, these ideas can only be shared with trusted analytic colleagues and friends. The implication is that the larger analytic community would not approve of these comments or, as one analyst remarked to me, "It would not be good for the profession."

The second series of events that inspired this chapter had to do with the recurrent reaction of colleagues to a case I had the opportunity to discuss over the same past two years in which the following occurred. A female patient whom I had been seeing three times weekly, using the couch, came into my office one day holding a magazine from my waiting room. She cheerily and spontaneously asked, before lying down, if she might borrow it. I suggested that we talk about it.

Later in the chapter, I will go into more detail concerning my thinking then and now about my taking this particular tack. For now, the important issue is not this case or what I chose to do or not do, but my colleagues' reaction to the position I took with my patient. I was quite surprised with the intensity of the negative reactions I received to my not simply lending my patient the magazine. My colleagues' reactions appeared to me to be more charged than one might expect over theoretical differences. They seemed to be related to much more powerful feelings about one's analytic identity and what constitutes being a good analyst.

What was striking to me was that, even before I had the opportunity to more fully discuss the thinking behind my approach with my patient, I was met by stiff opposition. I was told that I was too rigid, withholding, and depriving. A recurrent theme was that I was behaving like a classical dinosaur, and that I was relying on an outdated technical stance that interfered with a deeper engagement with my patient. While I think it is essential to our continued professional evolution to agree to disagree, I also think that the intensity of my colleagues' disagreement with me was a reflection of a deeper discordant note within each of us as analysts.

The intersection of these two series of events, that is, the taboo comments made to me by analysts about the practice of psychoanalysis, and the reactions of analysts to my technical stance with my patient, resonated with, and made me more aware of, my own inner sense of discord. The feeling that came forth for me during each of the aforementioned events had to do with feeling underappreciated and misunderstood. I also recognized that feeling devalued as a psychoanalyst was something with which, in recent times, I had become all too familiar. It has been disheartening to try to explain and justify my work to managed care operatives whose main incentive is cost control. It has been frustrating to witness the propaganda espoused by the financially powerful pharmaceutical companies as they attempt to reduce the human condition to faulty neurotransmission. Theirs is a brain theory, wherein mind does not matter, wherein interpersonal relationships have little role in determining what ails us. They would have had us believe that Lady Macbeth's compulsive hand washing was the result of a biochemically driven obsessive compulsive disorder, and not a function of her inner turmoil over having had a hand in the murder of her king. None the less, much of the public would choose psychopharmacology over psychoanalysis. The pharmaceutical companies offer a pill and the promise of quick relief, while we offer nothing tangible, only the hope of change through a slower, more deliberate, painstaking process. For contemporary psychoanalysts, it is not easy to maintain one's sense of professional value and self-worth in our culture.

My brief, impassioned digression into the current atmosphere within which we all practise serves as an important "adaptive context" (Langs, 1976) for the central idea of this paper. The self-conscious jokes that I noted above reflect the tension induced in us by society's general disparagement of our profession. One way we may be managing this tension is to join in. Through secretly disparaging ourselves in these taboo comments to one another, we are identifying with the aggressor. The thought might be that we are not so serious that we cannot find humour, even if it is at our own expense. We may rationalize that poking fun at ourselves is a form of healthy self-acceptance. I would argue differently. I believe that these taboo jokes among analysts reflect a deeper sense of disenfranchisement. I believe that the sentiments underlying the self-conscious, self-deprecating jokes have a profoundly negative effect upon our identity as analysts, and that they impact on how we practice, how we understand and interpret theory, and, perhaps, even how we shape contemporary theory.

Some basic assumptions about psychoanalysis

When I think of psychoanalytic treatment, I think of a traditional model: three or four sessions per week using the couch. My conceptualization has been most influenced by my own analysis. For the most part, it worked for me and was a life-changing experience. In this regard, my definition of psychoanalysis with respect to session frequency and use of the couch is similar to Bergman's observation (1999) that if one feels that one's own analysis was successful, one will not need to look for a new theory.

I believe that I do my best work with patients whom I see at least three times per week. I was taught that this is the optimum way of working and it seemed to work well enough in my own analysis and the analyses of those patients whom I was able to see with this frequency. It is only when I see patients multiple times per week that I find that I am able to enter a mutually regressed state wherein I can best use my own unconscious processes to gain access to what is transpiring in the patient, in me, and in the treatment.

Despite Merton Gill's (1994) observation about the unreliability of frequency of sessions as a measure of whether or not what transpires between patient and analyst constitutes psychoanalysis, most of us would agree that session frequency is an essential feature of psychoanalysis. Moreover, most of us would also prefer to see our patients more often.

I believe that it is a deep disappointment to all of us that we rarely practise our profession at the level at which we were trained. A simple fact is that the vast majority of us are not practising the craft that we were trained to practise.

While this is a rather obvious conclusion to draw from the evidence presented and from the experience of the vast majority of practising analysts, I feel somewhat like a heretic for stating it publicly. This is precisely the point. To speak of a taboo is to risk censure. Unfortunately, the history of censure for speaking about psychoanalytic taboos is as long as that of the profession itself.

Taboo and the history of psychoanalysis

In its founder, psychoanalysis had a leader who expanded our range of awareness of thoughts and feelings that had been banished to the unconscious, primarily through a courageous sharing of his own self-analysis. Despite his unprecedented openness, Freud had little patience for his dissenters. His reaction to Adler and Jung was to treat them as traitors to the mission, which he referred to as *die Sache*, the cause. In so doing, he exemplified the very meaning of taboo: "A proscription devised and observed by any group for its own protection" (Morris, 1979). Perhaps because of the conflict within his group of founders, and because of the larger society's resistance to his ideas, Freud also demonstrated that he was not impervious to the questioning of his ideas. His need to be appreciated was nowhere more apparent than in his soliciting support in his correspondence with Fleiss. I mention Freud's need for appreciation here because I think the need for all of us analysts to feel appreciated is an additional factor in our current dilemma, which I will develop more fully later in the paper.

According to Roazen (1999), the most telling example of psychoanalytic taboo also involved Freud. Roazen argued that there is a huge gulf between what analysts espouse in theory and write for publication, and how they actually practise. This, he stated, was nowhere more apparent than in Freud's largely secret treatment of his daughter, Anna. Freud did not talk about it, Anna refused to answer questions about it, and before Roazen's research (1969, 1975, 1993) it was not written about. Furthermore, Roazen revealed that the analytic community initially censured him for writing about Freud's analysis of Anna.

Rachman (1999) observed that the analytic community has traditionally followed an unwritten rule regarding those analysts who might violate policies and practices deemed sacrosanct. He called this the rule of *Todschweigen*, or death by silence. Dissidents within the profession were not to be spoken about; their names were not to be mentioned. Rachman stated that this was the approach taken by training institutes to the teachings of Ferenczi and Fromm, among others. It has only been in recent times that it has become safe to discuss their contributions to the field.

In his thoughtful book, provocatively entitled *The Death of Psychoanalysis: Murder? Suicide? Or Rumor Greatly Exaggerated?*, Prince (1999) provided a forum in which many leading contemporary psychoanalysts examined the state of the profession. Although many taboo subjects were explored regarding psychoanalysis's decline, there was only one reference to the fact that fewer analysts than ever were seeing patients with the traditional frequency associated with a true (at least as it was originally conceived) psychoanalysis. Moreover, this observation was made by a historian (Hale, 1999) not a psychoanalyst.

Lionells (1999), in her contribution to Prince's book, suggested that contemporary analysts might suffer from a professional developmental pattern similar to that of the "shamed child", as described by Fiscalini (1993). In Fiscalini's paradigm, the shamed child is a bright, outstanding child who was idealized and envied by his/her parents. The child's sense of shame appears when he/she becomes aware of having fallen short of his/her parents' expectations. In Lionells' analogy, analysts might suffer from similar fears of shame. She suggested that the rigours of analytic training subtly induce in analysts in training an expectation to please the institute, his/her supervisor, and especially his/her training analyst. Along with these expectations, she posited, comes the fear of falling short of these expectations. She concluded that contemporary analysts struggle with their sense of professional self-worth primarily because of the nagging fear of falling short of the expectations they acquired during their training. While this is an interesting and useful observation, Lionells neglected to mention the fact that few analysts see very many patients in the traditional three or four (let alone five) times per week sessions that were required in their training. This must also be a major factor in analysts' sense of shame. Most of us, at least when we began our training, had the fantasy that at some point when we became fully-fledged analysts, we would primarily practise psychoanalysis. Having fallen far short of that goal has perhaps generated a secret, if not unconscious, sense of shame in many of us. A collective sense of shame is fertile ground for the generation of consensual taboo.

It is ironic, yet strangely consistent with psychoanalysis's proclivity for contradiction and paradox, that a theory of the mind and a therapeutic process that focuses on the liberating within the individual of debilitating taboos could simultaneously encourage the creation of taboos within its tradition as a profession. Our individual professional lives and our existence as a profession have been devoted to helping our patients to speak the unspeakable, yet we are often afraid to talk to one another. We may identify ourselves as analysts, but do we truly feel like analysts when we rarely see our patients with analytic frequency?

The need to be appreciated and its effects
upon transference and taboo

It is nice to be appreciated. When I received the call for papers for this international conference on taboo, I thought that theme of the conference was a wonderful idea. Then I had some ideas of my own and submitted a proposal. The selection committee must have been interested in my ideas, and invited me to share them with the audience at the conference. It was most gratifying to me to think that my ideas were interesting and appreciated by my colleagues.

At its most basic, the sharing of ideas is one way to conceptualize the way in which we work with our patients. A patient comes to us with some problem or other and we say, in effect, "I have an idea about this." On some level, we have hope that our ideas, which are often, though not exclusively, couched in the form of clarifications and interpretations, are helpful. If these ideas prove helpful, then our patient feels that he/she has been appreciated and understood. As analysts, we feel gratified by alleviating some discomfort in our patient and derive some satisfaction in having our ideas (interpretations and the like) appreciated by our patient.

We also know that the transaction of ideas between patient and analyst is hardly this simple. Complicating the process of whether or not our ideas are helpful and appreciated is the transference. One of psychoanalysis's central tenets is that whatever the patient perceives his/her problems to be, the essence of these problems will be unconsciously expressed in the relationship with the analyst. Patients coming to see us for problems with their work/marriages/ children/parents/friends soon begin to learn that they are encountering some of the same problems with us. From the patient's perspective, they might come into treatment for difficulties experienced as primarily residing outside themselves, only to discover that the problems lie within, and are gaining new life and being repeated in their relationship with us. I am aware that I am restating and over-simplifying a well-known analytic fact, but I think it bears repeating here to sharpen our focus on the patient's experience in psychoanalysis and the effect it has upon both patient and analyst.

In the context above, the patient may come into treatment expecting one thing and we offer another. Transference is a peculiar thing. It is primarily for this reason that I always feel a bit presumptuous when making an interpretation. I am always keenly aware that no other relationship permits this. If one has any doubt about this, one has only to attempt making an interpretation to a relative or friend. For the patient and the analyst, the transference, as Freud was first to discover, is indeed "the hardest part of the analysis" (1905e, p. 116).

What does all this have to do with taboo? What relevance does it have to the derisive comments analysts make about seeing patients with less than desired frequency? Surely we know that the transference has always been a burden for the analyst, but I think that contemporary changes in our understanding of the transference have brought additional pressures upon the analyst. I believe that these pressures, combined with the declining opportunity to see patients more frequently, are major contributors to the cynicism in the analysts' comments noted at the beginning of this paper.

Changes in our conception of transference and the analyst's burden

In Freud's original formulation, although the management of the transference was an arduous task, there was solace provided by analytic anonymity. The analyst had the relative safety of the "not me" experience. The patient, in the transference, may have loved, hated, admired, needed, feared, been jealous of, or doubted the analyst. It was, however, really not the analyst himself/herself, but some resurrected imago projected on to the analyst. It then followed from this perspective that if the analyst were well analysed, it did not matter whom the analyst was. Given the same clinical material and the same transference paradigm, theoretically all analysts of that time would arrive at the same interpretation. The emphasis in that era was upon the patient's mental contents. The transference was seen as a pure projection arising as whole cloth out of the patient's unconscious with nary a thread borrowed from the analyst as a person. Although a weighty matter for the analyst, the transference still belonged to the patient and his/her pathology.

We now understand, and even the most resolute contemporary Freudians would agree, that there is no such thing as absolute analytic anonymity and neutrality. Our patients, in ways that we might not imagine or anticipate, know us. The way in which we now view transference has been forever changed via the contributions from the interpersonalists, the intersubjectivists, and the relationalists. In some way or other, each of these schools has reached the common ground that the analyst's conscious and unconscious participation in the treatment is an indelible part of the analytic interchange.

In contrasting more contemporary views of the transference with the classical position, Gerhardt, Sweetnam, and Borton (2000) suggested that in Freud's original conception of the transference the analyst's task was to comport himself like the character Marcello in Puccini's *La Boheme*, who tied himself to a chair in order to resist Musetta's seductive temptations. Like Marcello, the classical analyst, Gerhardt and colleagues argued, is tied to the chair by the restrictions of neutrality in order to resist the patient's passions. Clinical experience has taught us, however, that no matter how we may choose to consciously bind ourselves, there is no resisting emotional engagement with our patients. The treatment is shaped by how we experience and manage this engagement. In this model, it is the analyst's reflections and mental preoccupations that inform the work via "the continuous tacking between experience and reflection-interpretation-negotiation of meanings" (*ibid.*, p. 8).

Contemporary analysts, primarily intersubjective and relational theorists, have posited that whether in the form of enactment, sustained use of countertransference, reverie, or some other form of unconscious becoming conscious, the analytic dyad is triangulated by a third mediating voice (Gerhardt, Sweetnam, & Borton, 2000). Or, as in Ogden's (1992) particularly elegant conceptualization, the work involves an investigation by patient and analyst of a "dialectically constituted/decentered subject of analysis".

Although he may have disagreed with contemporary technique, I believe Freud would have concurred that working as an analyst is, in itself, a decentring experience. In today's view, however, rather than to gird ourselves against the pulls of engagement, and remain tied to the chair, we have been encouraged to embrace and to follow this decentring experience, since it promises to deepen our work. This is much more complicated and complex than what Reik (1948) had in mind when he suggested that analysts listen with a "third ear". How we listen, think, understand, react, interpret, and interact with our patients is more complex than ever.

Although I believe that these recent developments in our conception of transference have been extremely helpful in broadening the understanding of our co-creation and co-participation in the psychoanalytic dyad, I think that it has made the "hardest part" of the analysis even harder. At a time when we are seeing fewer patients in three or four times per week psychoanalysis, our theory has evolved and informs us that we need to be more aware of our involvement in the analysis than ever before. Fewer patients in analysis mean fewer opportunities to conduct deep analyses and fewer opportunities for us to discover the subtlety of our intended and inadvertent participation in shaping the tenor of the analysis. I would suggest that this combination of fewer opportunities and the greater scope required of our "evenly hovering attention" has made the task of managing the transference more difficult and burdensome, and might cause us to buckle under its weight.

How, you may ask, does this digression into contemporary views of transference relate to the analytic taboo I note at the beginning of this paper? I will attempt to make my position clearer through the discussion of the following clinical material.

Clinical vignette

I had been seeing a middle-aged woman who had been referred to me by a colleague who was seeing her teenage son for treatment. In the course of his therapy, it had become clear to my colleague that issues related to his patient's mother were significant, especially his feeling that she did not understand him and that she was too controlling and perfectionist. She agreed to see me under the condition, as she then stated it to me, "Only if it is to help my son." She had little awareness of her own inner turmoil and certainly would not have sought treatment on her own.

I initially suggested that we meet twice weekly. She wondered if this was excessive, but agreed to this arrangement if I thought it was necessary. She readily deferred to my suggestion, and her demeanour throughout this early phase of our work was co-operative, respectful, and almost ingratiating. She appeared to be the quintessential "good girl" to her ageing parents, her husband, and her four children. She knew how to "get things done" and would frequently wonder concerning our sessions, "How long is this whole thing going to take?"

Her life was her family, and it soon became clear that she had little sense of an internal life, let alone a life of her own outside the demands of wife, mother, and homemaker. She claimed that she had no childhood memories and could not recall anything before the age of ten or eleven. She had no recollection of any dreams either present or past, and seemed not to be able to identify much in the way of emotion except anger and frustration when she could not get things done. These early sessions were filled with material about her son and family. She had almost no awareness of her role in any conflict, and my attempts at interventions always seemed to fall short of moving the work in a more reflective direction. The sessions seemed locked into the boring deadness of manifest content. In fact, the patient would occasionally comment after a brief silence, "I'm stuck." I was not able at that time to say or do enough to help her (and me) become unstuck.

The first time that I felt a sense of hope in our work was when, after one of her pauses, she smiled and sheepishly said, "You know, this is weird, but I keep seeing something in the tiles in your ceiling." Seeming now more painfully shy than compliant, she stated, "I see a little girl's face. It's like she's peering over something, like the back of a chair or couch." She said this with such innocence and naïveté, as if there were a little girl in the ceiling.

She had no associations to this image, or any thoughts as to what seeing this in my ceiling might have to do with her or me. I suggested a number of things to her over the course of the session, including that she might be the little girl who was afraid to peer over the couch at me. She acknowledged being intrigued by my interpretation, but my sense was that she was quite sceptical of my looking beyond the surface meaning of her perception. It was only much later in our work that I learned just how important the issues of seeing and not seeing were to her. Despite my initial hopefulness in that session, subsequent sessions reverted to themes that seemed impenetrable to attempts to move beyond the surface. This manner of working continued for some months.

One day, Mrs C walked into my office with a magazine from my waiting room in her hand. She appeared to be more buoyant and cheerful than was her custom. Before lying down on the couch, she casually asked if she might borrow the magazine. Her question clearly required a direct and immediate answer, since she stood in front of me, waiting. I gestured toward the couch and said, "Let's talk about it."

This was one of those times in treatment where my heart goes nearer to my throat. In microseconds, my thoughts and feelings identified this as a precious moment. I wanted to be careful not to disrupt this gesture from Mrs C, but I also wanted to provide as optimal conditions as I could on the spur of the moment in order that we could best understand what was transpiring. I experienced her request as being for something well beyond the magazine, and I think I recognized some change in her in that she made this request. I suspected that something was now going to change in our relationship that held the promise of moving our work in new directions. I was conscious of not wanting to offend her, or to be off-putting in my demeanour. After all, she just wanted to borrow it. I could have simply said yes, then suggested we take a look at it. But I had a stronger urge to hold the tension of this moment without immediately granting or rejecting her request. I made this decision, as far as I am aware, not because of an adherence to some technical posture, but out of a deep conviction that my taking action via a simple yes or no answer might cause us to miss an opportunity.

I do not believe that everything is analysable. If my first action had been to accept or refuse her request, everything would have been changed. I do not believe that you can have it both ways. That is, I do not believe you can take an action, then step back and say, "OK, what did my agreeing to lend you the magazine mean to you, or my not lending the magazine mean to you?" Coming down on one side of the request or the other mitigates the tension of the moment. I attempted to engage Mrs C in a middle ground, one in which we could both become curious about this obviously new interaction between us.

I realize that my suggestion to Mrs C that we talk about her request is a form of action taken through what might be perceived as the relative "inaction" of reflection. I recognize that everything I say and do, or do not say or do not do, is an enactment. What I am suggesting here is that, for this particular patient and this particular analyst, at that time, the best thing seemed to be to wait. I will never know what might have happened had I simply said, "Sure", or "I don't think it's a good idea."

I have found Aron's (1996) observations about analytic choices particularly helpful in situations such as this. He stated that, as analysts, we are forever making choices in our work. We may listen and intervene differently from one another, and from patient to patient. He argued that there is no one correct way in which to conduct this work, but suggested that we be cognizant of our choices and mindful of the directions alternative paths may have taken us.

I will not go into detail here about the result of my actions with this particular patient. I should add, however, that it was personally very difficult for me not to just lend her the magazine. This is how I would react with a friend, colleague, or even an acquaintance. I demurred with the hope that perhaps we might find something more substantial in her gesture.

I share with you how personally difficult it was for me not to lend her the magazine because it represents one small example of how difficult it is to do the work we do. No matter which analytic choices we make, we must all cope with an enormous amount of restraint. This is a wonderfully intimate and yet strange profession.

As I indicated above, my purpose in presenting this vignette was not to discuss the details of the case, but rather the reactions I received from colleagues. I had the opportunity to present this case in a number of formal and informal settings. Each time I was surprised by how quickly my intervention was negatively judged, even before I explained some of the reasons behind my thinking. The main criticism was that I was being too aloof and withholding and, especially, that I was avoiding deeper engagement with my patient by hiding behind the archaic stance of analytic abstinence. While I cannot say that I particularly enjoy criticism, I am also not new to it. I have learnt a great deal from the critique of my work by teachers, supervisors, and my own analyst. The criticism around this case, however, seemed to be particularly emotionally laden for the critics, and, in turn, for me as well.

I recall having felt particularly stung. First, because I did not see it coming (at least, following my initial presentation of the case material) and second, because I feel that with those colleagues who know me, and especially with my patients, empathic attunement and emotional involvement are characteristic of my work. My initial thought then was that whenever this form of criticism occurred, I was being misunderstood. I wanted to let my peers know just how deeply thought out my position was, and that, based upon the turn that the analysis had then taken with Mrs C, my choice had seemed to work for her. (As I now write this, I recall that, ironically, the first place it took us was that it unleashed a fury that I did not quite know existed within Mrs C.)

After the second or third time that I received similar criticisms, I recognized that being misunderstood and unappreciated felt all too familiar. It was the same way that I felt whenever I attempted to obtain more sessions for my patients from some managed care official, or when I read in the newspaper about some new breakthrough in understanding the genetic and/or biochemical basis of emotional problems, or when I saw heavily financed advertising campaigns for the newest psychoactive drug. It was at times like these that it was difficult for me to feel valued and appreciated as an analyst.

I know that what psychoanalysis has to offer is rare and unique. Undergoing analysis has been a life-changing experience that has helped me grow in directions that, before analysis, I could not have conceived. I have had the pleasure to incorporate this experience into a rewarding career and to participate in the life-changing growth I witness in my patients. I tend to eschew certainty because it might limit discovery, but I am certain that analysis is the best form of treatment available.

I therefore find it frustrating that the public perception of psychoanalysis is that it is outmoded. I think there are many reasons for this perception and that we bear responsibility for some of these. (For a more thorough exploration of these reasons, see Prince, 1999.) Additionally, I find it frustrating not seeing patients with greater frequency. I recognize that there are things I cannot seem to help patients with in once-weekly therapy. While I still try to work as analytically as possible, I know that the limited time does not provide the safety and containment needed to reach certain states that need to be reached in order to be of most help. This is something to which I have given much thought in terms of making analysis more accessible and affordable to my patients. In the clinical example above, I might have acted differently if I knew that I would not see Mrs C for another week, rather than in two days. The deprivation (for me and for her) would have been too much. In not acceding to her request, I had the conviction that I had something that I thought was more valuable to offer: the resurrection of discarded aspects of herself in the transference. The existence of the transference is unalterable, but intensity facilitates its emergence.

I believe that I am not alone in my frustration. In fact, my thesis is that the taboo comments made to me that I cited at the beginning of this chapter serve as a barometer for similar sentiments among my colleagues: that we are all, to varying degrees, feeling some sense of professional devaluation. The content of these taboo statements reflects the leading edge of our sense of devaluation. The joke contained in the first comment, "At my current fee, I couldn't afford to see myself," is particularly revealing. Through poking fun at himself, the analyst is saying that he has become so important that few can afford to see him. This addresses his anxiety concerning rejection by the general populace. A second meaning of his statement suggests that he cannot afford to see himself. Oddly, then, his taboo joke serves the compromise of concealing by revealing. He can reveal to himself, and his friend, that he worries about the decline in his analytic practice, but perhaps conceals from himself ("I couldn't afford to see myself") that this is something at which he, and the rest of us, need to take a closer look.

I apologize to my friend and colleague if he recognizes his comment. He should not take offence, any more than should the little boy who had the courage to announce that the emperor had no clothes. We do have clothes. It is just that we may need to be a bit more self-aware, especially with respect to issues that may threaten our self-esteem. As we have discovered in our work with patients and in our own analyses, the taboo subject is not as terrible as having had to keep it a secret. It is to the subtle effects of this particular analytic secret that I would now like to turn as I conclude.

There is another rendering of the taboo comments that I originally cited, a rendering of which you have undoubtedly been aware. One shared meaning among the comments is that they are all self-deprecating. In effect, the joke is on us. There is also, however, a not so thickly veiled hostility toward the patient who does not find a way to avail himself/herself of our artistry (analysis as a "fine painting"). Beneath the hurt of rejection, and the soothing illusion of good humour at our plight, lies the anger of condescension directed at those who would not more fully appreciate us.

This reminds me of another taboo involving a "humorous" story told to me by another analyst regarding one of his patients. The previous night there had been a flood in a bathroom located above my colleague's office. He returned to work the next day to find that, because of the water damage, a large piece of plaster had fallen from the ceiling and had left a gaping hole. He was able to remove the chunk of plaster before his first patient arrived, but repair of the ceiling had to wait. My colleague then began to describe to me the various reactions of his patients when they lay down on the couch and first noticed the hole. Each of his patients had some comment or question for him, except one. This particular patient lay down on the couch as usual and, without missing a beat, launched into a recapitulation of the events of the weekend. My colleague complained to me that this patient was totally unaware of anything but himself, and that the patient was particularly unaware of him, the analyst, as a person. The analyst punctuated his story by declaring, "I could greet him at the door with an axe sticking out of the side of my head, and he would simply walk past me and lie down and begin talking about his weekend."

My colleague is a good analyst. He is also human. He had a very human reaction. He needed to have his patient notice that something had happened to his office, and, in some sense, to him. Since the event so obviously intruded into the treatment in the form of a gaping hole, it might have, for my colleague and his other patients, brought some small fragment of the realities of my colleague's life into the foreground, if only briefly. Except for this one patient. And it was this patient who stirred my colleague's ire. At that moment, perhaps beclouded by the distraction of an external event (the gaping hole in his office [his practice?]), my colleague's need to be seen and to be appreciated by his patient surfaced.

I recount this story now because it reiterates the dynamics that I think are inherent in the taboo comments the analysts made about patients being unwilling or unable to come for more than once weekly sessions. In an effort to shore up our damaged self-esteem, we might be unwittingly blaming the patient. Our sense of our profession having been devalued, and our own personal sense of devaluation arising from not seeing enough patients with analytic frequency, engenders hostility in us that may be difficult to manage.

Our frustration inevitably will be directed towards our patients. Our unconscious hostility towards our patients for rejecting us might make it difficult to bear their more intense affects, especially their anger towards us, lest we recognize aspects of our own projected hostility. Gray (2000) has re-emphasized that, historically, psychoanalysts had the most difficulty when it came to experiencing and tolerating their patients' aggression. If that aggression were directed at the analyst, it became even more difficult. One of the weaknesses Gray found in contemporary training was that supervision did not seem to assist candidates with their capacity to fully experience their patients' anger. He suggested that many candidates, and many analysts as well, tended to intellectually analyse their patients' anger in the service of distancing themselves from their patients' aggression. Gray observed that we cannot hope to help our patients be less afraid of their aggression if we retreat via a too intellectualized approach.

I am concerned that some degree of the shift in our theory of technique might be similarly influenced. Perhaps some of the desire to be more real to our patients in the form of greater self-disclosure is influenced by our need to defend against awareness of our aggression towards our patients and our concomitant need to defend against awareness of their aggression towards us. Moreover, by becoming friendlier, more forthcoming, and more giving as analysts, we might be unconsciously attempting to mitigate aggression, and unconsciously soliciting appreciation from our patients. In so doing, our patients may become more important to us than might be in their best interest.

In describing the essence of the adolescent's message in what he called "the anti-social tendency", Winnicott (1956) suggested that these dramatic acts "compels the environment to become important". He went on to state that, in such cases,

> There has been a true deprivation; that is to say, there has been a loss of something good that has been positive in a child's experience up to a certain date, and that has been withdrawn. [p. 309]

Although important advances have been made in our theory that have helped us to become more aware of the intersubjective nature and the mutual influence within the analytic dyad, I fear these advances might, at times, be misinterpreted. If we are too quick to act, to disclose, for example, rather than to reflect with the patient, we may be behaving in a manner similar to Winnicott's acting-out adolescent. We have endured true deprivation. All of us, to some degree, have had to contend with modifying our dreams of full-time practices devoted solely to three or four times weekly psychoanalytic patients. Managing this deprivation might sometimes "compel the patient to become important" in our attempts to restore that which has been taken away. We might need our patients' appreciation more than we realize.

Our taboo comments to one another about the practice of psychoanalysis should not remain forbidden inside jokes that we self-consciously share with only our trusted friends. As Freud first noted when he developed his theory of the mind, that which is taboo is that which will provide essential information about unconscious conflict. Rather than being slightly embarrassed by the taboo comments I referred to at the beginning of this paper, we should use them as a valuable source of information about ourselves and the work we do.

References

Aron, L. (1996). *A Meeting of Minds*. Hillsdale, NJ: Analytic Press.

Bergman, M. (1999). Do the enduring controversies within psycho-analysis endanger its future? In: R. M. Prince (Ed.), *The Death of Psychoanalysis: Murder? Suicide? Or Rumor Greatly Exaggerated?* Northvale, NJ: Jason Aronson.

Fiscalini, J. (1993). Interpersonal relations and the problem of narcis-sism. In J. Fiscalini & A. Gray (Eds.), *Narcissism and the Interpersonal Self*. New York: Columbia University Press.

Freud, S. (1905c). *Jokes and their Relation to the Unconscious. S.E., 8*: 1–243. London: Hogarth.

Freud, S. (1905e). *Fragment of an Analysis of a Case of Hysteria. S.E., 7*: 1–122. London: Hogarth.

Gerhardt, J., Sweetnam, A., & Borton, L. (2000). The intersubjective turn in psychoanalysis: a comparison of contemporary theorists: Part I: Jessica Benjamin. *Psychoanalytic Dialogues, 10*: 5–42.

Gill, M. M. (1994). *Psychoanalysis in Transition*. Hillsdale, NJ: Analytic Press.

Gray, P. (2000). On the receiving end. *Journal of the American Psycho-analytic Association, 48*: 219–236.

Hale, N. G. (1999). Does Freud have a future in American psychiatry? In: R. M. Prince (Ed.), *The Death of Psychoanalysis: Murder? Suicide? Or Rumor Greatly Exaggerated?* Northvale, NJ: Jason Aronson.

Langs, R. (1976). *The Bipersonal Field*. New York: Jason Aronson.

Lionells, M. (1999). Thanatos is alive and well in psychoanalysis. In: R. M. Prince (Ed.), *The Death of Psychoanalysis: Murder? Suicide? Or Rumor Greatly Exaggerated?* Northvale, NJ: Jason Aronson.

Morris, W. (Ed.) (1979). *The American Heritage Dictionary*. Boston, MA: Houghton Mifflin.

Ogden, T. (1992). The dialectically constituted/decentered subject of psychoanalysis. I. The Freudian subject. *International Journal of Psycho-Analysis, 73*:417–426.

Prince, R. M. (Ed.) (1999). *The Death of Psychoanalysis: Murder? Suicide? Or Rumor Greatly Exaggerated?* Northvale, NJ: Jason Aronson.

Rachman, A. W. (1999). Death by silence (*Todschweigen*): the traditional method of silencing the dissident in psychoanalysis. In: R. M. Prince (Ed.), *The Death of Psychoanalysis: Murder? Suicide? Or Rumor Greatly Exaggerated?* Northvale, NJ: Jason Aronson.

Reik, T. (1948). *Listening with the Third Ear*. New York: Farrar Straus.

Roazen, P. (1969). *Brother Animal: The Story of Freud and Tausk.* New York: Knopf.

Roazen, P. (1975). *Freud and his Followers.* New York: Knopf.

Roazen, P. (1993). *Meeting Freud's Family.* Amherst, MA: University of Massachusetts Press.

Roazen, P. (1999). Freud's analysis of Anna. In: R. M. Prince (Ed.), *The Death of Psychoanalysis: Murder? Suicide? Or Rumor Greatly Exaggerated?* Northvale, NJ: Jason Aronson.

Winnicott, D. W. (1956). The antisocial tendency. In: D. W. Winnicott (Ed.), *Through Paediatrics to Psychoanalysis* (pp. 306–315). New York: Basic Books, 1975.

PART VII

SELF-DISCLOSURE:
TO DO OR NOT TO DO?

CHAPTER SIXTEEN

Non-countertransferential self-disclosure in psychoanalysis[1]

Daniel Gensler

P sychoanalysts now recognize the value of occasionally telling patients about their own feelings. This possibility developed only after decades of suppressing Ferenczi's early experiments in this area. As Jacobs (1995) noted, the subject of self-disclosure has remained one of the strongest taboos in psychoanalytic practice partially because of the extreme and opposite positions that Freud (1912e) and Ferenczi (1933) took on this subject.

The current literature on self-disclosure has usually described the disclosure of countertransference feelings or ideas, i.e., telling the patient how the therapist feels about the patient and the therapeutic interaction (Ehrenberg, 1995; Maroda, 1991). Self-disclosure usually does not refer to disclosing personal information about the therapist's life. Yet, there are contexts in which sharing such personal information has therapeutic value.

It could be argued that a therapist who discloses personal information about his life to a patient does so out of unanalysed countertransference feelings, and that, therefore, there is no such thing as non-countertransferential self-disclosure. This argument collapses a useful distinction. While self-disclosure regarding personal experiences can certainly occur due to countertransference reasons, understanding its use and meaning is limited if this is the only way to conceive of such self-disclosure. Whatever the countertransference meaning, personal information may be shared for clinical purposes. These purposes might include providing company, relieving isolation, getting out of therapeutic impasses, giving hope, trying to relieve anxiety, modelling, or warning.

It is not a simple matter to propose this. The idea of sharing personal experiences, other than one's experience with the patient, is usually met with disapproval, anxiety, or at least uncertainty by psychoanalytic colleagues. These acts have not been conceived within psychoanalysis as appropriate. They are often met with the suspicion of unanalysed countertransference, wild analysis, or are labelled legitimate but non-psychoanalytic.

In the psychoanalytic literature, telling the patient of one's own life experience has not been considered a legitimate part of an analyst's activities. It has been taboo to consider whether such self-disclosure can be helpful, rather than harmful and wrong. The language used to distinguish countertransference self-disclosure from other kinds of self-disclosure shows the intensity of feelings involved. For example, Jacobs (1995) noted,

> Selective disclosure on the part of the analyst of what he is experiencing in this situation can sometimes be good, but not the disclosing of personal information about the analyst—that is quite another, and even more problematic, matter. [p. 245]

Literature

The subject of disclosure of countertransference feelings has received attention for many years among interpersonal psychoanalytic writers, dating back to the influence of Ferenczi (1933) on Thompson (1957). A review article by Moses & McGarty (1995) touched on the concepts of: participant observation (Sullivan, 1954); directness and giving up a professional façade (Fromm, 1947); analyst and patient as co-participant inquirers into transference and countertransference (Wolstein, 1975); disclosure of one's own dreams to patients (Tauber & Green, 1959); disclosure of negative feelings (Epstein, 1979); disclosure of intimate feelings (Ehrenberg, 1990; Searles, 1979); distinctions between unavoidable, unwitting and deliberate self-revelations (Mann, 1991); and such themes as disclosure of the analyst's pregnancy or illness.

Singer (1977) examined the inadvertent self-disclosure that occurs when a patient comes to understand that an analyst can be particularly empathic because the analyst has had personal experience with the matter about which the patient is talking. He wrote, "What analysts so fondly think of as interpretations are neither exclusively nor even primarily comments about their patients' deeper motivations, but first and foremost self-revealing remarks" (p. 183).

In recent years, the study of countertransference self-disclosure has widened. Burke's (1992) essay analysed a variety of considerations that should underlie the decision to disclose countertransference. What is the primary unit of study, the patient or the relationship? How much understanding should the therapist strive for regarding a self-disclosure before it is made? What are the patient's capacities to tolerate the analyst's disclosure? Who initiates such disclosure, and how frequently?

Renik (1995) argued against the concepts of neutrality and anonymity in psychoanalysis: "A blanket principle of analytic anonymity does not, in fact, help us determine which forms of self-disclosure are likely to oppose and which facilitate analytic investigation" (p. 474). He suggested that analysts try to ensure that a patient is privy to the analyst's own understanding of his or her analytic activity and participation in the analytic work. Renik (1996) advocated that analysts try to become aware of their intention to influence their patients, to realize the implicit judgments inherent in their communications, to recognize the sides they take and the feelings they bring to their choices of interpretation. But he did not refer to self-disclosure to the patient regarding facts about the analyst's life separate from their intentions, acts, and understandings within the treatment relation.

Aron (1996) summarized varieties of self-disclosure. Self-disclosure can be about what the analyst is thinking or feeling while with the patient; thoughts and feelings regarding the interaction between patient and therapist; thoughts the analyst had about the patient outside the treatment setting; why the analyst feels as he or she does, based on the analyst's character and history, or in response to a patient's questions about the analyst.

Disclosing personal information about the therapist's life occurs in therapy in two contexts. It can be in response to the patient's personal questions, such as: "Did you go through this when you were in analysis?" "Do you have these kinds of problems with your wife?" "Did you ever worry about your sexuality?" "Have you ever had the same kind of trouble with mood swings that I do?"

Disclosure of personal information can also be initiated by the therapist: "I think I made that slip not only for the reasons we have discussed regarding what happened between us, but also because something in our interaction reminded me of the way it used to be with people in my family."

A common factor underlies these two contexts: that is, the relationship between therapist and patient. Therapist-initiated self-disclosure can be in response to an unspoken appeal by the patient. The patient may ask personal questions after learning about the therapist's level of comfort with being open about personal matters.

Aron described other distinctions in the ways self-disclosure occurs. For conceptual clarity, these are put as polarities, though usually both occur to some extent. Self-disclosure can be purposeful or inadvertent. It can be considered or spontaneous. It also varies by the content area of what is disclosed. In a case illustration, Aron told a patient about his feelings about his own wife (and about his wife's feelings about him) with very useful effects. He shared this information in response to the patient's question, "Are there important things about your wife that you don't like?" He answered,

> "Yes, there are important things about my wife that I don't like . . . More significant perhaps, there are important things about me that my wife doesn't like . . . You know, there are important things about myself that I don't like—why should she have to like them?" [p. 225]

Aron's self-disclosure modelled tolerating ambivalence, made the patient feel less alone, distracted the patient from his painful feelings, demonstrated that the analyst was not exactly like the patient's father, and was a way for the analyst to show off and possibly outdo or intimidate the patient. Clearly, an act of self-disclosure has complex motives, intentions, and outcomes.

Reviewing other authors on the subject, Aron noted Searles' (1975) preference to reveal feelings and fantasies experienced during the analytic session itself, but not to reveal much about his life outside the office. Aron also noted Maroda's (1991) suggestion that early in treatment analysts share their immediate affective experience, and only later in the analysis reveal the origins of these feelings in their personal lives. Maroda also urged analysts to disclose countertransference feelings only at the patient's request or after having consulted with the patient about doing so.

Greenberg (1995) demonstrated that the analyst does not have a privileged position regarding reality. Even intentional self-disclosure reveals unintended motives and facts about the therapist. He also described how in every self-disclosure there is also self-concealing.

Bromberg (2006) examines how a therapist's decision about self-disclosure comes properly out of a focus on the patient's need for recognition and safety, in light of current enactments and dissociations on the part of both therapist and patient. He sees a therapist's revealing his own feelings about the interaction with the patient as not only inevitable but normal; not only permissible but a necessary part of the clinical process. In his view, going further and disclosing personal biographic information is appropriate when the therapist believes that such disclosure would "deepen an ongoing, affectively alive relational context in which here-and-now process experience is already being shared" (p. 146). Bromberg believes that when the therapist reveals personal history, he is obliged to be as attuned as possible to the patient's response to the therapist's possible motivation for the revelation, as well as to the content of what has been revealed. As one example, the patient could dissociate his own response to the therapist's disclosure, in order not to be overwhelmed affectively by what is taking place between them.

Case example

This topic is complicated to explore with colleagues. An analyst's disclosure of personal information is most genuinely and usefully done in a trusting relation, with analyst trusting the patient as well as the patient trusting the analyst. In such a relationship, both analyst and patient come to believe that the self-disclosure is for the sake of the analysis rather than for other motives. To come to this kind of trust, the analyst would need to work through other possible reasons for his or her self-disclosure. Motives for disclosure, besides being for the sake of the analysis, could include narcissism, impulsive self-indulgence, masochism, dependence, or need for attention. This working through would occur within the analyst and, to the extent that the analyst trusts the patient, between the analyst and the patient.

This kind of trust has usually not been established between an analyst and a professional audience, whether in a conference presentation or in a published article. Without such trust, the analyst presenting work on self-disclosure can become concerned that the self-disclosure will be taken as the expression of bids for attention, display, or punishment, either from the patient or the professional audience.

My patient is a man in his forties, married with two children, working full time and also doing art as a second vocation. He has been in analysis for ten years, three to four times per week. Presenting problems were intense anxiety and self-hatred, sexual problems with his wife, suicidal ideation, and deep uncertainty about his masculinity.

He was the only child of emotionally abusive parents. The family atmosphere was sadomasochistic and sexualized. His mother frequently threatened to beat him, and frequently showed an incestuous interest in him. It was never clear how much beating or incest actually happened.

His sexually exhibitionistic father collected pornography, whips, and bullets. He played a game with his son of torturing him with a thumbscrew to see if his son could take it. He would go to another city on weekends without telling his son or wife why.

My patient was taught to trust no one outside the family and to speak only with his parents about his concerns. He was told he should have been a girl and that he would probably only work in the post office. When he asked his father for help about the homosexual sadomasochistic beating fantasies that troubled him ever since early childhood, he was told that they were a normal variation of sexuality. "There are people like you, you'll get along."

His father was diabetic and obese, intentionally eating all the foods that were destructive to his health. "What does it matter?" he would answer to his son's and wife's pleas that he eat more carefully. He died of diabetic-related diseases when the patient was thirty-two.

When my patient came to analysis, he was tormented by chronic severe anxiety and by masturbation beating fantasies. He would occasionally enact these fantasies by getting himself beaten and tortured. This reduced his anxiety and also expressed the worthlessness that he felt. The fantasies included feeling cared for and understood by the man who beat him. The anxiety involved a profound conviction that he was bad and deserved to be punished. He also had deep inhibitions about trying to do anything to get ahead, and equally severe prohibitions against resting. He was phobic about anxiety itself, interpreting it as a sign that there was something wrong with him for which he was to blame. This was how his parents had always responded when he would complain of anxiety to them. His only relief from anxiety was in masochistic fantasies accompanied by frequent, compulsive masturbation. He also cut calluses off his feet with a knife, sometimes until they bled.

Treatment was stormy. The transference was often negative, especially in the early years. During these times he felt I was, like his father, detached, uncaring, and too neutral regarding tormenting aspects of himself. He treated me the way his mother treated him, demanding frequent verbal assurances of my caring, enquiring about me without regard to my privacy, and raging when I was not forthcoming. I responded by trying to understand the origins of his attitude towards me, recognizing the feelings he was experiencing and their legitimacy, and also arguing for the legitimacy of the frame of therapy, in which he paid me, sessions ended, and I maintained my privacy. He understood cognitively, but during emotional storms he understood emotionally only when there was a concrete sign of my caring for him. Sometimes, he would provoke my anger in order to feel it as a sign of my caring.

I took a position about his upbringing, describing certain aspects of it as incestuous, abusive, wrong, and sadomasochistic. Hearing me take the initiative in making these judgements relieved him of the obsessive worry as to whether he was making it all up just to be perversely unhappy. He felt freer to look at his own personality more closely.

He began to wonder what he was, diagnostically. How should he understand his sharp swings of mood, his alternation in his sense of himself between competent at work yet extremely anxious and lost inside, his dissociated periods, his deep uncertainty about sexuality, his trouble with intimacy with his wife, his intensity and rages, his tendency to act out self-destructively? Were there other people like him? I was a professional, a psychoanalyst: surely I had a construct, a treatment plan, a sense of where we were going and how we were going to get there. We spent time examining the idealization of me, the denigration of me, the effort to control me, and the desperate feelings.

By this time, he was on psychotropic medication (at first, Zoloft and Xanax; currently, Neurontin and Effexor). "Depressed" and "anxious" were not, however, specific enough terms to explain why he had such trouble getting through the day. We had used other terms to explain his troubles, all of which were disturbing to him. We had called it addictive, and he had gone briefly to a group for sexually addicted individuals. The members of that group were also heavily drug involved and he did not identify with them. We had also called his trouble compulsive and masochistic. The word perverse had been used, too.

At one point I told him that "borderline traits" described many of his problems. This was very upsetting to him. He had heard the term used pejoratively. He was also aware that therapists often did not like to work with borderline patients and that they had trouble helping them. He blamed me for not sufficiently preparing him for hearing this term. From the Internet and bookstores he assembled definitions and articles on the borderline concept. He asked his wife what she thought. Looking at the definition, she thought it matched much of what she knew of his problems and personality.

He came to consider that the term might apply to him, with some distinctions between borderline traits and borderline personality disorder. Struggling with his own self-condemnation for having borderline traits, he asked me for some company. He knew I had been in analysis. What was my diagnosis? He knew it was probably different from his, but did I ever go through feeling bad about myself in my own analysis? He would feel less denigrated and alone if I could join him as another person with difficulties.

This was not the first time he had asked me personal questions. Responses aimed at elucidating his associations to the questions he asked me, or his fantasies about the answers, led to intense mistrust and anger on his part, in what became a re-enactment of his relations with both parents. I had raised the issue of privacy as something valuable, both his privacy (which his mother had not respected) and my privacy. When I defended my privacy, he often felt as if I were his father excluding him and demeaning his wishes for closeness. He also felt like his mother, as if the boundaries between us were not important. He was open to considering a new way of thinking about privacy, although it was very painful for him.

I was aware that it was considered inappropriate for analysts to share personal information with their analysands. For example, Greenberg (1995) summarized Freud's concerns that the analyst's self-revelation makes resistances harder to overcome, makes patients insatiable to know more about the analyst, distracts the patient from analysing himself, and makes resolving the transference more difficult. On the other hand, my patient was in terrible pain in his struggle to accept the degree of his difficulty and the relevance of the diagnosis. He was trying to feel some sense of value and humanity to counter his self-denigration and his automatic assumption that he deserved to be punished. Given the impasse we were in and the suffering my patient was experiencing, answering his questions made sense to me.

I decided to answer his questions directly. I told him some of what I had learnt in my own analysis about my character and about how I dealt with anxiety. I also told him a little of its origins in my family, as I understood it. This was relieving to him. He felt company, that I trusted him enough to share something personal and important to me. He felt a mutuality that strengthened him to tolerate his own imperfections, rather than to feel isolated and to blame and punish himself.

He was also anxious about my self-disclosure. Along with believing that it was the right thing to do, he felt that in part he had pushed me into answering his questions, violating my own sense of privacy. So, this encounter felt sadomasochistic and challenging of my boundaries, as well as providing company and mutuality. He felt guilty, as well as satisfied, to have pushed me to answer personal questions.

In a complementary way, I felt anxious about having answered his questions. I wondered if I would regret compromising my privacy and if doing so would interfere with the work we were doing rather than further it. I also knew I was violating a psychoanalytic taboo against this kind of self-disclosure.

The sum of my feelings, however, was that it was appropriate in this context. Over the course of working with this patient, when I have felt this combination of anxiety and faith, I have concluded that the self-disclosure was right.

The results, while mixed, seem to have been worthwhile so far. There are still many times when he loses his orientation, feels worthless, and seeks satisfaction in sadomasochistic relief. These periods, while still intense, are fewer and shorter, and he can recover more quickly. When he loses perspective, he is able to move away from feeling he should be blamed and beaten to rejoin the therapy's purpose and me and act effectively in his own interest.

Feeling safe with me, his anxiety became less pervasive and more manageable, and he could think more clearly. His art has become deeper and richer, more textured, more evocative, and it has received a more positive response as he has become freer to experiment and to risk new modes of expression. His career has progressed substantially. He has used his good analytic ability to assert himself and his opinions, and he has taken on leadership positions at his job.

The progress in his art and career required him to face down shame over having made a mess of things at times. To have this degree of success, he had to turn away from joining an inner voice that condemned him for his anxiety, his perceptions, opinions, and occasional failures. The anxiety was great. It took courage to make these changes, as well as support from me.

He dared to confront his emotional and sexual needs in his marriage, first in the analysis and then openly with his wife. He came to feel the validity of his needs for closeness, and to distinguish the sexualized aspect of the sadomasochistic release from anxiety from other, non-sadomasochistic sexual interests. He started to ask his wife for what he wanted, emotionally and sexually, without sadomasochism, rather than to continue to have sexual intercourse while imagining being beaten. They started marital therapy to help improve their relationship.

Tolerating his wife's differing needs, the limits of her response, while also acknowledging her own interest in improving their love life, has been hard and is the subject of continued work. This work requires support from me and courage from him in order to face the anxiety. I have hope for this work because of the progress he has already made. He has also protected his children by not perpetuating on them the abusive upbringing he suffered.

My patient and I both believe that if I had not revealed important aspects of myself and if I had not continued to do so at other important junctures since then, the treatment would have had to stop. It was critical for him to feel that his problems were not his fault, and he could not feel this without hearing that others, myself included, have had to deal with personal troubles.

He could understand cognitively the difference between my maintaining my privacy and his father's detachment, but he could not tolerate the negative transference emotionally unless I was forthcoming at critical moments about myself. I came to believe that this kind of self-disclosure, negotiating my wish for privacy and my wish to respond to his need, as well as all the emotional involvement that accompanied it, was necessary for our work to continue.

I made other self-disclosures about my values. I told him that I hated violence. I told him I preferred values of growth and affirmation. I told him I valued effort over outcome. I told him that his problems were not his fault (a very different attitude from the one he grew up with), that they were his responsibility to try to do something about, and that I believed that this was true for all of us, including me. I also told him I thought acts that physically hurt him were not good for him and that he should try to stop getting himself beaten.

Hearing me tell him these values of mine was a complicated experience for him. He felt cared for, very differently from the way he felt when his father simply accepted that he liked to get beaten. He also worried that I did not really care about him, that I was only giving prescriptions with no personal interest in helping him. We had to analyse the hostility and despair in finding my caring never good enough.

He also found the new orientation deeply confusing, because, in telling him my values, I was inviting him to join me in those values and to separate from the sadomasochistic values he grew up with. The risk of leaving his parents behind, of turning away from their internalized voices and joining me, was scary to him. The shame of needing me so deeply was also painful.

These self-disclosures, as well as answering other personal questions, being responsive, and struggling with him through many episodes of doubt, resulted in his feeling able to trust and depend on me, feelings he never felt before, except in sadomasochistic enactments. He now turned to me for the sense of caring and close-ness that he had only felt before with the men who beat him, in fantasy or reality.

He had periods of intense dependence and attachment to me that both disturbed and gratified him. As he came to trust me to be steady during these periods, he became more able to experience periods of separateness and independence that were similarly disturbing and gratifying. Another discussion of values arose in this context: the value of independence as well as dependence, especially regarding his and my definitions of masculinity.

Trying to understand my patient's combination of deep depen-dence and effectively autonomous functioning, I have found Balint's (1968) concepts of benign and malignant regression useful, but too dichotomous. Benign regression, for Balint, allows a "new beginning" in a mutually trusting relation. This new beginning allows recognition of the patient's problems and is only moderately intense in its demands on the therapist. Malignant regression involves periodic breakdowns in the trusting atmosphere, frequent symptoms of desperate clinging, high intensity of demands, and the presence of genital or orgiastic elements, often in patients whom he described as having severe hysterical character disorders. The term borderline is not found in the index of his 1968 book, *The Basic Fault: Therapeutic Aspects of Regression*, but that diagnosis describes this kind of patient.

I have seen both kinds of regression in my patient. The kind Balint called "malignant" occurred under two circumstances. On my side, I sometimes rushed him into working on solutions before he felt emotional recognition and validation of the problem from me. On his side, he sometimes could not at first see any emotional difference between me and his parents (usually his father). He had to make a psychic space between his experiences of being with his father and being with me, and go through a period of working through the difference between us. This occurred when his requests for response from me went beyond what I felt able or comfortable providing, or when the responses I did have were too reminiscent of how his parents used to respond to him. We have always been able to restore our balance, usually painfully for us both, but at a more productive level, by processing such tense periods as genuinely as possible.

I have also been explicit in suggesting that he rely on me and on the therapy, rather than silently to hope that he do so. Suggesting this has raised the spectre of "fostering dependence", a spectre that was uncomfortable for us both. Dealing with it required both of us to consider our personal objections to having a patient rely on an analyst and to have an analyst suggest that a patient do so. We examined the positives and negatives for him of depending on me and of being independent of me.

Believing that our way of working is the right one for us is not a static matter. It is constantly challenged, reworked, and achieved again as we work through these issues.

Since this whole examination has been productive, and since it has been mutual rather than arising solely from the patient's side or mine, I find the term "malignant regression" a poor choice to describe a complicated, but useful process. I prefer to think of the process as working through periods that include frightening feelings of need and vulnerability, intense transference and countertransference related to those feelings, and painful times when the patient acted out. The latter occurred when the disruption in the therapy relationship was temporarily too much to tolerate.

I have discussed disclosures I made in this analysis related to my character style and its origins, and others related to my values. Another kind of disclosure became necessary, one more familiar in the literature on self-disclosure. I needed to disclose my countertransference, especially to admit when I was responding defensively. Sometimes, when I made formulations about his painful experience without spending time acknowledging the painful feeling itself, he felt rushed and confronted me angrily. At these times I defended my right to formulate and interpret his experience, and objected to his effort to dictate what I said and when I said it. He, in turn, confronted me with becoming defensive. It became valuable for the therapy for me to admit my defensiveness. To admit this, however, I had to make a distinction between my unwillingness to participate in a sadomasochistic enactment in the therapeutic relationship (by submitting to his angry criticism of me) and my acknowledgment that I did sometimes tend to leave him unbearably alone (by interpreting prematurely) without first acknowledging the emotional pain of what I was interpreting.

Summary

There is a powerful degree of closeness, and certainly risk and trust, involved in engaging in this kind of self-disclosure. I have referred to three kinds of self-disclosure in this case regarding some of my own diagnostic and characterological issues, my personal values (for example, about violence, injury, dependence, independence, masculinity), and my defensiveness. To engage in this kind of self-disclosure, for the purposes of offering company, support, and a new kind of example, leads to an intimacy with the patient. This intimacy involves both anxiety and pleasure. The intimacy, with its anxiety and its pleasure, should be acknowledged, including acknowledging it openly with the patient when to do so affords the recognition the patient needs.

Disclosure of personal information about the analyst, including countertransference and non-countertransference information, can occur productively with all patients, not just those with problems as difficult and painful as those of the patient I have been describing. Caution must be exercised. Dangers of such self-disclosure were described by Freud (1912e), referred to respectfully by many analysts since Freud, and reviewed above. These considerations are vital when the analyst is deciding when not to disclose countertransference feelings or personal information. Yet, I found with the patient I have been describing, that self-disclosure got us out of impasses, did not lead to an insatiable need to know more and more about me, and inevitably deepened the patient's self-knowledge, all contrary to the classical predictions and concerns.

Disclosure of countertransference or non-countertransference feelings and facts about the analyst can be useful when resistances and negative transferences are entrenched, when the therapist has made a painful or telling slip, during treatment impasses, and when the patient is stuck in feelings of isolation or despair. At these times, disclosure of both countertransference feelings and of personal information can have an effect quite different from the dangers Freud noted, not harming, but helping. Such disclosure is actually necessary at times to further the analysis. Additional study would be necessary to determine with greater specificity the nature of these contexts. When is disclosure of personal, non-countertransferential information useful? When is it not? When is it harmful?

Does it depend on the presence of impasse, intense negative countertransference, or the patient's isolation? For further study to occur, there must be a greater sense of legitimacy and openness regarding these questions. Anecdotes and comments from colleagues suggest that disclosure of non-countertransferential information about the analyst is more common than the literature would suggest. It is time to lift the taboo against discussing it.

References

Aron, L. (1996). *A Meeting of Minds: Mutuality in Psychoanalysis.* Hillsdale, NJ: Analytic Press.

Balint, M. (1968). *The Basic Fault: Therapeutic Aspects of Regression.* New York: Brunner Mazel.

Bromberg, P. M. (2006). *Awakening the Dreamer: Clinical Journeys* (Chapter 7, pp. 128–150). Mahwah, NJ: Analytic Press.

Burke, W. (1992). Countertransference disclosure and the asymmetry/ mutuality dilemma *Psychoanalytic Dialogues,* 2: 241–271.

Ehrenberg, D. (1990). Playfulness in the psychoanalytic relationship. *Contemporary Psychoanalysis, 26:* 74–95.

Ehrenberg, D. (1995). Self-disclosure: therapeutic tool or indulgence? *Contemporary Psychoanalysis, 31:* 213–228.

Epstein, L. (1979). The therapeutic function of hate in the countertransference. In: L. Epstein & A. Feiner (Eds.), *Countertransference* (pp. 213–234). New York: Jason Aronson.

Ferenczi, S. (1933). Confusion of tongues between adults and the child. In: *Final Contributions to the Problems and Methods of Psycho-Analysis.* London: Karnac, 1980.

Freud, S. (1912e). Recommendations to physicians practising psychoanalysis. *S.E., 12:* 111–120.

Fromm, (1947). *Man For Himself.* New York: Henry Holt.

Greenberg, J. (1995). Self-disclosure: is it psychoanalytic? *Contemporary Psychoanalysis, 31:* 193–205.

Jacobs, T. (1995). Discussion of Jay Greenberg's paper. *Contemporary Psychoanalysis, 31:* 237–245.

Mann, C. (1991). Self-disclosure on the part of the therapist and its meaning in the treatment process. Presented at the Georgia Association of Psychoanalytic Psychology, Atlanta, Georgia.

Maroda, K. (1991). *The Power of Countertransference: Innovations in Analytic Technique.* New York: Wiley.

Moses, I., & McGarty, M. (1995). Anonymity, self-disclosure and expressive uses of the analyst's experience. In: M. Lionells, J. Fiscalini, C. Mann, & D. Stern (Eds.), *Handbook of Interpersonal Psychoanalysis* (pp. 661–675). New York: Analytic Press.

Renik, O. (1995). The ideal of the anonymous analyst and the problem of self-disclosure. *Psychoanalytic Quarterly*, *64*: 466–495.

Renik, O. (1996). The perils of neutrality. *Psychoanalytic Quarterly*, *3*: 495–517.

Searles, H. (1975). The patient as therapist to his analyst. In: P. Giovacchini (Ed.), *Tasks and Techniques in Psychoanalytic Therapy, Volume Two* (pp. 95–151). New York: Jason Aronson.

Searles, H. (1979). *Countertransference and Related Subjects*. New York: International Universities Press.

Singer, E. (1977). The fiction of analytic anonymity. In: K.A. Frank (Ed.), *The Human Dimension in Psychoanalysis* (pp. 181–192). New York: Grune & Stratton.

Sullivan, H. S. (1954). *The Psychiatric Interview*. New York: Norton.

Tauber, E., & Green, M. (1959). *Prelogical Experience*. New York: Basic Books.

Thompson, C. (1957). *Psychoanalysis: Evolution and Development*. New York: Grove Press.

Wolstein, B. (1975). Countertransference: the psychoanalyst's shared experience and inquiry with the patient. *Journal of the American Academy of Psychoanalysis*, *3*:77–90.

CHAPTER SEVENTEEN

Analytic safety through the analyst's availability as a subject

Anton Hart

Introduction

What is it that makes another person *safe* to be with, particularly during the process of self-discovery and self-articulation characterizing the deepest, most growth enhancing analytic relationships? Is it that the other person has such a benign personality that in its absence of character it presents little that would impinge? Is it that the person is so ethical that all potential transgressions are kept in check? Is it an absence of desire that inherently secures by limiting the threats of expectation and demand? Is it the other's willingness to be fully open, even about private matters, such that the threat of there being unknown motivations—a hidden agenda—is neutralized?

Current understandings of the nature of all relationships, but particularly the relationship between analyst and analysand, suggest that each of these conceptions of interpersonal safety is, in some way, flawed. Complete openness is an impossibility, since the analyst's mental life is largely unconscious and, thus, unavailable, at least intentionally, for being absolutely revealed. Neither the analyst nor the analysand can ever become fully known. Bion's

(1967) injunction notwithstanding, it is hard to imagine a relationship devoid of desire; it is necessary to describe the most therapeutically compassionate relationships as thoroughly imbued with *passion*, fraught with the forces and the ambiguities of relational give and take. Ethics, while providing necessary foundations for the practice of psychoanalysis, fall short of providing a relationally dynamic and context-sensitive hedge against human imperfection and the complexity that accompanies it. And the ideal of a fully analysed analyst who will refrain from contaminating the analytic relationship with countertransference has been abandoned by all but the most idealistically wishful among us.

So, in the absence of a simply kind, fully analysed, impeccably ethical, desire-free, and freely disclosing analyst, how might the analysand become safe enough to risk the necessary losses (Bollas, 1999) of personal transformation ideally presented by the analytic endeavour?

The analyst's availability as a subject: the "analyst–analysand"

I propose that the key to the analysand's safety is the analyst's openness in the form of availability as a subject of analysis. There are two basic components of such availability:

1. *In relation to self*: the analyst perpetually engages his or her own associative experience while working, much as he would if he were in a personal analysis, approaching the work with the assumption that there are two analysands in the room, both of whom are involved in the unconsciously unfurling process of immediate experience. Although the primary focus is on the analysand, both analysand and analyst stand to be changed by the analytic experience.
2. *In relation to other*: the analyst continually strives to cultivate an internal state of receptivity to information about the analysand's experience of the analyst, both positive and negative, fantasy-based and reality-based, implicitly or explicitly communicated. Persistent effort is made to convey a willingness to be the (optional) object of the analysand's exploration, interpretation, supervision and criticism.

The analysand is secured to the extent that the analyst is both able to be available in these ways while, at the same time, not insisting on recognition of this availability. The overall focus on the analysand is retained, despite the analyst's working in a state of preparation to be scrutinized all along.

I consider my formulation of such a radically available "analyst–analysand" to go beyond a conceptualization of judicious self-disclosure (e.g., Stricker & Fisher, 1990) and to represent a resurrection of the idea of mutual analysis as first conceived by Ferenczi (1932) and his counterpart, RN. I intend here to develop the idea of an analytic praxis that is at once mutual and, at the same time, quite devoted in its orientation towards the growth enhancing, analytic needs of the analysand. I am incorporating the premise of mutuality, but, at the same time, defining necessary asymmetries that address some of the difficulties that have been associated with considerations of mutual analysis. The difficulties have been, most notably, the risks of exploitation of the analysand by the analyst, destructive attack of the exposed analyst by the (unaccountable) analysand, and a general sense of chaos and confusion about the direction and purpose of the analytic process.

There were significant reasons for Ferenczi's considering an attempt at mutual analysis when it was proposed to him by his patient, RN. Here is an abbreviated (and fictionalized) account of the exchange between them: RN said to Ferenczi, "Listen, I notice that there are some things that I cannot speak freely about in my sessions with you because I detect some qualities of your personality that interfere with my doing so. I sense that I could get in trouble with you if I am completely open. You are not yet analysed sufficiently for me to trust you enough to thoroughly address the issues that I need to as your patient."

"I follow what you are saying," said Ferenczi, admirably careful not to attempt to talk—read interpret—his patient out of her negative perceptions of him. "My trying to be a good analyst to you is not enough. What can be done?"

"Let's take turns," replied RN. If you are willing to submit yourself to me as an analysand, I will have the opportunity to learn more clearly about that which is dangerous in you and what is just my transference, the fears I bring with me from the past. I'll also have a chance to cure you of the particular pathologies you possess which pose the greatest danger to me given my own vulnerabilities."

Ferenczi already had significant experience in usefully working with patients' negative perceptions of him. He did not have the initial impulse to fault the patient when criticized, unlike other practitioners of his day, Freud included. (This is, perhaps a crucial ingredient in Ferenczi's apparent clinical giftedness in work with those who were most damaged; he developed an approach to the analytic process which emphasized the actuality of those things from which the patient was suffering, be they abuse at the hand of a parent or mistreatment in the conduct of the analyst.) Ferenczi balked at first in response to RN's request. Primarily, I think, he was concerned by the potential for exploitation, or at least the appearance of such, by himself as the ultimately responsible analyst.

Eventually, he did give in to RN's persistence. It would take me too far afield to address the details of what went wrong during the course of the experiment in mutual analysis that unfolded. Suffice it to say that RN's (apparently hard-earned) interpersonal destructiveness and Ferenczi's (apparently equally hard earned) masochism conspired against the experiment having a successful outcome. (See Ragen and Aron's [1993] discussion of Ferenczi's experiments with mutual analysis for an excellent exploration of the issues with which Ferenczi struggled at the time.) The latent wisdom in the co-created idea of mutual analysis would remain submerged in the years following the end of Ferenczi's experiments with mutual analysis and his untimely death.

I trace the lineage of my current reconsideration of the analyst as co-analysand back to Freud, who relied upon himself as analytic subject for the well-spring of his clinical and theoretical ideas, through Ferenczi, who courageously chose not to withhold explicit exploration of his psyche from his analysands, to Sullivan, who, influenced by Ferenczi via Clara Thompson, radically interpersonalized theory and practice, to Wolstein (e.g., Hirsch, 2000), who forcefully characterized analysis as being, in principle, mutual (yet not necessarily symmetrical in practice, with the analyst being inextricably linked to the analysand in a process of personal co-exploration and evolution). Other authors who have contributed to my current thesis include Searles, Wilner, Epstein, Bollas, and Ogden, each of whose contribution I will now briefly summarize as it pertains to my thesis.

Searles (1979) has written of the patient's basic need to be a therapeutic agent in relation to others, particularly the parents and then the analyst. He described such a need as originating from earliest childhood, usually incurring a significant amount of frustration, since the parents own insecurities have rendered them far from receptive to the shame associated with their child's curative attempts. For the purposes of the current discussion, there are two aspects of Searles' observations that I want to highlight. First, the analysand is constantly (though largely unconsciously) attuned to the analyst's emotional life, including that which is unconscious to the analyst. This is the case despite life experience having taught the analysand to subjectively obscure and externally conceal his persistent interpersonal curiosity in relation to the care-taking figure. Second, the analysand has a particular interest in serving as a *therapeutic* agent for those in whose care he resides, and upon whom he depends. In recognizing these things, Searles sought to participate in his analytic role in such a way that would both enable the analysand to feel he could be curious about the analyst's problems (without penalty of paranoid retaliation) and to receive and acknowledge the actual therapeutic impact that the analysand might have.

In a series of articles focusing on the analyst's using his immediate experience when working, Wilner (1998, 1999, 2000), influenced by Wolstein (e.g., 1994), has taken the use of the analyst's unprocessed associations as the primary vehicle for generative communication with the analysand. Immediate, interactive experience supersedes meta-theoretically informed interpretation and also intentional containing or holding functions. Wilner tries to present what comes to his own mind in parallel to the analysand's attempting also to do so. It is through the largely unconscious and emergent interplay of these two members of the analytic dyad that vividly rendered analytic truth can emerge, unencumbered by the veneer of theoretical allegiance. Wilner counters the assumption that such associative openness on the analyst's part is inherently dangerous or prone to misdirection. Instead, he argues, such openness enables a deeper and more vivid exploration of defensive relating.

Ogden's (1994, 1997) concept of "reverie" parallels and, I think, complements Wilner's expressive approach to the analyst's associations. He describes a contrasting emphasis on the cultivation of a private, internal state that is perpetually receptive to spontaneous associations during the process of analytic listening. Most of Ogden's associations are not directly articulated to the analysand; they represent the internal part of the analyst's dialogue with the analysand's own associations. Ogden attempts to maintain fidelity to the analysand's unconscious process through refined attunement to his own emergent experience. Deepening the Freudian tradition, he essentially engages in self-analysis as he works in the role of analyst to his analysand. Behind his apparently reserved temperament there is a stance of radical receptivity to emergent experience of self and other.

The contribution of Bollas (e.g., 1989, 1992, 1999) is also relevant to my discussion. Working within an avowedly interpretive tradition, Bollas attempts to create a condition in himself of maximal receptivity to his own associative process and he tries to bring his associations out when he believes his analysand is prepared to receive them as things to be used and played with. He draws on his own associative process, which he regards as consistently pertinent to the analysand's own associative process, in forming interpretive thoughts which are offered to the analysand for consideration. In this way, paralleling the others I have cited, analysis is carried out largely in the form of the analyst's self-analysis in the presence of the analysand. The analysand is indeed invited to engage his own associations and interpretations with those of the analyst. There are, thus, two persons engaged in both receptive–associative and interpretive activities at any moment during the course of an analysis. Yet, the parallel analysing stops short of being fully mutual, since Bollas sees the analyst's associative process mostly as a vehicle for the analysand's own unconscious elaboration. The analyst's "off the wall" thoughts are shared because they are viewed as induced. The analyst offers his associations so as to present the analysand with (unconscious) aspects of himself.

One more critical contribution must be noted before proceeding with my own ideas regarding the necessity of the analyst's availability as a subject of analysis. Epstein (1987, 1999) has emphasized the importance of the analyst's attention to, and receptivity to, communications from the analysand about his own negative impact upon the analysand, his own contribution to the analysand's sense of danger. Influenced by both interpersonal and object relations traditions, Epstein also builds on technical innovations introduced by Spotnitz (e.g., 1976). Spotnitz emphasized the necessity of the analyst's attention to resistances in the analysand, particularly those derived from the analysand's unconscious responses to perceived threatening aspects of the analyst's participation. He saw the illumination of transference resistance as having the primary purpose of freeing the analysand to continue using the ideally nourishing, maturational relationship that the analyst could potentially provide. Resistance analysis was not for the purpose of uncovering unconscious issues for their own sake. Instead, it was for helping the analysand to go on speaking freely to the analyst when transference issues were interfering with this. Taking things a step further, Epstein emphasizes paying attention to the actual (that is, not simply transference derived) negative impact that the analyst will inevitably have at moments in any analysis. For Epstein, it is the recognition of the analyst's counter-therapeutic impact that is most difficult for the analysand to bring forth. The analysand fears both the analyst's narcissistic collapse and the possibility of retaliation should he report this to the analyst. The analyst tries to convey that, despite these fears, he wants to hear about what he is doing that might be hurting. In attempting to secure the analysand in this essential way, the analyst attempts to cultivate conditions under which the analysand learns that he may speak freely about what the analyst's participation seems to be doing to him. The analyst tries to position the analysand as uniquely qualified to inform the analyst about what is good for him and what is not. The analysand's demarcations of negative impact are regarded as crucial pieces of information that will serve to guide the analyst in her work with the analysand. Their articulation might also help to detoxify them for the analysand. In this way, Epstein places the analyst in the position of being a subject of scrutiny for the analysand. The analyst strives to listen carefully to what the analysand is able to tell about the analyst's impact.

For these authors, taken together, safety is created for the analysand through the analyst's continuing efforts to be maximally in touch with his own capacity for associative experience while, at same time, taking a stance which communicates openness to the analysand's associations, "supervisory consultation", and criticism. The analysand's associations and supervision of the analyst ideally have the latitude—conveyed by the analyst's willingness to be used and scrutinized as a subject—to address *anything*, including detected aspects of the analyst that might be outside of the analyst's awareness. From this perspective, each analytic dyad would, in a sense, be comprised of two people actually in analysis: an analysand and an analyst–analysand. The primary therapeutic project is directed towards the analysand, yet the analyst–analysand aspires to being equally subject to the prospect of being moved, surprised, questioned, interpreted, discovered, or transformed. Simultaneously, the analyst–analysand is continually ready to receive communications from the analysand about negative impact and to take such communications as potentially useful, at least as supervisory indications that potentially reveal things about the analyst that the analyst could not have discovered alone.

This way of working goes beyond the idea of *using* "self-disclosure" as a way of enhancing the analytic process (Stricker & Fisher, 1990). The analyst's radical availability as a subject is not just an enhancement. It is the basis for analytic work. In order for the analysand to engage in the destabilizing process of psychoanalysis, the analyst must be willing to provide a context within which the analysand can sense him and explore him as an analytic subject.

The analyst's achievement of ongoing subjective openness

To be capable of the kind of responsive and responsible presence that Searles, Wilner, Ogden, Bollas, and Epstein portray requires of the analyst not so much achievement of character perfection, but, rather, the profound recognition of the complexity and elusiveness of personal and relational experience. To be an analyst–analysand, to be a subject of the analysis while working, involves a basic acceptance of the vast unknown-ness of one's own being and an awareness that one can be accurately known by others in ways that one is not known by oneself. Thus, it requires, in addition to humility, a stance that is never easy: a receptivity to the unexpected in each new analysis, in each session, ultimately in each moment. This involves a willingness to be changed, to risk being disturbed by the generative power of analytic revision as it transpires. I mean this quite emphatically: the analyst must be willing to be altered by each analysis in unforeseen ways, and will inevitably be changed when the analyst and the analysand are able to become truly engaged with each other.

It is not just that the analyst is *intellectually* aware of the unknown-ness of being. It is that he comes to experience his life as imbued with ambiguity, complexity, mystery, and unconsciousness. The analyst comprehends that he is largely unknown to himself and is always in the emergent process of self-discovery. In order to be a safe enough figure for the analysand, the analyst must approach his work ready both to work as an analyst and to be in it as well. It is the analyst's forgetting his own mysteriousness to himself that presents the primary source of danger to the analysand. This is so due to the fact that the analyst, in losing sight of his own subjective, relational emergence, has lost his ability radically to be a subject of analysis for self and for analysand. When the analyst is unavailable in this manner, the analysand loses the ability to process openly the danger-presenting aspects of the analyst in a way that could be received by (and potentially mutative for) the analyst himself.

A deep experience in personal analysis for the analyst in training (and beyond) *is* crucial. Theoretical tradition and psychoanalytic training praxis have held this to be so. Perhaps, however, it is not for the reasons that have traditionally been given, those having to do with analysing personal defects away so that they will not impinge on the analyst's "sound" conduct of the analysand's analysis. The real function of the personal analysis is the instilment in the analyst-to-be of a sense of the enduringly unconscious, ever-emergent, relationally constituted nature of who he is. Only when the analyst has had an analytic experience that has made this fact both self-evident and tolerable can he proceed in doing analysis without losing sight of this inherently self-destabilizing fact.

If the analysand is in possession of an analyst who both knows himself well and, yet, has a reliable sense of her own inherent personal obscurity, then the analysand can be free enough to explore the emergent contours of who the analyst is (and who the analyst becomes) during the process of working together. When the analyst has received this wisdom from her own analysis, she will be forever willing to have others serve in an analytic role in relation to her. Going through a deep analysis—perhaps all too rare an occurrence, given the common level of fear of such a potentially mutative endeavour—leaves one open, poised to make analytic gains in all subsequent interpersonal relationships. Such openness has no natural endpoint; it is, like curiosity, self-perpetuating. It is through this analyst's willingness to have the analysand play an analytic role in relation to the analyst that the analysand might hope to know the analyst and to help the analyst grow in ways that might be necessary for the analysand's own growth experience in relation to the analyst. This is the analysand's best hope for safety when facing the potentially perilous, destabilizing process of analysis. In encountering an analyst who is at once self-possessed and, at the same time, beholden to the vastness of that which is unknown, the analysand is finding an other who has real potential for providing a form of nurturance that is able to address both growth needs and safety needs.

Since a primary vehicle for the analyst's participation as analyst–analysand is the analyst's privileging of his own associative experience, the analysand attains increasing levels of interpersonal safety because he is with someone who is striving to be available as an analytic subject, aiming to counter his own tendency towards defensive mystification. The level of therapeutic responsiveness made possible by such analytic subjecthood on the analyst's part is not attained in any other way. No therapeutic stance derived from a position that precedes contact with the analysand can be responsive to the analysand as well as one that is transactionally based through the medium of subjective availability. Only through this dual role is the analyst able to be maximally resonant and non-intrusive at the same time. The resonance is borne of the willingness to be psychologically transformed by contact with the analysand in multiple ways. The non-intrusiveness comes from the fact that the analyst who is willing truly to be an analytic subject will be tremendously less likely than one who is not to use interaction with the analysand to mask, dissociate, or otherwise obscure anxiety-driven, intolerable aspects of self-experience engendered by encountering the analysand. The analysand has more access to the analyst's total subjectivity. Said another way, the analysand's safety with the analyst comes from the analyst's ongoing curiosity about, and associative engagement with, his or her self. This associative engagement militates against the analysand being insidiously used by the analyst as a vehicle for interpersonal extrusion of intolerable self-states.

Analytic disruption

Let me briefly state why I believe the issue of safety is so vital to an analytic relationship. It has to do with a sense in which psychoanalysis is inherently dangerous in that it seeks to disturb in the name of opening up new prospects for the analysand. This agenda of disturbing is inherent in the activities of "free" association, associative listening, or reverie, interpretation, and detailed inquiry. I have written about this destabilizing essence of analysis elsewhere, advocating an essentially disruptive role for the analyst through which change is made possible (Hart, 1999). I argued that the analyst intends to engender a generative sort of disruption that serves as a catalyst for the analysand's enlivenment and expansion. Only through the disturbance of conservative, limiting aspects of the analysand may hidden, alive aspects emerge. I illustrated that such expansion does not occur without a real sense of risk. Thus, I detailed the ambivalence and anxiety experienced by both analysts and analysands in relation to this subversive aim of the analytic process.

For such an aim to be fulfilled, there must be sufficient safety as the backdrop for disruption. This safety must be experienced by both analysand and analyst. Only in the context of such safety can their resistances to analytic disruption be surmounted. In the absence of such safety, there are too many potent defences against the analytic process having deep impact. Such defences, fuelled by annihilation anxiety, parallel those defences of everyday life, the characterological, stasis-maintaining ways people perpetuate stability in self-limiting efforts to be secure. These represent the reasons people often become increasingly resistant to change as they get older; they acquire greater skill in diminishing spontaneity and limiting the unpredictable impact of authentic engagement with others, and come to experience such skill as the foundation of their survival.

Given the backdrop of annihilatory dread derived from the truly threatening, disturbing, "undoing" agenda of psychoanalysis, a counterbalancing context of safety becomes crucial. In order to submit to such a process, the participants must have a sufficient sense of relational security. The purpose of designating the analyst as the "analyst–analysand" is to structure the analytic relationship in such a way that the analyst will be striving to be psychically accessible—to self and other—when in the analytic role. The designation, "analyst–analysand," places in the foreground the inherent, conscious, and unconscious co-participation characterizing the analytic relationship and seeks to promote the analyst's willingness to be available as a full participant. The analyst must be reachable, potentially available for the growth-enhancing efforts of the analysand. It is from such an analyst–analysand position that the analyst may be maximally receptive to the necessary insight, criticism, and correction that the analysand will provide.

If I am trying to be a subject of analysis while being the analyst, I will recurrently face internal questions as to which details from my associative experience would usefully be revealed. In my experience, these are not questions to be considered in isolation; they should be considered in consultation with the analysand. In such consultation with the analysand, I try to elicit his appraisal of the relevance and potential usefulness of my telling about my subjective experience. I find that analysands give information about this at many moments of the analytic process. There are ongoing opportunities for correction of my level of openness and whatever negative impact my non-optimal judgements might have had. Explicit *consultation* with the analysand regarding the impact of what I have said (or not said) is imperative if I am unable to identify such information in his consequent implicit communications. As I try to learn about my impact on the analysand, he is sensitized to my personal impact through my asking about it. Through the act of putting his response into coherent words, he learns to focus on the impact of the unfolding, mutually revealing, analytic process. I want to authorize him to become an increasingly astute, outspoken, and articulate consultant regarding my use of varying levels of explicit, personal openness.

Inherent in my relying on the analysand as a consultant are *both mutuality and asymmetry*. The process will be mutual in the sense of there always being two simultaneous analytic subjects. But the process will be asymmetrical in the sense that the therapeutic focus is primarily on just one of the subjects, the analysand, despite the fact that both of us may reveal things about ourselves and both of us are likely to derive personal gain. While a climate of emotional openness, especially to the analysand's negative experience, is critical for safety and, ultimately, for the analytic process to work, the place for addressing *my* negative experience as the analyst in relation to a particular analysand is almost invariably *outside* of the explicit analytic exchange. It is my responsibility to contain the analysand's negative impact and to bring that impact into an analytic relationship (perhaps designated as a supervision) in which the focus is on me. My analysands must not serve this purpose for me. In that case, these analyses would become inappropriately symmetrical, indeed exploitive. I do receive analytic attention from my analysands, some of which provides me with direct, growth-enhancing benefit. But such benefit must be serendipitous. I must ultimately go outside of my work as analyst for pursuit of my own growth.

Mutual, yet partly asymmetrical, analytic experience

There are two principles that, I believe, ought to structure and limit my expressiveness regarding my experience as an analytic subject during each moment of an analysis. First, I look to the analysand as a supervisory consultant in an attempt to optimize my participation as analyst. (I refer to the analysand as "supervisory consultant" in order to reflect the analysand's role in frankly and, at times, critically informing the analyst in order to facilitate the analyst's work with the analysand. I do not intend to suggest a common form of hypervigilance on the analysand's part [characteristic of analysands who have had to become their parents' supervisors from an early age], wherein there is pervasive resistance to allowing the analyst to serve with necessary autonomy in the role of analyst.) I seek to be attuned to the shifting, moment-to moment focus of attention in the session. My degree of expressiveness is to be determined by the direction of the analysand's focal shifts, conveyed on both overt and subliminal levels. I try to learn how I can provide an optimal opportunity for the analysand to discover and articulate himself. The analysand must not be under obligation to make similar adaptation to me, though a significant portion of any analysis might be devoted to the analysand's trying to know and to emotionally help me. While I try to be careful not to unwittingly use the analysand for my own personal, analytic needs, I do believe it is equally problematic to indiscriminately thwart the analysand's attempts to have therapeutic impact on me (see Searles, 1965, 1979).

The second limit of my expressiveness pertains to the fact that I must decide on how intentionally communicative I am *willing* to be with a given analysand at any particular moment. It is necessary to guard against being any more open than I am *willing* to be. This is a protection for both myself and, indirectly, for my analysand. I am careful not to override any hesitancy I sense about saying something. What would be most potentially perilous to the analysand is my forced self-exposure of some private aspect of my experience as I attempt to retain the position of subject in the analysis. The danger resides in my subsequent anxiety and possible defensive attempts to obscure what has been revealed or to transactionally restore personal security in some other, defensive way. The primary problem with such defensiveness is that it would damage my subsequent subjective availability for both myself and for the analysand. (For example, an analyst whose ability to be "in analysis" while working tends to be aided by the analysand's lying on the couch relinquishes this working arrangement because of a request for "more feedback". The analysand then gets an analyst who has accommodated her request, but she loses one who will be as able to be in contact with her associative thoughts and feelings while working. [I am not arguing here that the analyst should never adapt to the analysand; I am saying, however, that the analyst must give a high priority to paying attention to her own sense of safety while working. In this way the analyst's maintaining a position as a subject of analysis—a position vital for the analysand's own sense of safety— is protected.])

If I have sufficient analytic resources in place outside of the particular case within which I am serving as analyst, the analysand is privileged to have both an analyst who is available as a subject of attention *and* who, at the same time, does not *require* such attention. In this case, the analysand is rendered free to look away from me as the flow of his personal analytic process carries him away without fear of neglecting me.

To reiterate: the purpose of training analysis, rather than to eliminate the candidates' quirks (which, we are all aware, it usually fails to accomplish), is to establish the presence of portable capacity analysts can draw upon as they attempt to persist as analytic subjects. An analyst's being in a position of subject of analysis is made available to her analysand, but such availability must not depend on the analysand's attention for its subsistence.

Yet, conversely, it *is* reasonable for the analysand to depend on the analyst for securing the analysand's position as analytic subject and the analyst's maintaining her own. In effect, analysts, analogous to parents, must take responsibility for securing both their own and their analysands' safety. The analyst secures through looking to information about his impact from the analysand. He listens to the analysand's conscious and unconscious reactions to him and receives them associatively. He will inevitably *respond* to what comes his way. The expression of his response is guided by the agenda of persistent focusing on the analysand.

The analyst, as participant–observer, draws upon the capacity for being an observer in order to retain the focus on the analysand. But the fact that much, if not most, of the communication between analyst and analysand is unconscious and, thus, not subject to the limits of intentional control, limits the extent to which the analyst's efforts to maintain a therapeutic focus on the analysand can be fulfilled. How could the analyst rely on his own ability to limit his unconscious desire to be an analysand when such a desire would be outside of conscious awareness? Should the analyst feel confident that he is keeping the analysand in the role of primary beneficiary of the analytic relationship merely because he is "trained" to do so, is getting paid for his efforts, or *intends* to be in the role of the analyst? I dare say that analysts' exploitation of their analysands' therapeutic efforts is commonplace. Perhaps it is the lesser of two evils when the frequently encountered alternative is the analyst's use of the analysand not to make analytic progress, but to perpetuate his own neurotic strivings. At least in the instance where the analysand is analyst to the analyst, the analyst may—theoretically at least—make analytic progress such that he will be rendered increasingly available to serve in the role as analyst rather than analysand.

Experience has shown that the best insurance for the analyst's focusing on the analysand as primary in an analysis is the analyst's having available a separate analytic context within which he can be designated as the focus, as truly the analysand. It is through the securing of a personal analytic space—on an extended basis, I increasingly believe—that the analyst may trust his own willingness to be an analyst–analysand to the fullest extent possible without undue concern about displacing the analysand as the primary focus in the analysis. When there is an adequate analytic setting provided for the analyst, the analyst is both able to keep the analysand as the primary focus *and* the analyst is more available to be an analyst–analysand while working. The analyst is more able to be open without peril and more able to persistently (though largely unconsciously) re-designate the analysand as the focus of the work.

Aspects of my work as an analyst–analysand

I would like to mention some practical details of how I work which reflect my interest in creating the kind of safety I have described. I am interested in rendering my discussion of the analyst's availability as a subject less abstract than it has been in my description thus far. I present here selected details of my way of working rather than a case example, because there is no exemplary case for what I am proposing. Instead, I present details that are suggestive of a stance in which I try to make myself a subject of analysis while doing analysis.

In most cases my analysands lie down on the couch. I sit behind them in a reclining chair. I prefer this arrangement because I have found that I am much more able to allow myself private, associative experience from this position, freer from the normal demands of face-to-face contact. In contrast with received notions of the purpose of the couch, which focus on its role for the analysand, if there is anybody's "regression" I am trying to facilitate, it is my own. I am more able to pay attention to fleeting feelings, thoughts, and seemingly arbitrary images. From this position I am also able to sit longer in silence without feeling pressure to speak before speaking would seem useful. I have also found analysands can more readily partake in the essential experience of being silent, sometimes for extended periods, when they are on the couch. While at times I can be an overtly "active" participant and have extensive exchanges with analysands, I see silence as crucial for the analysand's (and my own) entry into feeling, analytic subjecthood.

I am generally reserved when doing analysis and this is only partly due to my character-based tendency towards shyness. This is an aspect of my emphasis on listening attentively to what the analysand might be conveying to me. Almost invariably, I tend to be slightly more reserved with my analysands than I sense they are prepared for me to be with them. I am cautious in this regard, vigilantly exploring (often explicitly with the analysand) the implications of an instance of my acting less reserved, more open, more vocal with my associations, more detailed in response to questions posed to me, or any of the kinds of participation that would represent a departure from the predominant task of listening closely on a moment to moment basis.

I do not assume that my relational carefulness comprises a stance of neutrality. I am not setting out to avoid contaminating the analytic field with my own subjective contribution. It is more as if I am trying to be a bit "quiet" so that I will be more able to "hear" as I work. Generally speaking, I can attend to what is going on better when I am not doing or talking too much. I have not seen a value (and I have seen consequences) in assertively imposing "authentic" conduct on the analysand. The negative impact of this kind of impingement far outweighs the potential negative impact of the kind of cautious action I am describing.

I usually write on a notepad. I use this as a way of privately thinking out loud as I listen. Sometimes, I write almost verbatim notes; sometimes, just words or phrases not consciously related to the happenings of the session. I prefer not to impose censorship on my notepad activities. I believe this pays off, since I have often found relevance in seemingly irrelevant, scriptural meanderings. Such writings provide a source of information about my level of engagement at any given moment. They allow for a kind of private, contained free association, so that I am less likely to feel pressure to say them aloud, using the analysand as a repository for my own associations. I write things I do not want to lose, things I might want to address later. I sometimes write things down I think of saying, then sometimes say them, sometimes not. I have found (echoing Winnicott) that it is quite gratifying to have a thought I believe is significant, wait to say it (sometimes by writing it to myself), then to hear it from the analysand without having spoken aloud.

Related to the issue of engagement, I have found that when I become absorbed in a session, or a moment of a session, my writing tends to slow down or stop unless I have expressly told myself to keep writing anyway in order to gather material I might want to keep. When my writing stops, I understand this as representing an intensification of my absorption. When I am most absorbed, I am more capable of being aware of multiple, simultaneous levels of meaning and enactment. It then becomes impossible to write down much of what I am experiencing. My writing trails off because my capacity to record my experience has been overwhelmed.

Going into a session partly feels as if I am going into my own analytic session. Indeed, I often feel as if I have had multiple personal analytic sessions after a day of work. There is a mentally aroused feeling, knowing I am about to enter into a familiar situation, in a familiar place, characterized by both possibility and uncertainty. I have the awareness, similar to the anticipation of personal analytic sessions, that I will be in contact with myself in a way that I am often not outside of a session. I would describe it as a welcome kind of solitude. Even though I will be with the analysand and my attention will be largely on what emerges from him or her, I have the distinct feeling that I will also be more profoundly with myself. While I have emphasized co-participation, characterizing the analyst's role as co-subject, solitude is a predominant experience when I am working.

I listen to what the analysand conveys, particularly regarding problems or complaints, as possibly being indirect references to "insights" about me. I expect such in-sights to be intelligent, yet largely unconscious. I listen for the implicit observations that I am able to detect regarding, for example, my mood, my appearance, the way I am talking or not talking. I am mindful of temporal sequence, constantly trying to consider what has come before the present moment, considering what my unwitting impact might have been. I try to discern the expectations I have conveyed, presently or in the past, which make it difficult to talk openly, and I try to bring this out. I tend, particularly, to focus on instances of the analysand's dismissal of her own perceptions. For example, in response to an analysand's saying, "I know this is all projection, but you seemed annoyed to see me in the waiting room," I might ask, "What made it feel like a projection rather than a perception?" Or I might say, "The way you put it implies that you seem pretty sure you're not seeing what you saw."

I have found it useful to not give in to my impulse to disabuse an analysand about what seems to me to be an erroneous perception (transference distortion) of me. The situation is different when the analysand asks about my sense of the accuracy of her observations. In that case, I reflect on my response to the question and consider what it would be like to convey my response directly. I use language in relation to an analysand's perceptions, implicitly holding out the possibility that the perceptions are accurate even if I am unable to immediately locate their truth in my own awareness. I try to find the truth in what I hear, even if this is uncomfortable or seems a remote possibility.

Here is a rather ordinary example of the kind of thing I am referring to: I am engrossed as I listen to an analysand describe, in more vivid detail than she ever has, a life-defining, traumatic experience with her mother when she was seven years old. Abruptly, she says, "I can't believe how boring I'm sounding. I know you are looking forward to the end of *this* session." As I am familiar with her tendency to dismiss her own feelings and to interrupt significant moments of engagement in our work, I am not quite as jolted as I have been at earlier, similar times. I think for a moment, and then say flatly, "Hmm. You're sounding boring and I'm looking forward to it being over." It is hard for me to feel that what I'm saying is true, but I hold it in my mind as a possibility as I say it, wondering how she comes to see me that way and what I might be like if it *were* true.

When I am asked a direct question by an analysand regarding a thought or a feeling in me that the analysand has become curious about, I tend first to consult with the analysand about his or her own observations that have led to the question. I often ask what the implications would be, as far as the analysand can be aware, of my speaking to the question. Having satisfied myself that I have sufficiently looked into the implications of speaking about myself, I will usually begin with a phrase like, "As far as I am aware", or "What

I am able to have access to at the moment is", or some such. I use this way of speaking not as an evasive trick, a manoeuvre away from owning my words, but as an attempt to accurately represent my view of what I am going to say. I am interested in conveying to the analysand that I am perpetually of the mind that what I am able to consciously access and articulate is only a part of what I really think and feel. Further, I want to convey, at least implicitly, that I believe the analysand might know much about the answer to his or her question that I do not.

I employ a consultant on a confidential basis whose scope of consultation is not restricted to my clinical work. I regard my consultant as both supervisor and analyst and do not make a funda-mental distinction between these two roles in our working rela-tionship. Having previously undergone years of analysis (with more than one analyst), I currently find much more limited, yet regular contact with my current consultant to be sufficient. I think there is wide variability from practitioner to practitioner regarding satisfactory frequency.

Summary and conclusions

This chapter has attempted to delineate a relationally-based manner for addressing the issue of analytic safety. I argued that no single frame, technique, or ethical code can adequately address the vast range of dangers presented by each analytic relationship. This was shown to necessitate a relationally conceived form of safety in which the analyst would be maximally sensitive and responsive to the analysand's communications regarding detected dangers during the course of the analysis. The concepts of the analyst's availability as subject of analysis and the analyst–analysand were introduced and described. These concepts can be seen to represent a resurrection of mutual analysis in that they involve the analyst's careful attention to his own associative experience while, at the same time, privileging the analysand's perceptions of, and articula-tions about, the analyst's associative and unconscious experience.

I have offered concrete information on the ways I engage in this work that make my own entry in to the analyst–analysand role possible. Other analysts might have their own ways of making this happen. Whatever form our attempts at securing our analysands take, I hope to have made a case for the need for specific, relationally-derived, rather than school-of-thought-derived, ways of addressing the need for safety in the psychoanalytic process.

The view that I have proposed that the analysand actually derives safety from the analyst's *openness*—which I have termed "the analyst's availability as a subject of analysis"—runs counter to long-standing views which hold that the ethical practice of analysis essentially depends on a highly developed form of self-conscious *censorship* and privacy of the analyst's experience. Boundaries, the vitally important ways of demarcating the rules, limits, and agreements of interpersonal contact have been misconstrued as needing to take the form of barriers to intimate access. I believe that psychoanalytic practice has laboured too long under the assumption that it is safer for the analysand if the analyst's immediate associative experience is kept separate. I have tried to argue that just the opposite is true, that it is through the analyst's willingness to be open that the analysand can face the relational danger presented by the analyst (and potentially work it through) in a more profound manner.

It is not hard to speculate about why it has seemed so risky for the analyst to be open. Perhaps it has to do with wanting to keep the child (analysand) out of the bedroom (analyst's unconscious mind), from seeing what goes on there, from being over stimulated by what is seen, from being enlisted in some form of incestuous exploitation. Perhaps it has to do with the analyst's fear of being revealed to be ordinarily human, and the belief that such a revelation would potentially compromise the analyst's power, particularly the power to conceal his own vulnerability. Perhaps it has to do with the analyst's fear of his own voracious, narcissistic appetite for attention; if the analyst is allowed to become a subject, then he may never be able to relinquish this position, forever displacing the analysand as the centre of attention.

I believe these fears have been misplaced. Boundary transgression, exploitation, and usurping attention are certainly not *prevented* by professionally sanctioned manners of hiding. The recommended openness will certainly not prevent these pitfalls either. But it will, through its combination of designating the analyst as subject and validating the analysand's analytic perceptions, afford the analysand a more informed basis for trusting the analyst and the situation. It might also allow analysts the opportunity to make sufficient personal progress while they are working, so that they will become safe enough for the analysand to allow the analysis to have real impact.

References

Bion, W. R. (1967). Notes on memory and desire. In: R. Langs (Ed.), *Classics in Psychoanalytic Technique*. New Jersey: Jason Aronson, 1981.

Bollas, C. (1989). *Forces of Destiny: Psychoanalysis and Human Idiom*. London: Free Association.

Bollas, C. (1992). *Being a Character*. New York: Hill & Wang.

Bollas, C. (1999). *The Mystery of Things*. New York: Routledge.

Epstein, L. (1987). The bad analyst feeling. *Modern Psychoanalysis, 12*: 35–45.

Epstein, L. (1999). The analyst's "bad-analyst feelings": a counterpart to the process of resolving implosive defenses. *Contemporary Psychoanalysis, 35*: 311–325.

Ferenczi, S. (1932). *The Clinical Diary of Sandor Ferenczi*. J. Dupont (Ed.), M. Balint & N. Jackson (Trans.). Cambridge, MA: Harvard University Press, 1988.

Hart, A. (1999). Reclaiming the analyst's disruptive role. *Contemporary Psychoanalysis, 35*: 185–211.

Hirsch, I. (2000). Interview with Benjamin Wolstein. *Contemporary Psychoanalysis, 36*: 187–232.

Ogden, T. H. (1994). *Subjects of Analysis*. New Jersey: Jason Aronson.

Ogden, T. H. (1997). Reverie and metaphor: some thoughts on how I work as a psychoanalyst. *International Journal of Psychoanalysis, 78*: 719–732.

Ragen, T., & Aron, L. (1993). Abandoned workings: Ferenczi's mutual analysis. In: L. Aron & A. Harris (Eds.), *The Legacy of Sandor Ferenczi* (pp. 217–226). Hillsdale, NJ: Analytic Press.

Searles, H. (1965). *Collected Papers on Schizophrenia and Related Subjects*. New York: International Universities Press.

Searles, H. (1979). *Countertransference and Related Subjects*. Madison, CT: International Universities Press.

Spotnitz, H. (1976). *Psychotherapy of Preoedipal Conditions: Schizophrenia and Severe Character Disorders*. New York: Jason Aronson.

Stricker, G., & Fisher, M. (Eds.) (1990). *Self-disclosure in the Therapeutic Relationship*. New York: Plenum.

Wilner, W. (1998). Working experientially in psychoanalysis. *Contemporary Psychoanalysis, 34*: 591–596.

Wilner, W. (1999). The un-consciousing of awareness in psychoanalytic therapy. *Contemporary Psychoanalysis, 35*: 617–628.

Wilner, W. (2000). A legacy of self: The unique psychoanalytic perspective of Benjamin Wolstein. *Contemporary Psychoanalysis, 36*: 267–279.

Wolstein, B. (1994). The evolving newness of interpersonal psychoanalysis: from the vantage point of immediate experience. *Contemporary Psychoanalysis, 30*: 473–499.

CHAPTER EIGHTEEN

To know without being told and to allow oneself to say[1]

Martha Hadley

"Cases of thought-transference during the analysis of suffering people are extraordinarily frequent. One sometimes has the impression that the reading of such processes encounters strong emotional resistance in us materialists; any insights we gain into them have the tendency to come undone, like Penelope's weaving or the tissue of our dreams"

(Ferenczi, 1932, p. 33)

U nconscious communication is not new to us. It is part of our lives as analysts and as people. However, beyond the more usual experience of intuitive knowing in our daily lives or in the context of the therapeutic situation, there are moments when we sit stunned in disbelief at uncanny incidents of the other person knowing what cannot be known. When a person speaks or dreams of something specific from our life experience that they could not have known about through any conventional means of communication, we resist and often do not speak. Analysts have noted such experiences as far back as Freud (1922a, 1941d) and Ferenczi (1932), but the tendency to be stunned, disbelieving, or simply confused about what to do next, remains. Should we contain the mystery of this kind of apparently telepathic knowing or acknowledge it and thereby disclose what seems to have been mysteriously communicated between us and the person with whom we are working? What are the implications?

The pursuit of these concerns and questions began for me several years ago with a patient I will call N. She was in her mid-forties, with twenty years of experience in various forms of treatment, that was followed by a hiatus of five years during which she had risen to the demands of motherhood. Her physician had perceived the anguish behind her various somatic problems and referred her to me. I found her articulate, perceptive, and likable, but tragic in her chronic paralysis and persistent self-criticism, even despising herself. She spoke of being unable to move out of her tiny, chaotic apartment where she had lived for more than twenty years, to change her oppressive job, or to begin to paint again, despite good training and a promising start in her early twenties.

Negation and despair permeated the sessions. Any progress, insight or good feeling was quickly followed by deprecating, dismissive comments. Although uncomfortable with both reflections on this pattern and attempts at work on transferential dynamics, she said that she felt "less adversarial" with me than her previous therapists and remained engaged. Slowly, she began to acknowledge the sadism that floated in the room, a ghostly inheritance from her angry mother's meagre and envious love, preventing her from being able to recognize her self or to make anything good last. "I can kill or erase anything," she concluded, with both triumph and despair. Any sense of accomplishment, order, or pleasure was sure to be followed by some negation or decay.

She lived in a life space where she and other, minimally related people waited for the end, working to stay alive in oppressive circumstances. Occasionally, there were magic moments in this life, such as holidays with good food, pretty dresses, and a celebratory mood tinged with cynicism, but shared with friends who were otherwise held distant. But these moments were soon followed by a return to resignation and the condemned space of her daily life.

During our first year of analytic work, she reported a number of very compelling dreams in which she expressed very little interest, experiencing them quite concretely, like the random throwaways of a night's sleep. Then, not long after a great struggle to find, then move into, a new apartment, she reported first one and then, several months later, a second dream, both woven with visual details and facts from *my* day-to-day life. These were details that I had never spoken about, nor could she have known about them directly. N did not work as a therapist, nor did she know, or know of, any of my colleagues or friends. She lived and worked in a different part of the city, had never been in my home, and did not associate me with the neighbourhood depicted in the dream. Further, she was not a notably curious or intrusive patient. She asked occasional, usual questions, such as where I had been on vacation, or how I was feeling after a winter cold, but these were expressions of interest or concern. I have no doubt that, over time, she had formed an image of my life and me outside the office, as patients do, but there was no indication of a press to know or investigate.

The dreams I will describe, with brief summaries of our work around them, were the first indication of a connection to my life outside the office. By way of introduction, I should say that as I listened to these dreams, with their seemingly telepathic know-ledge of my experience in other, distant contexts, I felt awe. My thoughts over the months that followed led me into an often neglected corner of our experience as clinicians, and one aspect of what is, in the early part of the twenty-first century, still taboo.

Dream one

N came in depressed, but seeking comfort rather than warding me off with her usual despairing self-report. She said she had a dream to tell me, with an air of bringing me something that she knew would please me, but which she regarded as of little interest.

The dream, said N, is about two apartments. One is mine that I now live in, and am trying to renovate. The other is a one-room, L-shaped apartment on the ground floor near the Park in the West 60s. It has a full picture window at the back, so when you sit on the bed or couch you can see the green of the Park. I'm trying to set it up like an extra apartment, a *pied à terre*. There is one door, sort of to the street, and one to the lobby of the building. I can see red-brick apart-ments being built that will block the view of Central Park. My friend Amy is there from Chicago, the one who said she would never come to New York, but now she is in my Manhattan *pied à terre*. We are consulting on where I should put the bookcases. She wants them in the corner. I would never have thought about it. Again, I see those

red-brick buildings. It's a pity they will block the view. In the apartment, I realize that the door that goes to the newsstand is near the
street. So people walk through my apartment from the newsstand to
the street. I go to the lobby to get a key and try to get in from the
lobby. I can turn the key to get into my apartment. I'm trying to find
out whose apartment it was before, or is it still theirs? Then the newsstand lady says it was hers. I can't remember if I'm buying or rent-
ing, or any transaction details. She tried to help me by going through
my calendars and papers. I'm not sure I like it, but she is trying to
help. I seem to remember that I had just looked at the apartment and
then moved my stuff into it. I never see my own apartment. But I
know my child is OK back at home. The stuff in this new apartment
is similar to what is really in my own apartment. I'm determined to
fit everything into one place, even though this is smaller.

She was pensive after telling the dream and spent time weaving various connections and stories to the different parts. Themes emerged,
having and making a home for herself, the concern about intrusion as
well as ownership, and a new feeling which she first described as a
"kind of optimism about the place". Finally, she said, "You know
what's important? I know I can fix this place up and I'm not worried
about my child back at home. I can do it for me. Maybe you are the
newsstand lady who helps me out. The apartment has somehow been
inherited from you."

As I listened and worked with her in her weaving of the dream's significance, there was a stunned part of me that I tried to keep hidden.
She had described the location and architectural details of my then
supervisor's new office in New York City. This is an office where I had
been going once a week to discuss this case for several months. I have
the feeling that I cannot believe what I am hearing. I ran the architectural details through my memory. The address was accurate. The
windows and trees fit the layout. Even the multiple doorways and
windows were the same. How could this be? I go to this office in the
mid-afternoon on a weekday when she is at work in a distant part of
town. I do not live or work anywhere near this address and have never
received mail from it, so she could not have seen an address in a directory or on an envelope. Even if she had seen me in this neighbourhood
on a day when she was out of work, many of the architectural details
described are not visible from the street of this doorman building.

In the moments after I heard the dream, my training and my gut
told me to work first with the dream's clear significance for her . . . a
place she can find and make herself a home. I said nothing about the

familiarity of the space and its significance for me. It did occur to me that she was able to use this dream far more symbolically and deeply than most she had had up to that point.

Later in the week, I told my supervisor, in the office in question, about the dream. His reaction included a mix of amazement and a kind of knowing irony. I recall his saying, "Yes, we love those trees," with a pensive look that suggested wonder at the process unfolding. The possibility of unconscious communication was, fortunately, not alien to him. We explored the implications of using his new office as a place where she could build a home for herself. His office of previous years was essentially windowless, smaller and without such architectural details.

It should also be mentioned that none of us—not the patient, my supervisor, or myself—have particularly marked psychic powers, nor profound beliefs about the occult. Like many others, I have wondered at stories about Aborigines communicating with each other across the desert or people somehow knowing where their loved ones were when they were lost, but I have had only mundane glimmers of such experiences in my own life. Further, N had never mentioned any such experience. In short, we were all new at this.

As I sat there processing the dream and its implications, I realized that I was worried and struggling with what to say to N. If I told her about her uncanny unconscious awareness of the office in question, she might be overwhelmed or spooked. I did not know what to make of this experience, nor did I know how to explain it to her. I felt a bit anxious, unsure, maybe even spooked myself. Her progress, so poignantly symbolized as finding a place where she could build a home, a self in a space she could take from me, felt fragile. In the course of our work, she had been consistent in running from too much excitement or possibility. To tell her she had somehow picked up information from me in an apparently telepathic way was exciting enough to unsettle me, let alone her. I did not understand or have enough confidence about what had happened to be able to hold her while conveying it. For the moment, we expanded on concrete elements of the dream (the architectural details, her friend's presence, the bookshelves, the buildings under construction that threatened to block her view, the newsstand lady helping her with her papers). We worked towards helping her explore the symbolic significance of building a self that is accessible from inside and out, with a sense of optimism and an ability to accept help as well as handle intrusion.

However, there was part of me that sensed I had not fully addressed or understood what had occurred. Then, several months later, a close friend of mine died suddenly. I was involved with her memorial service, giving one of several eulogies. As often happens in our profession, I was experiencing but trying to conceal my own grief while continuing to work with patients. At that time, N reported a second dream with uncanny parallels to my experiences outside the office.

Dream two

I am at a memorial service and have been asked to read a part of the eulogy. I am dressed in black; there are many people that I don't know. I am feeling ill at ease because I know that a friend has died but I'm not really sure who and I don't understand the text that I have been asked to read. There is a sense of awkwardness and embarrassment.

She immediately began to speak about her old friend, J, who is still alive, but whom she seldom sees. She wondered if she had "killed her or the friendship off", but does not really understand why, so can't figure out the eulogy she has been asked to read.

We explored these feelings and connections for a while. I considered the possibility that she might have picked up my sadness or that I could have inadvertently provided other clues. We work and live in different neighbourhoods and social worlds. She has never spoken of friends in my field, nor that of my deceased friend. There is no way I can construct a direct connection between my friend's death, the memorial service, and N's milieu. I had a growing feeling that this time I must say something. I began by telling her that it was her dream and I thought the meaning she had suggested made sense, but there is something else she should know. I told her that I was part of a service like the one she described several weeks ago. I asked if there was any chance that she had sensed some of my feelings about my own friend's death, feelings that are difficult to hide from a person as sensitive as herself. She was interested, sympathetic, and acknowledged that she had felt or suspected that I was sad, but had no idea that a friend of mine had died. In these cautious, exploratory moments where I began to share my questions with her, there was a closeness between us that had been rare in our relationship, despite our good rapport. She said, "So we have both lost a friend." Something shifted. She was no longer the woman who could not maintain a friendship, having to kill it off without knowing why. She was now someone who shared her grief with me and I let her know mine.

For me, there was a great sense of relief at not having to hold so much in. For her, there was an evident experience of strength in feeling that she could be there for me and with these feelings. We did not even try to wonder about how she could have known. By the end of the session, she expressed appreciation for my sharing this with her, something about my life. I mentioned her remarkable sensitivity and she was, for the moment, a little impressed, but also somehow disbelieving, or perhaps unable to grasp the capacity implied.

It struck me then that there is something less taboo and improbable about someone intuiting one's sorrow over a loss than knowing the architectural details and address of one's supervisor's office. The latter is so direct, so concrete compared to having a sense of the other's loss. I began to wonder if the images somehow come with or through the strong feelings.

Regardless, I continued to feel unsettled about her apparent tele-pathic knowing of facts from a familiar scene that I had never spoken about. I tried to sort out my unsettledness in terms of the transferential dynamics. There were several possibilities. By not telling her about the uncanny information in the first dream, was I re-enacting her family's inability to appreciate her astuteness, thereby depriving her of recognition? Was I worried about her feeling spooked and intruded upon, or was this really about my perme-ability and being ill at ease with her knowing what was in my mind? Was I, as the newsstand lady, censoring the news in some way that was significant to the treatment because I myself could not handle the implications? All the above, and probably other pos-sibilities, ran through my mind, but the feelings and confusion, countertransferential or not, did not dissipate.

I began to read and talk to others about their similar experiences. There seemed to be several kinds of unconscious communication described in the analytic literature: (1) tacit knowing of a mood, quality, or general experience of the other (e.g., sadness, excitement, depression, attraction, pain); (2) unconscious dynamics or dissoci-ated feelings conveyed through various kinds of enactments; (3) dreams in which the dynamics of patient and analyst were symbolized in ways that had not yet been grasped by either, but were readily recognized once the dream had portrayed the situation symbolically; (4) prescient knowing about the therapist's states such as pregnancy, illness, mourning, or desire; and (5) telepathic, sometimes prophetic knowing of details and events from the therapist's life.

The experiences I have described included several of these categories, but perhaps it is the last, the seemingly telepathic, direct knowing, which feels most outside the realm of our accepted theoretical frameworks or personal understanding. This knowing of details without being told is beyond the familiar constructs of transference, countertransference, unconscious fantasy, and re-enactment.

Many analysts, as far back as Freud (1922a), Ferenczi (1932), Devereux (1953), and more recently Stoller (in Mayer, 2001) have discussed unconscious communication, telepathic dreams, and simply telepathy in the therapeutic context. While contemporary psychoanalysts have written with great insight about unconscious communication in the therapeutic dyad, or shared unconscious states (Aron, 1991, 1996; Bollas, 1987; Bromberg, 1991, 1998; Lazar, 2001; Ogden; 1994; Wilner, 1975, 1987), unconscious transmission of particular, personal facts or "thought transmissions" (Freud, 1922a) seems to verge on the occult or inadmissible.

The unspoken assumption that most of us live and work with in our larger culture, as well as in the psychoanalytic milieu, is that we are, at least to some extent, the gatekeepers of our own minds. That is, while we are usually aware that others may intuit our mood or aspects of our character from non-verbal signals and be influenced by us when we do not intend it, it is our prerogative to choose to disclose or keep private facts about ourselves or our lives. The ongoing psychoanalytic discussion about disclosure is premised on the tacit belief that while unconscious re-enactments or expressions in slips of the tongue or dreams will probably occur, we can make conscious choices about what we reveal regarding the particulars of our lives outside the clinical situation.

In situations like the ones I have described, particulars of the therapist's life have not only become known, but gained significance in the analysand's psychic life without disclosure. Disclosure in such cases is not about revealing facts or feelings, but acknowledging that facts have become known without being told. Not only has "the blank screen" become transparent, but also the implications of withholding must be balanced with those of disclosure in the form of acknowledgement. I have wondered whether the feelings of uneasiness or awe many of us have around such direct unconscious communications are not similar to the discomfort and possible danger that early analysts felt when confronted with intense experiences of transference and countertransference. We do not yet understand it, and it is a truism that those things we do not understand often make us uneasy and defensive.

Reading and listening to analysts who have reported similar phenomena is useful. I have been particularly impressed with a paper by Robert Stoller, read at meeting of the Division of Psychoanalysis of the American Psychological Association (Division 39) in1998 and published with commentary by Elizabeth Lloyd Mayer (2001). The paper began with the sentence, "Although these experiences began in 1960, I have hesitated ever since to report them, they having as yet no respectable explanation" (p. 635). Stoller went on to report more than a dozen seemingly "telepathic dreams", one his own while in supervision, the rest reported by his patients. All these dreams included some kind of information about his recent private life: in one case, an accident involving his supervisor's son that could not have been known by the dreamer. It is interesting that a number of these apparently telepathic dreams included architectural details of places he had been or from his home. The others contained pieces of events in which Stoller had been involved, often pieces from unusual situations, like accidentally walking through a glass door. He described what had happened with great caution and anticipation that others might think he was "lying", repeatedly indicating that circumstances did not account for these uncanny dreams.

In Mayer's (2001) preface to the published paper, as well as in one of her earlier papers (1996), she encourages us to reflect on the implications of such seemingly "anomalous" experiences.

> If "telepathy" involves some form of communication currently considered anomalous, it is only through meticulous investigation of the communicative process itself that we will be able to understand what may or may not have been anomalous" (Mayer, 2001, p. 632). She questioned what such apparently telepathic dreams might mean for the subjectivity and intersubjectivity of the therapeutic dyad and the functioning of unconscious process. These are important issues, issues that we are theoretically and clinically ready to consider in contemporary psychoanalysis.

I would add that the fact that Stoller's paper remained in a drawer for twenty-five years because of discomfort with making his experiences public confirms our collective discomfort as a profession with such phenomena. In order for us to consider the implications of unconscious communications, or to reflect on how to deal with them in the context of our work, we must be able to speak about them.

The experiences described have led me to consider several qualities of this kind of unconscious communication in which a patient or analyst dreams details that suggest unconscious awareness of facts or scenes to which they have had no direct access. First, in the therapeutic dyad neither party seems to have control over such communications, yet both must be open or willing in order for such information to be afforded or accessed. Conversely, if either person shuts down or decides not to allow receptivity or transmission, it is very difficult for any further communication to occur.

Put differently, although at first such events may seem like random occurrences, they are not. There is, in Ferenczi's words a "dialogue of unconsciouses" (Ferenczi, 1932, p. 84) that has been achieved in such therapeutic relationships, a dialogue that can, and often does, shut down if one or both pull back. For example, at the end of Stoller's (2001) account he wrote that he decided at some point that it was "enough" and no further uncanny communications were reported. He had to stop receiving and allowing access. Less dramatically, all of us have had days when we more or less consciously decide to make certain facts or states inaccessible to patients and others, whether the facts refer to a loss, a pregnancy, a headache, or an all too human fantasy. This is not to say that we should shut down or allow access to such information, but that we naturally make some things less accessible when we feel it appropriate. However, *being open to each other's unconscious life is an achievement and being selectively open or selectively closed to the other when this kind of intimacy has been built is, by definition, not easy, or impossible, to control consciously.*

This kind of unconscious communication is often conveyed through imagery or a non-verbal, vague impression of a kind of place, event, state, person, etc. Such communications seem to come in bits of information, or in a sense of things that have transpired, that are then reconstructed by the sensitive, tuned receiver. For example, with the architectural details, aspects of a scene and a location were apparently picked up as fragments that were then woven into a setting that was integral to N's own story. The symbolic significance of having been able to find and take in this particular safe place where she felt she could build a self of her own suggests, however, an awareness of significance as well as facts. She did not find details of my back yard or dentist's office; she picked up bits and pieces from the setting (first dream) in which I had most actively held her in mind. One possibility is that, as we worked together, I had images of the office scene where I had been working on this case in supervision, and she picked them up. But, being a visual person, I know that I have images of all sorts of places and people in the course of an hour. It seems very likely to me that these particular images were afforded by the meaning and feelings they carried for me and the meaning she allowed them to have for her.

Finally, conscious discovery or awareness of unconscious communication has meaning in itself. The sender may not be conscious of providing access and the receiver may not be conscious of accessing, but when the person who is the source of an unconscious communication realizes what has happened, there is a feeling of distinct closeness, intimacy, and awe. Put differently, there is strong feeling that comes with acknowledging or making conscious the unconscious telepathic communication, acknowledging access and reception. As always, individual therapeutic situations must be the context in which we assess the wisdom of this or any other disclosure, but it has potential power as an affirmation of deep, unconscious, transformative connection.

By way of conclusion, almost six months after the first of the two dreams described, N and I were in the midst of a familiar kind of session. N's self-deprecation was being extended to the trashing of her own recent efforts at a job search, herself as a mother, and the worth of the treatment for her functioning in life. I mentioned that since I had met her she had achieved and found some things that were not about struggles of daily life. I reminded her of the two apartments dream and its meaning as she had constructed it, but this time I included the remarkable aspect of her having been able to know things from my life that had been woven into her dream. We spoke a little about the details, but the emphasis was on her capacity to be close and to take something from me for herself. She was struck silent at first, and then became thoughtful. She did not move into her usual stance of rejecting the importance or possible meaning of her dreams and my input. It was as if she were witnessing something that was not about belief or disbelief, but was real. That moment seemed to alter her perception of both herself and us. The dialogue and tone shifted from negation to recognition that she had accomplished things and changed in ways that were not about jobs, difficulties in raising a child, or the lack of order in her apartment. The sense of closeness and even humour began to return (me as the newsstand lady working so hard to bring her good news that she did not want to hear).

I can now say that what left me speechless and uneasy when I first heard it is now something which I accept with awe, no longer taboo, but no less powerful. It seems that there are layers of felt knowing and meaningful, presymbolic action that are implied in the phenomena of apparently telepathic unconscious communication. First, there is the access to, and reception of, meaningful information from within one person to the unconscious of the other. Second, the timing of the particular moments in the relationship/treatment when such communication occurs, in conjunction with the significance of the specific information that is picked up, suggests a meaningful, somehow selective, unconscious act. Finally, what the person makes of the information they have accessed, or how they weave it into the symbolic language of a dream or fantasy is a creative use of what has been afforded and accessed unconsciously. These are more intimate, complex versions of slips of the tongue or compulsions to repeat. They are the meaningful, creative confluence of unconscious minds.

Note

1. Presented at Joint International Conference, Niagara-on-the-Lake, Canada, 1 July 2000.

References

Aron, L. (1991). The patient's experience of the analyst's subjectivity. *Psychoanalytic Dialogues*, 1: 29–551.

Aron, L. (1996). *A Meeting of Minds: Mutuality in Psychoanalysis.* Hillsdale, NJ: Analytic Press.

Bollas, C. (1987). *The Shadow of the Object.* London: Free Association.

Bromberg, P. M. (1991). On knowing one's patient inside out: the aesthetics of unconscious communication. *Psychoanalytic Dialogues,* 1: 399–422.

Bromberg, P. M. (1998). *Standing in the Spaces: Essays on Clinical Process, Trauma, and Dissociation.* Hillsdale, NJ: Analytic Press.

Devereux, G. (Ed.) (1953). *Psychoanalysis and the Occult.* New York: International Universities Press.

Ferenczi, S. (1932). *The Clinical Diaries of Sandor Ferenczi.* J. Dupont (ed.). M. Balint & N. A. Jackson (Trans.). Cambridge, MA: Harvard University Press, 1988.

Freud, S. (1922a). Dreams and telepathy. *S.E., 18:* 197–220. London: Hogarth.

Freud, S. (1941d). Psycho-analysis and telepathy. *S.E., 18:* 177–193. London: Hogarth.

Lazar, S. (2001). Knowing, influencing and healing: paranormal phenomena and implications for psychoanalysis and psychotherapy. *Psychoanalytic Inquiry,* 21: 113–131.

Mayer, E. L. (1996). Subjectivity and intersubjectivity of clinical facts. *International Journal of Psychoanalysis,* 77: 709–737.

Mayer, E. L. (2001). On "telepathic dreams?": an unpublished paper by Robert J. Stoller. *Journal of the American Psychoanalytic Association,* 49: 629–657.

Ogden, T. (1994). *Subjects of Analysis.* Northvale, NJ: Jason Aronson.

Wilner, W. (1975). The nature of intimacy. *Contemporary Psychoanalysis,* 11: 206–226.

Wilner, W. (1987). Participatory experience: The participant observer paradox. *American Journal of Psychoanalysis,* 47: 342–357.

PART VIII

PROSCRIBED INTERVENTIONS

CHAPTER NINETEEN

A forbidden transaction: enactment or procedural interpretation?

Bruce Herzog

Introduction

W hen I first heard of the invitation to write about the theme of psychoanalytic taboos, I experienced a sense of anticipation and excitement. Perhaps those who took up the task would feel free to disclose some of the inevitable breaches in psychoanalytic technique that occur when working with our patients; the unconventional episodes which are all too rarely spoken about. With the exploration of taboos as our objective, we could be creating a forum where clinicians present incidents of "pushing the envelope," involving unusual analytic events that occur in order for us to be with our patients, events that, as often as not, apply to that portion of our clientele who may have been labelled as untreatable in the past.

I have always felt that the classification of a patient as "untreatable" was a dubious practice, being suspicious about how analysts could rationalize closing the door on people who were perfectly willing to come and work with them. Did this not contradict our mandate to help and explore? On the other hand, my scepticism might have derived from unrealistic ideals that dictated that analysts should be all things to all people. Whenever we say that people are difficult to treat, or are even untreatable, perhaps it has mostly to do with what we as therapists require of them in our consultation rooms. Some patients simply cannot abide the limitations we insist upon. In this way, we necessarily restrict ourselves in who we can treat. There can be considerable variation in what each therapist finds tolerable, however, and many of us, given the right circumstance, might be happy enough to experiment outside the framework of standard technique in order to respond therapeutically to a particular patient. When and how we are willing to extend ourselves, though, is subject to many individual factors.

One way to think of why a patient might appear to be difficult is to assume that a mismatch has occurred, where the therapist is unable to adjust himself sufficiently to develop a working alliance with a patient who cannot adapt to the therapist's requirements. The patient might be able to engage successfully in treatment, but only with a therapist who is comfortable working in the way that patient needs. For psychoanalysts to recognize this would require a belief that successful work in an analytic practice depends on both patient and analyst adjusting their behaviour to maximize the therapeutic potential of the analysis. If that view commonly existed, we would expect that many of our presentations would describe activities that are idiosyncratic to the particular dyad being discussed. Do we usually encounter this in our writing? Or do we still primarily limit ourselves to discussions of therapeutic interactions that are universally acceptable, leaving out conduct that might invite disapproval? This is why the exploration of taboos in psychoanalysis is so intriguing. It provides us with an opportunity to discuss forbidden territory, and suggest novel ways to facilitate treatment of our so-called "untreatables".

There are those of us who enjoy work that requires venturing outside of what is defined as a standard analytic position. In the context of professional meetings and journals, however, the introduction of what we have been experimenting with has never been good form. On the contrary, the ritual of attacking each other for our new ideas has been a time honoured tradition since Freud's pioneering efforts. We may not have yet progressed sufficiently in our tolerance for new viewpoints and techniques to allow ourselves to be entirely honest with each other about what we feel and do in our consultation rooms. Thus, much of what is potentially therapeutic may remain obscured by our fear of being publicly shamed.

The fear of being shamed made its presence felt when I began preparing for this chapter. I may have wanted to write with complete openness of something taboo that I have experimented with in my practice, but when I sat down to work on it, I was taken aback by my reaction of avoidance and dread. I could not convince myself that anyone else would be willing to take the risk of talking about forbidden activities in the therapist. In the patient possibly, but in oneself? If I was the only one of the writers who did, I might end up in the unenviable position of exclusively subjecting myself to the vilification of my colleagues, recklessly sticking my neck out, so to speak.

Following the first presentation of this paper, I had some interesting interchanges with a few of my colleagues about this issue. I was approached by one analyst who expressed genuine concern for my exposing myself in this way, while another mentioned that, for American psychologists, their code of ethics discouraged this sort of behaviour under the regulations involving "dual relationships". Yet another told a story of a highly respected, senior supervisor who privately admitted to her that he had engaged on a number of occasions in very similar transactions with his patients, but would never dare admit it publicly. Our concerns about making ourselves susceptible may have more pragmatic implications than just the fear of being shamed in front of our colleagues. We may also fear reprisal from our licensing bodies, and could face professional admonishment if we are judged to be outside of the standards of our profession. We may especially be at risk if our behaviour leads to unhappy results. So, although some of us would engage our patients in ways that are innovative, we may find it prudent to stay silent about it. Our professional regulations may intend to provide useful guidelines on how to approach our patients, but I worry about how they can function to prevent us from advancing our technical work and from having open discourse about our more controversial procedures. This could lead us to be secretive about our best therapeutic interventions, as well as predisposing us to be unable to fully make use of ourselves as therapists, creating in us a kind of professional paralysis.

There would be no point in doing this exercise if I were more interested in protecting myself than in attempting to explore a forbidden area in the way that has been suggested. Thus, I intend to join those analysts, past and present, who have been willing to throw caution to the wind, in order that we might objectively assess whether or not activities such as the one I have engaged in should become part of our therapeutic repertoire.

Theoretical background

It would be remiss not to outline the theoretical background which informs many of my decisions in the therapeutic process. Despite my somewhat agnostic fascination about how many legitimate ways there are to understand the analytic process, in practice I usually follow my own theoretical formulations derived from my experiences as a clinician and parent, analysand and child.

I believe that most of what we do in therapy revolves around understanding, and to some degree correcting, early failures in relatedness that occurred repeatedly between care-giver and child. A great deal of information about these failures is conveyed by the patient's direct recollection of his or her developmental history. In addition, much of what we need to know can be extrapolated from observations of our patients' habitual ways of interacting as adults, both with us and with others. This involves what many of us call transference, but I prefer to think of it as an expression of the patient's relational knowledge (see Lichtenberg, Lachmann, & Fosshage, 1992, and Stern et al., 1998); that is, implicit awareness of what consistently happened in the presence of significant others during development, which now manifests itself in the patient's expectations of us. It is especially at those times when our patients' assumptions about us do not coincide with what we already know about ourselves, that we have a very useful source of information about their way of relating.

This phenomenon comes up in the therapeutic process all the time, when the relational assumptions of the therapist and patient do not concur, and it is easy enough to demonstrate. As an example, one might think of the times in the treatment setting when a patient may tell a heartfelt story, something which touches the therapist deeply, only to startle the listener by following it up with a shocking invalidation of what was just said, such as the patient saying, "It's no big deal," or "I suppose I'm just being silly." The likelihood of the therapist experiencing surprise upon hearing this kind of statement is a reaction that provides significant information. Clearly, the response that the patient anticipates from the therapist is quite different from the one the therapist feels inclined to give. This difference allows the therapist to isolate and hypothesize about the patient's contribution to the interaction. In this way, the patient demonstrates what he has learnt to reflexively expect from others.

Although there are those who would suggest that efforts to do this may be fraught with interference from our own subjectivity, the judicious use of the therapist's subjective experience is precisely what is required to understand our patients. When our patients' relational experience distinctly contradicts our own, we are being given strong indications about how they approach relationships. This is an indispensable aid for us in our speculations about what forms of relatedness became established through early repeated experiences with care-givers.

What is automatically assumed about us by our patients effectively amounts to a cumulative memory of interactions that have occurred consistently enough in development to now become an integral, reflexive way of relating to others. Clyman (1991) has referred to this as a type of procedural memory, habitual behaviours that are as outside of someone's conscious awareness as the routine act of driving a car. I believe that the analyst needs to point out how these relational habits interfere with satisfactory relatedness (both in and out of the analytic setting), in addition to analysing their developmental source. This encourages the patient in his acquisition of insight into the origin and manifestations of his relational assumptions.

The analyst's increasing understanding of the patient's relational premises (for the purposes of this chapter, I am defining relational premises as what one automatically assumes about being with others, whereas the relational aspects of procedural memory, the habitual behaviours that I call "relational reflexes," involve what one automatically does when being with others) derives from the clinical situation, where the patient creates an evolving chronicle of traumatic patterns of relatedness that began with the prototypical relationship. The analyst can use this understanding to avoid retraumatization of the patient because the recollections of unhappy relatedness not only give insight into a patient's distress, but also subtly encourage the analyst to adjust his own behaviour. The resulting actions of the analyst, when circumventing the repetition of traumatic patterns of the patient's past, communicate within the realm of the patient's procedural memory because it is a realm of action. Such manifestations of analytic caring I call "procedural interpretations" (Herzog, 2001): behavioral communications of the therapist's deeply felt, authentic understanding of the patient's experience.

My concept of the procedural interpretation appears on the surface to be quite similar to Ogden's (1994) idea of "interpretive action", but in theory, and especially in practice, it is a very different entity. For Ogden, the therapist's action functions much like a verbal interpretation: it is another way to communicate the therapist's formulated thinking about his patient. Ogden's case examples appear to demonstrate that he is not intending to interpret at the level of the patient's relational knowledge (i.e., within the realm of non-verbalized, procedural experience), but rather is communicating, through action, what is known to the therapist in the symbolic, verbal realm. In contrast, a procedural interpretation is intended to function at the level of procedural memory, which involves unformulated experience (Stern, 1989, 1997). It is a behavioural communication of the therapist's intuitive understanding of the patient's relational knowledge. Because it intends to be heard at the level of the procedural realm, it must use its language, which is the language of activity, rather than words. It shows that the therapist "gets it": that is, has a non-intellectualized understanding of the patient. A procedural interpretation is an action, to be sure, but it delivers information that exists outside of the symbolic, language-dominated realm, the symbolic realm being what most psychoanalysts primarily write about. A procedural interpretation functions within the realm of experience that has not yet been known in words, a realm where the symbolic meaning of a verbal interpretation has little impact.

Repeated procedural interpretations, attempts by the analyst to behaviourally demonstrate awareness of the patient's vulnerabilities, can build a sustained experience of a new form of relating, which is a significant factor in the success of the analytic process. In fact, it is my contention that any effective analytic process necessarily involves a component of procedural interpreting which, by virtue of its healthy relational properties, is a crucial element in the evolution of more adaptive forms of relating.

I am not alone in assuming that certain established relational interactions in development are learned through repetition and eventually become relatively fixed, reflexive ways of relating. Many of us subscribe to this way of thinking, sometimes finding it more useful than more traditional notions of transference. Years ago, Stern (1985) called these interactive habits RIGs, early repeated interactions which become generalized models for ongoing relatedness. Bowlby (1988) named the internal representations of these fixed ways of relating "representational models". I prefer a different way of describing them. I have chosen to focus on observed clinical behaviours, calling any one habitual mode of behaving a "relational reflex". Associated groupings of relational reflexes are collectively referred to as a "relational template" (Herzog, 1998a). I use "template" chiefly because it is a simple word in common usage, evoking the image of a mould of relatedness that is created in early years, applicable to future interpersonal circumstance. I define the relational template as an individual's repertoire of reflexive interactive behaviours, which are activated within a specific relational context, with their associated cognitive, affective, unconscious, and conscious components, first learnt in childhood and then applied repeatedly to relationships throughout life. The concept of a relational template helps to illustrate and explain the human capacity to be able to take in certain aspects of relatedness (that is, those that fit the template), while having little access to other aspects (those that do not fit). Much of what is mutative in analysis involves new interactions that contradict the relational template, allowing a pull in the direction of health. Often, the task of the therapist is to challenge the template, in an effort to contradict its relatively fixed assumptions about relatedness. Shane, Shane, and Gales' (1997) concept of the therapeutic pull towards new relational configurations are in concurrence with this view. It is also in keeping with the ideas of the non-linear dynamic systems theorists Thelan and Smith (1994), which suggest that the "perturbation" of a seemingly invariant way of relating to others can lead to a different, ostensibly healthier form of relatedness. Any successful analysis inevitably serves to perturb a fixed relational pattern of thinking and behaving, or, as I would prefer it—to nudge, challenge, or unbalance non-viable elements of the relational template.

This notion can be applied to any analysis, no matter what the theoretical persuasion of the analyst might be. It is not difficult to understand, for example, how a patient who has had repeated exposure during development to a dismissive, unresponsive parent will eventually be moved by the attentive therapist to alter the assumption that people do not care to listen. In this way, all effective analysts are invariably working at challenging their patients' pathological relational templates, just by virtue of the more adaptive relational aspects of their particular analytic approach.

The clinical situation

The psychoanalysis of a middle-aged artist eventually led to an impasse, arising from her fixed belief that anything she had to offer was worthless. She experienced all attempts at verbal interpretation as simply the therapist doing his job. She could accept his ideas intellectually, but also knew that whatever was said could not change how she felt about herself.

Throughout her development, the relationship established between her and her parents included the implicit premise that she had no right to exist, nor did anything she produced. As far back as she could remember, her mother told her that she had been a disappointment since she was born, and that she had originally been slated to be an abortion. Her childhood interest in art involved an escape to the realm of objects, from a world where human relatedness represented a complete rejection of her wish to be connected to others. Through art, she could maintain a dependable attachment to nature by her loving study of its visual manifestations. Working as an adult artist was problematic, however, and not because of lack of ability. Rather, she had difficulty holding down various jobs; her belief that she was unlikeable and could never belong anywhere sabotaged her efforts. Increasingly dependent on doing freelance piecework, she again interfered with her ability to make a living by assuming that her productions were not worthwhile, making her prices unreasonably low. She even had difficulty signing her name to her work.

Her inability to promote herself had left her financially destitute. Yet, when she showed me her work, I found her to be a remarkably versatile artist, adept in the various media that she had used over the years. It was high quality stuff. All attempts to interpret the discrepancy between her negative opinion of herself and a more objective viewpoint were accepted with appreciation, but the patient admitted that whatever I said would never deeply reach her, because she could never entirely endorse any spoken interpretation. It was simply the therapist's hypothesis, and not the real truth. She told me that even if her professional efforts were of high quality objectively, she could never enjoy them, nor could she believe that others would either. She was well aware of the developmental origin of these beliefs about herself, being raised to feel of no use or interest to others. In therapy, she had grasped a thorough intellectual understanding of this, but insisted that she knew in her heart that she would never be deserving of love or recognition, and no matter how good her professional work was, she would never really consider herself to be a true artist.

The forbidden intervention

During the course of her analysis, I needed to commission a small painting for my home. The thought kept recurring to me that I should ask her to paint it. After all, she was desperately poor, so how could I, in all conscience, pay someone else to do it when I appreciated her work as much as anyone's? Despite this, I hesitated to mention it. What was stopping me? Of course, the idea that it could interfere with the clinical process worried me, but in retrospect I was more concerned with my colleagues' view of my behaviour than with derailing her treatment.

During the next few weeks I gave my decision a lot of thought. I recognized that my apprehension about my colleagues came from years of training where, all too often, the idea of the corrective emotional experience (Alexander, 1956) was viewed with disdain and ridicule, and my countertransferences were corrected. I had been taught that I must never gratify a patient; that I should not succumb to laughing at a patient's joke or return a greeting when someone walked into my office. I always viewed these suggestions with considerable defiance because they simply did not appeal to my common sense, which told me that I first needed to act like an accessible human being if anyone was to trust me as their therapist. I also could not understand why anyone would strictly adhere to notions of abstinence and neutrality, when Freud himself (see Jones, 1953) had no difficulty feeding patients and helping them out financially. Further, Anna Freud (see Young-Bruehl, 1988, p. 256) was known to buy presents for children and correspond with them after they left her care, demonstrating clinical habits as sensible as her father's. Lipton (1983) has written about the contrast between standard psychoanalytic technique and Freud's contradictory behaviour as an analyst, which could be sufficiently active when he felt the occasion called for it. So, I felt that my desire to set aside my inhibitions and come out with my request for a painting was not entirely without precedent. On the other hand, I had a worrying thought. What if I was imposing on a hapless patient my need to defy unpleasant supervisory experiences from years past? I eventually decided that my initial impulse was the best thing I could do as a therapist. It was my natural inclination, and I felt it could be of benefit to the treatment process. I had a strong sense that my commission, even if refused by her, could have therapeutic potential, by contradicting a traumatic relational template. Her family had never taken her work seriously, accepting her gifts of paintings only to humour her because they knew she could not afford to give anything proper. Her work was rarely displayed in anyone's home, and she was constantly being pressured to get a "real job". If I offered to purchase a painting, it could challenge her expectation that anything she created could never be valued by others.

In addition, I was also somewhat influenced by having grown up in a culture of small town businessmen, not more than a five minute drive from the location of the conference for which this chapter was originally written. These businessmen routinely hired their customers to promote goodwill. Where I grew up, it was expected that you hired those who hired you, because it was distinctly offensive to do otherwise. According to that way of thinking, a patient who has shown faith in my services is entitled to the same courtesy from me.

Once I had determined that I was going to ask her, I began to feel anxious about the idea. There were so many conceivable complications that could ensue, including (1) a potential shifting of the therapeutic dynamic to one which demanded compliance from her as an employee, (2) the possibility that any future need she might have to express anger towards me could become obscured by feelings of gratitude or a sense of obligation, (3) the anticipated criticisms of my colleagues that I was "acting in" secondary to my inability to tolerate her feelings of uselessness, and (the following worried me the most) (4) the myriad possibilities where I could be set up to have serious countertransference difficulties. For example: what if, heaven forbid, I did not like the painting? Regardless, I decided to go forward with the request. I believed that engaging her as an artist could function as a challenge to her relational assumption that proximity to others involved a lack of interest in what she had to offer.

When I attempted to frame the question, I wanted to convey my genuine wish to commission the painting without coercing her to comply through the force of my enthusiasm. I decided my approach should involve coming clean with what I thought I was doing, while presenting the potential dilemma it could cause. "I've been thinking for a while about something I might ask you to do for me, but I delayed asking for fear that I might end up pressuring you into doing something against your better judgement. Our bathroom has been designed with a place that needs a painting of a specific size. I'd like you to consider doing it for me, if you feel comfortable. Now this is not even remotely a normal psychoanalytic practice, so if you at all feel that it's not going to work out, it would be fine not to do it. What do you think?"

Her response was, "Why would you hesitate to ask? I think I can handle it. Just don't worry so much, and tell me what you need." We discussed my requirements, my misgivings (which she thought were mostly "not that big a deal"), and her feeling about it: she was delighted to do it and was quite animated whenever she talked about it or showed me her studies of what she was planning. The painting was soon finished, and we discussed at length what we both agreed would be a fair price. Needless to say, I was relieved to find that I loved the work, and she accepted the cash with some awkwardness, but soon put it to good use buying more art supplies.

This kind of activity is not something I do routinely. Nevertheless, I believe that there are times when such interventions can produce a significant impact at a non-verbal, procedural level that cannot be accomplished at the level of language-dominated communication. The request and transaction amounted to a procedural interpretation that demonstrated to her my understanding of the injustice of her family treating her good work with contempt, and my knowledge of her need for me to genuinely enjoy her artistic endeavours. Of course, as with all communication within the procedural realm, there is no guarantee that a behavioural message will necessarily be heard in the way the therapist intends. In this circumstance, however, the message seemed to have got through, and the experiment resulted in a positive outcome. One particularly dramatic moment occurred in the weeks following the completion of the transaction of painting for money when she suddenly sat up from the couch and announced, "My God, I just realized that yesterday while I was going about my business, I was actually thinking of myself as an artist. I'd never thought of myself that way before."

The intervention may have been risky, but not doing it had potential risks too. As soon as I needed a painting, I inadvertently became engaged in a clinical decision because I either was going to involve her, or I was not. I invite the reader to consider what this patient would have felt if she had ever found out that I commissioned someone else. After all, she had many artist friends in town, and word can get around. The procedural message communicated by that alternative could have confirmed some of the nastier aspects of her relational premises. Thus, once I had the need for a painting, I was presented with having to decide on whether the risk of trauma would be greater through exclusion or inclusion of her talent in my decision. Inclusion seemed to be the better choice.

The transaction and her later revelation did not occur in isolation from other analytic events, but I believe that this intervention had a significant therapeutic effect for her. It is now many years since we completed our work together, and she had done much through her own initiative to further her career as an artist. She took on private students, successfully competed for a teaching position at a prestigious institution, began charging competitive rates for what she produced, and learned to overcome her qualms about signing her work. She now continues to define herself as an artist, something she was never able to do before. But her analysis was not without its painful aspects. Her insight into her choice to be an artist led her to mourn for the loss of human relatedness that she had yearned for most of her life, and my fears that I would be encouraging her to sidestep any hostile feelings towards me were unfounded. After the purchase she had occasion to find me as unfair and uncaring as her parents ever were. My validation of her professional work seemed to successfully contradict the archaic relational template when it was activated, and this did much to deepen her insight. She became able to point out her contributions to disruptions in therapy, and recognize how her assumptions about others had sabotaged her ability to get what she needed.

Discussion

I would like first to consider our business transaction in light of how it might be defined by other psychoanalytic writers. I initially thought it would be considered an enactment of sorts, but this would not be in keeping with Chused (1997, p. 265) who clearly states that an enactment is "unconsciously determined, and is not a 'chosen' bit of behaviour." She also says that if the analyst is consciously aware of his action, it amounts to what she calls a "manipulation" (p. 264). Although her opinion appears to be some-what extreme, there seems to be a trend in the literature towards requiring the elements of spontaneity and lack of conscious aware-ness to be included in the definition of an enactment. Exceptions to this rule include Lazar's (1998) "facilitating enactments" and Lichtenberg's (1996) "disciplined spontaneous engagements", which both allow for some conscious activity on the part of the therapist while requiring the element of spontaneity in their formu-lations. I am in agreement with Lazar, who points out that it is diffi-cult to ascribe an absolute boundary between planned and unplanned interventions, emphasizing instead the importance of a quality of "emotionally driven spontaneity". The American Psycho-analytic Association Panel in 1992, on the other hand, seems to be at odds with this notion, defining an enactment as an actualization of the transference which must be mutually unconscious.

Regardless of the presence of some descriptions that are more inclusive, most definitions of enactment still currently appear to contain an inherent admonition against engaging in a consciously predetermined action. That could have something to do with the desire to distance the concept of enactment from the "corrective emotional experience" of Alexander (1956). Alexander deliberately acted out a specific therapeutic role according to what he felt was required by the patient, based on what he determined were parental inadequacies. Many have reacted unfavourably to Alexander's concept, characterizing it as dishonest and manipulative, but I suspect that the general psychoanalytic community has lost some of the more innovative aspects of his idea by discrediting him.

Unfortunately, within the discussion of the literature I have presented so far, there has been little said about therapeutic actions such as mine. My intervention was spontaneously felt at first, and would have involved an enactment as defined, except that I decided to delay acting upon it, doing so only after some contemplation. My behaviour was authentically motivated; I certainly felt inclined to do it. But it was also tempered by a therapist's reflection. It was an empathic response to what I sensed both instinctively and intellectually was a need of this patient. It demonstrates how a spontaneous impulse in the therapist can be delayed and acted upon later, allowing what would have been thought of as an enactment to be tempered with reflection and clinical acumen.

I have found it quite remarkable that analysts have written admirably about enactments as unconscious action by the therapist, but little has been said about spontaneous actions that have been reflected upon (I'm excluding Eissler's [1953] concept of parameters because he did not classify them as therapeutic events). Given that we are a group of professionals who value the capacity to contemplate and analyse, why would we not consider that some of us become aware of the wish to enact, delay it, think about it, but then still do it regardless? A therapist's behaviour can occur spontaneously, or can occur after considerable thought. Why would we decide to privilege or dismiss either eventuality?

Ultimately, I am less concerned about how to define this intervention than with the fact that I have found no clinical examples of its kind in the literature. We need to encourage more discussion of such interventions, even if they do not seem to fit our analytic framework, because they can be powerful therapeutic events. In regard to their therapeutic function for the patient, I would place this kind of activity under the rubric of procedural interpreting, where the therapist communicates a genuine understanding of the patient's relational knowledge through an interpretation using the language of the procedural realm: a language of action. My preference in using the term "procedural interpretation" permits me to bypass the exclusivity of the term "enactment" because it allows that awareness of communications occurring at the procedural level can vary considerably. Therapeutic actions residing within the procedural realm can occur either with or without the awareness of either patient or therapist. Perhaps the intuitive therapist's trademark simply involves a greater awareness of what is happening within the procedural realm, where the relational templates of both patient and therapist have their expression via clinical behaviour.

All therapists who are living and breathing engage in action, whether they like it or not. Thus, from the patient's point of view, therapists necessarily act within the procedural realm as a matter of course, albeit often more subtly than the dramatic example I have given. Whatever we do or do not do always has an element of our relational templates contained therein. Some of our more common behavioural adjustments to accommodate our patients amount to procedural interpretations—non-verbal messages that we "get it", that we really do understand. Perhaps we might be careful to be scrupulously punctual when someone finds it upsetting when we are late, or may decide to become more talkative or silent (or not) when someone requests it. We may or may not make accommodations like this, and we may be either aware or unaware that we have or have not done them.

With this patient, the impulse to purchase her work came from my wish to undo the insult of her being treated by her family as worthless. Inherent to some of my previous verbal interpretations was the message that I did not denigrate her abilities, and that her assumptions about the world were based on a pathological premise which she was taught by her parents. She understood this intellectually, but she was not sure what I said would ever feel to her to be more than just me doing my job. The purchase of a painting functioned as a procedural interpretation showing her that I "got it," that I felt the unfairness of her never being appreciated and wished to demonstrate to her that what was important to her could be of value to others. (A procedural interpretation can function as a communication of "affect sharing", where patients learn that their affect states have reverberated within the therapist, which I have previously shown has mutative, self-object properties [Herzog, 1998b]. In this case, my need to buy her painting was one of the many ways where I demonstrated that I was feeling some of the pride and pleasure she felt about her work.) My desire to put money on the table for something she produced demonstrated compellingly that I respected and enjoyed her work. My previous attempts to show her through verbal interpretation had had limited efficacy. It was not through words, but through action that I could most effectively comment on her family's mythology about her innate worthlessness. This was because, throughout her life, words had always been used to disavow her reality. My word-mediated interpretations were experienced by her as having attributes of what her family had already done—denying and explaining away their lack of authentic interest. Engaging in an action demonstrating my understanding, a procedural interpretation, got the message across. As the saying goes: "actions speak louder than words". It was only after an effective procedural interpretation like this that my verbal interpretations could have credibility.

I want to reassure any sceptics that I am not recommending behavioural activities take the place of verbal interpretation in psychoanalysis. I strongly believe that the role of verbal interpretation continues to be crucial, not only to the development of insight, but also as an act that has therapeutic properties outside of its words. I view the verbal interpretation as having both a symbolic, language-mediated element as well as a behavioural/procedural element (a point which has not been lost on Poland, 1986, who notes that there are messages contained in the action of an analyst's words). A verbal interpretation is not just words with meaning but also a behaviour, and, regardless of the accuracy or inaccuracy of its suppositions, it can communicate crucial information to the patient at the level of relational knowledge. For example, although the therapist may be mistaken in what he has said, his efforts can still communicate what is needed therapeutically: that he cares enough about his patient to try to help organize and explain her unformulated experience (Stern, 1997).

Any successful analysis invariably involves some kind of activity on the part of the analyst which gratifies the patient. Even the act of passively listening to someone who needs to be listened to, or working to understand someone who has rarely been understood, can be experienced by the patient as an activity which has a therapeutic effect at the procedural level. In fact, I would suggest that all successful therapies involve a series of sustained mutative actions, which invariably demonstrate our genuine caring for the patient. Exactly where we limit our behaviour, what we consider reasonable *vs.* unacceptable, has much to do with what each of us is individually comfortable with. Even if we feel that we are backed by theoretical considerations, the theories we have chosen to follow are, as often as not, reflective of our own personal biases and belief systems. Our therapeutic position can owe a lot to our own relational premises, derived from our upbringing, our cultural background, and a lifetime of relating to others in the best way we know how. That is why how we act with each patient should never be rigidly prescribed, but should be as varied as the two personalities represented in each analytic dyad. (This is the basic premise of specificity theory [Bacal & Herzog, 2003], which dictates that optimal therapeutic interactions are dependent on the specific capacities and limitations of the analytic couple.)

Conclusion

I hope I have shown that the analyst, through his or her actions, can deliver powerful procedural interpretations which communicate at the level of a patient's relational knowledge. The analyst's behaviour can demonstrate a deep intuitive understanding of the patient, allowing the patient to give more credence to the verbal interpretations that follow. In fact, if the therapist's act of verbal, symbolic interpreting is to be useful, it needs to exist in the context of healthy procedural relatedness. Without this milieu of healthy relatedness, an effective therapeutic process simply cannot take place. Further, certain interventions that may have been considered unacceptable in the past might sometimes be necessary for a therapeutic process to succeed, because of their mutative potential and their usefulness in helping circumvent therapeutic stalemates. One even has to wonder if we need to reconsider the conceptualization of "transference neurosis", because it could be an artefact of certain analytic approaches that attempt to exclude such interventions.

This case provides an example of how a business transaction initiated by the therapist can result in a significant therapeutic experience. It demonstrates how the delay of a spontaneous impulse in the therapist can allow what would have been thought of as an enactment to be tempered with reflection and clinical acumen. Such actions by the therapist are identified as procedural interpretations that can function to change a patient's entrenched ways of relating to others, often beyond what can be achieved by verbal interpretations alone.

References

Alexander, F. (1956). *Psychoanalysis and Psychotherapy: Developments in Theory, Technique and Training*. New York: Norton.

Bacal, H. A., & Herzog, B. (2003). Specificity theory and optimal responsiveness: an outline. *Psychoanalytic Psychology*.

Bowlby, J. (1998). *A Secure Base*. New York: Basic Books.

Chused, J. (1997). Discussion of "Observing–participation, mutual enactment, and the new classical models" by Irwin Hirsch, PhD. *Contemporary Psychoanalysis, 33*: 263–277.

Clyman, R. B. (1991). The procedural organization of emotions: a contribution from cognitive science to the psychoanalytic theory of therapeutic action, *Journal of the American Psychoanalytic Association, 39S*: 349–382.

Eissler, K. (1953). The effect of the structure of the ego on psychoanalytic technique. *Journal of the American Psychoanalytic Association, 1*: 104–143.

Herzog, B. (1998a). Compliance, defiance and the development of relational templates. Presented at the 21st Annual International Conference on The Psychology of the Self, San Diego, California.

Herzog, B. (1998b). Optimal responsiveness and the experience of sharing. In: H. Bacal (Ed.), *Optimal Responsiveness: How Therapists Heal Their Patients* (pp. 175–190). Northvale, NJ: Jason Aronson.

Herzog, B. (2001). Procedural interpretation and insight: the art of working between the lines in the non-verbal realm. Presented at the 24th Annual International Conference on The Psychology of the Self, San Francisco, California.

Jones, E. (1953). *The Life and Work of Sigmund Freud*. New York: Basic Books.

Lazar, S. (1998). Optimal responsiveness and enactments. In: H. Bacal (Ed.), *Optimal Responsiveness: How Therapists Heal Their Patients* (pp. 213–233). Northvale, NJ: Jason Aronson.

Lichtenberg, J. (1996). *The Clinical Exchange: Techniques Derived from Self and Motivational Systems*. Hillsdale, NJ: Analytic Press.

Lichtenberg, J., Lachmann, F., & Fosshage, J. (1992). *Self and Motivational Systems: Toward a Theory of Technique*. Hillsdale, NJ: Analytic Press.

Lipton, S. D. (1983). A critique of the so-called standard psychoanalytic technique. *Contemporary Psychoanalysis, 19*: 35–52.

Ogden, T. (1994). The concept of interpretive action. *Psychoanalytic Quarterly, 63*: 219–245.

Poland, W. S. (1986). The analyst's words. *Psychoanalytic Quarterly, 55*: 244–272.

Shane, M., Shane, E., & Gales, M. (1997). *Intimate Attachments: Toward a New Self Psychology*. New York: Guilford.

Stern, D. B. (1989). The analyst's unformulated experience of the patient. *Contemporary Psychoanalysis, 25*: 1–33.

Stern, D. B. (1997). *Unformulated Experience: From Dissociation to Imagination in Psychoanalysis*. Hillsdale, NJ: The Analytic Press.

Stern, D. N. (1985). *The Interpersonal World of the Infant*. New York: Basic Books.

Stern, D. N., Sander, L. W., Nahum, J. P., Harrison, A. M., Lyons-Ruth, K., Morgan, A. C., Bruschweilerstern, N., & Tronick, E. Z. (1998). Non-interpretive mechanisms in psychoanalytic therapy: the "something more" than interpretation. *International Journal of Psychoanalysis, 79*: 903–921.

The American Psychoanalytic Association Panel (1992). Enactments in psychoanalysis. M. Johan, Reporter. *Journal of the American Psychoanalytic Association, 40*: 827–841.

Thelan, E., & Smith, L. B. (1994). *A Dynamic Systems Approach to the Development of Cognition and Action*. Cambridge, MA: MIT Press.

Young-Bruehl, E. (1988). *Anna Freud: A Biography*. New York: Summit Books.

CHAPTER TWENTY

To touch or not to touch in the psychoanalytic arena[1]

James L. Fosshage

Psychoanalysis traditionally has placed an almost total interdiction on physical touch between patient and analyst within the analytic arena. Physical touch within psychoanalysis was initially hotly debated, beginning with Freud and Ferenczi. Ferenczi (1953) felt that nurturing touch could facilitate the analysis by helping a patient to tolerate pain that was characterologically defended against. Freud felt that physical contact would almost certainly lead to sexual enactments. In the heat of this controversy, Ferenczi's patient (Clara Thompson) boasted to one of Freud's patients that she was allowed to kiss "Papa Ferenczi" any time she wished. Freud strongly objected, admonishing Ferenczi that this sort of behaviour would inevitably lead to a downward spiral to full sexual engagement. Unfortunately, Freud's and E. Jones' subsequent silencing of Ferenczi, now well-documented (Rachman, 1989), forced the issue of touch to go underground.

While Freud's rule of abstinence and interdiction on touch has predominated in the psychoanalytic literature, there have been notable exceptions where physical touch has been seen as facilitative, even necessary, when dealing with periods of deep regression (Balint, 1952, 1968; Winnicott, 1954, 1965), with psychotic anxieties

and delusional transference (Little, 1990), and with deeply disturbed patients (see Mintz, 1969a,b, who describes the work of
Fromm-Reichman and Searles). More recently, additional reports of
the facilitative use of touch have emerged in our literature (Bacal,
1985, 1997; Breckenridge, 2000; Fosshage, 2000; Holder, 2000;
McLaughlin, 1995, 2000; Pedder, 1976; Pizer, 2000; Ruderman, 2000;
Schlesinger & Appelbaum, 2000; Shane, Shane, & Gales, 2000). In
addition, psychoanalysts of different persuasions in private
(Hamilton, 1996) frequently comment that physical contact in the
way of hand-shakes, hand-holding, hugs, and squeezes on the arm
occur and can be experienced by both analysand and analyst as
facilitative.

The emergence of psychoanalytic alternatives to classical theory,
including more detailed and comprehensive motivational models
(see Lichtenberg, 1989), and a vast array of empirical studies on the
neurobiological functions and psychological meanings of physical
touch is enabling us to readdress the meanings and uses of touch
within psychoanalysis. Recently, an issue in *Psychonalytic Inquiry* by
Ruderman, Shane, and Shane (2000) focused "On touch in the
psychoanalytic situation": a notable first to have a number of
psychoanalysts address the issue of touch and its role in psychoanalysis published in a major psychoanalytic journal.

The purposes of this paper are: first, to review the historical and
classical theoretical basis for the interdiction on touch in psychoanalysis; second, to provide a contemporary theoretical basis for the
use of touch; third, to provide a brief overview of the research on
physical touch; fourth, to review clinical reports of touch in the
psychoanalytic literature and relevant psychotherapy research; and
fifth, to lay down some guidelines for the use of touch in the
analytic setting and to provide several clinical vignettes.

Historical basis for the prohibition of touch

Mintz (1969b) delineated three historical factors that contributed to
the taboo against touch within psychoanalysis. First, psychoanalysis emerged within a cultural context of Victorian sexual prudery. It
was within this context that led Jones to write, "Freud and his
followers were regarded as . . . sexual perverts . . . a real danger to

the community. Freud's theories were interpreted as direct incite-ments to surrendering self-restraint" (Jones, 1955, pp. 108–109). In strenuous efforts to establish a respectable science, Freud and his group wanted to avoid any further misunderstanding that could have been wrought if physical touch entered the scene. With Freud's emphases on sexuality and aggression, any physical contact could easily be construed as sexually seductive or aggressive, plac-ing in jeopardy the whole psychoanalytic enterprise.

Second, the historical association of physical contact with the traditions of religion and magic provided additional incentive for Freud's adamant rejection of touch as part of his effort to bring human conflict within the orderly framework of the rational posi-tivistic science of the day. Physical contact was easily viewed as jeopardizing the psychoanalytic curative goal of rational insight.

Third, following his disappointment in hypnosis, Freud initially applied pressure, a remnant of hypnotic technique, by placing his hands on the patient's forehead, instructing the patient that in response to his pressure the appropriate memories and associations would emerge. Subsequently, he abandoned hypnotic technique altogether and distanced himself from it, including the avoidance of touching patients "in any way, as well as any other procedures which might be reminiscent of hypnosis" (Freud, 1904a, p. 250).

Classical theoretical basis for the prohibition of touch

The theoretical basis for barring physical touch in the analytic arena is anchored in Freud's drive and energy theory. In keeping with the pleasure principle, physical touch is viewed as gratifying (that is, allows for energy discharge of) the patient's infantile sexual longings. Gratification of these sexual longings, in turn, potentially fixates the patient at an infantile level. Refusal to touch, or non-gratification, forces infantile sexual wishes into awareness and articulation that ultimately facilitates their renunciation.

To aid the task of making the unconscious conscious, the analyst, through abstinence, anonymity, and neutrality, attempts to be a blank screen on to which the patient's childhood fantasies are displaced and projected. Within the classical conception of trans-ference, the goal is to prevent or remove any possible contribution from the analyst to the patient's experience in order to illuminate the patient's intrapsychically-generated projections and displacements.

Touch, as with any expressive, non-interpretive response by the analyst, is easily viewed as "muddying the waters" in that its deviation from the analytic stance of abstinence, neutrality, and a blank screen precludes the analysis of transference. Touch is understandably prohibited within the classical model, for it is seen as an intrusion of the analyst that interferes with the free associational process and the unfolding of the intrapsychically-generated transference. Based on this model, for example, Casement (1982) refused to hold the patient's hand out of a conviction that to do so would gratify the patient, in this instance the patient's longings for a good object, and would interfere with the full reliving of the trauma, including the patient's aggression generated by the trauma.

The dual motivational model of sex and aggression within classical theory renders touch as either sexual or aggressive. Other types of touch and, therefore, other meanings are excluded from consideration. If sexual feelings are kindled in the patient, they are assumed to be infantile in origin and, therefore, gratification will be fixating. Touch becomes a sexual enactment that interferes with the analysis. Not only are "adult" sexual feelings excluded (Hirsch, 1994) that, in turn, could become problematic, but it is assumed that gratification of infantile sexual feelings precludes a patient's and analyst's discussion and management of them.

A contemporary theoretical basis for the use of touch

Two major paradigmatic changes are transforming psychoanalysis: the shift from positivistic to relativistic science (or objectivism to constructivism) and the movement from an intrapsychic to an inter-subjective or relational model. These two changes have profound implications for the consideration of "to touch or not to touch" within an ongoing psychoanalytic process. The shift from positivistic to relativistic science has clarified that even our very act of observation affects that which is observed. The second paradigmatic shift, partially emergent out of the first, involves reconceptualizing the analytic relationship as an intersubjective (Stolorow,

Brandchaft, & Atwood, 1987) or relational (Mitchell, 1988) field in which there is bi-directional interactive influence (Beebe, Jaffee, & Lachmann, 1994). In combination, these changes in paradigms clarify that any action or non-action of the analyst variably affects the relational field and, therefore, the patient's experience of the analytic relationship.

In contrast to the classical or displacement model of transference in which transference is intrapsychically generated, within what I call the organization model of transference (Fosshage, 1994; Gill, 1984; Hoffman, 1983, 1991; Lichtenberg, Lachmann, & Fosshage, 1996; Stolorow & Lachmann, 1984–1985), patient and analyst variably co-contribute to the patient's transferential experience. Transference "refer[s] to the primary organizing patterns or schemas with which the analysand constructs and assimilates his or her experience of the analytic relationship" (Fosshage, 1994, p. 271). In other words, the patient tends to organize current perceptual events, to which both patient and analyst variably contribute, in keeping with the primary thematic emotional patterns established through lived experience. From the perspective of this model, neutrality, abstinence, and the blank screen are all *actions* of the analyst that variably contribute to the analysand's transferential experience.

The stringent avoidance of touch that is traditionally called for in psychoanalysis obfuscates that this very avoidance is not "neutral" and cannot create a blank screen. The avoidance of touch, just as touch, can have many different and profound meanings for analysands. Recognizing that the analyst variably contributes to the analysand's experience of the analytic relationship makes us far more aware of the subtle, complex, verbal and non-verbal communications that take place in the analytic arena (Lichtenberg, Lachmann, & Fosshage, 2002). In turn, it opens the door for us to consider a vast array of interventions, including touch, that may or may not be facilitative (Bacal, 1985, 1998; Fosshage, 1997).

On the basis of infant and neurophysiological research and psychoanalytic theory, Lichtenberg (1989) has posited a more complex motivational model (see also Lichtenberg, Lachmann, & Fosshage, 1992, 1996, 2002). Babies are born with five basic needs and innate response patterns. These needs and response patterns emerge within relational fields to become, depending on lived experience, variably functional or dysfunctional motivational systems. The motivational systems are psychological regulation of physiological needs, attachment/affiliative, sensual/sexual, exploratory/assertive, and aversive systems. Any one of these motivations, or a combination, could serve as underpinnings for touch. Importantly, touch can be either sensually soothing or sexually arousing. This more complex motivational model provides us with a broader understanding of a wider range of motivational underpinnings and meanings that touch can have.

Research on physical touch

While there were a few studies along the way, particularly beginning in the 1940s, it was not until the mid-1970s when an explosion of interest and research in the functions of the skin and touch occurred. In a seminal work, *Touching: The Human Significance of the Skin*, Ashley Montagu (1986) brought together the now vast array of studies that pertain to understanding the role of our skin and physical touch in human development.

Our skin is the largest sensory organ of the body. The various elements comprising the skin "have a very large representation in the brain" and the "nerve fibers conducting tactile impulses are generally of larger size than those associated with the other senses" (Montagu, 1986, p. 14). As a sensory system the skin, Montagu concludes, is the most important organ system of the body, for, unlike other senses, a human being cannot survive at all without the physical and behavioural functions performed by the skin. "Among all the senses, touch stands paramount" (*ibid.*, p. 17). The tactile system is the earliest sensory system to become functional (in the embryo) and might be the last to fade.

Research documents that tactile stimulation is necessary for the arousal and development of various physiological systems and is fundamentally required for healthy affectional relationships (Bowlby, 1952; Harlow, 1971; Harlow, Harlow, & Hansen, 1963; Montagu, 1986; among many others). For rhesus monkeys, Harlow (1971) concludes, "It is clearly the incentive of contact comfort [rather than feeding] that bonds the infant affectionately to the mother" (p. 19). In their study of bonding, Klaus, Kennell, and

Klaus (1995) demonstrated that those infants (human and non-human) who are stroked by their mothers at the earliest stages of their postnatal life do much better physically, emotionally, and interpersonally, as compared to those who do not get this experience of touch. The absence of touch may be most critical in accounting for an infant's failure to thrive (Field et al., 1986). Children who are denied close physical contact become anxiously attached (Ainsworth, 1978). Touch deprivation affects psychological as well as physical development (Cohen, 1987; Reite & Field, 1985). Moreover, the type of tactile contact pivotally affects behavioural development (Montagu, 1986). Montagu concluded:

> The study of mammal, monkey, ape, and human behaviors clearly shows that touch is a *basic behavioral need*, much as breathing is a basic physical need, that the dependent infant is designed to grow and develop socially through contact, tactile behavior, and throughout life to maintain contact with others ... When the need for touch remains unsatisfied, abnormal behavior will result. [p. 46]

Tactile communication forms an elaborate, powerful medium of communication among primates. Touch is each human's "first language" (Wilson, 1982). Physical contact can enhance or intensify communication. Stern (1990) writes, "The ultimate magic of attachment is touch. And this magic enters through the skin" (p. 99). Tactile stimulation has profound effects both physiologically and behaviourally. The mother's and father's holding and cuddling of the child create a sense of intimacy, love, safety, and well being. Children who have been inadequately held and touched suffer from an affect-hunger for such attention and, as adolescents and adults, experience difficulty in social and sexual development.

Miami's Touch Research Institute, a scientific centre devoted to exploring the effects of touch on health, has conducted more than fifty studies on massage, demonstrating its "positive effects ... on every malady TRI has studied thus far" (Colt, 1997). And, even more pertinent for psychoanalysis, Colt writes,

> A simple touch—a hand on a shoulder, an arm around a waist—can reduce the heart rate and lower blood pressure. (Even people in deep comas may show improved heart rates when their hands are held.) Touch also stimulates the brain to produce endorphins,

the body's natural pain suppressors, which is why a mother's hug of a child who has skinned his knee can literally "make it better". [p. 60]

So important is tactile stimulation for the development and maintenance of physiological and psychological regulation that recent research demonstrates that physiological and psychological regulations of persons of all ages are "righted" (Waddington, 1947) through physical holding and touch.

Published clinical reports of touch in psychoanalysis

In light of the important role that tactile stimulation and communication has for psychological development and interactive regulation, it is not surprising, in spite of the traditional interdiction on touch in psychoanalysis, that psychoanalysts have reported occasions of considered use of touch to facilitate treatment. (A whole level of discourse involving the potentially healing impact of touch from bioenergetics to expressive psychotherapies is of relevance, but goes beyond the scope of this paper.) Ferenczi, already cited, permitted behavioural enactments which at times included affectionate kisses (see Shapiro, 1992). He also used touch to facilitate bringing a patient back from a trance state to here and now reality. Fromm-Reichmann (1950) wrote, "At times it may be indicated . . . to shake hands with a patient, or, in the case of a very disturbed person, to touch him reassuringly" (p. 12). Searles (1965) indicates that "declining to provide physical contact" may be helpful, yet he mentions the undesirability of "being neurotically afraid of physical contact" (p. 701). Winnicott (1965), reported in his own writings and in those by his patient, Margaret Little (1990), would hold his patient and the patient's hand in efforts to create a sufficient "holding" environment. Little (1966) described a patient who despaired over his discovery that his "accidental" self injuries were intentional and needed the analyst to touch his hand. In his last lecture, Kohut (1981) described offering his two fingers to a patient to hold when the patient was in a state of deep despair (also reported in Bacal, 1985). Pedder (1986) described a deeply regressed patient who needed physical touch.

While published reports typically address the use of touch with very disturbed or deeply regressed patients, Mintz (1969b) suggested that physical touch might also be useful with the "healthy neurotic" in periods of deep regression when the patient is temporarily unavailable for verbal communication. Balint (1952) further expanded the circumstances of the emergence and meaning of touch and described patients' desire for touch towards the end of treatment, when the patients are better integrated, to communicate affection, mutuality, and a deeper connection. In contrast to erotic stimulation, touch under these circumstances can be a powerful form of communication that leads to a deeper intimacy and a "tranquil quiet sense of well-being" (*ibid.*, p. 231).

Recently, Breckenridge (2000) described a clinical situation in which allowing for physical contact conveyed a sense of acceptance and helped to modify a profoundly negative self image. Shifting away from the classical position on touch, McLaughlin (1995, 2000) wrote about physical and psychical touching with an increased ease and acceptance: "Handshakes come and go with some patients, stay consistent with others for the duration. The cue comes from the patient" (1995, p. 44). Rather than obstructing analytic work, he saw hand-shaking as

> having provided a surer sense of knowing I was there and in what kind of contact, before our longer relating through the verbal-aural reaching could be relied upon. It had been helpful that the handshake had been continued thereafter as another way to check in times of doubt. [p. 441]

McLaughlin notes his increasing comfort with holding the patient's hand, including when a patient on the couch reaches back for his. A patient may be reaching for "support, consolation, or for my presence in the face of the patient's not yet speakable yearnings" (p. 441). He finds that "this responsiveness facilitates, rather than hinders, the patient's consequent analytic seeking" (p. 442). In a recent issue of *Psychoanalytic Inquiry* (2000, *20*[1]), other psychoanalysts described their judicious use of touch.

Touch occurs much more frequently in the psychoanalytic arena than has been reported. In my recent private poll of approximately thirty analysts, every one had hugged or been hugged by patients. Reports have been limited for fear of slanderous criticism regarding "poor boundaries", gratification rather than analysis, and sexual seduction. The taboo against touch and its discreditation, augmented by our litigious society, can easily leave the analyst experiencing discomfort with physical contact even when it is initiated by the patient and feels non-sexual. (Cultures differ as to their assesement and availability of tactile experiences [Mead & MacGregor, 1951]. Within the USA, as children mature, physical contact is increasingly interpreted as sexual. Some writers note that the decreased opportunity for non-sexualized touch in our country has contributed to the observation by a number of authors that: "Americans, as a nation of people, are starved for nurturing physical contact" [Hunter & Struve, 1998].) Nevertheless, hand-shakes, a reassuring hand on the shoulder, a supportive squeeze of the arm, an affectionate hug at the door do take place. Recent contributions to psychoanalysis are including in our theory of technique the judicious use of touch as a form of communication.

Psychotherapy research on touch

Freud's interdiction on touch has variably affected most schools of psychotherapy except those that are body orientated (for example, Lowen's [1966] bioenergetic analysis). Research, however, has amply demonstrated that many psychotherapists, including psychoanalytic therapists, touch patients in order to express support, reassurance, warmth, caring, protection, or for other therapeutically motivated reasons (Gelb, 1982; Holroyd & Brodsky, 1977; Horton, Clance, Sterk-Elifson, & Emshoff, 1995; Hunter & Struve, 1998; Kardener, Fuller, & Mensh, 1973; Milakovich, 1992; Patterson, 1973). Emphasis has been placed in the literature on the undeniably harmful effects of erotic contact between patients and therapists (Pope, 1990). Yet, accumulative clinical and research evidence demonstrates that not all physical contact between therapist and patient (beyond a formal hand-shake) is a "boundary crossing", as Gutheil & Gabbard (1993) suggest, that places the relationship on a "slippery slope" of erotic gratification. Surveys of therapists fail to support the assumption that appropriate touch in therapy leads to inappropriate erotic touch (Pope, 1990). Touch, as with many actions, can trigger sexual feelings which, in turn, need to be discussed, understood, and managed, like any other feelings.

Two empirical investigations of the meanings attributed to non-erotic touch in traditional psychotherapy directly assess the experiences of patients in ongoing psychotherapeutic treatment. While Gelb's (1982) study was limited, with a small homogenous sample (ten female patients with male therapists), it identified four factors associated with patients' positive and/or negative evaluations of touch in psychotherapy. These factors are: (1) clarity regarding touch, sexual feelings, and boundaries of therapy (including the patient's sense that the boundaries are clear and unambiguous); (2) patient control in initiating and sustaining physical contact; (3) congruence of touch with the level of intimacy in the relationship and with the patient's issues; and (4) patient perception that the physical contact is for his/her benefit, rather than the therapist's. These four factors arising out of patients' reactions are, by and large, congruent with those emphasized by psychoanalysts in the clinical literature.

Horton, Clance, Sterk-Elifson, and Emshoff (1995) tested and extended Gelb's study. Their sample involved 231 adult (twenty years of age or older) patients who were or had been in psychotherapy for at least two months within the last two years and who had "experienced some sort of physical contact with their therapist (beyond accidental contact or a formal handshake)" (*ibid.*, p. 446). The sample included male and female patients and therapists, and heterogeneous and homogeneous pairs. The data supported the hypotheses that Gelb's four factors correlated positively with the patient's evaluation of touch occurring in therapy. "Congruence of touch with the level of intimacy" accounted for the largest portion of the variance. The hypothesis, "whether potential sexual attraction is inversely correlated with positive evaluation of touch in therapy, was not supported" (*ibid.*, p. 449).

In the patients' descriptions of touch two important themes emerged. Touch, reported by 69% of the sample, fostered a feeling of a stronger bond, closeness, and a sense that the therapist really cares, thereby facilitating increased trust and openness. Forty-seven per cent of the sample indicated that touch communicated acceptance and enhanced their self-esteem.

Sexually abused patients were more likely to attribute a corrective or educative role to touch in therapy, and to report feeling "touchable", "lovable" or generally better about themselves as a result of touch than were nonabused patients. [*ibid.*, p. 452]

Ten patients in this sample reported negative experiences with touch in their current therapy: six patients described that current therapist behaviour signalled their therapist's discomfort with touch, and four patients indicated that touch was accepted, but was not meeting "an expressed need of theirs" (*ibid.*, p. 452). Discomfort with touch in these cases was often alleviated by its open discussion. The authors concluded:

The results support the judicious use of touch with patients who manifest a need to be touched, or who ask for comforting or supportive contact. They also support Ferenczi's (1953) position that, contrary to orthodox opinion, "gratifying" the patient does not necessarily interfere with the patient's motivation to work in therapy, but may alleviate shame and help the patient tolerate the pain enough to face and work through issues more quickly, or on a deeper level. [*ibid.*, p. 255]

Touch and clinical work

Psychoanalysis, in keeping with our Western culture, has almost solely relied on verbal communication. Only recently have we begun to understand and to use with increased awareness the vast array of non-verbal communications. Montagu (1986) viewed touching as "chief among [the] languages of the senses" (p. xv). Touch, like other senses, can trigger important memories of past events, giving us access to preverbal or, yet to be verbalized, memories. In addition, touch is vital for survival and a sense of well being.

Psychoanalysts cannot afford to exclude such a powerful form of communication and connection as touch. Research and clinical experience amply demonstrate that for many patients, whether deeply disturbed or not, different kinds of touch, including "giving" as well as "receiving", can be facilitative of therapeutic moments and analytic work.

The use of touch within the psychoanalytic situation can create dangers of "the slippery slope" (Gabbard, 1994; Gutheil & Gabbard, 1993). An analyst's vulnerability, sensual and sexual deprivation, and self-deflation, are all psychological issues that can undermine the analytic spirit of inquiry and potentiate a sexual enactment. Nevertheless, touch as one form of broadened communication can occur safely as a disciplined, sometimes spontaneous, form of meaningful expression.

Temperament and lived experience affect a person's desire for, and comfort level with, touch, as well as a person's ease in the use of touch for communication. People differ as to sensuality and what is commonly known as "the gift of touch". The meanings and use (or not) of touch in the analytic dyad emerge out of a complex inter-action of two participants and their respective subjectivities. While certain kinds of touch can be facilitative of therapeutic "moments" and analytic work, touch can also be traumatizing. An overriding analytic "spirit of inquiry" (Lichtenberg, Lachmann, & Fosshage, 2002) facilitates joint awareness of meanings, especially important when touch has been problematic.

An analyst's comfort or discomfort with an analysand's request for hand-shaking, hand-holding, or a hug is revealing of the patient, the analyst, and the interaction. Occurring within a dyad, it needs the analyst to feel comfortable and authentic in order to create a facilitative interaction involving touch. (Six of the ten negative expe-riences with touch in the Horton, Clance, Sterk-Elifson, and Emshoff [1995] study were related to patients' experience of their therapists' behaviour to be communicating the therapists discomfort with touch ([and yet, still touching!].) The mix of genders and ages within the dyad undoubtedly affects meanings and comfort levels for both parties. On those occasions when we, as analysts, feel uncomfort-able and recognize that the discomfort is primarily "ours", openly acknowledging our discomfort (maintaining authentic engage-ment), rather than pathologizing the patient's desire for physical contact (e.g., "acting in"), will facilitate the analytic interaction.

Emanating out of research and clinical experience, the following guidelines are presented in summary form.

1. Touch must be in keeping with the desires and needs of the patient.

2. Touch must be in keeping with the level of intimacy in the relationship.
3. Touch, as initiated by analyst or patient, can have very different (positive and negative) meanings for each member of the dyad.
4. Hugs are more safely initiated by the patient because of the increased potential for erotic stimulation.
5. To remain authentically engaged, the analyst needs to accept and acknowledge comfort or discomfort with touch, especially when a patient is requesting physical contact.
6. Physical contact can create a sensual experience or stir sexual feelings (Lichtenberg, 1989; Lichtenberg, Lachmann, & Fosshage, 1992, 1996), as can a look, intonation, and verbal remark. When sexual feelings are stirred within the analytic encounter, they, like all feelings, need to be accepted, understood, and modulated.
7. A large study found that sexual attraction did not interfere with touch being experienced as positive (Horton, Clance, Sterk-Elifson, & Emshott, 1995), suggesting that sexual feelings can be appropriately modulated when touch is used as a form of communication.
8. While touch less frequently occurs during sessions because of the focus and potential for interfering with a patient's articulations, touch may be required to re-establish empathic contact particularly when trauma has been activated in the analytic encounter.
9. During sessions with periods of intense depersonalization and disorientation, touch, combined with simultaneous articulation of experience, can be used to foster a sufficient sense of protection and safety for the reintegration of dissociated memories and affect.
10. Occurrences of touch, like all interactions, need to be closely tracked and often discussed for understanding their meanings and for assessing whether they are facilitating or encumbering the therapeutic endeavour.

As for myself, I find myself liking and relatively comfortable with touch. I tend to communicate easily through touch. In the analytic arena, I find that hand-shakes with men and women create a sense of mutual respect and engagement. Sometimes, they become ritualized; often, they do not. I find myself easily touching the shoulder of a patient, man or woman, as they are walking out the door. Hugs at the door occur occasionally with men and women. And some patients I never touch, except at the end of treatment with a hand-shake.

As McLaughlin, I feel that I can usually (not always) sense the individual differences and can anticipate when touch will be facilitative or not. I try to make sure that the patient initiates hugs, for hugs can easily be experienced as an intrusion and as my agenda. Because of the nature of these hugs, they are rarely experienced as erotic. If so, we work with those feelings. Hugs, in my experience, are usually expressions of mutual affection and closeness, and at times gratitude. I will always discuss a hug, for it typically has more import and meaning. In contrast, a hand-shake, at times clasping both of my hands on my analysand's hand, or a squeeze on the shoulder, I will initiate sometimes to communicate my presence, warmth, and support of my analysand. At times the physical contact is discussed, sometimes not. Analysands, both those who have been deprived of touch and those who use touch to communicate, have often commented on how important and healing the touch has been.

While touch has occurred during sessions, I have personally found it rare, for I have experienced touch as potentially interfering with analysands' articulations of their experience. For preverbal trauma, however, touch may be required for establishing an empathic connection. Touch has occurred during sessions in which there are periods of intense depersonalization and disorientation and, on these occasions, touch, combined with simultaneous articulation of experiences, has helped to bolster a holding environment.

Clinical illustrations

I will present two clinical vignettes in which different forms of touch became powerful communications.

First clinical vignette

Samantha, a bright, attractive woman of thirty-seven, had entered a previous analysis with depression and suicidal ideation (see Fosshage,

1999, for a complete case description). The analysis went quite well for six months. She had never felt so understood. Following some hugs and driving the patient home at night (when she was her analyst's last patient), her analyst (I will call him Jay) precipitously disclosed his love, his desire to terminate treatment with her, and his wish to marry her. Three days later she had terminated treatment, and was living with him.

Two weeks later Samantha came into treatment with me. She was in the throes of love and an idealizing self-object connection with Jay. Over the next two months Samantha discovered that Jay, rather than understanding, was controlling and unavailable for discussion. De-idealization set in, and at the end of two months she had broken off the relationship with Jay and was back in her apartment. She was enraged with Jay. She also felt intense shame and guilt, for she felt that her discussion of sexual feelings and physical contact had contributed to their mutual seduction. She vowed never to have sexual feelings towards her analyst again, obviously directed towards me.

The analysis was a difficult one. Samantha had found little choice but to accommodate to her parents' powerful agendas. Both parents were quite successful, intrusive, and emotionally abusive. There had been an episode of sexual abuse with a neighbour. Samantha had become "a model Swiss–German girl", had frozen off her affective life, and suffered from depression. The transferential theme that I, like her parents and previous analyst, might also have an agenda for her, was periodically activated. Over time, Samantha felt sufficiently safe to access her emotional life, filled with intense shame, rage, tears, fear, and a sense of being lost.

After three years of an emotionally turbulent analysis, Samantha had improved considerably. Her affective experience was more available to her and more manageable. She felt more vitally alive and was better able to have and sustain genuinely positive feelings about herself. Her trust in me had grown immeasurably and she was becoming more expressive of loving feelings for me.

During the session on which I wish to focus, Samantha had been feeling particularly positive about herself and her life, having come through the "black clouds" and feeling "glad to be alive". In my experience, there was a palpable closeness between us. At the end of the session, we stood, and I, as usual, went to the door to open it. Before I opened the door, Samantha asked to hug me, telling me that she was feeling close and grateful and wanted to thank me for "hanging in" with her. We hugged comfortably and with mutual affection. Samantha's desire to hug, and our mutual comfort was made possible, I believe, because it was in keeping with the level of intimacy between us and emotionally quite fitting the moment. Our hug felt safe, for Samantha initiated it. For each of us, this was a poignant hug that powerfully communicated mutual trust, affection, and gratitude. I was particularly struck by it, for, as we discussed in the following session, it was an expression of Samantha's profound trust that neither of us would misinterpret it. It was like a watershed after what she had come through in her previous analysis. Subsequently, Samantha, upon parting, extended her hand for a hand-shake, wanted to have a brief hug, or preferred, especially when she was upset with me, to have no contact at all. For her to do what she felt, to initiate the action, was particularly important in light of her past experience of having to accommodate to her parents' agendas. Our routine was that she always initiated it and often expressed her feelings verbally as well. I am convinced that it deepened her affective experience, sense of safety, and the intimate connection between us.

Second clinical vignette

Susan, in her mid forties, was the first-born of seven children.[1] The core trauma was captured in a model scene (Lichtenberg, Lachmann, & Fosshage, 1992) in which Susan, as a little girl, stands at the doorway, wanting and hoping, but afraid to ask, for attention from her father, who is reading the newspaper. She recalled moments of intense closeness with her father, sitting and cuddling on his lap; yet, her father, more often, was experienced as self-preoccupied and non-communicative. In addition, he had an unpredictably explosive temper. The birth of her first sibling, a sister, when she was six, apparently captivated her father's attention, leaving her feeling "displaced" from her father's lap and rendered invisible. Susan's mother was not experienced as emotionally "present". As her other siblings arrived, Susan found her mother to be increasingly unavailable and unrelated to her children, frequently confusing their names. In contrast, she experienced her grandmother, who spoke in a language foreign to her, to be the one consistently affirming and comforting person. Her grandmother would express her love and caring through facial expressions and physical touch.

Susan valiantly fought to establish and maintain self-esteem, against easily triggered, devastating feelings of rejection and humiliation. She became a care-taker of her siblings, a model student, excelled academically, and was personally well liked. As an adult, with the same battle waging in her, she expressed and maintained her vitality through her efforts as a wife, mother, friend, and professional. Despite considerable success in her endeavours, the trauma of devaluation, rejection, and humiliation was always close at hand.

Susan longed for my affirmation and wanted to feel "special", in the sense of feeling valued, unique, and important in my eyes. Yet, she was convinced that she was not special or valued and, though she felt I liked her, she felt that I did not really see or respond to her as special. I was aware of my increasing fondness for her. Yet, to the degree that she remained protectively hidden (in response to her expectation of rejection), I felt that I could not see or respond to her sufficiently for us to be able to establish a sense of feeling valued. This relational config-uration tended to confirm, yet again, her negative percepts. Exploration and interpretive understanding of this relational scenario helped us to begin to extricate ourselves from it. She began, on occasion, to express herself with fuller affect that fostered reciprocally increased affective intensity in my responses. I, in turn, became more active in my inquiry: for example, shortening the length of silences between us, increasing my affective expression. My increased activity reciprocally increased Susan's expressiveness. Thus, our engagement gradually deepened, including an emergent, mutually reciprocal feeling that I "knew" her and valued her.

Gradually, an affirming, yet fragile, bond was formed, aided by a combination of empathic understanding and my more direct commu-nication of affirming feelings to her through my words, vocal tonality, facial expressions, and physical touch.

For Susan, physical touch was a particularly powerful and meaningful form of communication, for it was through touch that she had most poignantly connected with her father (sitting on his lap and cuddling) and non-English speaking grandmother (hugs). The moments of physical contact with her father and grandmother were the singular moments in her childhood when she had felt loved and valued. Susan, in addition, was temperamentally a very sensual woman who made touch an important form of communication.

For our purposes here, I wish to focus on the emergence of holding hands during sessions (an unusual occurrence in my experience). Susan's traumatic negative percepts of herself and of her analyst as insufficiently valuing her were easily triggered. We were well acquainted with these themes and their origins. On those occasions when a combination of my actions and Susan's constructions triggered her traumatic states, her negative percepts, marked with shame, humiliation, and deflation, took over and her reflective capacity vanished. Physically she began to shrink; her eyes partially closed, and her gaze dropped to the floor, rarely risking a glance at me for fear of what she might find. All of this was occurring in one particular session. This time, however, Susan, like the hesitant little girl at the doorway watching her father read his newspaper, hesitantly asked if she could hold my hand. Experiencing her taking a scary risk to reconnect, I responded in the affirmative, moved my chair forward, and reached out to her. Susan took my hand and then reached out for the other. We held both hands, sitting face to face. We sat in silence, feeling the connection. I felt and expressed warmth, caring, and affection toward her through squeezing her hands, and facially. She hesitantly dared to look at me, quickly turned away, then returned for a longer look. Slowly, she described what she was feeling. Holding hands and my facial expression powerfully communicated that I cared for and valued her, an experience she sorely needed. She was able gradually to re-emerge from her traumatic state, regain reflective capacity, and a different, far more benign, perspective on what had triggered the traumatic state.

Subsequently, when Susan was in the throes of these traumatic states, she or I on occasion would initiate hand-holding, which usually added the necessary ingredients of affection and reassurance for breaking through. My experience, as I told her, was that holding hands on these particular occasions had felt to me like a direct avenue to her heart, to her feeling valued again. And, of course, for this to occur, I needed to be feeling deeply that way towards her.

In these traumatic states, Susan often struggled with negative body images and feelings of repulsion. Holding her hands implicitly conveyed my sense of her physical "touchability" and her physical attractiveness (Kohut's gleam in the mother's eye) that helped her to emerge from her negative percepts and to reinstate more vitalizing feelings of attractiveness.

Would words have sufficed? Although we can never know for sure, in this instance I felt that touch, because of its particular meaning for this analysand, was needed to communicate at a fundamental level, to break through the traumatic states and co-create the needed, reassuring (holding) experience. Would touch have sufficed? Again we cannot know for sure, but I believe our discussions of the meanings of our hand-holding added immeasurably to our co-created experience and her growing self awareness.

Concluding remarks

Touch is a powerful form of communication. We cannot afford to eliminate a profoundly important mode of communication from our healing profession. As with any form of communication, verbal and non-verbal, we can use it advantageously, or not, for facilitating understanding, communication, and the analysis. As we recognize the communicative power of physical touch and expand our view of the possible meanings of touch, we are better able to understand our analysands' requests for touch and the spontaneous occurrences involving touch. It will afford analysts greater comfort and, regardless of whether analysts choose to touch or not, we will be better able to work with the meanings of touch in a more flexible and constructive manner.

Note

1. Several sections of this chapter have been previously published: Fosshage (2000).

References

Ainsworth, M. S. (1978). *Patterns of Attachment: A Psychological Study of the Strange Situation*. Hillsdale, NJ: Lawrence Erlbaum.

Balint, M. (1952). *Primary Love and Psycho-Analytic Technique*. London: Tavistock.

Balint, M. (1968). *The Basic Fault*. London: Tavistock.

Bacal, H. (1985). Optimal responsiveness and the therapeutic process. In: A. Goldberg (Ed.), *Progress in Self Psychology, Volume 1* (pp. 202–227). New York: Guilford.

Bacal, H. (1997). Optimal responsiveness and analytic listening: discussion of James L. Fosshage's "Listening/experiencing perspectives and the quest for a facilitating responsiveness". In: A. Goldberg (Ed.), *Progress in Self Psychology, Volume 13* (pp. 57–68). Hillsdale, NJ: Analytic Press.

Bacal, H. (Ed.) (1998). *How Therapists Heal Their Patients: Optimal Responsiveness*. Northvale, NJ: Jason Aronson.

Beebe, B., Jaffee, J., & Lachmann, F. (1994). A dyadic systems view communication. In: N. Skolnick & S. Warshaw (Eds.), *Relational Perspectives in Psychoanalysis* (pp. 61–81). Hillsdale, NJ: Analytic Press.

Bowlby, J. (1952). *Maternal Care and Mental Health: A Report on Behalf of the World Health Organization*. Geneva, Switzerland: World Health Organization.

Breckenridge, K. (2000). Physical touch in psychoanalysis: a closet phenomenon? *Psychoanalytic Inquiry, 20*: 2–20.

Casement, P. (1982). Some pressures on the analyst for physical contact during the reliving of an early trauma. *International Review of Psychoanalysis, 9*: 279–286.

Cohen, S. S. (1987). *The Magic of Touch*. New York: Harper & Rowe.

Colt, G. H. (1997). The magic of touch: massage's healing powers make it serious medicine. *Life* (August): 53–62.

Ferenczi, S. (1953). *The Theory and Technique of Psychoanalysis*. New York: Basic Books.

Field, T., Schanberg, S., Scafidi, F., Bauer, C., Vega-Lahr, N., Garcis, R., Nystrom, J., & Kuhn, C. (1986). Tactile/kinesthetic stimulation effects on preterm neonates. *Pediatrics, 77*: 654–658.

Fosshage, J. (1994). Toward reconceptualizing transference: theoretical and clinical considerations. *International Journal of Psychoanalysis, 75*(2): 265–280.

Fosshage, J. (1997). Listening/experiencing perspectives and the quest for a facilitating responsiveness. *Progress in Self Psychology, 13*: 33–55.

Fosshage, J. (1999). Forms of relatedness and analytic intimacy. Presented at the 22nd Annual International Conference on the Psychology of the Self, Toronto, 29 October.

Fosshage, J. (2000). The meanings of touch in psychoanalysis: a time for reassessment. *Psychoanalytic Inquiry, 20*: 21–43.

Freud, S. (1904a). Freud's psycho-analytic procedure. *S.E., 7*: 249–254. London: Hogarth Press.

Fromm-Reichmann, F. (1950). *Principles of Intensive Psychotherapy*. Chicago, IL: University of Chicago Press.

Gabbard, G. (1994). Commentaries on papers by Tansey, Davies, and Hirsch. *Psychoanalytic Dialogues, 4*(2): 203–214.

Gelb, P. (1982). The experience of nonerotic contact in traditional psychotherapy: a critical investigation of the taboo against touch. *Dissertation Abstracts, 43*: 248B.

Gill, M. (1984). Transference: a change in conception or only in emphasis? *Psychoanalytic Inquiry, 4:* 489–523.

Gutheil, T., & Gabbard, G. (1993). The concept of boundaries in clinical practice: theoretical and risk-management dimensions. *American Journal of Psychiatry, 150:* 188–196.

Hamilton, V. (1996). *The Analyst's Preconscious.* Hillsdale, NJ: Analytic Press.

Harlow, H. (1971). *Learning to Love.* New York: Albion.

Harlow, H., Harlow, M. K., & Hansen, E. W. (1963). The maternal affectional system of rhesus monkeys. In: H. L. Rheingold (Ed.), *Maternal Behavior in Mammals.* New York: Wiley.

Hirsch, I. (1994). Countertransference love and theoretical model. *Psychoanalytic Dialogues, 4:* 171–192.

Hoffman, I. Z. (1983). The patient as interpreter of the analyst's experience. *Contemporary Psychoanalysis, 19:* 389–422.

Hoffman, I. Z. (1991). Discussion: toward a social-constructivist view of the psychoanalytic situation. *Psychoanalytic Dialogues, 1:* 74–105.

Holder, A. (2000). To touch or not to touch: that is the question. *Psychoanalytic Inquiry, 20:* 21–43.

Holroyd, J., & Brodsky, A. (1977). Psychological attitudes and practices regarding erotic and nonerotic contact with patients. *American Psychologist, 32:* 843–849.

Horton, J., Clance, P., Sterk-Elifson, C., & Emshoff, J. (1995). Touch in psychotherapy: a survey of patients' experiences. *Psychotherapy, 32:* 43–457.

Hunter, M., & Struve, J. (1998). *The Ethical Use of Touch in Psychotherapy.* Thousand Oaks, CA: Sage.

Jones, E. (1955). *The Life and Work of Sigmund Freud, Volume 2.* New York: Basic Books.

Kardener, S., Fuller, M., & Mensh, I. (1973). A survey of physicians' attitudes and practices regarding erotic and nonerotic contact with patients. *American Journal of Psychiatry, 130:* 1077–1091.

Klaus, P., Kennell, J., & Klaus, M. (1995). *Bonding: Building the Foundations of Secure Attachment & Independence.* Boston, MA: Addison-Wesley.

Kohut, H. (1981). Lecture presented at the Annual Conference on Self Psychology, Berkeley, CA, October.

Lichtenberg, J. (1989). *Psychoanalysis and Motivation.* Hillsdale, NJ: Analytic Press.

Lichtenberg, J., Lachmann, F., & Fosshage, J. (1992). *Self and Motivational Systems: Toward a Theory of Psychoanalytic Technique.* Hillsdale, NJ: Analytic Press.

Lichtenberg, J., Lachmann, F., & Fosshage, J. (1996). *The Clinical Exchange: Technique from the Standpoint of Self and Motivational Systems*. Hillsdale, NJ: Analytic Press.

Lichtenberg, J., Lachmann, F., & Fosshage, J. (2002). *A Spirit of Inquiry: Communication in Psychoanalysis*. Hillsdale, NJ: Analytic Press.

Little, M. (1966). Transference in borderline states. *International Journal of Psychoanalysis*, 47: 476–485.

Little, M. (1990). *Psychotic Anxieties and Containment*. London: Aronson.

Lowen, A. (1966). *The Betrayal of the Body*. New York: Macmillan.

McLaughlin, J. (1995). Touching limits in the analytic dyad. *Psychoanalytic Quarterly*, 64: 433–465.

McLaughlin, J. (2000). The problem and place of physical contact in analytic work: some reflections on handholding in the analytic situation. *Psychoanalytic Inquiry*, 20: 65–81.

Mead, M., & MacGregor, F. (1951). *Growth and Culture*. New York: Putnam.

Milakovich, J. (1992). Touching in psychotherapy: the difference between therapists who touch and those who do not. Unpublished doctoral dissertation. Santa Barbara, CA: Fielding Institute.

Mintz, E. (1969a). On the rationale of touch in psychotherapy. *Psychotherapy: Theory, Research, and Practice*, 6: 232–234.

Mintz, E. (1969b). Touch and the psychoanalytic tradition. *Psychoanalytic Review*, 56: 365–376.

Mitchell, S. (1988). *Relational Concepts in Psychoanalysis*. Cambridge, MA: Harvard University Press.

Montagu, A. (1986). *Touching: The Human Significance of the Skin*. New York: Harper & Row.

Patterson, J. E. (1973). Effects of touch on self-exploration and the therapeutic relationship. *Journal of Consulting and Clinical Psychology*, 40: 170–175.

Pedder, J. R. (1986). Attachment and new beginning: some links between the work of Michael Balint and John Bowlby. *International Review of Psychoanalysis*, 3: 491–497.

Pizer, B. (2000). Negotiating analytic holding: discussion of Patrick Casement's *Learning from the Patient*. *Psychoanalytic Inquiry*, 20: 82–107.

Pope, K. S. (1990). Therapist–patient sexual involvement: a review of the research. *Clinical Psychology Review*, 10: 477–490.

Rachman, A. (1989). Confusion of tongues: the Ferenczian metaphor for childhood seduction and emotional trauma. *Journal of American Academy of Psychoanalysis*, 17: 181–295.

Reite, M., & Field, T. (Eds.) (1985). *The Psychobiology of Attachment and Separation*. New York: Academic Press.

Ruderman, E. (2000). Intimate communications: the values and boundaries of touch in the psychoanalytic setting. *Psychoanalytic Inquiry*, 20: 108–123.

Ruderman, E., Shane, E., & Shane, M. (2000). On touch in the psychoanalytic situation (Issue Eds.). *Psychoanalytic Inquiry*, 20: 1.

Schlesinger, H., & Appelbaum, A. (2000). When words are not enough. *Psychoanalytic Inquiry*, 20: 124–143.

Searles, H. (1965). *Collected Papers on Schizophrenia*. New York: International Universities Press.

Shane, M., Shane, E., & Gales, M. (2000). Psychoanalysis unbound: a contextual consideration of boundaries from a developmental systems self psychology perspective. *Psychoanalytic Inquiry*, 20: 144–159.

Shapiro, S. (1992). The discrediting of Ferenczi and the taboo on touch. Presented at the American Psychological Association Division 39 Spring Meeting, Philadelphia, PA.

Stern, D. N. (1990). *Diary of a Baby*. New York: Basic Books.

Stolorow, R., & Lachmann, F. (1984–1985). Transference: the future of an illusion. *Annual of Psychoanalysis*, 12: 19–37.

Stolorow, R., Brandchaft, B., & Atwood, G. (1987). *Psychoanalytic Treatment: An Intersubjective Approach*. Hillsdale, NJ: The Analytic Press.

Waddington, C. (1947). *Organizers and Genes*. Cambridge: Cambridge University Press.

Wilson, J. M. (1982). The value of touch in psychotherapy. *American Journal of Orthopsychiatry*, 52: 65–72.

Winnicott, D. (1958). *Collected Papers*. London: Tavistock.

Winnicott, D. (1965). *The Maturational Processes and the Facilitating Environment: Studies in the Theory of Emotional Development*. New York: International Universitites Press.

PART IX
REFLECTIONS

CHAPTER TWENTY-ONE

What is taboo and not taboo in psychoanalysis?

Rebecca C. Curtis

To understand what is taboo in psychoanalysis, we first need to have some agreement about what psychoanalysis itself is. For many clinicians and theorists alike, ideas about psychoanalysis have changed considerably in the past fifty years. In 1954, in a panel on the similarities and differences between psychoanalysis and dynamic psychotherapy, Fromm-Reichmann stated that the bases of psychoanalysis remained the doctrine of the importance of unconscious processes, the concepts of transference and resistance, and the significance of the childhood history. She added the significance of anxiety for the dynamics underlying personality. Psychoanalysts today probably agree with the major bases she described. There are, however, certain techniques and styles of conducting psychoanalysis that would, if used predominantly, render a treatment to be considered "non-psychoanalytic" by most in the field. Grotstein alluded briefly to such techniques as cognitive therapy, behaviour modification, guided imagery, psychodrama, and psychopharmacology in his chapter. Eagle dealt with the overdependency upon transference interpretations in psychoanalysis. The issue of the reliance upon the interpretation–insight model is one that psychoanalysts must grapple with more fully as the model of therapeutic action changes to one emphasizing new experiences. Most of the topics chosen by the contributors as potentially taboo, however, are concerned more with rules and traditions passed down by practitioners than with the differentiation of psychoanalysis from other forms of therapeutic treatment.

Grotstein and Eagle both address a number of different topics. Grotstein deals with the issues of acceptable theory in psychoanalysis, among other matters. He comments on the threat of suspension issued to the Los Angeles Psychoanalytic Society/Institute by the American Psychoanalytic Association over inclusion of Kleinians and the democratization of promotion to training analyst. Noting how so many were banned from mainstream psychoanalysis in its history if they differed too much, he concludes that a fear continues to loom over most psychoanalysts that if they go too far afield from accepted ideas and practices, they will be either excommunicated, or never included in the first place. Indeed, most of the contributors to this volume probably would not be considered to be psychoanalysts in the first place by some members of the International Psychoanalytic Association, who believe that a four-day per week analysis with one of their members is essential for qualification as a psychoanalyst. Grotstein suggests that there be guiding principles, but not taboos. How far theories and techniques can deviate from strictly Freudian ones and still be thought of as psychoanalytic is a question only history will decide.

Eagle is concerned about the reliance upon transference and countertransference in contemporary psychoanalysis. This concern, also expressed by Schacter (2002) and Curtis (2008), is part of the broader issue of the distinctiveness of psychoanalytic technique raised by Grotstein. This will probably become more of a "hot" topic within psychoanalysis, as some analysts see a wider range of patients and become more active than classical analysts have been. Eagle also raises the issue of the disjunction between the way some analysts embracing the "postmodern" turn within psychoanalysis see their work and what patients expect to be the analyst's job. Psychoanalysis has become less authoritarian in response to what patients expect and tolerate. The publication of the article by Eagle, Wolitsky, and Wakefield (2001) indicates that criticism of the disjunction between analysts' thinking they do not "know" what is going on in patients' minds and none the less making suggestions about what is going on is no longer a taboo subject, as the publication of their views has brought this topic completely out in the open.

Eagle, along with Tintner, Mellinger, Howard, Phillips, and Herzog, addresses the problem of money. The actual fee charged a patient is rarely reported. Because money reflects the value given to any activity, the taboo about this subject reflects a larger one in society and touches upon so many serious controversies regarding social and economic policies that it is likely to remain one that analysts are reticent to discuss openly for many years to come. The authors are to be applauded for bringing up their personal struggles regarding various financial matters.

Borg, Garrod, Dalla, and McCarroll address the issue of the application of psychoanalytic principles outside psychoanalysis proper. The attempt to apply psychoanalytic concepts to organizations has gone on at least since the Tavistock Centre was involved in attempts to advise the military in the first half of the twentieth century and Harry Stack Sullivan (Perry, 1982) participated with other social scientists in articulating principles for the prevention of war. Although some psychoanalysts are still active in attempts to reduce conflict and violence in the world (e.g., Volkan, 1988) and comment about consumerism and race (Wachtel, 1983, 1999), psychoanalysts have little influence overall in the fields of education, politics, government, and economics. If involvement outside psychoanalysis proper is not a subject that is taboo, as Borg and colleagues suggest, it is still one that is so complicated that it is usually met with the silence that Hansen mentions was given to Erich Fromm.

Another issue that Hansen raises is that of the number of patients actually being seen three or more times per week by most practitioners trained in psychoanalysis. Although training analysts, as well as practitioners in countries where psychoanalysis is reimbursed by the government, might have a good number of such patients, most psychoanalysts have fewer patients whom they see at least three times per week than they would like. Hansen bravely brings up the question, "Is psychoanalysis dying?" Psychoanalysis has never been a quick form of treatment or one easy to teach or easy to distribute, like medication. Still, interest in training is occurring in Eastern Europe, Japan, and in many moderately sized cities all over the USA. The discoveries of psychoanalysts are being rediscovered by psychologists and psychotherapists, who previously vociferously rejected concepts and ways of working inherent in psychoanalysis. For example, psychologists now accept that most workings of the mind are unconscious, although William James (1890) had banned the study of such "whimsical" processes from the discipline and the word "unconscious" was not found in cognitive psychology journals after the behavioural revolution until Marcel used it again in 1983. Around this time, unconscious processes were re-found (Greenwald, 1992; Kihlstrom, 1987). Cognitive therapists are now writing about the use of dreams, and cognitive behaviourists find free association useful at times: what Mahoney (1991) has called "streaming". Psychoanalysts interested in neuroscience are trying to investigate the implications of connectionism and various brain dysfunctions for analytic theories. The enthusiasm for this sort of integration has resulted in a new journal called *Neuro-Psychoanalysis*, and there are annual conferences on this topic. So, although the numbers or percentage of people seeking traditional psychoanalysis might not be great, psychoanalysis continues to have an effect on thinking in psychology and cognitive science.

Hadley addresses another issue that analysts talk about privately, but are afraid to mention publicly—the sense of telepathy. In addition to Stoller's (Mayer, 2001) paper, Rucker and Lombardi (1997) and I (Curtis, 2002) have also published examples of such uncanny experiences. Although we seem to be a long way from beginning to have a scientific explanation of what could be transpiring, perhaps eventually we shall have more "hard" knowledge about such processes, if they are indeed happening. For example, Gallese (2001) in Italy has found that the human brain picks up information from another person when the other person intends to engage in an action. Given that super-string theorists have found far more than three physical dimensions, it is possible that some sort of sixth sense will be discovered in the future that accounts for such seemingly uncanny knowledge.

Four authors bring up the possibility of psychoanalysts' harming their patients—Eagle, Kaley, Fonagy, and Ruskin. This topic needs considerable attention and discussion by psychoanalysts. Practitioners, especially of other forms of psychotherapy, have sometimes reported to me negative experiences in psychoanalysis. In a litigious society such as the USA, the case brought against Chestnut Lodge regarding failure to medicate a depressed patient and the rise of empirically supported treatments give psychoanalysts reason to question their treatments, even if ethical values alone would not lead to much questioning. Psychoanalysts could present and publish more interventions that do not turn out well and more failed treatments. Such a change in what is made public would probably require requests from conference organizers and journal editors. Although analysts may be reluctant to report on their own failings, supervisors could report on such cases and maintain the anonymity of the analyst. Panels could discuss openly conditions such as substance abuse and addictions, in which an attempt to demarcate better the point at which a treatment other than psychoanalysis, or as an adjunct to psychoanalysis, is advisable. Although Gensler and Hart have provided examples of disclosures other than countertransferential ones that have worked out well, analysts may also be able to provide instances where such revelations resulted in difficulties that might have been avoided. More empirical research conducted with both analysts and patients on what is helpful and hurtful would be useful in shedding light on some of these questions (cf. Curtis, Field, Knaan-Kostman, & Mannix, 2004).

Fonagy has dealt with the topic of when analysts should retire and suggested that re-accreditation be required. Institutes and/or professional organizations could set some guidelines regarding retirement, especially, perhaps, for analysts suffering from illnesses that are mentally incapacitating. A requirement of re-accreditation of all analysts by their individual institutes would have the benefit of not singling out particular analysts for attention. Institutes might find some of the principles used by hospital ethics committees useful in this regard.

It is possible to separate some of the issues discussed into categories of behaviour that probably should remain taboo, behaviours that are taboo but should not be, behaviours that are no longer taboo, and behaviours that remain very murky. Anything illegal or unethical will be likely to remain taboo. Although open discussion of financial matters and of practices not helpful to patients is taboo, this norm should likely be changed. A number of behaviours seem no longer to be always taboo. These include self-disclosure, including some that are not countertransferential, religious and spiritual beliefs, limited, non-sexual touch, and, perhaps now, uncanny experiences. Still, the implications of modern technology and the degree of deviance accepted from strictly Freudian theory and technique remain very unclear. Although many analysts may respond by saying that they deviate a great deal from strictly Freudian theory and practice, there is often still the criticism, "That is not psychoanalytic." This criticism can emerge when the analyst makes a decision to help the patient in a way that is not seen as furthering the "analytic process".

Trends towards behaving in a less conventionally "psychoanalytic" manner have become so pervasive that Hansen finds it taboo among his colleagues not to agree immediately to lend a patient a magazine. This raises a very interesting twist to our volume. Is it becoming taboo to conduct psychoanalysis in a traditional, classical style? Perhaps ironically, behaving in a classical manner has become one of the most taboo topics among American analysts in the relational/interpersonal tradition. Is psychoanalysis proper so distinct an experience that it is becoming a sort of arcane artistic or spiritual endeavour, like Tai Chi or Zen meditation, in some respects, or is the psychoanalytic approach becoming so well known, so embedded in our culture, and its practices so integrated by master therapists of all philosophical orientations, that it no longer represents a distinct form of theory and therapy? Perhaps another volume in twenty years will provide some answers to this question.

Psychoanalysis as a discipline, like cultures and religions, suggests that certain behaviours usually have harmful consequences and should remain taboo. Unlike religion, however, psychoanalysis has proposed that all topics are open to discussion. Unlike religion, the psychoanalytic tradition informs us that attempts to ban unacceptable thoughts from consciousness are often not successful and often not beneficial, even when the attempts are successful. When controversy is not allowed, psychoanalysis loses its distinction from religion. The topics in this volume all stir controversy. These contributions all further the sort of inquiry into often taboo subjects that is most central to the psychoanalytic endeavour.

References

Curtis, R. C. (2002). Termination from a psychoanalytic perspective. *Journal of Psychotherapy Integration*, 12: 350–357.

Curtis, R. C. (2008). *Desire, Self, Mind and the Psychotherapies; Unifying Psychological Science and Psychoanalysis.* Lanham, MD: Jason Aronson, Rowman & Littlefield.

Curtis, R. C., Field, C., Knaan-Kostman, I., & Mannix, K. (2004). What 75 psychoanalysts found helpful and hurtful in their own psychoanalyses. *Psychoanalytic Psychology, 21*: 183–202.

Eagle, M., Wolitsky, D. L., & Wakefield, J. C. (2001). A critique of the "new view" in psychoanalysis. *Journal of the American Psychoanalytic Association, 49*: 457–489.

Fromm-Reichmann, F. (1954). Psychoanalysis and general dynamics conceptions of the theory and therapy: differences and similarities. *Journal of the American Psychoanalytic Association, 2*: 711–721.

Gallese, V. (2001). The "shared manifold hypothesis: from mirror neurons to empathy. *Journal of Consciousness Studies, 8*: 33–50.

Greenwald, A. G. (1992). New Look 3: Unconscious cognition reclaimed. *American Psychologist, 47*: 66–779.

James, W. (1890). *Principles of Psychology.* Oxford: Dover, 1950.

Kihlstrom, J. F. (1987). The cognitive unconscious. *Science, 237*: 1445–1452.

Mahoney, M. J. (1991). *Human Change Processes.* New York: Basic Books.

Marcel, A. (1983). Conscious and unconscious processes: experiments on visual masking and word recognition. *Cognitive Psychology, 15*: 197–237.

Mayer, E. L. (2001). On "Telepathic dreams?" An unpublished paper by Robert J. Stoller. *Journal of the American Psychoanalytic Association, 49*: 629–657.

Perry, H. S. (1982). *Psychiatrist of America.* Cambridge, MA: Harvard University Press.

Rucker, N., & Lombardi, K. (1997). *Subject Relations: Unconscious Experiences and Relational Psychoanalysis.* London: Routledge.

Schachter, J. (2002). *Transference: Shiboleth or Albatross?* Hillsdale, NJ: Analytic Press.

Volkan, V. (1988). *The Need to Have Enemies and Allies: From Clinical Practice to International Relations.* Northvale, NJ: Jason Aronson.

Wachtel, P. L. (1983). *The Poverty of Affluence.* New York: Free Press.

Wachtel, P. L. (1999). *Race in the Mind of America: Breaking the Vicious Circle Between Blacks and Whites.* Florence, KY: Taylor & Francis/ Routledge.

CHAPTER TWENTY-TWO

Epilogue: Glancing back, facing forward. "Final" thoughts on taboo

Brent Willock

> "It can only serve the 'cause' Freud first started if we continue to ask all possible questions, considering nothing as too great a taboo to challenge"
>
> (Roazen, 1999)

I mmersing oneself in the topic of taboo, as the editors and contributors to this book (and now you) have done for a prolonged period, inevitably heightens awareness of this highly charged, dynamic domain located at the controversial frontier of what is thinkable and doable. A psyche so sensitized may be forgiven if, contemplating looking back, as would be appropriate at this point in our text, brings to the still freely associative mind the taboo against that very act that Lot and his family carried with them as they fled the imminent annihilation of Sodom and Gomorrah.

Embodying Freud's (1905d) portrayal of polymorphous perversity, denizens of that iniquitous metropolis flagrantly violated all manner of taboos. Lot, himself, is to be commended for wanting to protect the two male angels who were sojourning overnight in his home from the rowdy mob surrounding his abode, hungering to

sodomize these newcomers. The host beseeched the unruly crowd
to refrain from acting so wickedly. Attempting to placate the hostile,
horny throng by offering them a substitute object for their desire
might have been a crafty ploy, but was certainly less noble. Lot
proposed that if they would abandon their roiling urge to sodomize his guests, he would hand over his two daughters for them to
do with as they saw fit. As further enticement, he did not fail to
mention that his offspring were virgins. While this offer must have
been tantalizing, the horde was not to be distracted from its initial
impulse.

Abraham's hope that at least ten righteous men could be found
in the twin cities so that the citizenry as a whole could be spared
the Lord's wrath seemed unlikely to be fulfilled. The populace
doggedly incarnated Freud's imaginative view of our ontogenetic
condition prior to the establishment of oedipal taboos under the
auspices of the superego that prepare the way for the relative quies-
cence of latency. Although Lot himself seemed somewhat different
from his neighbours and was not without some moral values, one
would be hard-pressed to envision even him as a pillar of right-
eousness. He might be described as a salt of the earth type with a
value system that was, to say the least, deeply divided.

Just as Freud usefully underscored our profound temptation to
transgress taboos, so Lot's wife could not resist defying the divine
interdiction on looking back on the wild subculture from which
they were separating. (Her husband and daughters also manifested
reluctance to part from their home town and needed to be hustled
along by the angels.) Risking God's fury for one last visual pleasure
that must have seemed worth the danger, Lot's wife was, in consequence, transmogrified into a pillar of salt. The resultant sculptural
formation was, in itself, an intriguing phenomenon. Artfully com-
bining a sense of upright rigidity with a more subtle implication
that this formal stiffness could readily be dissolved (come the
rains), this unusual monument paralleled the nature of taboos that,
in their essence, also represent unyielding structures that, none the
less, enshrine potent urges, possibilities, and even suggestions to
melt their proscriptive authority to permit more fluid pleasures.

While glancing back in that Biblical narrative was clearly forbidden and dangerous, looking forward would have turned out to be
equally perilous. With their mother now solidly out of the picture,

reduced to representational status, Lot's daughters experienced a peremptory urge to propagate. They resolved to get their father drunk in order to undo his incest taboo. Whatever barriers against such thoughts and deeds they may have had evidently had already been dissolved by a more interior, hormonal wine.

While the proscription against looking back, the saline column, and other features of this renowned story are universally remembered, this difficult, second climax in the story is less well known, less frequently remembered, perhaps even repressed. The Book assists us with this forgetting process by bestowing no names on the daughters. We immortalized Onan for spilling his seed on the ground, creating a word, onanism, in his honour. We similarly memorialized the entire population of Sodom by naming a whole class of sexual activity after them that we also carved into legal statutes. For the young women who wanted to "preserve the seed of our father", however, we seem to have adhered to the taboo of not mentioning the name. (Nameless, they could, of course, represent anyone, and everyone.) Our selective attention in such matters is understandable, for the fantasies the no-name daughters enacted tend to evoke the most fundamental taboo on thinking, let alone living such depravities. Likewise, when it comes to the younger generation to whom these stories are routinely imparted, we might feel comfortable instructing them to obey certain authorities, particularly ones endowed with divinity and other forms of idealization. We might not be so at ease when it comes to opening up dialogue on what the one, comparatively good, family in that ancient town was up to.

Inclined to identify with Lot's nuclear family—the best of a bad lot—we tend to resist identification with the more clearly deranged townsfolk, at least consciously. In these identificatory processes, we may even overlook the otherwise troubling detail of Lot's offering his daughters to the rabid mob. Our relatively easy identification with this family turns out, however, to be anything but easy, as the skilful author of Genesis leads us, as the angels did Lot, forward to post-sodomitic life.

Accustomed to the idea that there are wicked people in the world, we often rely on that notion to sustain a convenient repository for our own projected, intolerable impulses. We are far less at home with the perturbing realization that what Freud (1900a) referred to as "evil" impulses reside in our own families and psyches. These urges within enable us to resonate with all facets of character portrayed in the Old Testament tale.

What would Lot's wife have thought if she could have looked forward? As oedipal mother, she might have had salty words for her offspring. One could imagine her threatening to visit a wrath like Jehovah's upon these young upstarts should they persist with their lusty plan, forcefully freezing them in their tracks. In the best of all worlds, she might have had some sage guidance to offer, helping her offspring negotiate the challenging journey from chaotic, polymorphous perversity through the perilous phallic–oedipal rapids toward the calmer land of latency. Given her tendency to look the other way, however, this latter, positive scenario would not seem highly likely.

Freud reflected to great effect on a classic, Sophoclean drama to shed light on what he came to call, in honour of the mythic tragedy, the Oedipus complex. Casting a psychoanalytic eye on the amazing story of Lot's family, a scholarly activity that might, in itself, transgress a taboo, one finds yet another, powerful source of support for Freud's bold theory, this time from the father–daughter perspective rather than the son's. Ancient authors knew a great deal about what transpires in both the conscious and unconscious reaches of our minds. Intuitively grasping the intricate dance between our phylogenetic inheritance, our culture, and our intimate relational surround, they comprehended the significance of taboos and temptations, and understood our longings to circumvent these prohibitions directly, indirectly, and through various compromise formations.

It can, then, clearly be dangerous to glance back, frightening to face forward. These bivalent terrors we know not only from Genesis, but also from our clinical and everyday experience. Psychoanalysis originated and evolved as a secular method of helping us (who can so easily become petrified and frozen in time) to find ways of looking back safely so that we will not be retraumatized by what we have witnessed. Psychoanalysis developed a theory, a technique, and a relational mode to facilitate our living more fully in the present, informed by the past, with an eye to a future that could now stand a chance of being novel, rather than just another, horrific repetition of the dreaded past.

In her comprehensive Introduction, Lori Bohm led us to peek forward, surveying the exciting chapters that would unfold in this volume. In her equally thorough review of the book, Rebecca Curtis facilitated our glancing back to carefully consider the implications of all that had been articulated by our talented array of thinkers. Although I imagine Dr Bohm and Professor Curtis might have felt challenged by the integrative demands of their twin tasks, they obviously were not frozen into writers' block. To pen further "terminal words" on our topic at this time would be redundant and, indeed, ironic in a book that hopes not to close any doors on dialogue, but rather to open up a spirited debate on the full panoply of issues that are problematic to face and discuss. It seems best, therefore, to learn from the Biblical scribes for whom brevity often seemed a virtue. The creators of that earlier Book of the Taboo elected to leave much to the reader's imagination, and plenty for exegesis by future generations of scholars (as did Freud, in his classic venture into totemic territory.) In our book of the taboo or not taboo, we should benefit at this point from their wisdom and foresight and embrace the ideal of concision.

As in planned therapeutic terminations, it is our hope that what the authorial collective in this volume has generously shared—with knowledge, courage, wisdom, and humour—may have enriched readers' internal worlds, as it has our own. If so, we can feel relatively confident that, closing this chapter, we will all venture forth more motivated and equipped to recognize and come to grips with whatever taboos we have, or will encounter in clinical practice, professional associations, thinking, writing, and other realms of conflictual living. Fortified by the stimulating ideas and inquiring spirit we have imbibed, we can surely look forward to a more open, enlivening discourse, with enhanced potential for advancing psychoanalysis's historic role as a fascinating and liberating discipline.

References

Freud, S. (1900a). *The Interpretation of Dreams. S.E.*, 4–5: 1–625. London: Hogarth.

Freud, S. (1905d). *Three Essays on the Theory of Sexuality. S.E.,* 7: 130–243. London: Hogarth.

Roazen, P. (1999). Freud and analysis of Anna. In: R.M. Prince (Ed.), *The Death of Psychoanalysis: Murder? Suicide? or Rumor Greatly Exaggerated?* (pp. 141–141). Northvale, NJ: Jason Aronson.

INDEX

Abraham, G., 212, 214, 223
Abraham, K., 5, 15, 134, 140, 144
abuse, 65, 108, 115–116, 139, 144,
    338
  child, 11, 56, 270, 342
  drug, 198, 357
  of patient(s), 52, 56–57, 59–61
  sexual, 52, 56–57, 59, 101, 115,
    141, 180, 342
affect, 14, 21, 26, 41–42, 51–52, 54,
    60–61, 66, 68, 70–73, 81, 84,
    86–88, 103, 111, 113, 133, 142,
    197, 202, 245, 255, 313, 322,
    330–333, 339–340, 342–344
  see also: self–affect–object
ageing, xxiv, 212–222, 239
aggression, xxi, xxv, 14, 18, 28,
    40–41, 47, 72–73, 82–83, 96, 129,
    134, 143, 154, 168, 213–214, 232,
    245–246, 329–330
Ainsworth, M. S., 333, 346
Albee, G. W., 204–205
Albus, K., 82, 91
Alexander, F., 7, 96, 116, 315, 320, 324

Alstad, D., 106, 118
Altman, N., 116, 194, 201, 205
ambivalence, 6, 13–14, 50, 55, 62, 84,
    98, 136, 139, 172, 174, 200, 221,
    254, 277
American Psychoanalytic
    Association (APA), 8–9, 56,
    319, 354
American Psychoanalytic
    Association Panel, The, 319,
    325
analytic dyad(s), xxi, xxv, 49, 52, 54,
    69–71, 78, 238, 246, 271, 274,
    298–300, 308, 323, 339–340
anger, xxi, xxv, 30–31, 42–44, 67,
    102, 124–127, 129, 140, 200–202,
    239, 244–245, 257–258, 263, 292,
    317
animism, 4, 14–15
anxiety, 23, 28, 39–41, 43–47, 51, 61,
    67, 82, 100, 135, 141, 197–198,
    204, 210, 214, 229, 243, 252,
    256–260, 264, 276–277, 280, 295,
    317, 327, 333, 353